MARXISM, REVISIONISM, AND LENINISM

MARXISM, REVISIONISM, AND LENINISM

Explication, Assessment, and Commentary

Richard F. Hamilton

Westport, Connecticut
London

Library of Congress Cataloging-in-Publication Data

Hamilton, Richard F.
    Marxism, revisionism, and Leninism : explication, assessment, and commentary / by
Richard F. Hamilton.
      p. cm.
    Includes bibliographical references and index.
    ISBN 0–275–96882–0 (alk. paper)
    1. Communism. 2. Communist revisionism. I. Title.
    HX73.H345 2000
    335.4—dc21   99–055874

British Library Cataloguing in Publication Data is available.

Library of Congress Catalog Card Number: 99–055874
ISBN: 0–275–96882–0

First published in 2000

Praeger Publishers, 88 Post Road West, Westport, CT 06881
An imprint of Greenwood Publishing Group, Inc.
www.greenwood.com

Printed in the United States of America

The paper used in this book complies with the
Permanent Paper Standard issued by the National
Information Standards Organization (Z39.48–1984).

10 9 8 7 6 5 4 3 2 1

Copyright Acknowledgment

The author and publisher gratefully acknowledge permission for use of the following material:

Quotations from V. I. Lenin in Chapter 4 from V. I. Lenin, *Imperialism: The Highest Stage of Capitalism* (New York: International Publishers, 1939), reprinted by permission of International Publishers.

Contents

Tables

Acknowledgments

Commenting on the intellectual enterprise, Aristotle wrote—I quote from distant memory—that "we cannot collectively fail." The notion was, and still is, appealing to me, even though I know it is mistaken. The best we can hope for is minimization of error. The more widely we consult, the better the final product. The best results depend on the help of capable and willing coworkers.

The following persons fit that description: Edward Bell, John R. Champlin, Edward Crenshaw, G. William Domhoff, Paul Eberts, Eric Fisher, John Higley, William H. Form, Roscoe Hinkle, James Kittelson, Neil McLaughlin, Anthony Mughan, Rick Ogmundson, John Pestana, Paul A. Rahe, Clayton Roberts, Lars Sandberg, Michael Smith, David F. Trask, Henry Ashby Turner Jr., Jonathan Turner, and Axel van den Berg. I wish to thank all these collaborators. Their generous assistance is very much appreciated.

Special thanks are due also to the Mershon Center, Ohio State University, for financial support and for many other kinds of assistance. I am much indebted to Richard Ned Lebow, the center's director, and to Mershon's superb staff, most especially to Wynn Kimble.

My friend, colleague, and coworker, Bill Form, deserves special commendation. For his services, a summa cum laude. He has read the entire manuscript several times over, and provided many pages of comments. Jim Kittelson deserves special credit: He spotted a serious problem and saved me much embarrassment.

A special note of thanks and appreciation goes to Young-Ho Kim, my research assistant during much of this work. For exceptional diligence and dedication, he too deserves a summa cum laude.

The many contributions of Irene Hamilton are likewise gratefully acknowledged.

MARXISM, REVISIONISM, AND LENINISM

Introduction

This volume will provide explications and assessments of three major social theories central to the understanding of 20th-century events: Marxism, revisionist Marxism, and Leninism. These theories, directly or indirectly, are responses to the claims of still another theory, liberalism. It too, accordingly, must be given some consideration. Some commentary and consideration of the wider implications of these assessments will also be provided.

As used here, the word *theory* refers to a set of general statements purporting to describe and explain a complex reality. In social affairs, one is dealing with an infinitude of fact. Finite minds cannot handle such quantity. All thought, therefore, whether one recognizes it or not, involves some arrangement for simplification; that is, some theory or theories.

For most persons, including academics and educated citizens, knowledge of those theories will ordinarily be rather limited. Apart from a small number of experts (those who teach social, political, or economic theories, or those dealing with intellectual history), that knowledge will be rough, approximate, incomplete, a "shadowy outline" rather than a comprehensive understanding. References to liberalism occur frequently in everyday discussion, but few educated persons are likely to have an adequate understanding of its meaning. Not many would know its intellectual history.

One could have a detailed and accurate knowledge of a theory's major claims but at the same time know nothing about the empirical status of those claims. One could, in other words, know the major propositions but know next to nothing of their validity. Many people in the social sciences and humanities speak knowingly of the Marxian theory, using its concepts and accepting at least some of its principal conclusions. Apart from the specialist historians, however, few academics would have sufficient knowledge of the political, economic, or social history of Britain, France, Germany, or the United States to assess any of the theory's major propositions.[1]

Limited knowledge means that miscues are a possibility, with "authorities" vouching for a handed-down theory without knowledge of its adequacy. Sociologists (and others) speak knowingly of Max Weber's *Protestant Ethic and the Spirit of Capitalism*, but it is a rare sociologist who has read either a history of the Reformation or an economic history dealing with the development of modern capitalism. Few of them appear to know that the leading specialists, the economic historians, see little or no value in the "Weber thesis." Elements of a theory from one field, moreover, occasionally drift into the "discourse" of another. Sociologists claim Max Weber as "one of their own," but members of other academic departments also refer to and accept his claims about the "Protestant ethic." Many people, in short, accept those claims on faith, trusting that the sociologists have done their work and done it well.[2]

To comprehend the modern world, an in-depth knowledge of liberalism is a prime requisite. One should know the rudiments of the theory and its principal variations. That poses some difficulty, since, unfortunately, there is no basic or canonic text. Posing much greater difficulty, one should also have a basic knowledge of liberal practice; that is, its implementation and subsequent development in Britain, France, Germany, the United States, and elsewhere. Chapter 1 of this book will provide a brief overview of both the theory and its practice.

The liberal plans and achievements brought opposition, understandably, from old-regime defenders. They pointed to the "unbridled" individualism, to the self-interested, egoistic behavior championed by many liberals. That brought about, so they claimed, a decline of community, the deterioration of all supportive group ties. Pointing to the experience of ancient Greece and Rome and the lessons of the French Revolution, the critics claimed that those powerless individuals were easy prey for various demagogues who offered simplistic solutions to individual and collective problems. That argument, later to be called the mass society theory, was a cautionary tale, one counseling, rather fruitlessly, retreat or abandonment of the new direction.

The critique from the "left" was to be of much greater importance. The most significant of these countering statements was Marxism, the theory developed by Karl Marx and Friedrich Engels. To comprehend the major events of the 20th century, one must have a basic knowledge of that theory and of its most important variants. This book will attempt to provide that basic knowledge.

The Marxian theory attacked the liberal achievement on all major points. The liberal economic reforms, it was claimed, were fundamentally flawed. Free mobility of individuals was promised, but the reality was another system of rigid classes. Capitalism created an economy with enormous potential, but one with a fatal flaw. The absence of any overall plan brought a cyclical development, with periods of growth followed by crisis, depression, and mass unemployment. This inevitable development, called the "anarchy of capitalist production," would lead to the development of class consciousness on the part of the workers and they, through revolution, would overthrow the capitalist regime. A new social order with a planned economy would follow. It would be a classless society. Except for the capitalists, all would benefit.

Unlike the mass society theory, Marxism gained important organizational support. Socialist parties, many of them explicitly Marxist, appeared in West European countries. Through to 1914, the development, as judged by voting support, was one of steady growth. In 1912, Germany's socialist party, the Social Democrats, gained one-third of the votes cast, becoming the nation's largest party. Those results gave plausible support for a key Marxist prediction, that of the inevitable victory. The same voting results, it should be noted, would have generated opposite feelings in the minds of liberals, capitalists, and other defenders of the "established" social order. The efforts of the various Marxist parties, moreover, were coordinated by a larger organization, the International. That organization operated under the general direction of the German Socialists, their party being seen as the most advanced in its theory, its organization, and its achievement.

These organizational embodiments meant that Marxism, as of 1914, had a resonance within West European societies far greater than any other dissenting movements of the period. The theory clearly "touched" large numbers of followers; for some as a consistent comprehensive worldview, for many others as a collection of meaningful slogans. Some millions of workers would presumably be moved toward the ultimate goal: revolution and the new beneficent society.

The Marxist theory will be reviewed and assessed in Chapter 2. For this purpose we have a basic or canonical text, the Marx–Engels *Communist Manifesto*, a brief overview statement first published in 1848. The "Marxism" reviewed there is the original exposition, a position sometimes referred to as "orthodox."

Around the turn of the century, a controversy occurred within the socialist parties about the adequacy of Marxist orthodoxy. This was the struggle over "revisionism." Marx and Engels saw the "revolution" as imminent, something that would come with the next crisis. But that prediction was not fulfilled. The real living standards of workers improved, a fact challenging their prediction of growing misery. The class structure was not changing as predicted. Events were not moving toward a "dialectical confrontation" of workers and capitalists. A class of salaried white-collar employees was growing. They, like the well-off workers, presumably favored moderate or reformist politics.

The lessons were simple: Revolution was ever less likely. To gain power, socialists would have to win elections. To secure majorities, they would have to abandon the orthodox or revolutionary position and develop moderate programs with appeals to those well-off workers. And, reaching across class lines, they would also have to appeal to middle-class moderates, to those salaried employees.

Revisionism was the subject of heated discussions within the socialist parties at the turn of the century. This intellectual "insurgency" was effectively quashed when the party leaders decided in favor of orthodoxy. But revisionism had a second birth in the 1950s and 1960s, when socialist parties adjusted to the new realities and adopted revisionist programs. Elements of this theory, as will be seen, were also adopted by university-based social scientists. The basic elements of this theory will be reviewed and assessed in Chapter 3.

As of 1914, at the outbreak of World War I, Marxism was a theory with a sizable following and a large institutional base in the Socialist parties and in the International. Although the *Manifesto* had predicted an imminent working-class revolution, more than six decades had passed and nowhere were the socialists "in power." That changed in November 1917 with the Russian revolution. Marxism had finally "arrived" within a major nation. The event was to bring substantial changes in Marxist theory and practice.

Vladimir Ilich Lenin's most significant intellectual contribution was to transform Marxism by giving a central place to imperialism. His theory, published just prior to the revolution, provided an explanation for the delayed revolution. It also purported to explain the change in location. Rather than Britain, France, Germany, or the United States as the most likely settings, the revolution, he argued, would occur first in colonial areas, in those exploited by the advanced capitalist nations.

Lenin's theory largely replaced the previous orthodoxy. The German dominance within socialism was instantaneously eclipsed. Left factions within the socialist parties broke away to form communist parties. A new international, the Third or Communist International (for short called the Comintern) replaced the moribund Socialist International. The new organization was to have a much stronger directive role than its predecessor. It had binding rules for membership, obligatory direction in questions of organization, and much closer control of party policies involving both domestic and international affairs.

The new arrangement, not surprisingly, was a major concern for the leaders of the capitalist nations. For some two decades, accordingly, their policies aimed to "contain" the Soviet Union and its influence. This changed with World War II, in the course of which that nation, unexpectedly, became a valued ally. In the aftermath, some eight East European nations became Soviet "satellites" and Marxism, or more precisely, Marxism–Leninism, was adopted as their official ideology. With the onset of the Cold War, containment again became the basic policy of the major capitalist nations. The Chinese revolution, completed in 1949, provided further confirmation of the Leninist position. With one significant emendation, the central role assigned to the peasantry, the Leninist position became the official ideology of the world's most populous nation.

In the course of the Cold War, for approximately four decades, the First World (the capitalist nations), and the Second World (the communist nations), struggled for influence in the Third World among the poor or "underdeveloped" nations, many of them colonies or former colonies of the "West." The Marxist–Leninist position found a ready following in the latter settings. Where successful—that is, where takeovers occurred—private properties were socialized and some kind of economic planning followed. The Leninist variant had its greatest resonance in those four decades. This theory will be reviewed and assessed in Chapter 4.

We ordinarily assume that an influential social theory will have a solid empirical base. Put differently, we assume that the elements of such a theory will "reflect" available evidence drawn from the societies being described and analyzed. A simile may prove useful: A theory is like a map. Both are simplified representations of complex realities. Both signal important variables and indicate their relationships. If a map proved inadequate (new roads were built, old ones were abandoned), we would discard it and get another. In the case of theories, however, many people react defensively. Unwilling to discard, they undertake revision and assert the continued usefulness of "their" map. Another problem involves the opposite reaction. On occasion theoretical preferences shift, a "map" is discarded and another adopted, without any clear and compelling evidential basis.

The rise and fall of social theories in the twentieth century shows something other than empirical adequacy to be operating in our collective intellectual efforts. In the first decades of the 20th century, for example, Herbert Spencer (1820–1903) had a towering reputation in the social sciences, at least of the English-speaking world. Late in his life, Spencer reported total sales of his books at 368,755 volumes. He argued an evolutionary perspective, with societies moving from simple to complex forms. Among other things, a competitive struggle drove this process. Called social Darwinism, a key concept was "the survival of the fittest."

Elements of this evolutionary perspective were picked up and transmitted in the writings of William Graham Sumner, a leading American sociologist. Spencer's commanding presence may be easily appreciated with a glance at the ample index listings in the leading sociology textbook from the 1920s and 1930s, that of Robert E. Park and Ernest W. Burgess. Spencer received thirty-two index references, some of these containing lengthy quotations from his work. There are twenty-five references to Sumner. In marked contrast, there are only seven index references to Karl Marx, all of them trivial with regard to substance, none more than one sentence in length. Those few comments, moreover, are all deprecating. This thousand-page book contains only seven brief references to "class."[3]

A second sociology text, second in time and influence to Park and Burgess, was that of Dawson and Gettys. A shift in emphasis appears here. Spencer received only five page references in the index, all to brief mentions or comments. Sumner received much more attention, sixteen references, some of these discussions running over several pages. No references are made to Marx. There are five brief references to "class" and "class consciousness," but none of those pages touch on Marxism.[4]

Roscoe Hinkle has undertaken a comprehensive review of the treatments of Marx and Marxism in sociology. His conclusion: "Marx remained of only minimal or marginal interest to mainstream American sociologists through the 1920s, 1930s, and 1940s." A few dissenters wrote approvingly of Marx, but even those judgments were qualified. Writing in 1912, Albion W. Small, one of the founders of American sociology, rejected Marx's program but predicted that his theory would "have a place in social science analogous with that of Galileo in physical science." That very positive assessment, however, follows a statement suggesting that Marx's conclusions were now passé: "I do not think . . . Marx added to social science a single formula which will be final in the terms in which he expressed it." A social theory text by James P. Lichtenberger gave ten generally respectful pages to Marx and his work, this at the end of a chapter on "Darwin and Evolution." Like Spencer, he wrote, Marx had "grasped the essential principles of evolution in advance of Darwin's demonstration." But the reader was also told that Marx was not the originator of "the theory of economic determinism" and that his "theory of class conflict is not new."[5]

A significant change in focus then occurred. The historian Crane Brinton, writing in 1933, put the question, "Who now reads Spencer?" His conclusion: "We have evolved beyond Spencer."[6] The man's influence lingered on in sociology, as did the routine denigration of Marx and Marxism, but by mid-century Spencer's position had suffered a near-total eclipse. Several other thinkers were now placed at the forefront of attention.

The shift within sociology was due, in great measure, to the influence of Talcott Parsons, a leading sociological theorist. His massive study, *The Structure of Social Action*, was first published in 1937, but its major impact came with the second printing in 1949. The subtitle points the direction: *A Study in Social Theory with Special Reference to a Group of Recent European Writers*. The group, or more precisely, the trio, consisted of Vilfredo Pareto, Emile Durkheim, and Max Weber. Spencer received only passing attention. The book opens with Crane Brinton's "who now reads" question and proceeds to inquire about his lost influence. Parsons's summary judgment reads, "Spencer is dead. But who killed him and how? This is the problem." Several pages of his book (along with an assortment of mentions) were given to Marx.[7]

Weber and Durkheim have been prominent in American sociology ever since. Pareto never gained a wide audience. For a while he was bracketed with two other writers, Gaetano Mosca and Robert Michels, that trio being referred to as "the elitists." Of the three, only Michels had a significant impact. But then, in the 1960s, even that influence waned and, for all practical purposes, the position was dropped from the active repertory.

Gradually, unexpectedly, Marx and Marxism replaced the elitists as the third position of sociology's theoretical trinity. It was an astonishing transformation. In the first decades of the century, Herbert Spencer was revered and commended; Marx was ignored, his work deprecated. From the 1960s on, Marx was revered and commended; Spencer was now ignored and his work deprecated. Current sociology texts routinely vouch for the work of Marx along with that of Durkheim and Weber. Jonathan Turner has indicated some understandable concern about the theorists who "genuflect at the sacred works of St. Marx, St. Durkheim, and St. Weber." At the same time, he adds, "We spit on the grave of Spencer because he held a moral philosophy repugnant to the political biases of many contemporary theorists."[8]

If those shifts in theoretical centrality resulted from detailed systematic review of relevant evidence, one could, perhaps, rest satisfied with the current tendency in sociology, with those three as the dominant paradigms. But if the changes and present "results" stem from some nonintellectual processes, from whim, fancy, tendency, *Zeitgeist*, personal charisma, special interest, or prejudice, as Turner suggests, there would be grounds for concern.

This book will undertake four main tasks: First, the principal propositions of the three major social theories will be formulated as testable claims.

Second, it will make an empirical assessment of the validity of those claims. A set of conclusions will be provided for each theory, indicating which propositions are supported, which are not supported, and what questions remain open because for one reason or other they cannot be immediately resolved.

The third task of this book is to consider the implications for subsequent analysis and research. Some theoretical propositions, those lacking empirical support, should be dropped from the active theoretical repertory. Those "things once believed" ought to be consigned to intellectual history courses. Our thinking ought to be guided by evidence; that is, by the propositions which have serious empirical support.

A fourth task of this book will be to consider nonevidential bases of intellectual outlooks. This refers to psychological factors (predispositions or response sets), social psychological factors (interpersonal influences), and social organizational (or social structural) factors. Theories are accepted both for reasons of real or apparent empirical adequacy and because of these other influences: Some authority figures, for example, vouched for them; some people saw the political utility of a theory (either to mobilize or to secure consent); some people are conformists, deferential followers, either unwilling or unable to raise objection. Where these nonevidential influences dominate, the possibility of whim, drift, or intellectual trendiness is enhanced. The fourth task, therefore, is to discuss and comment on these "extra-empirical" processes involving the psychological and social determination of beliefs.

These chapters cannot be regarded as final or definitive. Such standards are inappropriate for any scientific work. All such effort is ongoing, part of a continuous process in which new findings will appear and in which new formulations would certainly be appropriate. One might object to the specific propositions put forward here to summarize a given theory. An appropriate response would be to offer other formulations or to make some additions. One might object to the empirical assessments, pointing to misinterpretations of findings or neglect of some relevant research. An appropriate response would be to revise, rewrite, and/or supplement the summaries presented. Those responses could then be discussed and, possibly, incorporated into a subsequent revision.

Some academics object to precise formulations, such as the propositions put forward in the following chapters. Some people show a pronounced preference for murky formulations or, as it might be expressed in "scientific" language, they have a strong diffuseness-preference. Others will object to the empirical assessment of those propositions, preferring instead what in the 1950s was termed "data-free speculation." Antiempiricist positions have become much more elaborate in subsequent decades. Many argue against something called "positivism." A routine hermeneutical examination of those texts makes clear the underlying meaning of that term: It means "bringing evidence to bear on." The rejection of the positivist standard, that of "normal science," makes room for the new permissive epistemologies, those summarized by Paul Feyerabend, a philosopher of science, in his straightforward procedural rule: "Anything goes."[9]

The combination of the diffuseness-preference and a privileged antiempiricism yields a result that is not very helpful; namely, muddled thought. One eminent social scientist, Pierre Bourdieu, has discovered "structured structures predisposed to function as structuring structures."[10] I do not feel that such effort serves any useful intellectual purpose (although I am willing to be instructed). The present work, obviously, is not intended for the muddlers of this world.

Readers with specialized knowledge in a given area may find little new in some of the following chapters. Economic historians, for example, may learn little about imperialism. That discussion, based largely on their work, summarizes their findings. Specialists in some areas will know also that some of the topics considered here are not current issues in their fields. Again, those subjects are intended for other readers. Put differently, the problem is that some people, perhaps a thousand persons in the entire world, are very knowledgeable about recent work on the "cutting edge" of a given topic, but few others possess that knowledge. That means most people will be operating on the basis of some previous understandings, ones long-since discredited. Most experts know that Lenin's theory of imperialism has little to be said for it. Most educated persons, some millions of them, however, have little or no knowledge of those findings. The expert conclusion does not ordinarily appear in that clutter of events called a "university education." And unless one somehow came upon the relevant literature, the principal lesson would remain unknown.

Many people, in short, have little or no knowledge of the empirical validity of the major claims contained in these theories. Many "theory" courses review the central propositions with loving care, but little attention is paid there to evidence, either to that available at the time of the initial exposition or that produced subsequently. It is unrealistic to expect people to carry such knowledge in their heads. The alternative is to provide that information in written form, as something to which one can refer. The aim in the following chapters is to do just that: to provide a statement of the principal claims of three major theories and to indicate, through a review of relevant evidence, the empirical adequacy—the validity—of those claims. The task, put simply, is to take stock, to undertake an inventory of our theoretical holdings.

The work, necessarily, is interdisciplinary. It draws on the findings of many fields and attempts to synthesize those many diverse results. To assess claims about imperialism, for example, it is necessary to review narrative histories, political and diplomatic histories, biographies of key decision makers, military histories, and economic histories (including data on trade and investment patterns). For assessment of some aspects of other theories, particularly those focusing on mass or popular opinion, cross-sectional surveys of contemporary adult populations will be used.

A final consideration: The emphasis to this point has been the "knowledge" produced by various intellectuals. But that knowledge also has implications for practice. Liberalism was (and is) a major political action program, one that brought about the transformation of the institutions and attitudes of the modern world. Liberalism is still of central importance in domestic policy, most especially in the concern with equality of opportunity. It is still of central importance in international affairs, most especially in regard to trade arrangements.

The Marxian framework (along with its major variants) is also a plan of action. Thousands of people—revolutionaries, counterrevolutionaries, and innocent bystanders—died in revolutionary struggles guided by Marxist theory. And many millions died after the revolutions, most obviously in the Soviet Union and in China. The forty-year Cold War was fought over the issues generated out of liberalism and Marxism. Social theories, in short, have ramifications that extend far beyond university classrooms.[11]

NOTES

1. For a review and assessment of the Marx–Engels treatments of modern history, see Richard F. Hamilton, *The Bourgeois Epoch: Marx and Engels on Britain, France, and Germany* (Chapel Hill: University of North Carolina Press, 1991).

2. For a review of the Weber case, see Richard F. Hamilton, *The Social Misconstruction of Reality: Validity and Verification in the Scholarly Community* (New Haven: Yale University Press, 1996), ch. 3.

3. The leading sociology textbook was that of Robert E. Park and Ernest W. Burgess, *Introduction to the Science of Sociology*, 2d ed. (Chicago: University of Chicago Press, 1924). For an overview of the Spencer and Sumner impacts, see Roscoe C. Hinkle, *Founding Theory of American Sociology, 1881–1915* (London: Routledge and Kegan Paul, 1980), 50–53, 71–72; Roscoe C. Hinkle, *Developments in American Sociological Theory, 1915–1950* (Albany: State University of New York Press, 1994), 85, 103, 142, 310; and Jonathan H. Turner, Leonard Beeghley, and Charles H. Powers, *The Emergence of Sociological Theory*, 3d ed. (Belmont, Calif.: Wadsworth, 1995), chs. 4, 5.

4. Carl A. Dawson and Warner E. Gettys, *An Introduction to Sociology* (New York: Ronald Press, 1929). Both texts discussed here have many index listings under "status."

5. Hinkle, *Developments*, 283–284; James P. Lichtenberger, *The Development of Social Theory* (New York: Century, 1925), 291–302. The Albion Small quotation appears on p. 302.

6. Crane Brinton, *English Political Thought in the Nineteenth Century* (London: Benn, 1933), 226–227.

7. Talcott Parsons, *The Structure of Social Action: A Study in Social Theory with Special Reference to a Group of Recent European Writers* (Glencoe, Ill.: Free Press, 1949), 3.

8. Jonathan H. Turner, *Herbert Spencer: A Renewed Appreciation* (Beverly Hills, Calif.: Sage, 1985), 7. See, for example, the current best-selling introductory textbook, John J. Macionis, *Sociology*, 7th ed. (Upper Saddle River, N.J.: Prentice Hall, 1999), 245.

9. Paul Feyerabend, *Against Method: Outline of an Anarchistic Theory of Knowledge* (London: Verso, 1978), 23.

10. Pierre Bourdieu, *The Logic of Practice*, trans. Richard Nice (Stanford: Stanford University Press, 1990), 53.

11. The positions discussed do not by any means exhaust the theoretical repertory. Other major social theories, those that have had a wide following in the 20th century, would include the previously discussed mass society theory, the pluralist theory, and the theory of bureaucracy. They will be reviewed and assessed in a later work, *Mass Society, Pluralism, Bureaucracy: Explication, Assessment, and Commentary* (Westport, Conn.: Praeger, forthcoming).

CHAPTER 1

The Liberal Background

Liberalism was and is an intellectual system, a program of action, and a social movement that has shaped the modern world in one way or another for some three centuries. Because of its diversity, various emphases, and shifting character, definition is not an easy matter. The following statement describes some of its major characteristics:

Liberalism is the belief in and commitment to a set of methods and policies that have as their common aim greater freedom for individual men. . . . Liberal thought and practice have stressed two primary themes. One is the dislike for arbitrary authority, complemented by the aim of replacing that authority by other forms of social practice. A second theme is the free expression of individual personality.

Early liberalism emphasized freedom *from* arbitrary authority. . . . In place of traditional authority [liberals] have supported the authority of reason and of demonstrated, rather than revealed truth. Liberalism has stressed also the desirability of impersonal social and political controls: the rule of law and the market.

Also vital to liberalism has been the goal of an active freedom, the ideal that the individual has the opportunity and the capacity for free expression. To this end, liberals have supported a more equal distribution of liberty, the abolition of monopolies, the destruction of aristocratic privilege, and a law that was general and founded upon rational principles.[1]

The modern world begins with liberalism or, as it was known in the 18th century, with the Enlightenment. The terms refer, in the first line of analysis, to an intellectual framework designed to free people from the restraints of handed-down, outmoded, and irrational ways of life. From the 18th century onward, liberals targeted the old regime in all its aspects, pointing out the irrationality of the received social arrangements, the curiosities of its norms and values, the perplexing character of its political and economic institutions, and, especially, the absurdities of a hierarchy based on inheritance. With intelligence, logic, and some primitive research, the liberals subjected the old regime to a thorough going critique, one that, all things considered, was largely justified.

It was easy to point out the irrationalities. The old regime, whether in Britain, France, the German states, Spain, Italy, or Russia, was a hodgepodge of handed-down arrangements and procedures, the accumulation of hundreds of years of patchwork. Any large state, because of amalgamations, would have several legal systems, a diversity of rights, obligations, and procedures that were never unified (or "rationalized") even under the direction of the so-called absolute monarchs. There was a diversity of weights and measures within the land, multiple currencies, and varying tax laws and collection procedures. Many of those arrangements, liberals demonstrated, impeded the growth of industry and commerce, thus making nations poorer than they would be otherwise; that is, under enlightened rule. The legal arrangements, especially in criminal law, were filled with irrationalities and, typically, were also characterized by harsh, repressive, and vindictive punishment of offenders, many of them poor, downtrodden, and desperate.

Nowhere was the liberal critique more successful than with regard to the old regime's political institutions and the closely related arrangement of classes. The system of hereditary rule, for any thinking person, was obviously absurd. Based on accidents of birth, some people were destined to rule over states, making decisions that affected millions of lives. The hereditary arrangement could occasionally produce brilliant leaders: Philip II of Spain, Peter I of Russia, or Frederick II of Prussia are obvious examples. But it could even more easily produce incompetents, those of indifferent talents, or those who were capable but not especially interested in governance (that is, the lazy, the fops, or the dissolute). The prevailing censorship did not allow direct criticism of monarchs and their policies. But the point, formulated in a general critique, could be made in works of philosophy, economics, and fiction, and those lessons were easily appreciated.

One of the most striking examples of this kind of criticism appears in the play by Beaumarchais, *The Marriage of Figaro*, which opened in Paris in 1784. It dramatizes the struggle between Count Almaviva and Figaro, his talented valet. The count is seeking to take advantage of Susanna (the "droit de seigneur"). Figaro, who is engaged to Susanna, successfully thwarts the count's intention. In the final act, Figaro, in an angry monologue, condemns the aristocrat: "What have *you* done to deserve such advantages? Put yourself to the trouble of being born— nothing more." Mozart, two years later, set the play to music in an opera which still, two centuries later, entertains audiences throughout the world.[2]

The liberal program, in broad outline, called for the dismantling and removal of virtually the entire old-regime heritage. All those irrational leftovers, the entire arcane "system" of handed-down arrangements, all of the unjustified privilege would be removed. That regime was to be replaced by new rational procedures and arrangements. At its simplest, a constitution and a general system of law would replace the old hodgepodge. General rules of administration would be formulated and applied throughout society. A well-thought-out system of weights and measures would replace the previous odd-lot arrangements (the metric system is the obvious achievement here). Tax arrangements would be rationalized. Internal barriers to trade would be removed. Most important, the system of classes would be eliminated; inheritance of rank would be replaced by unhindered social mobility. One liberal formula declared that the aristocracy of birth would yield to the aristocracy of talent. Another formula announced "careers open to talent."

The 18th and 19th century liberal plans aimed to remove traditional social arrangements. In their place the only "social structures" of any importance would be provided by governments. The rational arrangements and procedures would be generated and implemented by enlightened rulers and administrators (in effect, by civil servants). The basic concern was that the procedures be rational; that is, intelligent, clear, easily understood, and nondiscriminatory. The liberal plan of government, it should be noted, assumed centralized and uniform rule.

Some commentators argue that liberalism is "antigovernment." The aim presumably is, whenever possible, to remove government from the direction of human affairs. Phyllis Deane, the noted economic historian, provides an important observation on such claims: "The real objective of the philosophical radicals [i.e., liberals] turned out to be not freedom from government but freedom from inefficient government; and efficiency meant effective and purposeful intervention in the economic system as opposed to ineffective and aimless intervention."[3]

Within that minimal framework of law and administration, the economy, it was assumed, would be organized by a multiplicity of entrepreneurs. Each of them would respond to market demands, each making adjustments based on their sense of changes in those demands. These responses were individual, uncoordinated, and dispersed activities. The entrepreneurs, after all, were competing for advantage. Unlike the old regime, the new arrangement would have no fixed classes (as with royal favorites granted monopoly privileges). Considerable social movement was envisaged, with the successful increasing their wealth and gaining social position while others would lose—justifiably—in both respects. Overall, the aggregate result would be positive—the entire society would benefit.

In a frequent misreading, economic liberalism is depicted as an extreme noninterventionist position. The proper role of government is to do nothing, as suggested by the expressions *laissez-faire* and *laissez-aller*. But few liberals have advocated that extreme. Adam Smith, for example, signaled defense, justice, public works, and education as appropriate tasks of government. Those are necessary tasks that could not ordinarily be left to private enterprise.[4]

The liberal plan is unusual among the world's philosophies in that it unambiguously commends self-interested behavior. That might be read as approval for unrestrained egoism. But Smith, a hard-headed realist, recognized the difficulty. In one often-quoted statement he declared that people "of the same trade seldom meet together, even for merriment and diversion, but the conversation ends in a conspiracy against the public or in some contrivance to raise prices." Smith thought it impossible to prevent such meetings by law. That would not be "consistent with liberty and justice." But later generations of liberals did approve government efforts to prohibit practices "in restraint of trade." They did approve antitrust laws and the creation of regulatory agencies such as the Federal Trade Commission, the Food and Drug Administration, and the Securities and Exchange Commission. The key concerns, very pragmatic ones, would be the extent and intelligence of any regulation. The principle of intervention itself was not in dispute.[5]

The liberal philosophy clearly does not aim for de facto equality of condition. The entrepreneurs, innovators, and hard workers generally would of course receive greater rewards than others, that being the central or driving concept. Unequal rewards are the normal condition of a liberal society. Those performance-linked rewards provide the incentives need to generate "the wealth of nations." The equalitarian concern, it should be noted, focuses on opportunity as opposed to result. Much of the discussion of liberalism, in both the 19th and 20th centuries, has been over the degree to which "equal opportunity" has been achieved. And, accordingly, subsequent reform plans, both then and now, have sought to better approximate that equality of opportunity with positive interventions, with free public education, later with the welfare state, and still later with equal opportunity legislation.[6]

The liberal theory is not a social theory. It is not a sociology, a science of human group relations and involvements. It has little to say about marriage and family.[7] Even less is said about community, religion, ethnicity, or nationality. That neglect, in effect, declares those factors to be of limited importance. More than simple analysis is involved. In some formulations, the argument is that those factors should be of limited importance: They are part of the ancient heritage, part of the system of restrictions that interfere with human betterment. Apart from the family (and possibly the community), the decline of those "irrational" social arrangements was welcomed by many liberals. It was the expected correlate of the continued progress of reason or enlightenment. One end result of this entire process was (or would be) a highly individualized society. The key actor in the liberal drama, after all, is the "individual." The talents and abilities of those many individuals would be the decisive determinants of both individual and collective outcomes. The theory is perhaps best seen as a political science. It is a statement about ideal government arrangements, a plan which, initially at least, called for minimal government and clear, unambiguous, and efficient administrative procedures.

The basic hypothesis underlying this theory may be put as follows: The human condition will be significantly improved through the adoption of those rational arrangements. Put somewhat differently, the argument is that the "free" society will allow maximal individual and collective improvement. Every removal of the old, the outmoded, or the irrational would contribute to that general improvement. As stated by most 18th- and 19th-century liberals, those claims were unsupported hypotheses. Little research was available to back up those claims. For the most part, the arguments were sustained with logic and crude analyses of the then-current experience. The arguments, on the whole, have been sustained in subsequent experience and investigation.[8]

The most striking proof of the liberal argument appears with respect to economic performance. Liberal economic reforms were followed by significant economic advances. The "history of all hitherto existing society" (to borrow a phrase) had been one of economic stagnation and general privation. Now there appeared the reality of significant growth and, for the first time, the possibility of ending that general privation. Although moving in fits and starts, disrupted by depressions and wars, the general upward movement in the last half of the 19th century was unmistakable. Two major wars and one major depression in the 20th century caused considerable disruption, but they also brought some new lessons and stimulated new and superior practice. For the economically advanced nations, the period from 1950 to 1970 saw one of the most rapid sustained advances in all of human history. Although moving at a slower rate after 1970, those advances have continued through to the 1990s.[9]

Modern administration, for all its faults, has achieved tasks that were unthinkable in the 18th century. The systems of taxation in economically advanced societies, despite many curiosities, are more equitable than anything achieved under the Habsburgs, Bourbons, Hanoverians, Hohenzollerns, or Romanovs. Few would fault the reforms of the legal system, with rights of counsel, confrontation of accusers, protections against self-incrimination, appeals procedures, and so forth. Humane goals were achieved through the creation of the welfare state, a set of new institutions made possible by the liberal economic achievement. Many 20th-century intellectuals have been reluctant to recognize the linkage, but the correlation of economic plenty and the social and political achievements is so striking one can hardly miss it. Most people would count the democratic achievement, the basic freedoms, educational opportunity, and extended welfare systems, as good things. Those who value the achievement, accordingly, should not be indifferent to, deprecating of, or hostile to the circumstances of their appearance.[10]

The liberal movement was not, and obviously is not, all of a piece. The agendas change, necessarily, with historical circumstances. With the demise of the old regimes the original issues effectively disappeared. A wide range of adjustment problems dominated subsequent agendas; that is, finding and implementing appropriate arrangements within new liberal regimes. There were struggles over the extent of freedom or, put differently, over the question of limits; that is, justifiable regulation. And there were also struggles about priorities and emphasis. Should economic freedom be central? Or, aiming for equality of opportunity, should one aid economically deprived groups? There were struggles over civil rights, over the extension of suffrage, and, a related issue, over the character of electoral systems. Intellectuals, those concerned with the production of culture, understandably emphasized freedom of expression. Liberalism was and is best seen as involving a broad and shifting coalition of forces which, both then and now, contains a wide range of emphases. Any discussion of the theory (and its practice) must therefore include some consideration of its variant readings and uses.

Some liberals focused on the economy. Many of them called for limited government, for a general laissez-faire policy, and for free mobility of people and resources. They sought the removal of government monopoly and of private producers' monopolies, such as those of the guild system. They advocated the creation of large trade territories, general administrative rules, and nondiscriminatory taxes. Some liberals advocated the largest possible trade territory, a single world market. The resulting interdependencies, they argued, would maximize productivity and wealth. It would also reduce the risk of war, ultimately eliminating it altogether.[11]

The large trade area made possible and encouraged the division of labor and specialization with consequent economies of scale and reduction of unit costs. Those innovations, it was argued, would solve the persistent age-old problem of poverty. The basic plan was spelled out and justified in Adam Smith's famous and influential book, *The Wealth of Nations*, first published in 1776.

Other liberals argued for significant modifications of that basic plan. The creation of a larger trade territory was easily justified but, for the moment at least, some opposed the moves for a worldwide market. One could remove internal restrictions within a larger territory, adopt general administrative procedures, have an extensive division of labor, specialization, and so on. But rejecting worldwide free trade, some liberals called for a protective tariff around that larger trade territory to protect the "infant industries." Given Britain's early start and advantages in technique, experience, and ready capital, all other countries, all the latecoming nations, it was argued, were at a serious disadvantage unless given that initial assistance. This was the argument, for example, of Friedrich List, a 19th-century German economist who was appropriately described as a national liberal. Earlier, in the United States, Alexander Hamilton advanced the same argument.

The national liberal option was instituted in many settings. The Prussian government undertook some sweeping liberal economic reforms in 1818. These were followed, in an important extension, by the Customs Union (*Zollverein*) of 1834, other German states then joining with Prussia. The partners agreed to remove internal obstacles to trade and gained the benefit of the external barrier and of increased tax revenues. Other European countries considered similar options, although with no equivalent success. For almost a century, the United States operated on national liberal principles, benefiting from its enormous internal market and high tariffs. The European Common Market is an extension of this liberal variant. Originally a customs union of six nations, its successor, the European Union, currently has fifteen member nations. American critics point to Japan as the foremost contemporary national liberal practitioner. But the argument is self-serving; the United States itself is among the leaders in this tendency.[12]

Because liberal arguments were so pointedly directed against established regimes, it is often assumed that such advocacy must have come from "the opposition"; that is to say, from "the rising bourgeoisie." But the either–or reading is mistaken. Liberal economic programs were often initiated within the old regimes for a very simple reason: to maximize benefits. Those policies would yield larger tax revenues for the government and might also improve conditions for the general population. The *Zollverein* accordingly was planned and developed within the Prussian government. Prussia's civil servants were not insurgents. They were following policies taught within the Prussian universities, by professors who were also civil servants. Liberal economics, in short, could easily be combined with old-regime politics.[13]

A second focus within the liberal coalition might be termed social. Any group that was disadvantaged under the old regime would ordinarily favor liberal reforms seeing some obvious benefits. Religious or ethnic minorities typically favored equal rights and equal opportunity. They opposed the special privileges enjoyed by the established church and its adherents. Short of disestablishment, one could favor an intermediary position, toleration, which would remove the disabilities imposed on dissenting minorities. In general, Protestants in Catholic countries were liberals; Catholics in Protestant countries were liberals; Jews throughout Europe, with rare exceptions, were liberals. Members of dissenting religions were ordinarily liberals. Those generalizations apply to the 18th and early 19th centuries. Later in the 19th century, in settings where liberalism came to be identified with anticlericalism, religious groups made other political choices. Ethnic minorities, those on the margins of the society, understandably also favored liberal policies, especially those involving emancipation.

A political concern, enfranchisement or participation, generated a third liberal constituency. Those who were shut out of political affairs, the overwhelming majority of any nation in the 19th century, had an interest in liberalism. On this issue, however, an important division appeared within liberal ranks. Some, especially the economic liberals, the owners of property, did not favor the extension of voting rights (universal suffrage). Their argument was simple: If the poor and dispossessed had the vote, they would make use of it to expropriate the rich and redistribute property. The masses, so it was thought, were either real or potential communists. For the well-off liberals, suffrage reform meant votes for property holders (or men of wealth) as opposed to a system based on inheritance. Suffrage extension would, at best, be a slow process, one coming in stages as more and more citizens became wealthy, acquired property, and thereby became "responsible." For one 19th-century political leader, gaining the vote was an easy task—François Guizot's recommendation was *"enrichissez-vous"* (enrich yourselves).

For the masses, suffrage was easily understood, an immediately attractive option which, from the time of the Chartists in the 1830s and 1840s, was to be a staple issue in Europe and elsewhere. Where liberal parties were hesitant or reluctant, continuing the restrictive practice, the issue was taken up and advocated, with much greater insistence, by Labor Parties and Socialists.

There was also a fourth concern, the cultural interest. Intellectuals and artists were generally liberal in tendency. Under the old regime, they chafed under the restrictions and limits set by their often none-too-wise patrons. They quickly discovered the advantages of liberalism, recognizing the creative and financial advantages to be gained in the free market. But for many, especially writers and journalists, there was the additional restraint of official censorship. And this obstacle led many of them, the overwhelming majority, into the "opposition." Intellectuals were major actors in the French revolutions of 1830 and 1848, with censorship a key issue in the former and suffrage extension central in the latter. One leading historian has referred to the events of 1848 as "the revolution of the intellectuals."[14]

Nowadays it is sometimes difficult to see this linkage of intellectuals and artists with the liberal insurgency. In part, the lessons have been lost. The revolutionary thrust of the poets Byron, Shelley, and Keats does not routinely appear in the contemporary classroom, that part of the lesson having been discreetly omitted. Mozart's *Marriage of Figaro* omits the valet's highly charged speech of the original play. For most modern listeners, the opera is simply "good fun" combined with brilliant arias, its revolutionary message perhaps not fully appreciated. But at the time, in the first appearance of the "modern" writer and artist, the political linkage was unmistakable. Victor Hugo, France's leading 19th-century author, wrote that "Romanticism is . . . nothing more than liberalism in literature."[15]

A romantic myth has distorted much of modern cultural history. The "artist" is portrayed as an otherworldly being, one far removed from the concerns of the marketplace. Several artists, most notably Mozart, have been portrayed, in defiance of evidence, as experiencing neglect and living in desperate poverty. In fact, Mozart was very attentive to popular demands and, on the whole, did remarkably well. He was easily within the top income decile during his ten years in Vienna, the last decade of his life. There was no neglect, no abject poverty. The poet Byron contributed to the myth with his portrait of the idealistic hero, the man moved by higher purposes and, at the same time, disdainful of crass, everyday material concerns. Only in the recesses of a biography does one find his declaration of the hidden truth: "I loves lucre."[16]

The liberal movement, this broad coalition of forces, understandably attracted very wide support and ultimately won sweeping victories. The Liberal Party was in power in Britain over much of the 19th century. The Conservatives appeared to be a hopeless minority until the party was revived under Disraeli's leadership. The liberal forces were strong in France throughout Louis Philippe's July monarchy, installed after the revolution of 1830. It was their pressure for suffrage extension that unexpectedly toppled the regime in February 1848. The liberals had a brief reign in the Second Republic, from 1848 to 1851, but were then toppled by Louis Napoleon. The Third Republic, 1871 to 1940, was the period of liberal dominance, with an array of liberal parties regularly forming the government. Italy was dominated by

liberal parties from unification in 1861 through to World War I. The
United States had no "old regime" and thus had no conservative party
defending an aristocratic heritage. Accordingly, the parties were in
the liberal tradition from the outset. Eventually, the Republicans came
to be "right" liberals, giving emphasis to the economic aspects of the
program. The Democrats came to be "left" liberals, giving emphasis
to the social aspects.[17]

Germany is an obvious exception to the general pattern of "liberal
triumph." Discussion of the German case has been cast, mistakenly,
largely within the Marxian framework. The bourgeoisie failed to perform its historic mission; an authoritarian regime was able to maintain itself in power long after its time by imposing a "revolution from
above." But this is theory-saving, an attempt that ignores two of the
most obvious facts of that nation's history.

The Catholic populations of Prussia strongly opposed the 1866 war
with Austria. Bismarck's effort stimulated a sharp reaction that led to
the founding of a Catholic party, the *Zentrum*. In the 1870s, Bismarck
precipitated the *Kulturkampf*, a major struggle against the Catholic
Church that increased and solidified support for the *Zentrum*. In subsequent decades, it was one of the largest parties in the nation. The
Zentrum gained voters who had previously supported liberal parties.
In 1871, in the first Reichstag election after unification, the National
Liberals took 30 percent of the vote and the Progressive groups (left
liberals) took 16.5 percent for a total of 46.5 percent. The Catholic party,
the *Zentrum*, took 18.6 percent. There are two big "ifs": If the liberals
had been unified, and if there had been no *Kulturkampf*, the liberals at
that point would have had a fair-sized majority.[18]

Later, Germany saw the rise of socialism, the Social Democrats, and
again Bismarck engaged in a major effort of repression. The growth of
socialism also meant losses for the liberals as workers shifted to the
new party. Germany, in short, differed from other European countries
in the timing of key events. Political Catholicism and Social Democracy both made early appearances there. The latter was a major presence in Germany two decades before the party's "takeoff" in other
European settings. Because of those two major defections, liberalism
did not or, more precisely, could not achieve the legislative majorities
found elsewhere in Europe. Those voter losses stemmed from the presence of successful competing parties, not from a "bourgeois failure"
or from a supposed authoritarian revolution.[19]

Italy would also have been an exception but for the different impacts of the same two factors, religion and socialism. The new government was anticlerical, the unification having come at the cost of Church
lands and privilege. In this case, however, rather than forming a Catholic party, the Vatican called for abstention. That, together with a later

development of socialism, allowed liberal victories until World War I. After the war, with the appearance of a large Catholic party, the *Populari*, and with sizable socialist gains, the liberal era was over.[20]

Those liberal victories, it should be noted, came prior to World War I, at a time when most nations had serious franchise limitations. The obvious conclusion is that the majority support for liberalism came from within the "privileged classes." Many accounts provide miscues as to the actual experience. The history was clearly not a struggle of conservative elites versus insurgent masses. The political struggles of that era involved segments of the upper- and upper-middle classes. It was, basically, the conflict of a conservative coalition against a liberal coalition, with the latter both larger and, at that time, generally more successful.

Some of the enthusiastic reaction to Beaumarchais's play came from within the heart of the old regime. Queen Marie Antoinette was a Beaumarchais supporter and arranged a private reading of the play. The king, Louis XVI, was appalled and forbade public performances. The court divided into pro- and anti-Figaro factions. Russia's Grand Duke Paul, Catherine's son and heir, was in Paris at this point. He and his wife suggested to Beaumarchais that the play could have its première in St. Petersburg. Marie Antoinette's faction ultimately won out. The performance of Mozart's operatic setting of Beaumarchais's work in Austria required the Kaiser's approval. An enlightened monarch, Joseph II saw some practical advantage in the critique of "the aristocracy." The later Byron enthusiasm was also located, of necessity, in the upper- and upper-middle-class ranks. In Paris, Rossini, who was sponsored by the reactionary regime of Charles X, wrote three immensely popular operas, all of them dealing with opposition to tyranny: *The Siege of Corinth, Moses and Pharoah*, and *William Tell*.[21]

Further testimony on this subject appears in an important work by Friedrich Engels. His account of the 1848 revolution in Germany begins, unexpectedly, with what might best be termed cultural arguments:

German literature laboured under the influence of the political excitement into which all Europe had been thrown by the events of 1830. A crude Constitutionalism, or a still cruder Republicanism, were preached by almost all writers of the time. It became more and more the habit, particularly of the inferior sorts of literati, to make up for the want of cleverness in their productions, by political allusions which were sure to attract attention. Poetry, novels, reviews, the drama, every literary production teemed with what was called "tendency," that is with more or less timed exhibitions of an anti-governmental spirit.[22]

Engels says nothing about the audience, the readers or listeners. Given the costs involved, the upper- and upper-middle classes are the obvious possibilities, especially in a decade of privation, the "hungry forties."

The liberal parties of Europe were ultimately overwhelmed. In most countries, suffrage extension came in the immediate aftermath of World War I (in France, Italy, and Belgium the extension followed World War II). The Socialist parties had grown and taken votes from left liberals. The socialists then divided, with left factions breaking away to form the new Communist parties. Fascist parties made their appearance, these drawing on diverse constituencies and, among other things, complicating the simple left–right dichotomies of the previous era. Christian Democratic parties took votes from the liberals in the interwar period and, to a much greater extent, after World War II. In Britain and Western Europe, the liberals became minor "third parties," to all appearances destined for permanent minority status, at best, partners in someone else's coalition.

None of those developments appeared in the United States. The Republican and Democratic parties maintained their major-party status and continued as agencies of, respectively, right and left liberalism. Canada had a similar pattern, with the Progressive Conservatives and Liberals representing the right and left strands of the broad liberal spectrum. Canada differs in that a left party, the New Democrats, is a regular contender, one that from time to time has formed provincial governments. In contrast to Europe, these two North American countries "lack a feudal past."[23] In this instance, the cliché points up, accurately and appropriately, an important fact. With no old regime to defend, neither country had a classical conservative party, one seeking to defend aristocratic privilege. In the North American context, "conservative" generally means right liberal. It refers to economic liberalism, to the defense of business interests, and, broadly speaking, to limited government.

An unexpected convergence occurred in the half-century following World War II. Socialist parties dropped two key aspects of their original aims. They no longer defined themselves as working-class parties, and they ultimately gave up the socialist aspiration; that is, the goal of taking over the "means of production." What remains is a focus on the development and extension of the welfare state and the concern with the condition and rights of the underprivileged. That means, in effect, a belated shift to a left-liberal program. The Christian Democratic parties, from the beginning, were committed to left-liberal social-welfare programs. The right-liberal parties of Europe and North American shifted from their initial opposition (or reluctance), and they too came to accept "the welfare state."[24]

The general acceptance of the welfare state occurred in a period of dramatic increases in national incomes and real living standards. It is easy to accept substantial welfare charges when the costs are no longer prohibitive. In earlier times, one could legitimately read some demands as "excessive," and beyond the ability of the nation. The conservatism of many opponents, in short, might have been based on realism as opposed to hard hearts. It is, of course, difficult to establish motives, especially in long-past decades. A 1910 survey of 25,000 American employers provides an important clue. It found that 95 percent of them "favored compensation as a matter of right for industrial accidents; few had the resources to institute such programs privately."[25]

The West European Communist parties, originally "hard left" in orientation, became rather moderate in the 1960s and 1970s. They too dropped many elements of previous doctrine and made program shifts that brought them to a left-liberal position. All this occurred before the general collapse of the communist world in the early 1990s.[26] All major parties, in short, converged on the left-liberal position. This meant a general acceptance of both the market economy and the welfare state.

Liberal practice did not always measure up to its initial high promise. The reasoned critiques of the old regime came easily, but developing rational policies for the new regimes often proved difficult. All could agree on the removal of obvious "rot" in the old system, but the new, "rational," centralized plans ran up against regional interests and, accordingly, federalist compromises proved necessary. The old obstacles to trade were removed, but then groups within the liberal ranks put forward their demands for assistance or benefits. And these, typically, would be met with some compromise solutions. In the course of time, the liberal parties became notorious for such "compromises," for their wheeling and dealing, horse trading, back scratching, and so on. The French Third Republic came to be known as the *"république des copains"*—the republic of pals. Given the liberal commitment to individualistic values, party discipline was difficult if not impossible. In practice, liberalism meant a sprawling undisciplined coalition of forces, a situation in which the compromisers, or worse, the "dealers," came to the forefront. The movement that achieved success on the basis of its idealism, its rational critique of a "rotten system," was itself sullied in the exercise of power. The array of ad hoc compromises, as often as not, became a new "rotten system."[27]

For some groups with religious commitments, the anticlerical struggles of the late 19th century also sullied the notion of liberal idealism. This long-latent struggle was probably inevitable. Liberalism was at root a secular theory. Its basic formulations made no provision for religion in any of its manifestations. From the beginning of the movement, church leaders everywhere were alert to the threat: an attractive theory that had no role for God, church, revelation, sin, miracles, or the afterlife.

In France, in 1848, the new Minister of Education, Hyppolyte Carnot, saw the schools as instruments in the political struggle and called on "the village school-teachers to counteract the clergy by spreading the republican faith." It was the beginning of "the ideological struggle between the *curé* and the *instituteur*." The struggle reached an acute phase late in the 19th century: Who was to educate the forthcoming generations? Would it be the nuns, priests, and laymen chosen by the local clergyman? Or would it be the small army of secular teachers, those trained in the new normal schools, those now ready to embark on the liberal mission? In later accounts in the dominant (and partisan) liberal histories, the anticlericals are portrayed as "forces of enlightenment" and their victories are counted, unambiguously, as progressive achievements. There was, however, a hidden cost: Those who were liberal *and* religious turned to, or were driven to, other parties. Where liberals were favorable to religion, the party had greater success, the most obvious case being that of Great Britain, especially under Gladstone's direction.[28]

Another serious loss and corrosion of "the ideals" appeared with respect to economic liberalism. The movement came to be divided against itself, with left liberals challenging the integrity of the right liberals. It was, in essence, the political, social, and cultural liberals, including most of the liberal intelligentsia, arrayed against the "right" (free-enterprise businessmen), against economics (referred to as the "dismal science"), and against profit seeking, money grubbing, "dark, satanic mills," smoking chimneys, slag piles, and steam locomotives. Much of this criticism and division appeared early on in the "condition of England" literature of the 1830s and 1840s. It is regular fare in later literature; for example, in Dickens's portrait of Thomas Gradgrind. For those authors, the world was divided into two camps: the sensitive and virtuous arrayed against the calloused and the unfeeling, those who, one way or another, caused much suffering.

Much of that denigration is caricature, much of it "poorly researched." The mills, for example, were not dark; they had giant windows to bring in the light. How else could one see the work? Smoke and slag piles were unquestioned correlates of steel manufacture. But in this respect the criticism is partial or incomplete. If no smokestacks, what then? Would the critics have stopped the industrial revolution so as to save the English countryside? Would they have preferred an untouched peasantry? The critique provides an ugly aesthetic vision that is set in opposition to another ideal. One can commend "merrie olde England" with its "sturdy yeomen," but that begs the question of its realism. The basic question is this: Was a more humane course of economic development possible?[29]

The criticism is misleading—and ultimately false—in another respect. Adam Smith's *Wealth of Nations* begins with a chapter on the division of labor. It is a famous discussion that reviews two ways of manufacturing pins. In the first, the traditional procedure, a worker would perform "about eighteen distinct operations." In the second arrangement, ten workers would each perform one or two operations. Each task—sharpening the points, for example—would be repeated again and again. It would, clearly, be the ultimate in simple, repetitive labor. Smith's point was that for a given expenditure of effort the new procedure would yield hundreds of times more pins than the traditional procedure and the cost of pins would be dramatically reduced. It was the first of many lessons on increasing the "wealth of nations" and, so it was hoped, of those nations' inhabitants. The entire effort, the entire plan, was a design to end the ancient and persistent scourge of poverty.

As with the smokestacks, some critics of liberalism focus on the unattractive consideration, repetitive jobs, and neglect the principal lesson, the possibility of reducing or ending want. They suggest knowledge of realistic alternatives, but that vision too fades on closer inspection. In one episode of revulsion, a group of intellectuals and journalists in the early 1970s predicted a "rebellion in the workplace" if the organization of work were not changed. Among other things, some Swedish experience was recommended wherein the assembly line was abandoned and replaced by self-paced three-member teams with a weekly rotation of tasks in the manufacture of Saab engines. But they avoided an obvious lesson that Adam Smith or any other economist would have pointed up in an instant: The Saab was (and is) a very costly automobile. The recommended procedure, in short, was akin to traditional pin manufacture.[30]

Those critics of liberalism suggest that they have realistic alternatives. But in fact, they have not thought through the recommendation—abandoning the division of labor—let alone investigated the possibility. Economics might well offer many "dismal" conclusions, but if one has not thought about and researched those conclusions and somehow established the viability of the alternative, the criticism is dishonest. If one were to implement the recommendation it would mean fewer goods, higher-priced goods, and consequently increased want for economically marginal consumers. This "aesthetic" variety of liberalism, curiously, loses sight of one of the most important of liberal goals, ending material want.

Liberalism promised improvement. Under the guidance of liberal principles, so it was claimed, the world would make exceptional progress. The latter term was taken as a synonym for liberalism, with many liberal parties calling themselves Progressives. But then, unexpectedly, early in the 20th century, a world war broke out, the largest, most intense, and bloodiest in the history of the world. The two-decade peace that followed saw the appearance of Fascist and Communist parties, both decisively rejecting liberalism and attacking it and all its pretensions. The worldwide depression also contributed to "breaking the spell." Then came the second of the world wars, larger and bloodier than the first. The Holocaust dispelled any lingering illusions about modern times, about the liberal era, as an "age of progress."

Many commentators, reassessing their earlier positions, responded to those events with sweeping pessimistic judgments that condemn the entire modern age. Writing in 1941, the eminent historian, Carleton J. H. Hayes, remembered that as a student many years earlier he had viewed the last decades of the 19th century as a "stage, indeed a glorious stage, in the progress of Europe and our Western civilization toward ever greater liberty, democracy, social betterment, and scientific control of nature." He still remembered those decades that way but now also saw them "even more clearly as a fertile seedtime for the present and quite different harvest of personal dictatorship, social degradation, and mechanized destruction of the twentieth century." He refers to the "dual character of the age—at once climax of enlightenment and source of disillusionment."[31]

A significant problem appears here: Liberalism is being faulted for the sins of its enemies. Some key questions are these: Were the events of August 1914 the results of liberal plans and programs? Or did those events stem from some other "system" or arrangement? Was imperialism a root cause of the war? If so, was that imperialist drive a product of liberal plans? Or was it the result of some other plan, one regularly opposed by liberals? Should liberalism be blamed for the programs and depredations of fascists and communists?[32] One might with greater justice point to liberal failings with respect to the Great Depression. Again, inquiry is useful: Was it an inherent flaw of liberalism that caused the crash? Or was antiliberalism at fault? Was it the high tariffs, the new protectionism, that broke up and fragmented the world market, thus causing the collapse?[33]

That "disillusionment," that pessimistic reading, is based largely on the catastrophes of three decades from 1914 to 1945. What of the later experience, that of the subsequent five decades? The advanced capitalist nations have learned some important lessons and now make regular use of countercyclical or, more recently, monetary economic policies. The alarming swings seen in the previous century now seem largely contained. Some fluctuation continues, to be sure, but none so violent as the crises and long depressions typical of the prewar era.[34]

The three previous paragraphs cannot adequately deal with the questions raised here. They merely point up a problem with the ready acceptance of the pessimistic reading, with the easy judgments about "the failure of liberalism." Many liberals of the 18th and 19th centuries were remarkably naïve in their beliefs about the power of reason, the impact of rational administration, and the effects of an unleashed human potential. Voltaire's mockery of Panglossian optimism was justified. Some skepticism about the "dialectical opposite," about naïve or unreflective pessimism, is also justified. Reflection and investigation are always appropriate. And partitive judgment is always a possibility.

Liberalism, as indicated, was and is a broad, wide-ranging movement with many diverse emphases. There are the right and left poles and the many intervening positions. One also finds the economic, political, social, and cultural emphases, allowing a wide range of combinations.

Over time, we have seen gradual changes in the possibilities and emphases. In the 18th century, with states everywhere being poor, a focus on welfare-state liberalism would have been utopian. The welfare state became a possibility and a reality only with the subsequent economic takeoff and general affluence slowly generated in the late 19th and early 20th centuries. The more rapid advances of national and personal real incomes in the 1950s and 1960s, an upward movement that continued at a slower rate to the end of the century, allowed a wide range of new possibilities.

The liberal theory has suffered a curious fate. Liberalism is the common sense of the modern age, at least in economically advanced nations. Despite its remarkable overall success, the theory's basic principles are taken for granted and, accordingly, receive little attention in much of the scholarly literature. Only rarely are liberal principles and practices reviewed and discussed in general textbooks; for example, those of sociology or political science.[35] Since most people do not know the history of their own common sense, they cannot fully understand it. They cannot appreciate the liberal achievement and, more important, they cannot adequately defend it when defense is appropriate.

NOTES

1. David G. Smith, "Liberalism," *International Encyclopedia of the Social Sciences*, vol. 9 (New York: Macmillan, 1968), 276.

Michael W. Doyle begins his description of the "principles of liberalism" as follows: "There is no canonical description of Liberalism. What we tend to call Liberal resembles a family portrait of principles and institutions, recognizable by certain characteristics—for example, individual freedom, political participation, private property, and equality of opportunity—that most Liberal states share, although none has them all." See Doyle, *Ways of War and Peace: Realism, Liberalism, and Socialism* (New York: Norton, 1997), 206–212. John Zvesper lists the following as the "foundations of liberal thinking": "the absence of positive moral guidance in nature, the priority of liberty over authority, the secularization of politics, and the promotion of constitutions of government and principles of law that establish the limits of government and the rights of citizens against government." See Zvesper, "Liberalism," in *Blackwell Encyclopaedia of Political Thought*, ed. David Miller (Oxford: Blackwell Reference, 1987), 285–289. For still another useful definition, see Michael Howard, *War and the Liberal Conscience* (New Brunswick: Rutgers University Press, 1978), 11.

For a sweeping critical overview, see Anthony Arblaster, *The Rise and Decline of Western Liberalism* (Oxford: Basil Blackwell, 1984). See also David Spitz, *The Real World of Liberalism* (Chicago: University of Chicago Press, 1982); Richard Bellamy, *Liberalism and Modern Society: An Historical Argument* (University Park: Pennsylvania State University Press, 1992); and Stephen Holmes, *Passions and Constraint: On the Theory of Liberal Democracy* (Chicago: University of Chicago Press, 1995).

2. For a brief review of Beaumarchais's life, the play, and its reception, see Simon Schama, *Citizens: A Chronicle of the French Revolution* (New York: Knopf, 1989), 138–146. For a more extended treatment of Beaumarchais's life, see the intelligent popular biography by George Lemaitre, *Beaumarchais* (New York: Knopf, 1949). The play and its reception is described on pp. 215–219. For the play itself, see Beaumarchais, *The Barber of Seville and the Marriage of Figaro*, trans. and with an introduction by John Wood (London: Penguin, 1964). The quotation is from p. 199.

3. Phyllis Deane, *The First Industrial Revolution*, 2d ed. (Cambridge: Cambridge University Press, 1979), see especially ch. 13, "The Role of Government." The quotation is from p. 232. The chapter ends with this observation: "The new techniques of government control of the economy . . . had their own built-in tendency to develop, grow and multiply" (p. 237).

4. Adam Smith, *An Inquiry into the Nature and Causes of the Wealth of Nations*, ed. C. J. Bullock (1776; reprint New York: Collier, 1937), 447–467. For an intelligent recent discussion of the role of government, see Milton Friedman, *Capitalism and Freedom* (Chicago: University of Chicago Press, 1982). "The existence of a free market," he writes, "does not of course eliminate the need for government. On the contrary, government is essential both as a forum for determining the 'rules of the game' and as an umpire to interpret and enforce the rules decided on. What the market does is to reduce greatly the range of issues that must be decided through political means, and thereby to minimize the extent to which government need participate directly in the game" (p. 15). See also Samuel Brittan, *Capitalism with a Human Face* (Aldershot, U.K.: Edward Elgar, 1995), especially ch. 14.

5. Smith, *Inquiry*, 131–132. Smith's quotation is often cited as "proof" of an insistent business tendency. But by itself the statement is an unsubstantiated hypothesis. Such usage is ad hominem—the statement is presumed to be true because Adam Smith said it.

6. Those later emphases change the content of liberalism. Friedman, *Capitalism and Freedom*, 5–6, describes the transformation as follows: "The nineteenth-century liberal regarded an extension of freedom as the most effective way to promote welfare and equality; the twentieth-century liberal regards welfare and equality as either prerequisites of or alternatives to freedom. In the name of welfare and equality, the twentieth-century liberal has come to favor a revival of the very policies of state intervention and paternalism which classical liberalism fought."

7. A few summary sentences cannot do justice to all of those writers ordinarily counted as liberals. Sociological concerns are a continuous presence in the work of Alexis de Tocqueville; John Stuart Mill wrote an important essay on the subjection of women.

8. For overviews, see Deane, *Industrial Revolution*; David S. Landes, *The Unbound Prometheus: Technological Change and Industrial Development in Western Europe from 1750 to the Present* (Cambridge: Cambridge University Press, 1969); Peter Mathias, *The First Industrial Nation: An Economic History of Britain, 1700–1914*, 2d ed. (London: Methuen, 1983); N.F.R. Crafts, *British Economic Growth during the Industrial Revolution* (Oxford: Clarendon Press, 1985); Rondo Cameron, *A Concise Economic History of the World*, 3d ed. (New York: Oxford University Press, 1997); and David S. Landes, *The Wealth and Poverty of Nations: Why Some Are So Rich and Some So Poor* (New York: Norton, 1998).

For comprehensive historical accounts of European liberalism, see Frederick B. Artz, *Reaction and Revolution, 1814–1832* (New York: Harper, 1934), ch. 4; William L. Langer, *Political and Social Upheaval, 1832–1852* (New York: Harper & Row, 1969), chs. 3–5; and Hiram Caton, *The Politics of Progress: The Origins and Development of the Commercial Republic, 1600–1835* (Gainesville: University of Florida Press, 1988).

9. Many discussions of economic achievement in the 19th century reach starkly negative conclusions about "early capitalism"; for example, in the "condition of England" literature. For a review of that literature and criticism of the very doubtful methods used, see R. M. Hartwell, G. E. Mingay, Rhodes Boyson, Norman McCord, C. G. Hanson, A. W. Coats, W. H. Chaloner, W. O. Henderson, and J. M. Jefferson, *The Long Debate on Poverty: Eight Essays on Industrialisation and "The Condition of England"* (London: Institute of Economic Affairs, 1972). Of special note is the chapter by J. M. Jefferson, "Industrialisation and Poverty: In Fact and Fiction." For another useful overview, see Friedrich A. Hayek, ed., *Capitalism and the Historians* (Chicago: University of Chicago Press, 1954).

See Chapter 2, note 48, for additional sources on the 19th-century experience. Evidence on the economic trends in the half century since 1945 will be reviewed in Chapter 3.

10. Michel Foucault has written at length on the unsuspected nefarious character of the liberal achievement. His criticism, however, is based on dramatic (and largely unrecognized) scholarly failings. For review and comment, see Richard F. Hamilton, *Social Misconstruction of Reality: Validity and Verification in the Scholarly Community* (New Haven: Yale University Press, 1996), ch. 6.

11. On this point, see especially Howard, *War and the Liberal Conscience*. There is a sizable research literature on this question. For an overview, see John R. Oneal and Bruce M. Russett, "The Classical Liberals Were Right: Democracy, Interdependence, and Conflict, 1950–1985," *International Studies Quarterly* 41 (1997): 267–294.

12. One major liberal achievement came in 1846, when the British Parliament opened the domestic market to foreign grain with the repeal of the Corn Laws. On Friedrich List and the national liberal option, see Douglas A. Irwin, *Against the Tide: An Intellectual History of Free Trade* (Princeton: Princeton University Press, 1966), ch. 8. For accounts of the later protectionist efforts, see Alexander Gerschenkron, *Bread and Democracy in Germany* (Berkeley and Los

Angeles: University of California Press, 1943); Herman Lebovics, *The Alliance of Iron and Wheat in the Third French Republic* (Baton Rouge: Louisiana State University Press, 1988); and Peter A. Gourevitch, *Politics in Hard Times: Comparative Responses to International Economic Crises* (Ithaca: Cornell University Press, 1986). For a comprehensive overview of the incidence and effects of free trade, see Paul Bairoch, *Economics and World History: Myths and Paradoxes* (Chicago: University of Chicago Press, 1993), chs. 2–4 and, for summary statements, pp. 164–165, 170. On contemporary Japan and the United States, see Jagdish Bhagwati, *A Stream of Windows: Unsettling Reflections on Trade, Immigration, and Democracy* (Cambridge: MIT Press, 1998), 99–100, 125–126, 134, 153–154, and chs. 15, 16, 18–21.

13. On the Prussian Customs Union, see W. O. Henderson, *The Zollverein* (Cambridge: Cambridge University Press, 1939); and Hans-Werner Hahn, *Geschichte des Deutschen Zollvereins* (Göttingen: Vandenhoeck and Ruprecht, 1984). See also Richard F. Hamilton, *The Bourgeois Epoch: Marx and Engels on Britain, France, and Germany* (Chapel Hill: University of North Carolina Press, 1991), 127–129. For a review of the British experience, see Michael Mann, "The Industrial Revolution and Old Regime Liberalism in Britain, 1760–1880," vol. 2, ch. 4 of *Sources of Social Power* (New York: Cambridge University Press, 1993). An efficient economy, it should also be noted, made possible a more effective military. On this point see John Brewer, *The Sinews of Power: War, Money and the English State, 1688–1783* (Cambridge: Harvard University Press, 1990).

14. Lewis Namier, *1848: The Revolution of the Intellectuals* (London: Oxford University Press, 1946), Hamilton, *Bourgeois Epoch*, ch. 3, and pp. 197–205.

15. The Victor Hugo quotation is from the Preface to *Hernani*, ed. David Owen Evans (London: Thomas Nelson, 1936), 73. For an outstanding portrait of the literary scene in Britain just after the Napoleonic wars, see Ian Jack, *English Literature: 1815–1832* (Oxford: Clarendon Press, 1963), ch. 1. See also Marilyn Butler, *Romantics, Rebels, and Reactionaries: English Literature and Its Background, 1760–1830* (New York: Oxford University Press, 1981); Howard Mumford Jones, *Revolution and Romanticism* (Cambridge: Harvard University Press, 1974); Jürgen Rühle, *Literature & Revolution* (New York: Praeger, 1969); and Renée Weingarten, *Writers and Revolution: The Fatal Lure of Action* (New York: Franklin Watts, 1974).

16. On the Mozart case, see Hamilton, *Social Misconstruction*, ch. 2. The Bryon quotation appears in Elizabeth Longford, *The Life of Byron* (Boston: Little, Brown, 1976), 171–172. Longford reports that at age thirty-four, through inheritance, Bryon "was henceforth to command an income of some £6,000 a year." An industrial worker in Britain was lucky to command £50 a year. A farm worker had even less.

The romantic imagery, the portrait of the poor (or neglected) artist, is sustained through "selection" of atypical cases and misrepresentation of even that experience. Among the composers, the argument is made with the Mozart and Schubert biographies, both of which, in the popular versions, are seriously distorted. Beethoven, whose history is also distorted, was well-off. Richard Wagner, after some initial difficulties, achieved considerable affluence. Brahms required a business agent to handle his finances. See Johannes Brahms, *Briefwechsel mit dem Mannheimer Bankprokuristen Wilhelm Lindeck 1872–1882,*

Sonderveröffentlichung des Stadtarchivs Mannheim, no. 6 (Heidelberg: Heidelberger Verlagsanstalt und Druckerei, 1983); also Jan Swafford, *Johannes Brahms: A Biography* (New York: Knopf, 1997), 427–428. By any reasonable standard, Rossini, Verdi, and Puccini were very wealthy men.

17. Similar developments—that is, histories of liberal dominance—appeared in smaller European democracies in The Netherlands, Belgium, Scandinavia, and also Canada. See Sigmund Neumann, ed., *Modern Political Parties: Approaches to Comparative Politics* (Chicago: University of Chicago Press, 1956). See also Yves Mény, *Government and Politics in Western Europe: Britain, France, Italy, and Germany*, trans. Janet Lloyd, 2d ed. (Oxford: Oxford University Press, 1993).

18. See Sigmund Neumann, "Germany," in *European Political Systems*, ed. Taylor Cole, 2d ed. (New York: Knopf, 1959), 349. For a brief discussion of the struggle, see Gordon A. Craig, *Germany, 1866–1945* (New York: Oxford University Press, 1978), 69–78. On the shift of German Catholics from the liberals to the *Zentrum*, see Jonathan Sperber, "The Shaping of Political Catholicism in the Ruhr Basin, 1848–1881," *Central European History* 16 (1983): 347–367, and Margaret Lavinia Anderson, "The Kulturkampf and the Course of German History," *Central European History* 19 (1986): 82–115. For more detail, see Jonathan Sperber, *Popular Catholicism in Nineteenth-Century Germany* (Princeton: Princeton University Press, 1984), especially chs. 4–6; and *The Kaiser's Voters: Electors and Elections in Imperial Germany* (Cambridge: Cambridge University Press, 1997). See also Helmut Walser Smith, *German Nationalism and Religious Conflict* (Princeton: Princeton University Press, 1995).

19. This brief paragraph cannot do justice to all complexities of the German case. The liberals in Germany were divided into right and left camps and, prior to the Bonn republic, never "got it together." For comprehensive overviews, see James J. Sheehan, *German Liberalism in the Nineteenth Century* (Chicago: University of Chicago Press, 1978); Dieter Langewiesche, *Liberalismus in Deutschland* (Frankfurt am Main: Suhrkamp, 1988); Dieter Langewiesche, ed., *Liberalismus im 19. Jahrhundert: Deutschland im europäischen Vergleich* (Göttingen: Vandenhoeck and Ruprecht, 1988); and Konrad H. Jarausch and Larry Jones, eds., *In Search of a Liberal Germany: Studies in the History of German Liberalism from 1789 to the Present* (New York: Berg, 1990).

A note on the complexities: Goethe called himself a liberal as did the young Bismarck (Sheehan, *German Liberalism*, 5). In 1933, a German industrialist wrote, "I have always been liberal, in the sense of Kant and Frederick the Great." Quoted in Henry A. Turner, *German Big Business and the Rise of Hitler* (New York: Oxford University Press, 1985), 22.

20. Denis Mack Smith, *Italy: A Modern History*, rev. ed. (Ann Arbor: University of Michigan Press, 1969), chs. 8, 9, 39; and *Modern Italy: A Political History* (Ann Arbor: University of Michigan Press, 1997), chs. 39–41.

21. For the struggle over the performance of *Figaro*, see Lemaitre, *Beaumarchais*, 273–280. On Mozart and Kaiser Joseph II, see Volkmar Braunbehrens, *Mozart in Vienna: 1781–1791*, trans. Timothy Bell (New York: Grove Weidenfeld, 1990), 209–215. On Rossini, who was no revolutionary, see Hamilton, *Bourgeois Epoch*, 263–264.

22. Friedrich Engels, "Germany: Revolution and Counter-Revolution," in *The German Revolutions*, ed. Leonard Krieger (Chicago: University of Chicago

Press, 1967), 134. See also Eda Sagarra, *Tradition and Revolution: German Literature and Society, 1830–1890* (New York: Basic Books, 1971), chs. 5–8; and Robert C. Holub, "Young Germany," in *A Concise History of German Literature to 1900*, ed. Kim Vivian (Columbia, S.C.: Camden House, 1992).

23. For overviews, see Seymour Martin Lipset, *Continental Divide: The Values and Institutions of the United States and Canada* (New York: Routledge, 1990); and Janet Ajzenstat and Peter J. Smith, eds., *Canada's Origins: Liberal, Tory, or Republican?* (Ottawa: Carleton University Press, 1995).

24. For discussion of the changes, see Stephen Padgett and William E. Paterson, *A History of Social Democracy in Postwar Europe* (London: Longman, 1991); Christiane Lemke and Gary Marks, eds., *The Crisis of Socialism in Europe* (Durham, N.C.: Duke University Press, 1992); Herbert Kitschelt, *The Transformation of European Social Democracy* (Cambridge: Cambridge University Press, 1994); and Donald Sassoon, *One Hundred Years of Socialism: The West European Left in the Twentieth Century* (New York: New Press, 1996).

25. James Weinstein, *The Corporate Ideal in the Liberal State: 1900–1918* (Boston: Beacon, 1968), 47.

26. See Howard Machin, ed., *National Communism in Western Europe: A Third Way to Socialism?* (London: Methuen, 1983); and Daniel Chirot, ed., *The Crisis of Leninism and the Decline of the Left: The Revolutions of 1989* (Seattle: University of Washington Press, 1991), see especially ch. 9 by Seymour Martin Lipset, "No Third Way: A Comparative Perspective on the Left." Similar processes occurred throughout Africa. The socialist regimes, after long experience with failure, shifted to market systems. The most dramatic change of all came in China, with Deng Xiaoping's second "long march." See John King Fairbank, *China: A New History* (Cambridge: Belknap-Harvard, 1992), ch. 21.

27. For useful case studies, see Herbert Luethy, *France Against Herself*, trans. Eric Mosbacher (New York: Praeger, 1955); and Nathan Leites, *On the Game of Politics in France* (Stanford: Stanford University Press, 1959).

28. See Alfred Cobban, *A History of Modern France*, 2d ed., vol. 2 (Harmondsworth, U.K.: Penguin, 1965), 141. For more detail, see Alfred Cobban, "The Influence of the Clergy and the 'Instituteurs Primaires' in the Election of the French Constituent Assembly April 1848," *English Historical Review* 58 (1942): 334–344. In Quebec, liberals were simply defined as anticlericals, as *les rouges*, this position being thrust upon them by a suspicious church hierarchy which based its conclusion on the European experience. See Mason Wade, *The French Canadians: 1760–1967*, rev. ed., vol. 1 (Toronto: Macmillan, 1968), ch. 7. For a brief discussion of Gladstone's policies, see John Vincent, *The Formation of the Liberal Party, 1857–1868* (London: Constable, 1966), xvi–xxii. For a rich array of detail, see H.C.G. Matthew, *Gladstone 1809–1874* (Oxford: Clarendon Press, 1986), especially 1–2, 37–48, 62–66; and *Gladstone 1875–1898* (Oxford: Clarendon Press, 1995), 86–88.

29. For a portrait of life in what was once the world's largest textile mill, one with giant windows, see Tamara K. Hareven and Randolph Langenbach, *Amoskeag: Life and Work in an American Factory-City* (New York: Pantheon, 1978). Comparing life on the farm in Canada with her factory job, one worker said, "It was paradise here in Manchester [New Hampshire]." Another, also com-

paring farm and factory, described the latter as "a good life" (pp. 203, 384). For further evidence on this question, see Chapter 2.

30. See Richard F. Hamilton and James D. Wright, *The State of the Masses* (New York: Aldine, 1986), 261–272, for a review of job redesign studies. For the Saab experience, see Arthur S. Weinberg, "Six American Workers Assess Job Redesign at Saab-Scandia," *Monthly Labor Review* 98 (1975): 52–54; and Robert Schrank, *Ten Thousand Working Days* (Cambridge: MIT Press, 1978), 214–218. For a review of some later experience, see Barnaby J. Feder, "The Little Project That Couldn't," *New York Times*, 21 February 1998, p. D1.

31. Carleton J. H. Hayes, *A Generation of Materialism* (1941; reprint New York: Harper Torchbooks, 1963), xi; see also ch. 2, "The Fruition of Liberalism." Spitz reviews several similar "indictments" of liberalism, these too based on "persistent misunderstanding." See Spitz, *Real World*, 1–2.

32. H. W. Koch declares, "However thin and tenuous it may be, the connection exists between the liberal belief in progress, the march of science and Auschwitz," in Koch, ed., *The Origins of the First World War*, 2d ed. (London: Macmillan, 1974), 342.

33. A significant reversion, a shift away from economic liberalism, occurred in the period from the late 1870s to the 1930s (see note 12). For an overview, see Cameron, *Concise Economic History*, chs. 12, 14.

34. See ibid., ch. 15. A brief paragraph cannot begin to indicate the complexities of economic theory, research, and policy making. On countercyclical policies and their problems, see Michael R. Smith, *Power, Norms, and Inflation: A Skeptical Treatment* (New York: Aldine de Gruyter, 1992), 24–37.

35. The current best-selling sociology textook, that of John J. Macionis, has no index listing under liberalism. A reference is made to "liberal politics," a brief discussion of present-day usages. See Macionis, *Sociology*, 7th ed. (Upper Saddle River, N.J.: Prentice Hall, 1999), 434–436. A leading political science textbook, James MacGregor Burns, J. W. Peltason, Thomas E. Cronin, and David B. Magleby, *Government by the People*, 17th ed. (Upper Saddle River, N.J.: Prentice Hall, 1998), gives several pages (pp. 180–187) to contemporary meanings of liberal and conservative, along with data on public choices and understandings. A wide array of sources is provided.

A variety of treatments appear in history textbooks. Donald Kagan, Steven Ozment, and Frank M. Turner give some fifteen pages to liberalism, touching on British, French, Belgian, and Russian experience. See Kagan, Ozment, and Turner, *The Western Heritage*, 4th ed. (New York: Macmillan, 1991), 746–761. Philip Lee Ralph, Robert E. Lerner, Standish Meacham, Alan T. Wood, Richard W. Hull, and Edward McNall Burns, *World Civilizations: Their History and Their Culture*, 9th ed., vol. 2 (New York: Norton, 1997), gives the subject an entire chapter, "The Rise of Liberalism (1815–1870)." A single disdainful paragraph on liberalism appears in Richard Goff, Walter Moss, Janice Terry, and Jiu-Hwa Upshur, *The Twentieth Century: A Brief Global History*, 4th ed. (New York: McGraw-Hill, 1994), 18. Their discussion moves immediately to a two-page discussion of Karl Marx, identified as "one of the world's most important political theorists." On the same page, under a picture of the man, the lesson is restated: "founder of one of the most influential modern ideologies."

CHAPTER 2

Marxism

The term Marxism refers to a theory developed in the writings of Karl Marx (1818–1883) and Friedrich Engels (1820–1895). There are more than forty-five volumes in their *Collected Works*, containing a range of commentary and analysis that touches, in one way or another, on most of the world's history. The authors' principal focus, however, was the bourgeois epoch. Most of their work deals with the three leading capitalist nations: Britain, France, and Germany. Marxism, in short, provides an analysis and criticism of the functioning of "capitalism." Put somewhat differently, Marxism is a critique of the theory and practice of right liberalism.

In its early years, the Marxian theory was borne by various coteries and advocacy groups. It was later adopted "officially" by some continental European Social Democratic (i.e., Socialist) parties where it was sustained, elaborated, and recommended to a much wider audience. In the 1920s, it became, with significant modifications, the official doctrine of a major nation, the Union of Soviet Socialist Republics, where it was taught in schools and universities. The Soviet Union also arranged for extensive subsidized publication of Marxist texts and commentaries, both for domestic and foreign consumption. Ultimately, Marxism (or a variant thereof) became the official doctrine in the world's most populous nation, China. It held that privileged position also in a range of smaller nations of Eastern Europe, along with North Korea, Vietnam, and Cuba.

Marxism has also had a significant impact in the noncommunist world. In academic settings in Britain, France, Germany, Italy, the United States, Canada, Australia, and throughout Latin America it has been a "major fact," although the extent of its acceptance in any of these settings would be difficult to estimate. The collapse of the Second World in the late 1980s revealed that the Marxist presence in the communist nations was more appearance than reality. It was never the "common sense" of those nations, as liberalism was in the First World. The Marxist presence has continued within the First World, less exuberantly than before and perhaps with somewhat attenuated aspirations. To understand the 20th century, one must understand both the original Marxian argument and its principal revisions.

EXPLICATION

The appropriate beginning point is *The Manifesto of the Communist Party*, a brief programmatic statement first published in February 1848. It contains an array of summary claims about the major developments of the capitalist epoch. In the forty-five-plus volumes of the *Collected Works* there is no better overview of the Marxian theory.

Several cautionary observations are perhaps necessary. First, the focus of this chapter is Marxism as formulated by Marx and Engels. Two major revisions, the most important of many subsequent efforts, will be treated in Chapters 3 and 4.

Second, some commentators view the *Manifesto* as a work of limited intellectual value. Their claim is that the "real" contribution is to be found elsewhere, in some more sophisticated works. But Marx and Engels judged the *Manifesto* differently. In seven later prefaces their judgments are unreservedly positive. In the preface to the German edition of 1872, for example, they wrote, "However much the state of things may have altered during the last twenty-five years, the general principles laid down in this Manifesto are, on the whole, as correct today as ever. Here and there some detail might be improved."

Third, some Marxists have put forward a Marx versus Engels argument. The claim, basically, is one of underlying fundamental differences. Various good things in the Marxian theory (and in subsequent practice) are associated with Marx; the bad things are associated with Engels. The argument is, to say the least, implausible.[1]

Marxism: An Exposition

The text begins with a powerful single-sentence summary: "The history of all hitherto existing society is the history of class struggles." In support of that claim, the authors provide an illustrative listing of the contending classes of earlier periods: "Freeman and slave, patrician and plebeian, lord and serf, guild-master and journeyman, in a word, oppressor and oppressed, stood in constant opposition to one another."

The fight ended, each time, "either in a revolutionary re-constitution of society at large, or in the common ruin of the contending classes" (482). In those earlier epochs, the arrangements, almost everywhere, were complicated and untidy. In ancient Rome one found "patricians, knights, plebeians, slaves; in the Middle Ages, feudal lords, vassals, guild-masters, journeymen, apprentices, serfs; in almost all of these classes, again subordinate gradations." The modern epoch, "the epoch of the bourgeoisie, possesses . . . this distinctive feature: it has simplified the class antagonisms. Society as a whole is more and more splitting up into two great hostile camps, into two great classes directly facing each other: Bourgeoisie and Proletariat" (485).

In a note to the 1888 English edition of the *Manifesto*, Engels provided two relevant definitions: "By bourgeoisie is meant the class of Modern Capitalists, owners of the means of social production and employers of wage-labour. By proletariat, the class of modern wage-labourers who, having no means of production of their own, are reduced to selling their labour-power in order to live" (482).

Leaving the text for a moment, one may summarize the theory with three general observations: First, Marx and Engels saw history as divided into discrete epochs. They delineated ancient society, feudalism, and modern or bourgeois society. The pattern of historical change was not a continuous linear movement, as suggested in the liberal worldview; it was not a series of gradual, cumulating improvements. Rather, they saw sharp breaks, revolutionary reconstitutions, separating one period from the next.[2]

Second, each epoch was seen as having a distinct class formation, a specific arrangement of dominant and subordinate classes. These were defined by their relationship to the means of production. They are, essentially, owners and nonowners or, in other words, exploiters and exploited. The dominant class, the one giving the epoch its name, owned the means of production of that era.

Some commentators have mistakenly treated all discussions of "class" as if they were distinctively Marxist. But Marx himself, in an unusually clear formulation, indicated that he did "not claim to have discovered either the existence of classes in modern society or the struggle between them. Long before me, bourgeois historians had described the historical development of this struggle between the classes, as had bourgeois economists." His distinctive contribution, he wrote, was "to show that the *existence of classes* is merely bound up with *certain historical phases in the development of production*."[3]

Third, processes of change were said to be operating within each epoch. Various forces were moving events and these, ultimately, would end the prevailing pattern of domination. The changes, as will be seen, are necessary, which is to say they occur without any special will or effort. They occur independently of, or even contrary to, will or intention. The dominant class, after all, seeks to perpetuate its rule. It is, however, destined to be overthrown. Those driving forces, the principal dynamic elements, are located within the economy. The economy of an epoch constrains or sets outer limits to human effort. Changes within the economy require or, more precisely, force changes in all other institutions of the society. The dependent effects include even the society's basic thought patterns.

The *Communist Manifesto* gives a synoptic overview of the transformations occurring within the bourgeois epoch. The changes brought about by the bourgeoisie create the proletariat or working class. That class was formed quantitatively, its numbers being vastly increased; it would, ultimately, form the majority of modern societies. The proletariat was also formed qualitatively, meaning that it would achieve an understanding and awareness of its condition and historical mission. That historically determined class-consciousness would lead workers to the revolutionary overthrow of the bourgeois regime.

Part I of the *Manifesto*, entitled "Bourgeois and Proletarians," opens with an overview of the changes occurring within the already-existing capitalist societies.[4] The major claims, hypotheses actually, will be reviewed in the following pages.

Early on in their overview, Marx and Engels announce that the bourgeoisie "has played a most revolutionary part." A summary paragraph of elaboration follows, which describes the liberal achievement reviewed in the previous chapter. Wherever the bourgeoisie has "got the upper hand," it has

put an end to all feudal, patriarchal, idyllic relations. It has pitilessly torn asunder the motley feudal ties that bound man to his "natural superiors," and has left remaining no other nexus between man and man than naked self-interest, than callous "cash payment." It has drowned the most heavenly ecstasies of religious fervour, of chivalrous enthusiasm, of philistine sentimentalism, in the icy water of egotistical calculation. It has resolved personal worth into exchange value, and in place of the numberless indefeasible chartered freedoms, has set up that single, unconscionable freedom—Free Trade. In one word, for exploitation, veiled by religious and political illusions, it has substituted naked, shameless, direct, brutal exploitation. (486–487)

As a description, a summary account of the de facto achievement, the statement is generally consonant with liberal claims. The liberals proceeded to dismantle the old regime, to end feudal relations, to discard the motley feudal ties. But a marked disparity appears with respect to the evaluations. Where liberals saw the achievement as a good thing, all of the modifying expressions contained in this paragraph make strong negative assessments.

An array of specific hypotheses follow this introduction. Each of these, typically, appears as the opening sentence of a paragraph. Most of them are accompanied by some elaborating commentary. Here, for convenience and to facilitate the later discussion, the hypotheses have been numbered and given a label. The hypotheses are then presented either literally or in brief paraphrase and some elaboration is provided. The first set of hypotheses deal with the bourgeoisie.

1. The requirement of innovation: "The bourgeoisie cannot exist without constantly revolutionising the instruments of production." Competition forces innovation, the development of new tools and new processes, and requires their use. The result, in contrast to all earlier epochs, is "uninterrupted disturbance of all social conditions, everlasting uncertainty." The end result is that "man is . . . compelled to face . . . his real conditions of life, and his relations with his kind" (487).

2. National breakdown; the requirement of internationalism: "The need of a constantly expanding market for its products chases the bourgeoisie over the whole surface of the globe." The bourgeoisie is forced to break down localism, regional particularism, and national boundaries. In place of "the old local and national seclusion and self-sufficiency, we have intercourse in every direction, universal inter-dependence of nations." The impacts are felt throughout the society. For workers the "modern subjection to capital . . . in England as in France, in America as in Germany, has stripped him [the worker] of every trace of national character" (487–488, 494).

3. The requirement of great cities: "The bourgeoisie has subjected the country to the rule of the towns. It has created enormous cities, has greatly increased the urban population as compared with the rural. . . . The bourgeoisie keeps more and more doing away with the scattered state of the population, of the means of production, and of property. It has agglomerated population" (488). This is a key consideration: The exploited population in the feudal epoch was scattered, never came together, and could hardly develop a common consciousness, let alone organize for collective purposes. But the bourgeoisie brings workers together. It is forced to do so, thus facilitating development of their understanding, their organization, and their ultimate historical task. In an earlier work, Engels declared, "The great cities are the birthplaces of labour movements; in them the workers first began to reflect upon their own condition, and to struggle against it; in them the opposition between proletariat and bourgeoisie first made itself manifest."[5]

4. The concentration of property: The bourgeoisie has "concentrated property in a few hands" (488). The early liberal economists, as

we have seen, anticipated decentralized production organized by thousands or tens of thousands of small entrepreneurs. This proposition points to an early-appearing tendency; that is, growing capital requirements, a resultant centralization of the means of production, and a concentration of control. The large producers, the bourgeoisie, would be able to dominate the entire society.

5. Political centralization. The concentration of property brings with it a concentration of political control. The point is forcefully stated: "The necessary consequence of this [concentration of property] was political centralisation." Loosely connected provinces with separate interests were brought together "into one nation, with one government, one code of laws, one national class-interest, one frontier and one customs-tariff" (488–489).

6. Bourgeois domination: The new economic arrangement, they write, was "accompanied by a social and political constitution adapted to it, and by the economical and political sway of the bourgeois class" (489). The bourgeoisie has "conquered for itself, in the modern representative State, exclusive political sway. The executive of the modern State is but a committee for managing the common affairs of the whole bourgeoisie" (486).

7. Economic crises: Marx and Engels begin here with a striking acknowledgement of the capitalist achievement: "The bourgeoisie, during its rule of scarce one hundred years, has created more massive and more colossal productive forces than have all preceding generations together." The point, developed at some length, recognizes the success of the liberal economic program, at least in one major respect. But along with that success there appeared also a major failure; namely, "the commercial crises that by their periodical return put on its trial, each time more threateningly, the existence of the entire bourgeois society." Capitalist production gives rise to a distinctive absurdity, "the epidemic of over-production." The capitalists solve the problem by "enforced destruction of a mass of productive forces," by "the conquest of new markets," and by the more thorough exploitation of old ones. This does not solve the problem, however. It is merely "paving the way for more extensive and more destructive crises . . . diminishing the means whereby crises are prevented" (489–490).

The authors' discussion of crises is the most extensive of all the claims reviewed here. The periodic economic collapse is of key importance to their position. The potential for well-being evident in the contemporary productive forces contrasts dramatically with the fact of economic breakdown. The latter demonstrates the irrationality of the system, one that, if arranged otherwise, would yield continuous growth and material benefit. The argument, although not spelled out in the *Manifesto*, is that planned production could easily avoid the overproduction crisis; it would end the "anarchy of production" inherent in capitalism. But that was something for the future, something that would occur after the revolution.

For their argument, the key point was that the revolution would occur in the course of the economic crisis. It was the distinctive conjunction of promise and failure that would generate the workers' revolution. When the economy collapsed, the workers would be moved to action, and to realize the obvious potentials of "the productive forces at the disposal of society."

The next set of hypotheses focus on the condition of the workers. The authors begin again with a comment on the actual operation of the liberal program.

8. The quality of work: The extensive use of machinery together with the division of labor has transformed the character of work which, they say, has lost "all charm." Another famous phrase appears here: The worker has become "an appendage of the machine" (490–491). It is, presumably, another grievance for the modern worker, another reason for joining in the ultimate revolt.

9. The immiseration thesis: Marx and Engels argue an absolute decline in workers' wages. Given the previous claim of skill reduction, it follows that "the cost of production of a workman is restricted, almost entirely, to the means of subsistence." The point is made in another strong and unambiguous formulation: "In proportion, therefore, as the repulsiveness of the work increases, the wage decreases" (491). The logic of the argument is easy: Capitalists are forced to use machinery and to divide the labor; competition forces them to reduce costs, among them wages, in order to survive. It is, presumably, an inescapable logic.

10. The aggregation of workers: In contrast to the "little workshop" of the patriarchal master, one now finds "the great factory" of the modern capitalist. There "masses of labourers" are crowded together and "organized like soldiers . . . under the command of a perfect hierarchy of officers and sergeants" (491). This everyday despotism in the service of gain, according to Marx and Engels, is experienced as hateful and embittering. Although not explicitly indicated here, it is also, like the aggregation of workers in the large cities, a circumstance that facilitates communication, organization, and collective action on the part of workers.

Hypotheses 8, 9, and 10, it will be noted, involve separate and distinct aspects of the workers' condition. In this text, Marx and Engels signal them all as having a common effect, all contributing to the development of revolutionary sentiment. One could have unattractive work and subsistence incomes in combination with dispersed populations, the obvious example being the peasantry. Deprivation without aggregation ordinarily makes revolution difficult. One could have aggregation in conjunction with increasing real incomes, a condition that could hardly be denied later in the 19th century. It was that recognition, even in the authors' lifetimes, that forced rethinking and revision of Hypothesis 9.[6]

The *Manifesto* concentrates on the emerging bipolar struggle of bourgeoisie and proletarians. Three other groups are given some attention, each of them "assigned" a task in the developing conflict. These are the petty bourgeoisie, the *Lumpenproletariat*, and some bourgeois intellectuals.

11. The petty bourgeoisie: This expression refers to "the lower strata of the middle class, [to the] small tradespeople, shopkeepers, and retired tradesmen generally, the handicraftsmen and peasants." The basic prediction is one of downward mobility: "All these [segments] sink gradually into the proletariat." Their "diminutive capital" does not allow them to compete successfully against the large capitalists; their "specialised skill is rendered worthless by new methods of production" (491–492). The initial discussion points simply to the downward mobility, indicating the resultant increase in the size and importance of the proletariat.

At a later point in the *Manifesto*, the expression "lower middle class" is used as a direct equivalent of "petty bourgeoisie." There, a brief description of the political orientations of that class is provided: "All these [segments] fight against the bourgeoisie, to save from extinction their existence as fractions of the middle class. They are therefore not revolutionary, but conservative. Nay more, they are reactionary, for they try to roll back the wheel of history" (494). Nothing is said about their attitudes after "sinking" into the proletariat. They presumably assimilate, becoming an undifferentiated component of the growing revolutionary class.

12. The *Lumpenproletariat*: This German term might be translated as ragtag proletariat. The translation refers to it as the "dangerous class," the "social scum," and "that passively rotting mass." Here and there it might be "swept into" the revolutionary movement. But its "conditions of life" make more likely "the part of a bribed tool of reactionary intrigue" (494).

13. The bourgeois intellectuals: Eventually, as the struggle develops, "a small section of the ruling class cuts itself adrift, and joins the revolutionary class. . . . Just as . . . at an earlier period, a section of the nobility went over to the bourgeoisie, so now a portion of the bourgeoisie goes over to the proletariat, and in particular, a portion of the bourgeois ideologists, who have raised themselves to the level of comprehending theoretically the historical movement as a whole" (494). They "supply the proletariat with fresh elements of enlightenment and progress" (493–494).

14. The organizational development: The bourgeois epoch will see the formation of large, comprehensive working-class organizations. Early on, the workers formed "an incoherent mass scattered over the whole country," a mass "broken up by their mutual competition" (492). But with the development of industry, the proletariat is concentrated in greater masses, thus easing the task of organization. The workers first "club together," forming trade unions to keep up wages. Ultimately, a larger organization, a political party, develops, representing the interests of the entire class. The development is not without momentary reverses. It is continually "upset by the competition between the workers themselves." But then the organization "rises up again, stronger, firmer, mightier" (493). Ultimately, out of that initial formless diversity comes the proletarian movement, the "self-conscious, independent movement of the immense majority" (495).

15. The proletarian revolution: All of the foregoing processes result in the creation of an organized, self-conscious revolutionary class that, inevitably, will overthrow the bourgeoisie. The revolution will occur in the course of an economic depression, when the grievances are most intense and the failure of capitalism most transparently obvious.[7]

Before undertaking the task of assessment, some summary observations about the Marxist theory may prove useful. It is, first of all, a materialist history. The mode of production and the social relations linked to it determine the major events of an era. "Ideas" are not the driving forces; they are mere "reflections" of the underlying material forces. Adam Smith's ideas did not make the capitalist era. His ideas were generalizations derived from observation of the unfolding events. Capitalists did not need Smith to tell them how to organize production or how to manufacture pins. The materialist framework rejects the claims of "idealistic" history (whether derived from Smith or Hegel). It likewise rejects the so-called great-man theories, the claims that some major figures—Martin Luther, for example, or John Calvin, Frederick the Great, or George Washington—"made" history. As expressed in the now-familiar cliché, events made the man, not vice versa.[8]

Second, the Marxian theory is a deterministic view. The principal actors are not free to choose among a wide range of options. Individual capitalists have no serious choice. Their choice, effectively, is to do what is required or "go under." The capitalists who do not "revolutionize the means of production" will be less efficient producers and will lose out in competition. Great cities pose a serious threat to the stability of capitalist societies. But the capitalists are forced, nevertheless, to further that development. In those large cities workers will come together and they will organize. These two points are summarized in the expression, "economic determinism."

Third, the theory is also characterized, in another summary expression, as "dialectical materialism." A dialectical history is one involving opposition, a struggle between contenders. In this case it refers to the struggle of contending classes. The rising class is formed within the old society. It comes into conflict with that society's ruling class. It ultimately replaces the old society with a new, higher-level achievement, one that incorporates the accomplishments of the preceding era. The dialectical history stands in opposition to the claims of "liberal history" and the notion of a linear development of gradual improvements, as with a series of reform acts.

Fourth, the theory is announced as scientific. It is regularly set in opposition to various "utopian" ideas with their "fantastic pictures of future society" (515). Those views seek to move people to action through depiction of some attractive future condition. The portraits of a new society, of some New Harmony or Icaria, are condemned as groundless idealism, as hopeless dreams. That is not the way "society" or "history" operates. The Marx–Engels arguments, in contrast, involve testable scientific claims.[9] Those claims deal with antecedent causes that can be shown, presumably, to be linked with some specified subsequent effects. Workers in large factories (as opposed to those in small shops) will be "more aware." They will organize; they will engage in revolutionary activity.

Fifth, the Marx–Engels writings focus on the dynamics of the capitalist epoch. The authors provide "scientific" analyses of processes seen within existing capitalist societies. That point has an important correlate: It means that very little is said about processes in the next epoch, the socialist or communist era. In the entire corpus, there are fewer than a dozen pages that, in any way, discuss "how things will be." That omission, in a scientific work, was entirely appropriate. It was, however, inappropriate to state or to assume that the future would be better, since no evidence is (or, more precisely, was) available on such matters. The "determinant" processes driving history could just as easily have been moving events toward a catastrophe rather than toward "a new realm of freedom." The theory, in short, came embellished with an important "utopian" component. Unlike the work of their competitors, however, Marx and Engels did not provide "fantastic pictures." They offered a promissory note.[10]

ASSESSMENT

The Marx–Engels formulations involve what might be called *presentism*. They put in the present tense what at best were developing tendencies. In describing trends or rapid social developments, they avoided the complicated formulations required; that is, base points, statements of rate, and details as to the extent at the time of writing. Instead, they depicted things as de facto achievements rather than on-going processes. Steam and machinery, for example, "revolutionised in-dustrial production." Britain had made considerable progress in this direction as of 1848, but quantitatively most of that revolution was still to come. Elsewhere, in France, Belgium, and the German states, steam power had made only a trivial appearance. These formulations were clearly intended for "dramatic effect"; that is, for rhetorical purposes.

The processes described, all of them, contributed to the proletarian revolution, an event that Marx and Engels assumed to be imminent. Their expectation was that the revolution would come in the course of the next economic crisis. If not then, it would happen in the subse-quent and more serious crisis. In 1895, Engels wrote a brief introduc-tory note reviewing the crisis–revolution linkage, to accompany Marx's *Class Struggles in France*. The 1848 revolution, he wrote, followed "the great commercial crisis that broke out in England in 1847." But then "the prosperity of trade and industry" that came in "the course of 1848 and increased still further in 1849 paralysed the revolutionary upsurge and made possible simultaneous victories of reaction." Marx's text, written in 1850, stated the point more forcefully: "*A new revolu-tion is possible only in consequence of a new crisis. It is, however, just as certain as this crisis*" (emphasis original). Engels was still arguing the claim in 1895, despite repeated failures of the prediction.[11]

The failure of the key prediction, as will be seen later in this chapter, forced continuous modifications and adjustments. In the discussion that follows, the assessments, unless otherwise indicated, will be based on the entire subsequent 150 years of experience. Marx and Engels pre-dicted what was happening or would happen in the bourgeois epoch. This account will, in a summary way, ask what has happened. Other re-vised readings, to be sure, are both possible and justified. At this point, however, we are considering the original Marx–Engels claims.

1. The requirement of innovation: Does the bourgeoisie "constantly revolutionize the means of production"? To address that question one must first specify some meanings. Change is an omnipresent fact. How much change must occur in a given technology for it to be counted as revolutionary? And, a second concern, what time span is involved? Is it a matter of years, decades, or generations? Those meanings must be provided in order to assess the claim; they are necessary prerequisites for any informed conclusion.

An instructive case study is provided by the cotton industry, the example figuring so prominently in Marx and Engels's writing. The industrial revolution in Britain, for all practical purposes, began with a series of remarkable breakthrough inventions in the manufacture of cotton cloth. Phyllis Deane's review of the history lists six innovations: the flying shuttle, the carding machine, the spinning jenny, the water frame, the steam engine, and the cotton gin. The first of these was introduced in the 1730s but gained wide adoption only in the 1750s and 1760s. The spinning jenny was patented in 1770. Whitney's cotton gin was introduced in the last decade of the century. The steam engine was first used in a spinning mill in 1785. Its introduction "on a considerable scale," however, came only in the 1820s, 1830s, and 1840s.[12] This world-historical technological breakthrough, Marx and Engels's exemplary case, required a century for its completion.

The next episode in the history of the textile industry also deserves attention: The industry operated with essentially the same technology for the next century.[13] "Constant revolutionizing" assumes continuous innovation. But invention, especially those bringing revolutionary breakthroughs, are not inevitable; they are not "in the cards." Put simply, if there is no invention, no revolution of production follows. The development of technology brings with it an increase in the costs of innovation. The early inventions were the work of talented mechanics and artisans. But later on, trained scientists, engineers, and expensive laboratories and test sites are required. Innovation, other things being equal, requires research-and-development funding and effort. Highly competitive fields, such as textile manufacture and the garment industry, have low profit margins and little surplus for research and innovation. That is the condition for stagnation, not for constant revolution.

The apparel industry provides another example of a major breakthrough followed by stagnation and then, much later, another episode of dramatic change. The sewing machine was developed by Howe, Singer, and Wilson in the period from 1846 to 1854. Some lesser innovations followed in subsequent decades, but the next "revolutionary" change did not come for a century, with robotization and computerized production.[14]

The persistent focus on "breakthroughs" leads us to overlook the opposite experience of technological persistence or stagnation. For many commentators, "modern times" began with the automobile. The major breakthrough here was Henry Ford's introduction of the assembly line just before World War I. But the basic manufacturing process remained constant for the next half-century until the gradual appearance of robotization. The main- and sub-assembly lines became longer, the product was much more complex with many more parts than the Model T, but the basic assembly process remained unchanged.[15]

A constancy of technology may be seen elsewhere. One of the most important industries in all countries of the modern world is construction. That breaks down into several components: roads and highways, factories, high-rise office and apartment buildings, special purpose (dams, levees), and home construction. Major innovations have occurred in most of those fields; picks and shovels, for example, being replaced by earth-moving equipment in road building. Home construction, until recent decades, has shown a remarkable constancy. Most tools used in the 18th century building trades, those seen in science-and-industry museums, have easily recognized 20th-century counterparts. The power saw replaced the handsaw as a general-purpose tool in the late 1940s. The hammer has been the basic tool in construction for several millennia. In recent years, the nail gun has replaced the hammer for some routine tasks. Electricians, plumbers, roofers, and sheet-metal workers use slightly different more advanced tools and better materials, but the work itself has changed little over the last half century.

A systematic bias appears in this focus on the technological breakthrough. Basically, the innovation is newsworthy; stagnation or constancy is not. Electronic data processing is "news." IBM and mainframe computers, Apple and desktop computers, Microsoft and Windows are news. Unchanged technology in construction or in auto manufacture is not news. At one point in the 1980s, the addition of several hundred thousand computer programmers to the labor force was "news." The addition of the same number of truck drivers, however, was not. It is a problem of sampling bias. The bias in things brought to our attention leads to a second one involving things thought about or things analyzed. We are led to think about "constant revolutionizing." We are not led to think about the causes of stability. Home construction, for example, could long since have been a mass-production industry with prefabrication of floors, sides, and roofs, but the diversity of municipal building codes in combination with a range of union work rules made such rationalization impossible. One result has been more costly housing.[16]

On the basis of this brief review, a more differentiated judgment seems appropriate. As opposed to the constant-change assumption, it is clear that some industries have revolutionized, some have not. Even in the former, the process is not continuous. It is perhaps better to think in terms of episodes, of significant advance followed by stability and then, later, another advance.

One must also consider the question of the rate of change. The initial changes in textile manufacture occurred over the course of perhaps four generations. That was undoubtedly greater overall change than in any previous era. Since then, the rate of change, the speed with which innovations appear and are adopted, has increased considerably. The electric motor was invented in 1821. Its year of first application was 1886. The invention–application gap for the transistor was three years, 1948–1951. For the solar battery it was two, 1953–1955.[17] Frequent innovation is clearly the rule in modern times. The two linked conclusions, "uninterrupted disturbance of all social relations" and "everlasting uncertainty," however, appear to be overdrawn. Personal computers bring some elements of disturbance, but the problems are hardly "uninterrupted." E-mail, providing instant communication, helps to reduce uncertainty.

2. National breakdown: Did nationality break down and disappear with the emergence of international capitalism? A review of the European experience in the period following the Napoleonic Wars casts considerable doubt on this claim. There was, first, the long struggle for the independence of Greece. Then, in 1830, two national uprisings occurred, one a success, the other a failure. The Flemish and Walloon regions of the United Netherlands broke away to form an independent Belgium. A Polish uprising against Russian rule was defeated. The Polish aspirations, incidentally, were championed by advanced intellectuals throughout Europe; Marx and Engels were active supporters of Polish nationalism. Another Polish rising occurred in Cracow in 1846. It too was suppressed.[18]

A series of revolutions swept the European continent in 1848, beginning in Palermo in January. Marx and Engels described these as class struggles, an interpretation that has gained wide acceptance even in non-Marxist circles. Nationalism, however, from the start, was an insistent fact throughout the revolutionary period. The "five glorious days" of armed struggle in Milan sought to throw off Austrian rule. The struggle in Hungary, the longest and most stubbornly fought of the period, was also national, an attempt to end Austrian rule. Prussia was involved in two national struggles that year, one to gain Schleswig and Holstein, and the other to defeat a Polish rising in Posen.[19]

The Crimean War was fought in 1854–1856. Then came the Austrian–Italian War of 1859. The unification of Italy was achieved in 1861. Another Polish insurgency came in 1863. German unification, in some ways the most important event of the era, came in 1871. A series of national struggles led up to the latter event, with Prussia pitted against Denmark in 1864, against Austria in 1866, and against France in 1870. Prussia made use of the national "weapon" in the struggle with Austria; it supported Hungarian nationalists in an attempt to break the Empire's strength. Recognizing the threat, the Austrian government subsequently provided a new constitutional arrangement that gave considerable autonomy to Hungary. The same weapon, nationalist subversion, was considered in the Franco–Prussian War. Persistent national questions in the Balkans led to two wars there in 1912 and 1913. And then, in August 1914, a major conflict began. It was to be the largest conflict of nations in the world's history—until surpassed, a generation later, by an even larger conflagration. In the course of World War I, Germany supported nationalist movements in Russia and there, especially in the Ukraine, they had considerable success.[20]

The period from 1815 to 1914 saw a growth of national consciousness and concerns. World War I was an apotheosis, a culmination of "the national question." A range of social innovations made nations more viable entities than they had ever been in previous centuries. Improved administrative technique allowed greater efficiency in the collection of taxes, in the training and education of the citizenry, and in policing. The administrative technique and the resulting revenues also made possible the formation of stronger, more effective armed forces. The 19th century, moreover, saw the appearance of voluntary associations. Among these were various advocacy groups, some supporting the assertion of national interests, some arguing for the requisite means, a stronger army, a more effective navy, better weapons, and so forth.

The nation-building tendencies continued after 1918. The Versailles negotiators created new states. Poland was restored, several others were formed out of the Austrian empire, the Balkans were rearranged, and in the Baltic region four new states were made out of once-Russian territories. The twenty-year interlude between wars has sometimes been called the "period of fascism," the term referring to the dedicated nationalist parties that appeared after the war.

The aspirations of German, Italian, and Japanese leaders brought about World War II, this conflict more awesome in extent and impact than the first. The early postwar decades saw an extensive decolonization. As a result of outright grants of independence and national liberation struggles, still more states appeared, either revived ones or those formed for the first time.

The "historical movement" was clearly running contrary to the direction announced by Marx and Engels. This was known and recognized by them and, accordingly, two positions are contained in the *Manifesto*. The first, that just reviewed, argues the breakdown of nationality. Through its exploitation of the world market, the bourgeoisie has "given a cosmopolitan character to production and consumption in every country" (488). Only a few pages later the de facto persistence of nations was recognized and a second position spelled out. The concentration of property and the resultant political centralization occurs within nations and the class struggle, accordingly, is at first "a

national struggle." The proletariat must "first of all settle matters with
its own bourgeoisie" (495). The latter is involved "at all times" in a
struggle "with the bourgeoisie of foreign countries." In these battles,
the bourgeoisie is "compelled to appeal to the proletariat, to ask for its
help, and thus, to drag it into the political arena (493).

On the following page, returning to cosmopolitanism, one is told
that "subjection to capital" has stripped the proletariat "in England as
in France, in America as in Germany . . . of every trace of national
character." Later, the point is stated with ultimate simplicity: "The
working men have no country" (502). "National differences and antagonisms between peoples," the authors report, "are daily more and
more vanishing, owing to the development of the bourgeoisie, to freedom of commerce, to the world market, to uniformity in the mode of
production and in the conditions of life corresponding thereto" (503).

Marx and Engels could not avoid "the nationality question" in their
subsequent writings and had to deal repeatedly with such matters.
Those contributions, however, occupy a distinct "second place" in most
of the Marxist literature, there being a clear bifurcation in treatment.
The "major writings" deal with the "Marxian theory." A range of minor, and largely unknown, writings address the irrepressible national
issues, the questions of *Realpolitik*.[21]

3. The great cities: Urban growth is an undoubted fact in the modern
era. That said, a review of relevant evidence is useful. As will be seen,
some specification and some further thought on the subject is required.

London was and is the largest city of Europe in modern times. It is
easy to assume that capitalism and modern industry are the relevant
and appropriate causes. But the growth of London far antedates the
appearance of "modern industry." The city had 400,000 inhabitants
by the mid-17th century, a half-century before the industrial revolution usually associated with cotton manufacture. One major factor
contributing to the growth of cities, London and elsewhere, was the
demographic revolution, the sudden, dramatic increase in population
which began in the mid-17th century. But much of London's growth
had occurred even earlier. At best, that early growth would have to be
linked to some premodern industry.

Most discussions of urban growth, it will be noted, are both casual
and dataless. Most discussions of the British experience comment on
London, the metropolis, and then move quickly to Manchester, the
archetypical industrial city. But few would know the actual rank-
ordering of cities at mid-century. In 1851, London was clearly first with
2,491,000 persons. But then came Liverpool, a port city living on trade

and commerce, with 376,000. The third largest was Glasgow with 345,000. Only then, in fourth position, came Manchester with 303,000. Other industrial cities follow, Birmingham fifth, Leeds seventh, Bristol (another port city) eighth, and Sheffield ninth. Edinburgh, an administrative center (and former capital), was sixth. If one knew the history, that is, if one knew the timing of London's growth, and if one knew the full list of cities, then at minimum a more complex account of urban growth would be required. The simple formula, the declaration that the bourgeoisie "has created enormous cities," is not adequate.[22]

An examination of urban growth on the European continent provides some additional unexpected lessons. The five leading cities there, again at mid-century, were Paris, 1,053,000; St. Petersburg, 490,000; Vienna, 431,000; Naples, 415,000; and Berlin, 378,000. All of them, it will be noted, were considerably larger than Manchester. None of them were centers of "modern industry." There is, however, an easy alternative: They were all centers of government and of premodern handicraft industries. The dominance of governments is evident even later in the century. Adna Weber's figures for 1890 show the following order: London, Paris, Berlin, Vienna, St. Petersburg, and Moscow. Seventh on the list was Hamburg-Altona, Germany's leading port city. And only then, eighth on the list, does one find a modern industrial city, Manchester.[23]

The points made here are reinforced by a more detailed examination of the urban development within the German territories of Europe. The largest cities there at mid-century, as just seen, were Vienna and Berlin. The next largest cities were much smaller, none of them having more than 150,000. Six of them had more than 100,000, those being Breslau, Cologne, Dresden, Hamburg, Munich, and Prague. Five of the six were capital cities, of provinces or of an independent state (Bavaria). Hamburg, a free city-state, was a major port city. The next range, cities with 50,000 to 99,000 persons, contains another twelve cities. Here one finds still more provincial and national capitals (Graz, Brünn, Stuttgart, and Hanover), and more trading centers, centers of traditional manufacturing, or port cities (Frankfurt am Main, Leipzig, Nuremberg, Bremen, Triest). These cities were all contained within the German Bund, a loose federal administrative arrangement having the same boundaries as the earlier Holy Roman Empire. One large German-speaking city, Königsberg, was located outside the Bund territory. It was a provincial capital and an important port on the Baltic.[24]

Some sense of the economic development in one of those large cities, Cologne, may be gained from a mid-century encyclopedia account. It was Prussia's third largest city, with a 1849 population of 94,789 persons. It had an extensive steamship trade with The Netherlands and, upriver, with Frankfurt and Strassburg. Trade was also growing because of the new railroad lines. "Among the factories," the Brockhaus encyclopedia reports, "the most important are those producing *Eau de Cologne*, of which there are about 30, and tobacco, particularly, snuff. In addition, there are factories in wax, soap, sugar, hats, paper, lacquered wares, ropes and hawsers, musical and optical instruments, dyestuffs, glazed pottery, gold- and silverware."[25]

The major point may be seen in another way, through consideration of some "negative findings"; that is, of the cities not on the list, those not yet having 50,000 inhabitants. Friedrich Engels's home city, Barmen, was an important manufacturing city as of 1848. Engels's father was a leading member of the city's bourgeoisie. As of 1850, Barmen had only 36,000 persons. In contrast to Manchester, it had grown by only 5,000 in the previous decade. Essen, home of the Krupps, was destined, in 1933, to be the sixth-largest city in Germany, but in 1850 it had not even passed 15,000. Gelsenkirchen, which in 1933 would have more than 300,000, at this point had only about 3,000. The largest city in the Ruhr region in 1850 was Düsseldorf, the provincial capital. It had 26,500 persons.[26]

Those great cities, ones that were large and growing prior to the appearance of "modern capitalism," were centers of "modern administration." This observation has a striking implication for the Marxian theory, specifically for the class nomenclature. It points up the importance of "bureaucracy" and of salaried white-collar employees. Had they recognized the existence and importance of this class, they could have placed it in their theory as of 1848. Put differently, they could have conceptualized and analyzed "the new middle class" long before its "discovery" a half-century later by the Marxist revisionists.

4. The concentration of property: Has production been centralized in a few hands? The answer is a qualified yes. The general pattern was clear from the mid-19th century onward. There are, however, some important exceptions and, as will be seen, the tendency has limits, typically ending with several producers rather than with monopoly. Given the rising capital costs, in automobile manufacturing for example, concentration was inevitable. In the United States, in 1921, eighty-eight firms were making automobiles. The number had fallen to six in 1953. In 1976, there were four. In 1987, 90 percent or more of U.S. domestic production was dominated by four or fewer companies in motor vehicle and car-body manufacture, electric lamp bulbs, cigarettes, and chewing gum. Between 80 and 90 percent of production was held by the top four in cereal breakfast foods, malt beverages, refrigerators, flat glass, turbines, and turbine generators. The high level of concentration in most fields is eminently clear.[27]

The literature on concentration points to an important specification. In the United States no industry has pushed to the end point; that is, to monopoly, to 100-percent domination by a single producer. Many 20th-century Marxists misrepresent the development with their use of a catchphrase, "monopoly capital." The reality, however, in the overwhelming majority of fields, is oligopoly, meaning a small number of producers. The pure monopoly in capitalist nations typically involves a government enterprise: the post office, public transport, the water works, or, here and there, gas, electricity, telephones, and telegraph.

Marxist commentators typically stress the power of the "monopolist." The giant firm with its immense capital resources is able to dominate its market. But economic specialists point to a distinctive weakness of "dominant" firms. That very dominance makes them sluggish and unresponsive. At the same time, the high profit margin (the "monopoly profits") attracts new, more aggressive competitors. Both processes halt the concentration tendency somewhere short of the monopolistic endpoint independently of any government antitrust efforts. The Standard Oil Company once controlled nearly 90 percent of U.S. oil production. But the firm was indifferent to the exploration of new fields. When Spindletop, a famous Texas "gusher" came in, they had no leases in the area. The company's neglect of the southwest fields made possible the appearance of new competitors, among them Texaco, Gulf, and Sun Oil.[28]

At its founding in 1901, the U.S. Steel Company controlled roughly 65 percent of domestic production. It was the creation of J. P. Morgan, the nation's leading "finance capitalist." Shortly thereafter, it became even larger, with the acquisition of the Tennessee Coal and Iron Company. But then, as a result of struggles in management, some knowledgeable executives left the firm and founded a competitor, Bethlehem Steel. The new firm was designed for a new market, sheet steel for automobiles, and became an important challenger. As of 1938, U.S. Steel controlled approximately one-third of the nation's steel production. In 1988, it controlled less than a sixth. The history of the firm was one of persistent management failure. By the 1960s, Bethlehem Steel was also sluggish and unresponsive; it too paid a heavy price for managerial incompetence.

The history of the American steel industry in the 20th century, it should be noted, is a striking exception to the "rule" of concentration, the history being one of deconcentration. Barnett and Crandall conclude their review, *Up from the Ashes*, as follows:

By the end of this century, the U.S. steel industry will be somewhat smaller, but the larger, integrated companies will be substantially smaller. These integrated companies have already shed 30 percent of their mid-1970s capacity. And they are likely to lose nearly 50 percent of the current capacity by the end of the century. During the same period, the more dynamic new minimills will double their current output and capacity. In short, the complexion of the steel industry will have changed dramatically by the end of the century. No longer will U.S. steel simply be Big Steel.[29]

The Ford Motor Company was once dominant in automobile manufacturing, gaining its ascendancy with the famous Model T. But Henry Ford proved to be peculiarly indifferent to public tastes and demands and, for nineteen years, continued with an unchanged product long after the appearance of more attractive competitors. General Motors produced a range of offerings and brought out new models each year. Henry Ford's managerial failure almost brought the company to collapse. In a later period, the managerial indifference of General Motors, Ford, and Chrysler created an opportunity for foreign competitors, first Volkswagen and then several Japanese producers. The "dominant" firms, in effect, gave away important shares of "their" market.[30]

General Electric, holding the major Edison patents, was once the undisputed giant of the electrical industry. But one of its leaders, Thomas A. Edison, whose inventions made the firm possible, had a stubborn preference for direct current, a choice that for several reasons had disastrous implications for the firm. That "immobility" allowed a competitor, Westinghouse, to make considerable advances through the sale of alternating-current generators.[31]

International Business Machines was once the undisputed giant in electronic data processing. But in the 1980s, its management made some major errors of judgment, among them the decision to continue their emphasis on mainframe computers. The major demand in that decade, however, was for microcomputers. In a brief span, the company's share of the personal computer market dropped from 80 percent to less than 20 percent. The company was suffering heavy losses in the early 1990s, and the 1992 loss was "the biggest annual loss in American corporate history."[32]

The sluggish performance of the oligopolies was to have far-reaching consequences. Until the early 1960s, the major steel producers engaged in a legal form of collusion called administered pricing. One firm would take the lead by announcing its new schedule of increased prices for basic products and the others would follow, adopting the same price list. The arrangement worked well in the booming 1950s and the companies showed commendable earnings. The consumers paid the price but, in those good times, that caused little strain. Unions made heavy wage demands in the period and the companies acceded with little resistance, knowing that those costs too could be passed on to consumers. While successful in the short run, this managerial practice brought long-run disaster. American steel products came to have high costs. This circumstance, as in automobile manufacture, brought new, more serious foreign competition.

In a sharp confrontation in 1962, President Kennedy, demonstrating remarkable independence, blocked a round of steel price increases, successfully thwarting the aims of the oligopolist producers. Later in the decade, the steel industry was facing serious losses in domestic and foreign markets. "By the 1980s," as Walter Adams and Hans Mueller put it, "the steel oligoply seemed moribund—a collection of helpless giants begging for government relief from self-inflicted injury." The impacts of the easygoing managerial practices of the 1950s extended far beyond a couple of major industries. Those management arrangements contributed to the appearance of "rust belt" cities and, inadvertently, helped to create "the urban underclass."[33]

5. Political centralization: Centralization efforts had been underway for centuries. Ferdinand and Isabella, it is said, had unified Spain. The later "absolute" monarchs were ardent centralizers. The *fronde* wars in France slowed the process, but ultimately Cardinal Mazarin and Louis XIV defeated the aristocratic challenge. Peter the Great, Charles XII of Sweden, and Frederick the Great were all centralizers. The process continued with even greater zeal under Napoleon Bonaparte, his policies having a lasting impact throughout the continent. All of that centralization, it will be noted, occurred long before the appearance of modern industry or bourgeois hegemony. Those efforts were initiated by *political* leaders; it was not the work of a "rising bourgeoisie." On this point Marx and Engels have cut the evidence to suit their theoretical purpose. The supposed causal factor, the "concentration of property," came long after the movement for "concentration of political control."

It might be the case that the bourgeoisie, when in power, continued those long-term centralization efforts. If so, a specification of the cases and some demonstration of the bourgeois initiatives would be appropriate. The unification of Germany might qualify as a decisive step toward centralization. Marx and Engels both showed considerable enthusiasm for Bismarck's achievement. In August of 1870, Marx wrote Engels declaring, "*L'Empire est fait*, i.e. the German Empire." Engels replied, "Now, as in 1866, Bismarck is doing a bit of our work, in *his own* way and without meaning to, but all the same he is doing it. He is clearing the deck for us better than before."[34]

Several problems appear in this connection. Marx and Engels had predicted a bourgeois takeover. The bourgeoisie, they announced in 1848, would imminently be in power. But in the 1848 revolution the Prussian bourgeoisie had "failed miserably." They had not carried through "their" revolution and in short order the old regime was back, apparently in full control. Was Bismarck then, in 1870, acting as a representative of the old regime? Or was he somehow an agent of a nonrevolutionary bourgeoisie? If the former, some reconciliation of fact and theory was (and would still be) appropriate, since a major prediction had not been supported. If one wished to argue "agency," some evidence, some documentation of the point would be appropriate. One should present, for example, some letters or memoranda showing Bismarck carrying out the will of Ruhr industrialists.[35]

Still another problem appears in this episode. Bismarck's accomplishment fell far short of Marx and Engels's aspirations. In a letter to August Bebel in 1884, Engels recognized the Empire to be "a thoroughly revolutionary creation." But he reproached its planners for being "only wretched revolutionaries" for having failed to go further to annex all of Germany. Still later, in 1891, Engels wrote that "the system of small states must be abolished—just try to revolutionise society while there are the Bavarian–Württemberg reservation rights— and the map of Thuringia, for example, is such a sorry sight. . . . What should take its place? In my view, the proletariat can only use the form of the one and indivisible republic."[36] Bismarck, it seems, had done a poor job of it. He had unified only part of the German-speaking peoples, adopting the "Small German" solution. And worse, he had created a federal system.

Again, a prediction had not been supported. But rather than reconsidering the prediction, Engels was blaming Bismarck and the recalcitrant facts. Centralization, from the beginning, was a key demand in the Marxian agenda; the centralized arrangement would facilitate the proletarian revolution. The mixing of scientific and practical efforts gave rise to a continuous problem. Their practical needs were driving the formulations of their "science."

6. Bourgeois domination: This claim, in its boldest form, assumes a clear and unambiguous takeover; that is, a bourgeois revolution. But this argument, despite widespread acceptance, was problematic from the outset. Marx and Engels had difficulty locating "the bourgeois revolution" in England, the most obvious possibilities being in the 17th century. The difficulty is indicated by their diverse dating of the event: 1640, 1648, and 1688. But "the bourgeoisie" was then only in its very early development, certainly not in a position to "take power." Few of the leaders of the English Civil War or of the Glorious Revolution could be described as members of the bourgeoisie, not as Marx and Engels typically used that term. Late in the 19th century, in

private correspondence, Marx and Engels expressed their puzzlement about the continuing presence of the aristocracy in the highest offices of the British government.[37]

The bourgeoisie, it was claimed, took power in France in 1789. But that too was (and is) difficult to sustain by reference to historical sources. One would have to assume that the Constitutional Assembly was dominated by (or was the instrument of) the bourgeoisie, the leaders of modern industry. And, presumably, one would have to say the same for the Jacobins. Bonaparte's 1799 coup would also pose a problem. Was he bourgeois? Or was he an agent of the bourgeoisie? But those difficulties did not interest Marx and Engels; they did not address the issues involved but simply repeated, again and again, their basic claim. The 1830 and 1848 revolutions in France are both portrayed as bourgeois revolutions. The coup of Bonaparte's nephew, Louis Napoleon, in 1851 posed an obvious problem and an "explanation" was hastily extemporized.[38]

No bourgeois revolution occurred in Germany; the German bourgeoisie "failed" in its historical task. The bourgeois revolution thesis, in short, cannot be satisfactorily sustained in any of the three major European contexts. One might reasonably substitute a bourgeois evolution thesis, but that would postpone the appearance of bourgeois rule. It would then become a complex history of steps or episodes with much accident or contingency. Faced with the problem of flimsy supporting evidence, Marx's solution was to fall back on metaphor and insinuation. The bourgeoisie is regularly portrayed as operating "behind the scenes" (*hinter den Kulissen*). In another frequently used image, Marx is "unveiling" the otherwise obscure linkages. In one exuberant literary display, he has an array of public figures performing their very public (and easily documented) roles while "the real commanders sat behind the counter."[39] Literary legerdemain is of course no adequate substitute for evidence.

Marx and Engels argue direct instrumental control. No murky "structuralism" is to be seen, for example, in their claim about the state as a committee for the management of the bourgeoisie's common affairs. The appropriate test of that claim would require extensive research, a sweeping review of decision making in governments throughout the entire epoch. The following paragraphs provide a brief review of political events in the United States from 1896 to 1914. This limited sample of experience can obviously serve only as illustration of the kind of research needed and the possible diversity of results.

In the 1890s, a group of bourgeois notables led by Marcus Alonzo Hanna chose William McKinley as their candidate for the presidency and, in 1896, succeeded in their aims. That experience provides an unambiguous documented example of direct bourgeois domination.

Early in McKinley's first term, some groups began agitation for a war with Spain over the Cuban question. McKinley, Hanna, and most other business leaders opposed the war, but in this case, the "executive committee of the bourgeoisie" lost the contest.

In 1900, McKinley was again the favored candidate. At this point, Theodore Roosevelt, the popular wartime hero and later governor of New York, was accepted as the vice presidential candidate. Roosevelt was not welcomed by those bourgeois notables, nor by the Republican bosses. He was an interloper, an unwelcome presence. Hanna was vociferous on the subject. At the convention he asked, "Don't any of you realize that there's only one life between that madman and the Presidency?" The assassination of McKinley in the following year made Roosevelt president of the United States. Hanna, known for pungent speech, said they now had to deal with "that damned cowboy."[40]

Roosevelt's presidency is known for, among other things, its antitrust activity; that is, government efforts to break up some of that "concentration of property." The most important of these, a suit instituted by the Justice Department, led to the breakup of the Standard Oil Company. In an important opposite move, one that "served the interests" of J. P. Morgan, he approved U.S. Steel's acquisition of Tennessee Coal and Iron.

Declining the possibility of a third term, Roosevelt chose his former Secretary of War, William Howard Taft, as his successor, a decision, it will be noted, that bypassed the bourgeois notables. Even more antitrust actions were instituted during Taft's administration, the most important of these stemming from U.S. Steel's acquisition of the Tennessee company. These government antitrust actions demonstrate the independence or autonomy of "government." They challenge a staple Marxist argument, that governments simply "reflect" the wishes of powerful monopoly capitalists.[41]

In 1912, Taft held the powers of office and, defeating Roosevelt's challenge, again secured the Republican nomination. Woodrow Wilson, the progressive governor of New Jersey, was the Democratic candidate. Roosevelt then chose to run as a third-party candidate, also as a progressive. This split the Republicans and gave the presidency to the progressive Democrat. The conservative bourgeois notables lost twice in this contest: They could not block the insurgency within "their" party and they lost control of the presidency. In the first years of Wilson's administration, his progressive years, the high tariffs, generally referred to as Republican tariffs, were cut. Those high tariffs provided a sizable portion of the government's revenues. To make up the lost revenues, Wilson and the Democratic Congress instituted an income tax.[42]

A first lesson to be drawn from this brief sample of experience is that a differentiated conclusion is appropriate. In some instances big business won; in others it lost. A loss meant that some other group or coalition was stronger than the coalition of major capitalists. As opposed to the claim of exclusive bourgeois domination, those losses make clear that other options are possible within capitalism. At minimum, those other options should be recognized; some explanation, some appropriate extension of the theory, is required.

One should consider other alternate substantive possibilities. Business might win regularly in one era but do poorly in another. Big business, for example, might have done well early on, in the 1870s and 1880s, the period of the "robber barons." But later, opposition to the interests appeared first with the populists and then with the progressive movement. The progressive forces lost out in the 1920s, in a period of conservative Republican resurgence. But then, with the coming of the New Deal and the victory of liberal forces in the Democratic Party, business came to be a frequent loser.[43]

7. Economic crises: This claim, as noted, is given considerable prominence in the *Manifesto*. The crises, it was argued, were unavoidable; they were an inherent or necessary concomitant of the capitalist arrangement. The problem, the authors announced, would become more severe; one would see "more extensive and more destructive crises." Economic crises had appeared regularly in the capitalist world and would continue to appear over most of the subsequent century. It was not, however, a history of cumulating intensity. Through to 1930, a general upward economic movement was seen in all major capitalist nations, accompanied by wide cyclical swings with years of prosperity followed by years of depression. The major economic catastrophe came in the 1930s. It was the most serious collapse of the entire modern era.

The experience of the years following World War II does not support the basic claim. The postwar history was one of dramatic economic growth with only modest cyclical swings. The period from 1950 to 1970 saw what was probably the greatest and most sustained economic growth in all of human history. The knowledge required for controlling those swings, the basic countercyclical policy options, had been available for some time before 1930. But the use of that information had been prevented. Business leaders and conservative politicians refused to use the Keynesian procedures, viewing them as economic heresy or, worse, as communistic. Marx and Engels regularly portrayed the bourgeoisie as rational, informed, and knowledgeable. But in this case, their shortsighted policies created the disaster. One consequence was that the disaster led to a change in outlooks and brought more informed economic policies that have dominated now for a half-century.[44]

8. The quality of work: A dramatic decline in the quality of work came, supposedly, with the division of labor. We do not, of course, have serious studies of attitudes toward work before and after that transition. The claim, accordingly, rests on a plausible logic; namely, that artisan or craft production, with all its diverse operations and individual control, must have been more satisfying than divided labor with its endless repetition. But skepticism is always appropriate, especially with respect to the purely logical case. How much charm would remain after the first few weeks for the craftsman who performed all eighteen steps in pin manufacture? How much charm lingered on for the shoemaker after years of cutting, stitching, and hammering?

The argument is problematic in another respect. It is based on atypical experience; it separates out what, even in the mid-19th century, would have been the experience of a small minority in the labor force in economically advanced nations. Most work in the Western world, for several millennia, had been agricultural. Much of it, initially, involved use of the hoe; later, it would have been a combination, some people working with a plow and many others still hoeing. It was an endless round of planting, weeding, and harvesting. A priori it seems unlikely that such work provided much charm. Even without biblical guidance, most people, during all those millennia, would have easily agreed with the text of Genesis that bread was earned only with "the sweat of thy face."

Systematic studies of work began to appear early in the 20th century; their number and quality increased considerably after World War II. The studies in recent decades have shown, with remarkable consistency, large majorities reporting some degree of satisfaction with their work. The most frequent response in one important series, the National Opinion Research Center's General Social Surveys, is "very satisfied." That option was chosen by roughly half of the respondents in the nineteen studies covering a quarter-century of recent experience.[45] Another three-eighths, approximately, indicated they were "moderately satisfied" (see Table 2.1). Those results are for full-time employed persons. A slight decline is indicated in this period; all of the 50-percent-or-more results occurred in 1985 or earlier. The corresponding increase, a matter of a few percentage points, appeared in the "moderately satisfied" response.

Some commentators have argued that routine-work-satisfaction questions like those used in Table 2.1 involve a serious response bias. Respondents, it is said, are reluctant to admit to interviewers that their jobs are unattractive. To maintain (or to communicate) a positive self-image, many people supposedly give more favorable reports than is

Table 2.1
Work Satisfaction (NORC General Social Survey)

Year	Very Satisfied	Moderately Satisfied	A Little Dissatisfied	Very Dissatisfied	Total
1972	49 %	37 %	11 %	3 %	746
1973	50	37	9	4	643
1974	51	37	9	4	632
1975	57	32	8	3	607
1976	56	33	9	3	611
1977	50	39	10	2	761
1978	52	37	8	3	712
1980	46	37	13	4	685
1982	48	39	9	4	686
1983	53	35	9	3	731
1984	47	35	12	6	714
1985	50	39	8	3	736
1986	49	41	9	1	694
1987	47	38	12	3	762
1988	49	38	10	4	724
1989	49	38	9	4	758
1990	48	39	9	4	700
1991	48	42	7	4	701
1993	45	42	10	4	809
1994	47	40	10	3	1,588
1996	46	40	10	4	1,634

Note: The question was, "On the whole, how satisfied are you with the work you do— would you say you are very satisfied, moderately satisfied, a little dissatisfied, or very dissatisfied?" Responses are for those currently working full-time only. Excludes those working part-time and temporarily not at work as well as those retired and keeping house.

actually the case. This hypothesis, it is claimed, gains support in ethnographic studies of work. Observational studies allow closer contact and in-depth probes, it is claimed, and yield considerably less positive results.

One specialist, Randy Hodson, had graduate students read 101 ethnographic studies of work and code them on a wide range of characteristics, one of these being job satisfaction. The ratings assigned in these studies were as follows: very high, 4; high, 32; average, 23; moderately low, 33; and very low, 9. These results are not as positive as those reported in Table 2.1. But the 101 studies, it should be noted, are not representative of the labor force. They are, moreover, doubly mediated: Investigators chose the sites, saw things, selected among those things, and reported findings; graduate students then provided summary judgments based on their reading of the texts. One indication of the difficulties was that five of the nine monographs rated as showing "very low" satisfaction were based on experience in the United Kingdom.[46]

The degree of satisfaction, not surprisingly, varies generally with the income, status, and/or responsibility of the job. But even in the least attractive occupations, in the semiskilled, unskilled, and service jobs, satisfaction was reported with much greater frequency than dissatisfaction (Table 2.2). The class differences, it should be noted, are rather small. Among the males, comparing the two groups of operatives (machine operators, semiskilled workers) and the two high-status middle-class groups, the professionals and managers, one finds a difference of roughly 20 percentage points in the "very satisfied" reports. Comparing the crafts (skilled workers) and professionals, the difference is effectively zero. For all of the discussion about "the importance of class," this result shows only a modest impact.

In recent years, some commentators and researchers, bypassing this nonconfirming evidence, have argued a de facto "degradation of labor." In some accounts, the supposed tendency is referred to as "deskilling." This revival of the older claims stimulated some research on the topic. William H. Form, a leading industrial sociologist, reviewed these studies and concluded that the claim was unsupported. The skill-degradation argument was based on an unrepresentative sample of experience; the claim "found most support in early case studies of dying crafts." The later "historical research into a wider set of occupations demonstrated that these early findings could not be generalized." Later studies covering all occupations in the labor force found "little or no aggregate skill change" in recent decades.[47]

The skill-degradation claim runs counter to one of the most easily established conclusions about work in modern times; that is, the decline in unskilled labor. In 1900, farm and nonfarm laborers together formed one-third of the male labor force. In 1950, they formed only one-seventh of that total. Those onerous tasks have, for the most part, been mechanized. The backbreaking labor, the "toting and hauling" of previous generations, was now done with cranes, conveyor belts, assembly lines, and forklift trucks. This change, it should be noted, is one of the most important occupational transformations of the entire modern era.[48]

Table 2.2
Occupation and Work Satisfaction for Nonfarm Males and Females: Full-Time Employed (NORC–GSS Merge 1990–1994)

| | Nonmanual Occupations | | | Manual Occupations | | | | |
	Professional, Technical	Manager, Sales, Administrator	Clerical	Crafts	Operatives Excluding Transport	Transport Operatives, Laborers	Service	Total
Males								
Very Satisfied	52 %	51 %	41 %	50 %	35 %	32 %	45 %	47 %
Moderately Satisfied	38	37	46	40	48	50	42	41
A Little Dissatisfied	7	8	11	8	13	15	10	9
Very Dissatisfied	3	4	2	2	4	3	3	3
N =	(368)	(519)	(138)	(378)	(158)	(225)	(176)	(1,962)
Percentage Across	19	27	7	19	8	12	9	= 100
Females								
Very Satisfied	60 %	50 %	43 %	45 %	23 %	39 %	43 %	47 %
Moderately Satisfied	33	39	44	37	59	41	42	40
A Little Dissatisfied	5	9	11	12	13	14	10	9
Very Dissatisfied	2	3	3	6	6	6	4	3
N =	(430)	(390)	(487)	(51)	(111)	(49)	(249)	(1,767)
Percentage Across	24	22	28	3	6	3	14	= 100

The "critical" argument, the lost-charm or degraded-work claim, in summary, has been sustained through the use of questionable intellectual procedures. These include use of the untested logical argument, avoidance of serious contrary evidence of the work satisfaction studies, selective (or purposeful) sampling of experience (artisan shops versus agriculture, dying crafts versus the more typical cases of growth), and neglect of (or failure to report) one of the most important occupational changes of the modern era, the decline of unskilled labor.

9. The immiseration thesis: This claim is closely related to the skill-degradation argument. Skill levels would be pushed downward and wage rates would be reduced accordingly. Competitive pressures would force the capitalists, all of them, to move in this direction. But subsequent experience did not support this claim. In later decades, real wages were clearly rising; they were not being reduced, "almost entirely, to the means of subsistence." This proposition, therefore, had to be abandoned, and revision was necessary.[49] The modifications appeared in Marx and Engels's later writings. More forceful statements, those of the revisionist writers, came around the turn of the century. A second major revision was provided subsequently by V. I. Lenin. Both of those readings will be considered in later chapters.

10. The aggregation of workers: Abandoning the "little workshop," the modern capitalist is forced to bring workers together in "the great factory." W. O. Henderson has given us a summary account of employment in the British textile industry in the years prior to publication of the *Manifesto*, that industry being the prime case for Marx and Engels's analysis:

While the total labour force in the textile industries amounted to nearly a million and a half in 1841, the factory inspectors' returns for 1839 showed that under half a million workers were employed in the textile factories of the United Kingdom. Over a million textile workers—665,000 of them living in Ireland—did not work in factories. Most of them were handloom weavers or worsted wool combers. As late as 1850 about half the woollen workers in Yorkshire were still outside the factory system.[50]

Given the later "evidence," easily seen in major industrial centers, one could hardly doubt the validity of the aggregation claim. As always, however, it is useful to check impressions against systematic evidence. The questions of extent and trend should be considered. What proportion of workers were employed in great factories, say in 1880 or in 1900? What proportion are employed there today? And what is the current tendency?

Some useful data on this question come from Germany, where the industrial takeoff occurred in the last third of the 19th century. In 1882, early on in that process, almost half of the industrial labor force was employed in shops of one to five persons. If "giant factory" meant one employing 1,000 or more persons, those units accounted for about 5 percent of the total. The proportions had changed considerably by 1907, but even then the smallest category was still the modal case, employing approximately three-tenths of the total. The giant units at that point did not employ even one-tenth of the industrial labor force. In 1925, the giant units had almost "caught up," but still had not eclipsed the little workshops. Both categories employed just under one-fifth of the total. The majority, clearly, were employed in medium-size units, approximately equal numbers being found in the categories 11 to 50, 51 to 200, and 201 to 1,000 workers. At that late point, therefore, the result still did not accord with the Marx–Engels claim made some seventy-five years earlier.[51]

A major study of the U.S. adult population from the early 1970s, the Quality of Employment Survey, contained the following question: "About how many people work at the location where you work—I mean all types of workers in all areas and departments?" Approximately one-quarter (26%) of all employed persons worked in units of one to nine persons. Another quarter (24%) were found in the next category, units of ten to forty-nine persons. Only one in seven (14%) worked in units of 1,000 or more. A separate examination looking at the results for male blue-collar workers showed fewer in the two smallest categories and more in the middle categories. The equivalent figures for these categories were 19, 22, and 14 percent, respectively. Those results, to be sure, focus on individual locations as opposed to the entire firm or government unit.[52]

Marx and Engels pointed to a significant de facto working-class presence in the large factories, with the movement presumably continuing in the foreseeable future. While the movement, as seen in the German experience, was in the predicted direction, both the rate of change and the extent of the accomplishment were rather limited. More recent evidence shows that the majority of workers are still employed in small or middling establishments. Work in the giant factory is typical of only a small minority.

A comprehensive review of evidence on the size of the workplace appears in a very informative 1984 article by Mark Granovetter, "Small Is Bountiful."[53] The major finding is indicated in the title. A second finding involves the trend. While much popular commentary assumed continuing growth in the size of the workplace, his evidence showed some reversal in recent decades.

The evidence reviewed thus far addresses one specific question, the size of the workplace. The related questions of the quality of work, of work satisfaction, of hierarchy and social relations, of the union presence, and of political attitudes and party choices are separate and independent concerns requiring different lines of research. Juan Linz provided a detailed review of West German experience based on surveys from the early 1950s. Support for the Social Democrats among male workers did increase with size of plant, going from 37 percent in units with less than ten persons to 56 percent in units with 1,000 or more. Workers in the large plants were more likely to favor "constant struggle with the employers." They were more likely to think the unions "too soft." The differences between the extremes in these three measures were moderate, less than 20 percentage points.[54]

Discussions of giant enterprises and the presumed impacts on workers often neglect a range of other factors. Workers in larger shops are better paid, have more extensive fringe benefits, have more job security, and have more opportunities for advancement. Another relevant consideration is that unions are more likely to be present in the large shops.

The accounts stressing hierarchy, impersonal authority, and the "military regime" of the factory, together with claims of a collective worker response, often neglect the personal histories and the communal ties of those workers, counting such matters as unimportant. An insightful study by R. Blank pointed out, with evidence, that German industry was concentrated in the Ruhr, in Silesia, and in Alsace. All three were heavily Catholic regions and that meant a largely Catholic working class with strong ties to the Center Party (or to a fringe party representing the Polish minority).[55] That fact hindered the development of Social Democracy and of its allied trade unions in the Ruhr. It meant also that the party's strength would be located elsewhere, in other less-developed regions, in smaller shops, and in Protestant regions. Decades later, the Christian Democrats continued to outdo the Social Democrats in the Ruhr area (Nordrhein–Westfalen). The first reversal of that pattern, the first Social Democratic plurality, came in 1969.

Marxism, along with liberalism and the mass society theory, assumes that irrepressible secularizing tendencies are present in all modern societies. The assumption is that all communal bases of human existence, whether religious, ethnic, regional, or national, would be eroded and, ultimately, eliminated. Given that assumption, the neglect of those factors seems entirely justified. Religion, accordingly, is treated as a waning factor, one of ever-diminishing importance. Given the assumption, it would not seem necessary to inquire about Catholic and Protestant workers in the giant factory. The refusal to consider those communal factors means that theorists, commentators, and researchers are poorly prepared for their analytical tasks.[56]

11. The petty bourgeoisie: The main prediction here is one of downward mobility: This segment will "fall into the proletariat." It was to be a central issue in the conflict over revisionist Marxism. Consideration of this segment will be deferred to the next chapter.

12. The *Lumpenproletariat*: The authors' concern with this, the "dangerous class," is a peculiar one. In Marx's first major historical analysis, his account of the 1848 revolution in France, he assigned the *Lumpenproletariat* an important role in the June Days. The *Garde mobile*, he claimed, was recruited from those ragtag elements and used to defeat the working-class insurgency. More than a century later, Mark Traugott demonstrated that Marx's conclusion was mistaken. The barricade fighters and the members of the *Garde* proved to have nearly identical backgrounds. Marx's conclusion, in short, proved to be without justification.

Marx used the concept again in his second major historical analysis, the *18th Brumaire*. Again, the portrait was scathing, more excoriation than analysis. In later writings, references to this problematic group became less frequent. Most subsequent depictions of the classes and their activities did not even mention the *Lumpenproletariat*. With "history" providing no clear support, Marx and Engels simply abandoned the concept.[57]

13. The role of the intellectuals: Marx and Engels's reference to earlier experience, to the "small section of the ruling class" that "joins the revolutionary class," refers to a key event in the French Revolution. In the early procedural struggles within the National Assembly, the defection of some members of the first and second estates, the clergy and nobility, gave the insurgents within the third estate a decisive advantage, moving events further toward the collapse of the monarchy. The most dramatic of those shifts was that of Louis Philippe, the Duc d'Orléans, a cousin of the king, who soon, in the spirit of the age, changed his name to Philippe Egalité. Later, under considerable pressure, he cast a vote for the execution of his cousin.[58]

Marx and Engels doubtlessly had themselves in mind when writing of "the bourgeois ideologists" going over to the proletariat and providing "fresh elements of enlightenment." It was an unusual combination, with Dr. Karl Marx and his friend and collaborator Friedrich Engels, the son of a factory owner, mixing with the artisans and journeymen at meetings of the *Bund der Kommunisten*.

Two decades later, the key figures in the founding of Germany's Social Democratic Party were Ferdinand Lassalle, Wilhelm Liebknecht, and August Bebel. Lassalle was a very well-off lawyer, the son of a Breslau silk merchant. Liebknecht was descended from three generations of civil servants. He attended university but did not graduate, turning instead to journalism as a career. Bebel was one of the few socialist leaders of the period who could claim any proletarian connection. His father, a noncommissioned officer, died of tuberculosis when the son was in his teens. Shortly thereafter, his mother succumbed to the same disease. Bebel was apprenticed as a woodworker, served as a journeyman, and was a wage worker for some years before opening his own business. Karl Kautsky, for years the party's intellectual leader, came of an artistic family; both parents "were professionally associated with the Austrian theatrical world." In his memoirs Kautsky sought "to establish a vague proletarian pedigree for himself," but as one biographer put it, "his immediate family was not proletarian by any stretch of the imagination." He spent nine semesters at the University of Vienna but did not take a degree.[59]

The leaders of the Social Democratic Party's left wing, Karl Liebknecht and Rosa Luxemburg, also had no proletarian roots. Liebknecht, a son of the party's founder, was raised in considerable affluence in one of the better sections of Berlin. He held a doctorate in law. Luxemburg held a doctorate of philosophy. Half of the members of the founding committee of the German Communist Party held doctorates. The founders of the Communist Party in Italy, Gramsci and Togliatti, both had doctorates. Gramsci came from an impoverished lower-middle-class family. Jean Jaurès, the leading figure of the French left, came from a modest lower-middle-class background and was a graduate of the prestigious Ecole Normale. Eugene Victor Debs, the charismatic leader of the American Socialist Party, was the son of a prosperous Terre Haute, Indiana, store owner and the grandson of an Alsatian textile manufacturer. Norman Thomas, his successor and longtime leader of the party, was descended from three generations of Presbyterian ministers.

The significant presence of bourgeois intellectuals in the parties of the left has long been noted. In an important account, first published in 1911, Robert Michels reviewed the European experience and pointed to the tendency for the intellectuals in the socialist parties to favor the left. The "strongest impulse to the reformist tendency in Germany," he wrote, "was given by the trade-union leaders, by persons therefore of proletarian origin. . . . Generally speaking the working-class lead-

ers of proletarian origin have a special tendency to adopt the reformist attitude." The radical or revolutionary tendency was sustained primarily by intellectuals, by persons of bourgeois origin. Intellectuals,
however, were divided. Michels found them distributed in nearly equal
proportions among the two tendencies.[60]

Although not spelled out in detail, the logic of Marx and Engels's
argument is clear enough. Workers engaged for long hours in routine
tasks would not see or understand the larger picture. They would,
understandably, give almost all their attention to wages and hours
questions, to work conditions, and to "bread and butter" issues. In
later discussions, this narrow focus was termed "economism" or
"workerism." Such demands could be met through normal trade-union
efforts within capitalism, all without ever rising to the political level.
Where Marx and Engels assumed that the movement from economic
to political questions would come easily, later Marxists, Lenin in particular, argued a sharp disjunction. Workers, because of their limited
experience, would not ordinarily make that leap. The revolutionary
intellectuals, because of their wide-ranging education, could see the
larger connections and could formulate the needed lessons. To make
the linkage of the economic and the political, the intellectuals' efforts
were indispensable.

The *Manifesto* statement has workers and intellectuals operating together in easy harmony: Workers need tutelage and intellectuals supply it. The lessons, presumably, would be readily accepted and the
historical process would move accordingly. In practice, however, the
process did not move as they suggested. In the 1840s, Marx and Engels
had formed various Correspondence Committees to spread their views
and to gain influence in working-class circles throughout Europe. Those
efforts, however, were not successful. They then turned their attention
to the League of the Just, an organization they saw as providing access to the working class.

The League was the creation of some talented, self-taught workers,
artisans, and journeymen, most of them German exiles living in Paris,
London, and elsewhere. The relationship was not an easy one. Marx
made a sharp personal attack on one of the founders, Wilhelm Weitling,
and wrote a strong criticism of another, Hermann Kriege, in an effort
to displace them. There was, understandably, some distrust of the "literary characters in Brussels" because of that "intellectual arrogance."
But some of the working-class leaders also recognized that they needed
intellectual guidance, and negotiations continued. The organization
was renamed, at Marx's request, and became the League of Communists. It was agreed that Marx and Engels would write the group's
manifesto, which would be adopted as their official position. Shortly
thereafter, Marx became the head of the Central Committee.[61]

In May 1846, Marx had written to Pierre Proudhon, the French working-class leader, asking him to write for their Correspondence Committee. As far as France is concerned, he wrote, "we can find no better correspondent than yourself." Proudhon sensed something in the tone of the letter and, in his reply, cautioned against the possibility of "a new intolerance." "Let us . . . encourage all dissent, let us outlaw all exclusiveness," he wrote. In July 1847, Marx published a monograph condemning the thinking of this proletarian leader. Proudhon, unlike Marx's other opponents considered here, survived the onslaught.[62]

The League history was repeated later in Cologne in 1848 and 1849. In the early days of the revolution there, Andreas Gottschalk, a doctor working among the poor, organized a Workers' Association (which, incidentally, he viewed as an extension of the Communist League). It had considerable success, having recruited 8,000 members. Shortly after Marx's arrival in the city, he attacked Gottschalk's leadership. David McLellan writes that differences between the two "were inevitable." Marx joined and became a leading figure in a rival organization, the Cologne Democratic Society, in part with a view to "making contacts" that would benefit his newspaper, the *Neue Rheinische Zeitung*. Gottschalk was jailed from July to December 1848. On his release, he found his organization "largely in the control of the Marxists and . . . no longer interested in his advice or leadership." In February 1849, the organization was "under Marx's leadership." In this case, the middle-class intellectuals dominated the workers' organization from the beginning.[63]

Two decades later, in the struggle for control of the International Workingmen's Association—the First International—the conflict was between Marx and Michael Bakunin, neither of them in any way of proletarian background. Bakunin was the son of a Russian estate owner.

The lesson to be drawn from Marx and Engels's own experience, from their *Praxis*, was that intellectuals would displace workers in the leadership of the working-class movement. Intellectuals went beyond the provision of a service, "supplying enlightenment," and took control of the movement.[64]

The disjunction required systematic misrepresentation. The Socialist and the later Communist Parties declared themselves to be working-class parties. But the leaders of those parties were typically not workers, nor were they of working-class origin. The misrepresentations took various forms. Fictional biographical elements were provided, containing some "proletarian" antecedents or linkages. Where that was implausible, the accounts provided a history of martyrdom stemming from years of service in the proletarian cause. Marx and his family, it is said, suffered extraordinary privations for many years in their "exile" in Britain. For an American audience, one unlikely to know the man's actual circumstances, Wilhelm Liebknecht was described as a man "satisfied with the merest necessities of life, so long as he can serve his cause."[65]

Another tactic used to give plausibility to the working-class character of a party was the use of a "front man," a person with unquestionable working-class credentials who would willingly accept the direction provided by the party's actual leaders. One striking example of this manipulative practice involved Ernst Thälmann in the German Communist Party in the later Weimar period. The Communist Party in the United States made similar use of William Z. Foster, the charismatic leader of the 1919 steel strike and, in the process, destroyed his credibility. To give the appropriate appearance, the French Communist Party required its units to have a minimum number of workers in leadership positions and on candidate lists. The resulting "evidence" was then publicized and used to their advantage, particularly vis-à-vis the "bourgeois" socialists. To bridge the gaps in backgrounds, knowledge, and abilities, pairing arrangements were developed. For their mutual advantage, a party intellectual who could provide theory, history, and bureaucratic skill would join forces with a working-class leader who could provide knowledge of local conditions and appropriate credentials.[66]

A conclusion: The working-class movement, from an early point, was not led by workers. The organizations and parties, with only rare exceptions, were directed and managed by people of middle-class origin, most of them from rather privileged backgrounds.

14. The organizational development: Marx and Engels anticipated a shift from the initial incoherent and scattered "mass" to the "clubbing together" in trade unions and, finally, to the comprehensive "independent movement of the immense majority." A seesaw process was foreseen, with gains, losses, and then further more comprehensive gains.

The trade unions did develop in most countries, especially where prior liberal victories allowed two basic freedoms, those of expression and assembly. Working-class parties appeared also, in most instances coming in the predicted sequence, after the unions. The relationships of the unions and the parties, however, were not those predicted. Some unions clubbed together to secure job monopolies, basically to exclude other workers, a tendency persisting in some instances for decades. Unions, moreover, had to give considerable emphasis to job-related issues. The left parties, with the "larger" perspective, pushed a different range of issues, these often running counter to the "immediate concerns" of the unions. The conflict of the economic and political concerns gave rise to irreconcilable problems. Even in the closely controlled communist unions, the political line could not be simply imposed. Where it was imposed it brought disenchantment among the supporters and a serious loss of members. Manipulation was at best a short-term aid. In the longer run, such *Praxis* eroded the credibility and the strength of the party.[67]

The development of the left parties brought another issue into view. In the early 20th century, the German Social Democratic Party (SPD) was by far the world's largest and most advanced socialist party. By any measure, it was a giant enterprise with large numbers of employees, many specialized operations, and multiple layers of hierarchy. Robert Michels's detailed analysis of the socialist parties, which focused on the SPD as the archetypical case, pointed up something else— the absence of internal democracy. His conclusion, first published in 1911, was that a large organization inevitably meant oligarchic rule, a conclusion formulated as an "iron law": "He who says organization says oligarchy." Michels's conclusion challenged the claim of the party as the movement of the "immense majority." Where socialism promised a "new realm of freedom," the principal "instrument" of the movement proved to be another restraining device. That well-documented conclusion cast some serious doubt on the beneficent promise of socialism, before the appearance of the first successful socialist revolution.[68]

15. The proletarian revolution: Marx and Engels, as noted, anticipated that the workers' revolution would occur in the downswing of the next economic cycle. The economic collapse would aggravate workers' grievances and, simultaneously, demonstrate clearly the basic failure of capitalism. The empty factories and the widespread unemployment would stand in sharp contrast to the productive potential created by capitalism. Any lingering "false consciousness" would be dispelled by those "hard" economic realities.[69] But the predicted revolution did not occur. Britain, the central case for their argument, never experienced a proletarian revolution. Almost a century after the *Manifesto*, the Labour Party secured a parliamentary majority and, in the next legislative session, instituted sweeping changes, including the socialization of much heavy industry. But even that belated achievement proved disappointing. It did not bring a "qualitative transformation" in the lives of workers.[70]

France had a revolution in 1848, which inadvertently overturned the July monarchy and brought in the Second Republic. A working-class uprising occurred in Paris in June of that year. In his first historical monograph, Marx declared the "June days" to be a decisive struggle, a preview of events to come. As history, the monograph was a poor achievement. At almost every point, Marx cut and distorted so as to give plausibility to his larger claims. The next working-class uprising came two decades later, again in Paris and again it was defeated. Marx wrote his third (and last) historical monograph on this occasion. He again depicted the event as providing proof for his basic claims. No proletarian revolution occurred in the ensuing century. The greatest victory for socialism occurred in 1981 with the election of Francois Mitterand as president of the Fifth Republic. The sweeping changes that were instituted proved rather problematic, and retrenchment followed.[71]

On the last page of the *Manifesto*, Marx and Engels wrote, "The Communists turn their attention chiefly to Germany, because that country is on the eve of a bourgeois revolution that is bound to be carried out under more advanced conditions of European civilisation, and with a much more developed proletariat . . . and because the bourgeois revolution in Germany will be but the prelude to an immediately following proletarian revolution" (519). A month after publication, a revolution did occur in Germany and two bourgeois notables took office, as prime minister and finance minister. But within months the two were out of office and a somewhat wiser old regime was back in power. No subsequent bourgeois revolution followed.

In November 1918, at the end of World War I, a revolution occurred in Germany and brought in a socialist government. A socialization commission was constituted which offered some very modest recommendations. But the first election, in mid-January 1919, failed to produce a socialist majority, so even those recommendations had little practical result. Within two years, the socialists were out of power and were replaced, in a reversal of the predicted sequence, by a succession of "bourgeois" governments. There was no subsequent proletarian revolution.[72]

In the course of Marx and Engels's lifetimes, it was clear that the United States was the rising capitalist nation and, given the trend lines, was destined to eclipse Britain. It could not be ignored and, accordingly, received considerable attention. In this case, the basic prediction was modified and an evolutionary possibility was indicated. Socialism might come to the United States through a gradual electoral advance. But that expectation also failed. The American Socialist Party gained its greatest success in the 1912 presidential election: 6.2 percent of the total.[73]

The basic conclusion to be drawn from this review of the four leading capitalist nations is that the central Marx–Engels proposition, imminent working-class revolution, was not supported. Marx and Engels attempted to save the proposition with revised claims about the timing, but that merely avoided the obvious conclusion: The key prediction failed repeatedly. At present, the time span involved from the publication of the *Manifesto* is more than seven score years.

The location and circumstances of revolutions in the 20th century provide two further challenges to the Marx–Engels predictions. Those revolutions occurred in settings that were far from the centers of capitalism. And they did not come in the downswings of economic cycles; they came in conjunction with or in the immediate aftermath of wars. A review of this experience provides some instructive lessons.

The 1905 revolution in Russia came in the aftermath of the Russo Japanese War. The 1917 November Revolution in which the Bolsheviks took power occurred in the midst of World War I. The revolution had overthrown the government of a backward agrarian country, one in the earliest stage of capitalist development, one in which no bourgeois take-over had occurred, and one with only a small proletariat.[74] The success of this "Marxist" revolution led to a significant revision of Marxism.

Revolutions occurred in Germany and Austria-Hungary a year later, in November 1918. In both cases, the new governments were socialist, both officially announcing Marxist commitments. But moderate socialists dominated in Germany and Austria. In Hungary, the revolutionary regime of Bela Kun had a 100-day existence. These events paralleled the earlier Russian case; they occurred in the course of the war, specifically as the old regimes were collapsing. Another war-linked revolution brought an end to the Ottoman empire in 1922.[75]

After a quarter-century pause, more revolutions occurred, beginning in the mid-1940s. These came in the course of or immediately following World War II. They too occurred far from the leading centers of capitalism. Most of them could, with considerable justification, be termed national liberation struggles. Tito's insurgency in Yugoslavia ousted both the old regime and the German occupiers in 1944 and 1945. The Chinese communists escalated their efforts considerably in 1945. Defying all odds, they defeated the Chiang Kai-Shek regime in 1949, taking control of the world's most populous nation. A peasant-based revolution, it pushed out the corrupt and authoritarian regime; it also pushed out and expropriated the imperialists.[76]

The withdrawal of the Japanese imperialists from Southeast Asia at the end of World War II created a sensitive moment for many nations in the area: Would the European imperialists return and take control of their former colonies or would those populations become independent? A complicated sequence of events brought the French back to Indochina, this leading to the long and stubbornly contested revolution there. The French phase of the struggle ended effectively in 1954. The American phase ended in defeat, the final episode an ignominious withdrawal in 1975.[77]

The Dutch returned to Indonesia in 1945. They too soon faced armed forces fighting for independence. In 1949, pressured by the United

States, they gave up the struggle and returned home.[78] The threat of insurgency led the British to abandon all of their former possessions in Southeast Asia: Burma, Malaya, and, the most important of them, India, was given up in 1947. When the imperialists were forced out of mainland China in 1949, only Hong Kong and Macao remained in Western hands.[79]

The significance of these transfers of power is sometimes not appreciated by those trained in Eurocentric or North America–centered worldviews. In terms of population, China and India were, by considerable margins, the first and second largest nations in the world. Indonesia at that time was the fifth largest (after the Soviet Union and the United States).

The colonists retreated also from Africa. Britain gave up almost all holdings there. Where armed struggle was involved, it was usually stimulated by white settlers (as in Kenya, Rhodesia, and South Africa) rather than by British capitalists and/or by the Foreign Office. Belgium gave up the Congo. After Vietnam, France faced serious armed conflict in Algeria between 1956 and 1958. This struggle too was driven largely by French colonials in alliance with members of the French army. The Algerian struggle was an offshoot of the Indochina War. Algerians who had fought for the French in Vietnam learned some lessons, independence and how to fight for it, and applied them at home. The French army, humiliated by the defeat in Indochina, sought to restore its lost prestige.[80]

Portugal was the last of the European nations to give up its African colonies. Settlers were again key to the perpetuation of the struggle and they also, as in Indochina and Algeria, were supported by the military. In this case, after their defeat the military conducted its own revolution and brought down the conservative, authoritarian Salazar-Caetano regime and created a parliamentary democracy.[81]

The war–revolution link is easily appreciated. Wars, especially in the modern era, require the arming of the eligible citizenry. Workers and peasants are given weapons and taught their use. They learn how to fight; they also gain some leadership experience, at least for tactical struggles. Many new things would be seen and appreciated, things they would never know otherwise: cities, countries, and peoples. Management errors, an inevitable correlate of all large-scale struggles, discredit established leaders, both military and civilian. The problems of legitimacy cumulate, most especially for the losers. The errors typically range from the serious to the disastrous. Apart from the calamities at the front, shortages of food, fuel, and medical supplies are likely, all combined with serious inflationary pressures. All these factors erode traditional loyalties and "set the stage for" insurgency.[82]

An assessment of hypotheses may yield one of four possible results:

Confirmation. Evidence supports the original claim.

Rejection (or disconfirmation). Evidence does not support the original.

Mixed results. The original claim might be contingent, that is, supported only in given circumstances, or the factual claim might be confirmed but the causal implication either questioned or rejected.

Uncertainty. The available evidence does not allow an empirically based conclusion; evidence might be lacking entirely, or it might be of such poor quality as to make the drawing of conclusions inappropriate.

For the fifteen hypotheses, we have the following results:

1. The requirement of innovation: Mixed. It is a contingent hypothesis. Technological innovation begins with invention; lacking invention, a given industry will show constancy, not change. Innovation is, in part, a function of research and development. Such efforts will vary with the profitability of an industry. Managerial choices also play some role.

2. National breakdown: Rejected. The history of the modern world is a history of growing national development.

3. The great cities: Mixed. Cities have unquestionably grown, but they were growing prior to modern industry and the appearance of the bourgeoisie. Most large cities of the 19th century were centers of government. The causal processes are different and more complicated.

4. Concentration of property: Mixed. The general tendency is confirmed in most industries. Some specification is needed, however, since the process stops short of the monopolistic endpoint, with oligopoly being the typical experience. Giant producers, with remarkable frequency, tend toward sluggishness and incompetence.

5. Political centralization: Mixed. The tendency had been there for several centuries. Again there is a question about the causes, since the tendency was present long before the coming of modern industry. As with the great cities, some other causes appear to be operating. There are questions also about the extent.

6. Bourgeois domination: Mixed. There are serious doubts as to the historical takeovers in Britain and France. The German case has always been problematic, that is, nonconforming. It is not at all clear that bourgeois interests regularly dominate or win out in contemporary capitalist societies.

7. Economic crises: Mixed. These appeared throughout the 19th century and into the 20th. The most serious crisis of the modern era, that of the 1930s, was followed, from the 1950s on, by remarkable economic growth and sharply attenuated cyclical swings.

8. The quality of work: Rejected. Most people in capitalist societies make positive assessments of their work. The arguments for decline and degradation typically neglect the extensive array of studies in the area, making their case with atypical examples and with untested logic. The century-long decline of unskilled labor goes against that logic.

9. Immiseration: Rejected. Evidence available in the lifetimes of Marx and Engels made this claim untenable. The general claim disappeared in their later writing.

10. Aggregation of workers: Mixed. Factories did become larger. There is some question about the extent and significance of the development. The tendency has reversed in recent decades.

11. The petty bourgeoisie: The assessment of this proposition will be undertaken in the following chapter.

12. The *Lumpenproletariat*: Rejected. Lacking support in Marx and Engels's lifetimes, this claim disappeared from their later writing.

13. The bourgeois intellectuals: Mixed. They do play an important part in working-class movements. As opposed to the predicted service role, the provision of enlightenment, intellectuals replaced the workers, taking over the leadership of those movements.

14. The organizational development: Rejected. The organization of workers does not rise up "stronger, firmer, mightier." Unions and parties tend to have different leaders and different interests. Both show tendencies toward sluggishness or immobility.

15. The proletarian revolution: Rejected. The workers' revolution never occurred, not in the period and locations predicted. All 20th-century revolutions occurred in different circumstances; that is, in ones not originally predicted.

COMMENTARY

A theory, one hopes, would show an outstanding record of supported predictions. But here, as seen, the record is very poor, lacking even a single clear confirmation. Two of the mixed results involve general support with regard to the principal tendency, cities and factories grew in size. But even there, some emendation was necessary. The attribution of city growth to the bourgeoisie proved mistaken, a serious miscue that led the authors to neglect the class of administrators, the bureaucracy. The growth of the factories was by no means as rapid as assumed; the implication or assumed consequence, revolutionary workers, has remained an unfulfilled hope. The immiseration hypothesis was rejected "by history" and accordingly disappeared from the repertory of claims along with the notion of a "dangerous class," the *Lumpenproletariat*. The most important of the hypotheses, those involving the growth of working-class organization and the resulting proletarian revolution, have been decisively rejected in the last 150 years of "advanced capitalism."

Despite the poor record and failure of these, the original scientific claims, the Marxian theory has enjoyed remarkable success in the 20th century. One commentator, Robert G. Wesson, has referred to this paradoxical phenomenon as the "success of a failed theory."[83] That success, in part at least, depended on subsequent changes or adjustments. The history of Marxism has been a history of revisions made necessary by the failure of the key claims. Two major revisions, those provided by Eduard Bernstein and V. I. Lenin, will be considered in the following chapters.

NOTES

1. All quotations from the *Manifesto* are from the edition contained in Karl Marx and Friedrich Engels, *Collected Works*, vol. 6 (New York: International Publishers, 1976), 477–519. Specific page references appear in the text in parentheses. This is the English edition of 1888, one edited and approved by Engels. It differs from the German original at many points. In subsequent notes, the *Collected Works* will be referred to as *MECW*. For detailed comments, see the notes in Frederic L. Bender, ed., *The Communist Manifesto* (New York: Norton, 1988). All the passages cited here have been checked against the German-language version contained in Karl Marx and Friedrich Engels, *Werke*, vol. 4 (Berlin: Dietz Verlag, 1964), 459–493.

For the 1872 preface, see Bender, *Manifesto*, 43. Max Weber rejected the critical theses of the *Manifesto* but, at the same time, declared it "a work of scholarship of the highest order." See Weber, "Socialism," in J.E.T. Eldridge, ed., *Max Weber: The Interpretation of Social Reality* (New York: Scribner's, 1971), 205.

For a brief review and criticism of the Marx versus Engels position, see Richard F. Hamilton, *Bourgeois Epoch: Marx and Engels on Britain, France, and Germany* (Chapel Hill: University of North Carolina Press, 1991), 10–12. For book-length reviews and criticism, see J. D. Hunley, *The Life and Thought of Friedrich Engels* (New Haven: Yale University Press, 1991); and S. H. Rigby, *Engels and the Formation of Marxism: History, Dialectics and Revolution* (Manchester: Manchester University Press, 1992).

2. Those three epochs describe the Western world; it is European history that is being analyzed. Elsewhere, the authors discuss the "static" Asiatic mode of production. It is a minor entry, a poorly developed sketch, one that has received much less attention. For an overview and appropriate references, see Bryan S. Turner, "Asiatic Society," in *A Dictionary of Marxist Thought*, ed. Tom Bottomore, 2d ed. (London: Basil Blackwell, 1991), 36–39.

3. The passage appears in a much-cited letter (dated March 5, 1852) written to Joseph Weydemeyer. In it, he summarizes his intellectual achievement (*MECW*, 39: 62–65). One could have "wealthy classes," powerful classes (e.g., praetorians, Caesarists, the military), bureaucratic domination (as in China), or coteries without any special base in "the productive process." Classes per

se are such an obvious fact in any given history, it would have been a miracle if they had not been recognized long before the announcement of the *Manifesto*. For further discussion, see Hamilton, *Bourgeois Epoch*, 205–209.

4. The *Manifesto* and most other Marx–Engels works are truncated. They give only cursory attention to the origins of the bourgeois epoch. When did the "bourgeois revolution" occur? Various dates were offered for England—1640, 1648, and 1688—none of them really plausible. For France, the "obvious" option is 1789. But both of these historical claims, both "cornerstone" assumptions for the theory, are untenable. For review, criticism, and assessment, see Hamilton, *Bourgeois Epoch*, chs. 2 and 3.

5. From his *Condition of the Working Classes in England* (*MECW*, 4: 418). Unlike most mass society theorists, Marx and Engels expressed no regret about the tendency. This development, they wrote, "rescued a considerable part of the population from the idiocy of rural life" (488).

6. Marx, however, was still arguing the immiseration thesis as late as 1867, in his most famous work. With the development of capital, Marx wrote, "grows the mass of misery, oppression, slavery, degradation, exploitation; but with this too grows the revolt of the working class, a class always increasing in numbers, and disciplined, united, organised by the very mechanism of the process of capitalist production itself." See Marx, *Capital: A Critique of Political Economy*, vol. 1 (New York: International Publishers, 1975), 750 (*MECW*, 35).

The peasantry, in contrast, is deprived but, because of its territorial dispersion, could not organize as a self-conscious revolutionary class. Their economic grievances often stimulated insurgency, during the Reformation for example, but the superior skills and organization of the aristocracy meant regular defeat. For a typical analysis, one that follows Engels on the point, see Franz Mehring's treatment of the Peasant War in Mehring, *Deutsche Geschichte vom Ausgange des Mittelalters* (1910; reprint Berlin: Dietz Verlag, 1947), 35–39. The argument of peasant helplessness was subsequently rejected in the Mao Tse-tung revision.

7. This brief summary cannot begin to deal with all of the specific hypotheses contained in the *Manifesto*. One hypothesis, for example, links capitalism to family breakdown, this also, to some degree, contributing to the revolution. I feel this claim to be of less importance than those spelled out in the text.

8. The cliché is widely accepted but difficult to test. Did "events" make Peter the Great? If genetics and the royal succession had produced Peter the Daft, and had he been in command at Poltava in 1709, would Russia have survived? Would the subsequent history have been roughly comparable to the one we have known in the 20th century? If Prussia had seen the reign of Frederick the Hopeless, would that nation have become a major European power? Would it have survived? Would Germany have been unified under the Hohenzollerns? Would German unification under the Habsburgs have produced the 20th century as we have known it? For a thoughtful and provocative "what if" study—What if Adolf Hitler had died in the automobile accident in the summer of 1930?—see Henry A. Turner, Jr., "Hitler's Impact on History," in *From the Berlin Museum to the Berlin Wall: Essays on the Cultural and Political History of Modern Germany*, ed. David Wetzel (Westport, Conn.: Praeger, 1996), ch. 6.

9. In an earlier work, *The German Ideology*, Marx and Engels put heavy emphasis on the importance of the scientific investigative effort: "Empirical observation must in each separate instance bring out empirically, and without any mystification and speculation, the connection of the social and political structure with production" (*MECW*, 5: 35).

10. This use of the rhetoric of science gave Marx and Engels a considerable advantage vis-à-vis the utopian socialists. For some comment on their equivocal procedure in this regard, see Hamilton, *Bourgeois Epoch*, 207–208.

Marx and Engels did produce some "fantastic pictures" early in their careers, one example appearing in *The German Ideology*, written in 1845–1846 but not published in their lifetimes. With the division of labor, they wrote, "each man has a particular, exclusive sphere of activity, which is forced upon him and from which he cannot escape." In contrast

In communist society, where nobody has one exclusive sphere of activity but each can become accomplished in any branch he wishes, society regulates the general production and thus makes it possible for me to do one thing today and another tomorrow, to hunt in the morning, fish in the afternoon, rear cattle in the evening, criticise after dinner, just as I have a mind, without ever becoming hunter, fisherman, shepherd or critic. (*MECW*, 5: 47).

Engels explained the anticipated future arrangement in a lecture given in Elberfeld on February 8, 1845. "In communist society," he announced, "it will be easy to be informed about both production and consumption. Since we know how much, on the average, a person needs, it is easy to calculate how much is needed by a given number of individuals, and since production is no longer in the hands of private producers but in those of the community and its administrative bodies, it is a trifling matter *to regulate production according to needs*" (*MECW*, 4: 246). Utopian elements appear also in the *Manifesto*, especially in Part II; for example, "In Communist society, accumulated labour is but a means to widen, to enrich, to promote the existence of the labourer" (499).

11. *MECW*, 10: 132, 135.

12. See Phyllis Deane, *The First Industrial Revolution*, 2d ed. (Cambridge: Cambridge University Press, 1979), 88–91. A few paragraphs of discussion can only scratch the surface of a complex and extensive literature. For an overview, see Nathan Rosenberg, *Inside the Black Box: Technology and Economics* (Cambridge: Cambridge University Press, 1982). His opening chapter reviews "The Historiography of Technical Progress." The second chapter discusses "Marx as a Student of Technology." See also David C. Mowery and Nathan Rosenberg, *Technology and the Pursuit of Economic Growth* (Cambridge: Cambridge University Press, 1989).

13. In the early 1960s, the introduction of shuttleless weaving again brought revolutionary changes in the industry with speeds that far surpassed any prior accomplishment. In the 1980s, electronic monitoring of production brought further major transformations. With 1990 employment in the industry at about half the 1940 level, production was at an all-time peak. See McAllister Isaacs III, "World Class Manufacturers Cut Labor Needs in Half," *Textile World* 139, 10 (1989): 71–76; and the special issue of *Textile World* 140, 10 (1990), especially the overview article by Isaacs, "Manufacturing: Pace of Change is Breathtak-

ing," 21–30. See also International Labour Organization, *Working Conditions in the Textiles Industry in the Light of Technological Changes*, Report 2 (Geneva: International Labour Office, 1991). For a 200-year overview of the industry, see Kitty G. Dickerson, *Textiles and Apparel in the International Economy* (New York: Macmillan, 1991).

14. David S. Landes, *The Unbound Prometheus: Technological Change and Industrial Development in Western Europe from 1750 to the Present* (Cambridge: Cambridge University Press, 1969), 294–295; and Deane, *Industrial Revolution*, 293. For the recent changes, see Dickerson, *Textiles and Apparel*, chs. 6, 9.

A long period without significant innovation "sets the stage for" another dynamic. When technological change is not decisive, labor costs take on greater importance. Britain's leaders, in both business and government, did what they could to protect their industrial secrets, but ultimately the industries were destined to move elsewhere. In the United States, the textile industry and much of the apparel industry moved from New England and New York to the south and the southwest. Ultimately, much of the garment industry moved to China and other low-wage Pacific Rim countries. See Jeffrey S. Arpan, José de la Torre, and Brian Toyne, *The U.S. Apparel Industry: International Challenge, Domestic Response*, Research Monograph no. 88 (Atlanta: College of Business Administration, Georgia State University, 1982); and Dickerson, *Textiles and Apparel*, ch. 9.

15. Walter Adams and James W. Brock, "The Automobile Industry," in *The Structure of American Industry*, ed. Walter Adams, 8th ed. (New York: Macmillan, 1990).

16. For an account of developments in home construction reporting on the recent increase in the factory assembly of homes, see Thomas E. Nutt-Powell, "The House That Machines Built," *Technology Review* 88, 8 (1988): 30–37.

17. Seymour L. Wolfbein, "The Pace of Technological Change and the Factors Affecting It," in *Manpower Implications of Automation* (Washington, D.C.: U.S. Department of Labor, 1965), 15–28. There is an extensive literature on the subject. For a start, see Louis A. Girifalco, *Dynamics of Technological Change* (New York: Van Nostrand, 1991).

18. For overviews, see Frederick B. Artz, *Reaction and Revolution: 1814–1832* (New York: Harper, 1934); and William L. Langer, *Political and Social Upheaval: 1832–1852* (New York: Harper & Row, 1969).

On the Belgian case, see E. H. Kossmann, *The Low Countries, 1780–1940* (Oxford: Clarendon Press, 1978), 151–160; and Samuel Clark, "Nobility, Bourgeoisie and the Industrial Revolution in Belgium," *Past and Present* 105 (1984): 140–175. The 1830 revolution there was basically a national liberation struggle, a rejection of Dutch cultural domination. That revolution recapitulated an earlier effort, a brief successful rejection of Austrian "cultural" domination in 1789. See Kossmann, *Low Countries*, 47–64; and Clark, "Nobility," 157–158.

19. For the 1848 events, see Langer, *Political and Social Upheaval*, chs. 10–12; Priscilla Robertson, *Revolutions of 1848: A Social History* (Princeton: Princeton University Press, 1952); Hamilton, *Bourgeois Epoch*, chs. 3, 4; and Jonathan Sperber, *The European Revolutions, 1848–1851* (New York: Cambridge University Press, 1994).

20. See A.J.P. Taylor, *The Struggle for Mastery in Europe: 1848–1918* (London: Oxford University Press, 1954), especially chs. 21, 22. On the Austro–Prussian

War and the support for Hungarian nationalism, see Fritz Stern, *Gold and Iron: Bismarck, Bleichröder, and the Building of the German Empire* (New York: Knopf, 1977), 89–90. On the German role in Russia, see Oleh S. Fedyshyn, *Germany's Drive to the East and the Ukrainian Revolution, 1917–1918* (New Brunswick: Rutgers University Press, 1971).

21. For an overview, see Walker Connor, "Three Strands of Nationalism in Marx and Engels," in *The National Question in Marxist–Leninist Theory and Strategy* (Princeton: Princeton University Press, 1984). Where the "national question" was unavoidable, as in Eastern Europe, "Marxism" was adjusted accordingly and that fact given much greater prominence. This refers to the "Austro–Marxism" of Otto Bauer and Karl Renner. Lenin too had to deal with the issue.

22. B. R. Mitchell, *Abstract of British Historical Statistics* (Cambridge: Cambridge University Press, 1962), 24–27. For a comprehensive overview see Paul Bairoch, *Cities and Economic Development: From the Dawn of History to the Present*, trans. Christopher Braider (Chicago: University of Chicago Press, 1988).

23. Adna Weber, *The Growth of Cities in the Nineteenth Century* (Ithaca: Cornell University Press, 1899), 450. Other cities larger than Manchester in 1890 were Constantinople, Bombay, Rio de Janeiro, and Calcutta. The Manchester-centric view of the modern (or bourgeois) world points to a distinctive cultural determinism. Engels's first book, *The Condition of the Working Class in England*, published in German in 1845 (*MECW* 4: 295–583), gave considerable attention to Manchester. At one point he referred to it as "the second city in England." For discussion of the book and its reception together with extensive references, see W. O. Henderson, *The Life of Friedrich Engels*, vol. 1 (London: Frank Cass, 1976), ch. 2. See also Gary S. Messinger, *Manchester in the Victorian Age* (Manchester: Manchester University Press, 1985). Counting Salford, a suburb, with the city's total, Messinger reports, made Manchester the "second most populous town of Great Britain" in 1801 (pp. 8–9, 16).

24. These figures are taken from J. C. Bluntschli and K. Brater, *Deutsches Staats-Wörterbuch*, vol. 2 (Stuttgart and Leipzig: Expedition des Staats-Wörterbuchs, 1857), 725–737.

25. The description of Cologne is from the *Conversations Lexikon*, 10th ed., vol 9 (Leipzig: F. A. Brockhaus, 1853), 112. Marx lived in Cologne from October 1842 to March 1843, where he edited the *Rheinische Zeitung*, and from April 1848 to May 1849 as editor of the *Neue Rheinische Zeitung*. Although the discussion here focuses on "industry" (old and new) and administration, most of the cities would have had some nontrivial military presence. Many persons at that time were engaged in domestic service.

26. Bluntschli and Brater, *Deutsches Staats-Wörterbuch*.

27. U.S. Department of Commerce, "Concentration Ratios in Manufacturing," Subject Series MC87-S-6, in *1987 Census of Manufactures* (Washington, D.C.: U.S. Government Printing Office, 1992). For more detailed discussions, see Ralph L. Nelson, *Concentration in the Manufacturing Industries of the United States* (New Haven: Yale University Press, 1963); and Frederick M. Scherer, *Industrial Market Structure and Economic Performance*, 2d ed. (Chicago: Rand McNally, 1980).

28. See Stephen Martin, "The Petroleum Industry," in *The Structure of American Industry*, ed. Walter Adams, 8th ed. (New York: Macmillan, 1990). The Standard Oil Company controlled 90 to 95 percent of U.S. refining in 1880. It was

losing its dominant position prior to the Supreme Court's decision in 1911, at that point controlling 64 percent. See Harold F. Williamson and Ralph L. Andreano, "Competitive Structure of the Petroleum Industry, 1880–1911: A Reappraisal," in *Oil's First Century*, compiled and ed. the Staff of the Business History Review (Cambridge: Harvard Graduate School of Business Administration, 1960), 70–84; and Daniel Yergin, *The Prize: The Epic Quest for Oil, Money, and Power* (New York: Simon & Schuster, 1992), 80–95.

29. Donald F. Barnett and Robert W. Crandall, *Up from the Ashes: The Rise of the Steel Minimill in the United States* (Washington, D.C.: Brookings, 1986), 114. See also Walter Adams and Hans Mueller, "The Steel Industry," in Adams, *Structure*, ch. 3. The data on concentration appears on p. 76; William Scheuerman, *The Steel Crisis: The Economics and Politics of a Declining Industry* (New York: Praeger, 1986); John Strohmeyer, *Crisis in Bethlehem: Big Steel's Struggle to Survive* (New York: Penguin, 1987); John P. Hoerr, *And the Wolf Finally Came: The Decline of the American Steel Industry* (Pittsburgh: University of Pittsburgh Press, 1988); Trevor Bain, *Banking the Furnace: Restructuring of the Steel Industry in Eight Countries* (Kalamazoo, Mich.: Upjohn Institute, 1992). The American steel industry made a modest recovery in one area with small and efficient minimills. See Barnett and Crandall, *Up from the Ashes*, and also Robert S. Ahlbrandt, Richard J. Fruehan, and Frank Giarratani, *The Renaissance of American Steel: Lessons for Managers in Competitive Industries* (New York: Oxford University Press, 1996). For recent developments in the industry and a portrait of recovery led by the new producers and by a transformed Bethlehem, see John Holusha, "A Flexing of Muscle in American Steel," *New York Times*, 5 July 1998, sec. 3, p. 4.

30. On the automobile industry, see Adams and Brock, "Automobile Industry." For data on the imports, see p. 132. See also the accounts by David Halberstam, *The Reckoning* (New York: William Morrow, 1986). This book reviews the Ford history, the growth of Nissan, and also, on pp. 82–84, the Spindletop history mentioned just above. See also Maryann Keller, *Rude Awakening: The Rise, Fall and Struggle for Recovery of General Motors* (New York: William Morrow, 1989), and *Collision: GM, Toyota, Volkswagen and the Race to Own the 21st Century* (New York: Currency-Doubleday, 1993).

31. On General Electric and Westinghouse, see Matthew Josephson, *Edison: A Biography* (New York: McGraw-Hill, 1959), 345–350; and Robert Conot, *A Streak of Luck: The Life & Legend of Thomas Alva Edison* (New York: Seaview, 1979), 252–255, 300–302.

32. On IBM, see Paul Carroll, *Big Blues: The Unmaking of IBM* (New York: Crown, 1993). The quotation is from Steve Lohr, "I.B.M. Posts $5.46 Billion Loss for 4th Quarter," *New York Times*, 20 January 1993, D1.

33. On administered prices, see John Kenneth Galbraith, *The New Industrial State* (Boston: Houghton Mifflin, 1967), 179–197; Scherer, *Industrial Market*, 176–195; and Adams and Mueller, "Steel Industry," 84–88. The quotation is from p. 73. On Kennedy's defeat of "big steel," see Grant McConnell, *Steel and the Presidency, 1962* (New York: Norton, 1963).

The automobile industry also had administered pricing arrangements. These too brought major short-run advantages to the firms (and to autoworkers) but had serious long-run consequences. An opportunity was thus created for foreign small-car manufacturers that ultimately allowed them to gain almost a quarter of the domestic market. Labor productivity in the industry rose 39 percent between 1967 and 1980, while wages, in a process of labor–management collusion, rose by 214 percent. This too contributed to the collapse of the traditional centers of industry and to the appearance of "rust belt" cities. For details, along with discussion of a range of other contributing managerial practices, see Adams and Brock, "Automobile Industry," 139–140, 146–158.

34. Marx letter to Engels, 8 August 1870, *MECW*, 44: 38; Engels to Marx, 15 August 1870, *MECW*, 44: 47.

35. For a discussion of Prussia's bourgeois leaders in 1848 and of Engels's disgusted reaction, see Hamilton, *Bourgeois Epoch*, 146–148. Engels's diatribe against the bourgeoisie shifts attention from the basic problem: the failure of a basic Marxist prediction. For a recent discussion, see David Blackbourn and Geoff Eley, *The Peculiarities of German History: Bourgeois Society and Politics in Nineteenth-Century Germany* (New York: Oxford University Press, 1984). Germany, according to Blackbourn, experienced a "silent" bourgeois revolution (pp. 176–205).

36. Engels's letter to Bebel, 18 November 1884, appears in Werner Blumenberg, ed., *August Bebels Briefwechsel mit Friedrich Engels* (The Hague: Mouton, 1965), 194. The second passage appears in "Critique of the Draft Social-Democratic Programme of 1891," *MECW*, 27: 227–228. This comment on the party's Erfurt Program was for private consumption. It was first published a decade later.

37. Hamilton, *Bourgeois Epoch*, ch. 2.

38. Ibid., ch. 3.

39. Marx, *The Eighteenth Brumaire of Louis Napoleon*, *MECW*, 11: 104. See also Hamilton, *Bourgeois Epoch*, 100, 104–105.

40. Margaret Leech, *In the Days of McKinley* (New York: Harper, 1959), ch. 3; Wayne Morgan, *William McKinley and His America* (Syracuse: Syracuse University Press, 1963), chs. 10, 11; Thomas Beer, *Hanna* (New York: Knopf, 1929). The cowboy quotation appears in Matthew Josephson, *The President Makers: The Culture of Politics and Leadership in an Age of Enlightenment, 1896–1919* (1940; reprint New York: Frederick Unger, 1969), 110.

41. In 1902, Roosevelt's government launched an important antitrust action, the Northern Securities case, against an important J. P. Morgan creation. In his second term, thirty-five antitrust actions were undertaken. See Lewis L. Gould, *Reform and Regulation: American Politics from Roosevelt to Wilson* (New York: Knopf, 1986), 40, 97–98; for more detail, see Lewis L. Gould, *The Presidency of Theodore Roosevelt* (Lawrence: University Press of Kansas, 1991), 47–53, 105–106, 212–218, and 279–281. On the Steel case and subsequent Roosevelt–Taft split, see Robert H. Wiebe, "The House of Morgan and the Executive, 1905–1913," *American Historical Review* 65 (1959): 49–60; James C. German, Jr., "Taft, Roosevelt, and United States Steel," *The Historian* 34 (1972): 598–613; and also, a popular account, William Manners, *TR and Will: A Friendship That Split the Republican Party* (New York: Harcourt Brace Jovanovich, 1969).

On the Standard Oil antitrust case, see Scherer, *Industrial Market Structure*, 528–529; for the U.S. Steel case, see pp. 530–531. A 1920 Supreme Court decision in the latter case went against the Justice Department. But then, as indicated earlier, management failure did what federal policy could not achieve.

42. Arthur S. Link, *Woodrow Wilson and the Progressive Era, 1910–1917* (New York: Harper, 1954), ch. 3.

43. Democrats were persistent winners in the Congress from 1933 to the mid-1990s. They controlled the U.S. Senate for fifty-two years of the sixty-two-year span from 1933 to 1994; they controlled the House of Representatives for fifty-eight of those years. Some of the Democratic losses at the presidential level were self-inflicted, as, for example, in 1968 due to the Vietnam involvement beginning in 1965, and in 1972 due to a related set of issues.

44. The Keynesian procedures, to be sure, have now been largely replaced by monetary policies.

The inevitable crises claim was stated with only a faint line of argument in the *Manifesto*, this pointing to overproduction. An underconsumption argument was spelled out at length in Marx, *Kapital*. On the crises of the 19th and early 20th centuries, see Peter Gourevitch, *Politics in Hard Times: Comparative Responses to International Economic Crises* (Ithaca: Cornell University Press, 1986). For accounts of the 1930s, see Charles P. Kindleberger, *The World in Depression 1929–1939*, Rev. ed. (Berkeley and Los Angeles: University of California Press, 1986); Peter Temin, *Lessons from the Great Depression* (Cambridge: MIT Press, 1989); Peter A. Gourevitch, "Breaking with Orthodoxy: The Politics of Economic Policy Responses to the Depression of the 1930s," *International Organization* 38 (1984): 95–129; and Ekkart Zimmermann and Thomas Sallfeld, "Economic and Political Reactions to the World Economic Crisis of the 1930s in Six European Countries," *International Studies Quarterly* 32 (1988): 305–334. The linkage of economic crisis and revolution will be considered later.

45. These are national cross-sectional samples of the adult (eighteen and over), noninstitutional, U.S. population. They are all multistage area samples. The earliest studies, those of 1972 through 1974, were modified probability samples, allowing a quota element at the block level. The 1975 and 1976 studies were transitional, half full probability and half block quota. From 1977 onward, the studies have been based on full probability samples. For further details, see James Allan Davis and Tom W. Smith, *General Social Surveys, 1972–1993: Cumulative Codebook* (Chicago: National Opinion Research Center, 1993), 811–822.

46. See Randy Hodson, "Organizational Ethnographies: An Underutilized Resource in the Sociology of Work," *Social Forces* 76 (1998): 1–34. For a general discussion of the problems involved with job satisfaction, see Randy Hodson, "Workplace Behaviors: Good Soldiers, Smooth Operators, and Saboteurs," *Work and Occupations* 18 (1991): 271–290.

Researchers, from the outset, were (and are) aware of the problems of validity; that is, whether a given question actually and appropriately measures the thing intended. The subject has been extensively researched with results broadly consonant with those shown in Table 2.1. For overviews, see C. J. Cranny, Patricia Cain Smith, and Eugene F. Stone, *Job Satisfaction: How People Feel About Their Jobs and How It Affects Their Performance* (New York: Lexington Books, 1992); and Paul E. Spector, *Job Satisfaction: Application, Assessment, Cause, and Consequences* (Thousand Oaks, Calif.: Sage, 1997).

The response-set argument has, on occasion, produced paradoxical results. In the early 1970s, it was claimed that "angry workers" experiencing growing dissatisfaction were challenging the authority of their employers and about to "tear apart" the factories and offices. But those same workers, it was said, intimidated by the interviewers, could not freely express their feelings.

The General Social Surveys put a related question: "If you were to get enough money to live as comfortably as you would like for the rest of your life, would you continue to work or would you stop working?" This should be less "threatening"; that is, easier for dissatisfied workers to answer. Sizable majorities at all points from 1973 to 1996 said they would continue working (the range was from 65 to 77%). The responses are age related, with older workers, those near retirement, more likely to say they would stop working.

47. William Form, "On the Degradation of Skills," *Annual Review of Sociology* 13 (1987): 44. For a comprehensive review of work and work-satisfaction studies, see Hamilton and Wright, *State of the Masses*, 65–95, and ch. 6. For a recent update, see Glenn Firebaugh and Brian Harley, "Trends in Job Satisfaction in the United States by Race, Gender, and Type of Occupation," in *Research in the Sociology of Work* 5 (1995): 87–105.

Among those arguing the quality-decline thesis, we have Harry Braverman, *Labor and Monopoly Capital: The Degradation of Work in the Twentieth Century* (New York: Monthly Review Press, 1974); Richard Edwards, *Contested Terrain: The Transformation of the Workplace in the Twentieth Century* (New York: Basic Books, 1979); and Dan Clawson, *Bureaucracy and the Labor Process: The Transformation of U.S. Industry, 1860–1920* (New York: Monthly Review Press, 1980). For a more recent entry, one that neglects all contrary evidence, see Walter Licht, "How the Workplace Has Changed in 75 Years," *Monthly Labor Review* 111, 2 (1988): 19–25, especially pp. 21–22.

48. Based on U.S. Bureau of the Census, *Historical Statistics of the United States: Colonial Times to 1957* (Washington, D.C.: U.S. Government Printing Office, 1960), 74. Most unskilled labor was and is done by men. A decline appears also among the women in the labor force, with the unskilled-labor category going from 15.7 percent to 3 percent between 1900 and 1950.

49. For overviews, see R. M. Hartwell, "The Standard of Living Controversy: A Summary," in *The Industrial Revolution*, ed. R. M. Hartwell (New York: Barnes and Noble, 1970); R. M. Hartwell, ed., *The Long Debate on Poverty: Eight Essays on Industrialisation and "The Condition of England"* (London: Institute of Economic Affairs, 1972); and Arthur J. Taylor, ed., *The Standard of Living in Britain in the Industrial Revolution* (London: Methuen, 1975). For a later summary with evidence and sources, see Peter H. Lindert and Jeffrey G. Williamson, "English Workers' Living Standards During the Industrial Revolution: A New Look," *Economic History Review*, 2d ser., 36 (1983): 1–25; and the subsequent comments in M. W. Flinn, "English Workers' Living Standards During the Industrial Revolution: A Comment," 88–92; and a reply by Lindert and Williamson, 94. See also Guy Routh, *Occupation and Pay in Great Britain, 1906–1960* (Cambridge: Cambridge University Press, 1965). On Germany, see Gerhard Bry, *Wages in Germany, 1871–1945* (Princeton: Princeton University Press, 1960); and Ashok V. Desai, *Real Wages in Germany, 1871–1913* (Oxford: Clarendon Press, 1968).

Another measure of well-being, in many respects a better one than wages, is height. Real incomes might improve with little or no impact on well-being due to infectious disease. Until late in the 19th century, money had little impact on health. For comprehensive reviews, see Roderick Floud, Kenneth Wachter, and Annabel Gregory, *Height, Health and History: Nutritional Status in the United Kingdom, 1750–1980* (New York: Cambridge University Press, 1990); John Komlos, ed., *Stature, Living Standards, and Economic Development: Essays in Anthropometric History* (Chicago: University of Chicago Press, 1994); and Richard H. Steckel and Roderick Floud, *Health and Welfare during Industrialization* (Chicago: University of Chicago Press, 1997).

50. W. O. Henderson, "The Labour Force in the Textile Industries," *Archiv für Sozialgeschichte* 16 (1976): 283–324.

51. W. L. Guttsman, *The German Social Democratic Party, 1875–1933: From Ghetto to Government* (London: George Allen and Unwin, 1981), 25–26. No source is given but, judged by the indicated dates, the results were derived from national census data.

Juan Linz's comprehensive study of post–World War II in the Federal Republic of Germany found 24 percent of male blue-collar workers employed in units of 1,000 or more. More workers, by a small margin, were found in units of 50 to 299. Many more, roughly a third, were in units of 49 or less. See Linz, "The Social Bases of West German Politics" (Ph.D. diss., Columbia University, 1959), 377. Female workers were located, overwhelmingly, in smaller units.

Routinely omitted from most discussion is the impact of laws or administrative regulations. Guttsman's graphs show an unexpected but persistent pattern in the distribution of the industrial labor force of Germany. At all four time points, relatively few workers appear in units of six to ten persons. Many more are found in the adjacent smaller and larger categories, but for some reason employers avoided this specific option. Many welfare and tax arrangements exclude the smallest units. One possibility is that a significant cost would have been incurred by the employment of a sixth worker. Such arrangements might thus contribute, independently, to the structure of the labor force.

52. Based on Robert P. Quinn, Thomas W. Mangione, and Stanley E. Seashare, "1972–73 Quality of Employment Survey" (Ann Arbor: Survey Research Center, 1975). The percentages are calculated from figures in the code book and, for the male blue-collar workers, from an original run. Women workers are less likely to be employed in large shops. For further discussion, see Richard F. Hamilton, *Mass Society, Pluralism, and Bureaucracy* (Praeger, forthcoming), ch. 3.

53. Mark Granovetter, "Small Is Bountiful: Labor Markets and Establishment Size," *American Sociological Review* 49 (1984): 323–334.

54. For discussions and evidence on correlates of large versus small shop employment, see Linz, "Social Bases," ch. 11; and Richard F. Hamilton, *Affluence and the French Worker in the Fourth Republic* (Princeton: Princeton University Press, 1967), ch. 10. The differences in outlooks associated with size of plant in France were smaller than those found in Germany. See also Frederick M. Scherer, "Industrial Structure, Scale Economies, and Worker Alienation," in *Essays on Industrial Organization*, ed. Robert T. Masson and P. David Qualls (Cambridge, Mass.: Ballinger, 1976).

55. R. Blank, "Die soziale Zusammensetzung der sozialdemokratischen Wählerschaft Deutschlands," *Archiv für Sozialwissenschaft und Sozialpolitik* 20 (1905): 510–513.

56. A majority of the blue-collar workers in the German Federal Republic were Catholic. Linz's ("Social Bases," 248) analysis of data from the early 1950s found 36 percent of male Catholic workers supporting the Christian Democrats. Among equivalent female workers, a majority, 54 percent, did so. Christian democratic support among Protestant workers, although lower, was not insignificant, the respective percentages being 16 and 24. There was, clearly, a 20-point difference in the support by Catholic and Protestant male workers. The difference associated with religious community was roughly equivalent to that associated with size of workplace. That being the case, attention should be given to both factors.

57. Mark Traugott, *Armies of the Poor: Determinants of Working-Class Participation in the Parisian Insurrection of June 1848* (Princeton: Princeton University Press, 1985). See also Hamilton, *Bourgeois Epoch*, 77–85.

A brief summary discussion by Tom Bottomore indicates the difficulties with this problematic concept. Some of Marx's scathing comments in the *18th Brumaire* are quoted but without any specific analysis or review of its history or justification. That discussion provided the basis, Bottomore reports, for some "occasional references" in discussions by later Marxists of the rise of fascism. Even then, he notes, "this notion does not have a very prominent place in their analysis." See Bottomore, *Dictionary*, 327. For an encyclopedic review of Marx and Engels's use of the term, see Hal Draper, *Karl Marx's Theory of Revolution*, vol. 2, *The Politics of Social Classes* (New York: Monthly Review Press, 1978), 453–478.

In 1870, Engels wrote a brief preface for the second edition of his *Peasant War in Germany*, in which he summarized the events of the previous two decades. It contained another sweeping condemnation of the *Lumpenproletariat*. The *MECW* volumes 22 to 29 contain the works written after 1871. These have only four index references under "*Lumpenproletariat.*" Even these represent editorial inference, since those pages contain references to possible kindred groups: the declassed, "robbers and murderers," and "declassés." In a late letter (5 June 1882), Marx provided a whimsical account of his life in Cannes: "No plebeian 'masses' here, apart from the *garçons d'hotels, de café*, etc., and *domestiques*, who belong to the *Lumpenproletariat*" *MECW*, 46: 272.

58. J. F. Bosher, *The French Revolution* (New York: Norton, 1988), ch. 5; William Doyle, *The Oxford History of the French Revolution* (Oxford: Clarendon Press, 1989), ch. 4; and Schama, *Citizens*, ch. 9. See also George Armstrong Kelly, "The Machine of the Duc D'Orléans and the New Politics," *Journal of Modern History* 51 (1979): 667–684. To guard against possible misinterpretation, Bosher's summary is worth repeating here: "To interpret the ensuing political conflict as a phase in the struggle of two warring social classes, the nobles and the bourgeoisie, is attractively simple but no longer seems tenable except to dogmatic Marxists" (p. 119).

59. Gary P. Steenson, *Karl Kautsky, 1854–1938: Marxism in the Classical Years* (Pittsburgh: University of Pittsburgh Press, 1978), 12.

60. Robert Michels, *Political Parties: A Sociological Study of the Oligarchical Tendencies of Modern Democracy*, trans. Eden Paul and Cedar Paul (Glencoe, Ill.: Free Press, 1958). See Part Four, "Social Analysis of Leadership," especially, pp. 247–260. The quotations are from pp. 336–337, 338.

Britain's Labour Party, in contrast to the continental socialist parties, was reformist in orientation. It was "overwhelmingly working class in its social origins. . . . The parliamentary party was wholly working-class. Of the 51 individuals who sat as official Labour MPs between 1900 and 1914 all were of working-class birth. . . . Only three did not begin their lives as industrial labourers. . . . No MP had any sort of university education and only MacDonald was born of parents not of the industrial working classes." From Ross McKibbon, "Why Was There No Marxism in Great Britain?" *English Historical Review* 99 (1984): 298–331. The quotations are from p. 324. Ramsey MacDonald was a teacher, a journalist, and party propagandist. On the relationship between MacDonald and several other intellectual leaders and the workers, see p. 325.

61. David McLellan, *Karl Marx: His Life and Thought* (London: Macmillan, 1973), 154–158, 167–193.

62. Ibid., 159–166.

63. The Cologne episode is described in P. H. Noyes, *Organization and Revolution: Working-Class Associations in the German Revolutions of 1848–1849* (Princeton: Princeton University Press, 1966), 116–123, 286–288. See also McLellan, *Karl Marx*, 194–196, 211–213.

64. McLellan, *Karl Marx*, ch. 7.

65. Wilhelm Liebknecht, *Socialism: What It Is and What It Seeks to Accomplish* (Chicago: Charles H. Kerr, n.d.), 2.

66. On Ernst Thälmann, see Ossip K. Flechtheim, *Die KPD in der Weimarer Republik* (Frankfurt: Europäische Verlagsanstalt, 1969), 194–196, 204, 215–216, 228–231. On the American Communist Party's use of Foster, see Theodore Draper, *American Communism and Soviet Russia* (New York: Viking, 1960). Intellectual–worker pairings appear throughout Draper's book. Foster had contempt for the intellectuals' "estrangement from the American working class about which, he felt, they talked much and knew little. But he suffered from inferiority in their favorite pastime of theorizing and intellectualizing." John Pepper, an intellectual, Comintern representative of Hungarian origin, and recent arrival in the United States gained considerable influence in the party. He "could overwhelm [Foster] with analogies and precedents from European history or with just the right quotations from Marx, Engels, and Lenin." To counter Pepper, Foster formed an alliance with "his" intellectual, Alexander Bittelman (p. 89). The two "clung to each other for many years . . . because one complemented the other." Pepper, incidentally, provides another example of an intellectual displacing working-class leaders. Within a year of his arrival in the United States he became the "real leader" of the American communist movement (pp. 43, 61). For an early example of the pairing arrangement from Paris in 1848, see the discussion of Louis Blanc and "Albert the worker" in Hamilton, *Bourgeois Epoch*, 187–189.

67. For some discussion of the strains between the party and its related unions see Hamilton, *Affluence*, 29–30; Richard F. Hamilton, *Who Voted for Hitler?* (Princeton: Princeton University Press, 1982), 287–308; Bert Cochran, *Labor and Communism: The Conflict That Shaped American Unions* (Princeton: Princeton University Press, 1977); and Adolf Sturmthal, *Left of Center: European Labor Since World War II* (Urbana: University of Illinois Press, 1983).

68. Michels, *Political Parties*, part 2. For a brief overview, see Seymour Martin Lipset, "Robert Michels and the 'Iron Law of Oligarchy,'" in *Revolution and Counterrevolution: Change and Persistence in Social Structures* (New York: Basic Books, 1968). Lipset is a coauthor, with Martin A. Trow and James S. Coleman, of a major empirical study of the Michels thesis. See Lipset, Trow, and Coleman, *Union Democracy* (Glencoe, Ill.: Free Press, 1956). Robert Michels was closely associated with Max Weber, the "iron law" argument, obviously, being entirely consonant with Weber's theory of the bureaucratization of the modern world.

69. The anticipated radicalization of workers should be evident in voting patterns during the recessions. But this evidence shows no clear and unambiguous shift "to the left." In the United States, for example, both socialist and communist strength remained minuscule throughout the 1930s. Working-class votes were cast, overwhelmingly, for the Democrats. For an overview and some evidence from Germany, see Hamilton, *Who Voted*, 107–108, 439–442, 546, n. 18.

70. Kenneth O. Morgan, *Labour in Power, 1945–1951* (Oxford: Clarendon Press, 1984); Henry Pelling, *The Labour Governments 1945–51* (London: Macmillan, 1984); Peter Hennessy and Anthony Seldon, *Ruling Performance: British Governments from Attlee to Thatcher* (Oxford: Basil Blackwell, 1987), chs. 1, 2; and Alec Cairncross, *The British Economy since 1945: Economic Policy and Performance, 1945–1990* (Oxford: Basil Blackwell, 1992).

71. For a detailed review of *The Class Struggles*, see Hamilton, *Bourgeois Epoch*, ch. 3; and Traugott, *Armies of the Poor*. The working-class uprising known as the June Days was fought for "reformist" ends, to retain a threatened job-creation program. Only a minority of the workers participated. More workers were engaged on the government side. The majority did not participate; they sat it out. Also sitting it out were the left intellectuals. They had provided much enlightenment, but were notably absent from the barricades. The Paris Commune of 1871 led to the third Marx monograph, *The Civil War in France*.

We have a curiosity here. Marxism is a theory of history; the authors purport to have found the key to historical change. For documentation, support, and backup of this awe-inspiring claim, they produced four brief (hundred-page), off-the-cuff monographs. This is counting, in addition to the two just mentioned, *The Eighteenth Brumaire* and Engels's *Germany: Revolution and Counter-Revolution*.

For the recent French experience with socialism, see George Ross, Stanley Hoffmann, and Sylvia Malzacher, eds., *The Mitterrand Experiment: Continuity and Change in Modern France* (Cambridge: Polity Press, 1987); and Walter Laqueur, *Europe in Our Time: A History, 1945–1992* (New York: Penguin, 1992), 479–487.

72. For a brief account of the 1918–1919 events in Germany, see Steenson, *Karl Kautsky*, 211–228. The 1919 socialization commission had an illustrious membership. Among others, it included Karl Kautsky, Emil Lederer, and Rudolf Hilferding. Walter Rathenau, the emininent businessman, intellectual, and later statesman, was a member. Later, Joseph Schumpeter was appointed (pp. 220–221).

73. See two collections, Karl Marx and Friedrich Engels, *Letters to Americans: 1848–1895*, ed. Alexander Trachtenberg (New York: International Pub-

lishers, 1953); and Henry M. Christman, ed., *The American Journalism of Marx and Engels: A Selection from the New York Daily Tribune* (New York: New American Library, 1966). There was no larger systematic study, no monograph even.

74. A.J.P. Taylor provides ten useful tables showing the relative position of six major powers in the decades prior to World War I. See Taylor, *Struggle*, xxvii–xxxi.

75. Robert A. Kann, *Habsburg Empire: A Study of Integration and Disintegration* (New York: Praeger, 1957), ch. 9. On Germany, see Erich Eyck, *A History of the Weimar Republic*, trans. Harlan P. Hanson and Robert G. L. Waite, vol. 1 (New York: Atheneum, 1970), ch. 1; and Arthur Rosenberg, *The Birth of the German Republic, 1871–1918*, trans. Ian Morrow (London: Oxford University Press, 1931), ch. 7. Also, see Marion Kent, ed., *The Great Powers and the End of the Ottoman Empire* (Boston: Allen and Unwin, 1984).

A tense atmosphere existed elsewhere, stimulated by the Russian experience and by postwar price rises (for example, in Italy and in the United States). People on the left, then and now, sensed an impending revolution. But there is an easy alternative reading: bread and butter concerns. With the return of price stability, the "revolutionary" atmosphere disappeared.

76. John King Fairbank, *The Great Chinese Revolution: 1800–1985* (New York: Harper & Row, 1986), chs. 13, 14; Jonathan D. Spence, *The Search for Modern China* (New York: Norton, 1990), chs. 17, 18.

77. Bernard B. Fall, *The Two Viet-Nams: A Political and Military Analysis*, 2d rev. ed. (New York: Praeger, 1967); Joseph Buttinger, *Vietnam: The Unforgettable Tragedy* (New York: Horizon Press, 1977); Stanley Karnow, *Vietnam: A History*, rev. and updated (New York: Viking Penguin, 1991); William J. Duiker, *Sacred War: Nationalism and Revolution in a Divided Vietnam* (New York: McGraw-Hill, 1995); and George C. Herring, *America's Longest War: The United States and Vietnam, 1950–1975*, 3d ed. (New York: McGraw-Hill, 1996).

78. George McTurnan Kahin, *Nationalism and Revolution in Indonesia* (Ithaca: Cornell University Press, 1952); Anthony Reid, *The Indonesian National Revolution 1945–1950* (Hawthorn, Victoria, Australia: Longman, 1974).

79. Michael Barratt Brown, *After Imperialism*, rev. ed. (New York: Humanities Press, 1970). On Britain's retreat from India, see Peter Hennessy, *Never Again: Britain, 1945–1951* (New York: Pantheon, 1993), ch. 6.

80. L. H. Gann and Peter Duignan, *Burden of Empire: An Appraisal of Western Colonialism in Africa South of the Sahara* (Stanford: Hoover Institution Press, 1967). For the French experience, see John Talbott, *The War without a Name: France in Algeria, 1954–1962* (New York: Knopf, 1980); Mahfoud Bennoune, *The Making of Contemporary Algeria, 1830–1987: Colonial Upheavals and Post-Independence Development* (Cambridge: Cambridge University Press, 1988); and, covering two cases, David L. Schalk, *War and the Ivory Tower: Algeria and Vietnam* (New York: Oxford University Press, 1991).

81. On Portugal, see Thomas C. Bruneau, *Politics and Nationhood: Post-Revolutionary Portugal* (New York: Praeger, 1984), ch. 2.

82. The war–revolution linkage appears also in earlier centuries. The American revolution came in the aftermath of the French and Indian War. The Austrian Netherlands revolted in 1789 when Joseph II was occupied with the

Turkish War. Almost all of Latin America broke away in the course of (and in the aftermath) of the Napoleonic Wars. See John Lynch, *The Spanish American Revolutions: 1808–1826*, 2d ed. (New York: Norton, 1986); and E. Bradford Burns, *A History of Brazil* (New York: Columbia University Press, 1970), ch. 3. In the course of the Italian War of 1859, where France and Piedmont fought against Austria, four revolts occurred, in Tuscany, Modena, Parma, and Romagna. The insurgents then joined with Cavour to form a unified Italy. The Paris Commune came in the aftermath of the Franco–Prussian War.

83. Robert G. Wesson, *Why Marxism? The Continuing Success of a Failed Theory* (New York: Basic Books, 1976).

CHAPTER 3

Revisionism:
The Reformist Argument

The term *revisionism* refers to the first of the efforts to transform the original Marxian framework. The intention was to bring that theory into accord with evidence about advanced capitalist nations, evidence that had accumulated by the end of the 19th century. This effort occurred within the German Social Democratic Party (SPD), which was the world's largest socialist party as measured in terms of members, size of organization, number of voters, and share of the electorate. Marx and Engels had given much attention to that party, seeing it as the principal agency for their political practice. With considerable income from membership dues, the party was able to support many newspapers and journals and that, in turn, meant it had a large "staff" of intellectuals. At that time, apart from the churches and the universities, there was probably no equivalent collection of specialized activist–writers to be found anywhere in the modern world. The combination of organization and intellectuals gave the SPD a unique position among the world's socialist parties. The SPD was dominant within the Second International. The other socialist parties looked to the Germans for guidance. The SPD leaders and intellectuals were more than generous in its provision.[1]

The leading figure in the revisionist struggle was Eduard Bernstein, a friend and coworker of Engels. At one time a member of the party's left wing, he later changed position, the revisionist argument being basically moderate or reformist. The original English translation of his major work was given the title *Evolutionary Socialism*. The argument, as will be seen, was still heavily focused on class and class dynamics. In contrast to the original, however, a different nomenclature, a different set of classes, was indicated. The predictions about the growth, decline, and transformation of the classes were much changed. And the predictions about class-specific outlooks were significantly altered. The most important of these was the claim of a dwindling revolutionary potential within the working class.[2]

The Social Democratic presence within Germany had major implications for German scholarship, particularly for the social sciences and history. Many German academics were forced to confront the issues raised by socialist intellectuals. The subject of class, accordingly, occupied a central place in German scholarship, and capitalism also became a major theme. The work of Werner Sombart, Max Weber, and Theodor Geiger provide the most obvious examples. Sombart's works all focused, in one way or another, on the development of modern capitalism. Max Weber's most famous work, *The Protestant Ethic and the Spirit of Capitalism*, addresses the same issue and, it is often said, was intended as a challenge to Marxist materialist assumptions.[3] Weber was the original editor of a series of volumes that appeared under the collective title *Grundriss der Sozialökonomik*. More than a dozen volumes were produced between 1914 and 1930, which included Weber's *Economy and Society*. The two volumes of the ninth "division" (*Abteilung*) contained extended empirical contributions on "The Social System of Capitalism." The first of these, a 500-page work, dealt with social stratification in capitalism. It contained nine long analyses, including ones on the aristocracy in the capitalist era, German farmers in the capitalist era, middle-class questions, the new middle class (by Emil Lederer and Jakob Marschak), and, by Robert Michels, a discussion of the psychology of anticapitalist mass movements. Michels's most famous work, *Political Parties*, also addresses themes from the same repertory.

In the 1930s, exiles from Hitler's Germany transported elements of the Marxist and revisionist views to other nations, especially the United States. One of those exiled scholars, Hans Gerth, joined with a talented graduate student, C. Wright Mills, and brought out a volume of Max Weber's essays. Mills later applied many elements of the intellectual heritage, Marxian, revisionist, and Weberian, to the American experience in his 1951 book, *White Collar*. Even more influential was the work of Seymour Martin Lipset, *Political Man*, published in 1960. A compendious review–synthesis, it brought together theory and research from several traditions (Marxian, revisionist, and pluralist) to provide the basis for a new central direction within American sociology, a political sociology with a strong, explicit focus on class and class dynamics. A key chapter, entitled "Elections: The Expression of the Democratic Class Struggle," signaled the moderate or reformist emphasis, clearly in the revisionist tradition. Some important elements of the revisionist framework, as will be seen, were used in the "affluent" 1950s for the analysis of events in the United States and in much of Western Europe. In the 1950s and early 1960s, class was introduced and legitimated in American social science. In this moderate version, it had become socially acceptable.[4]

EXPLICATION

The central Marx–Engels proposition, the basic summary claim about the tendencies of the bourgeois epoch, it will be remembered, was, "Society as a whole is more and more splitting up into two great hostile camps, into two great classes directly facing each other: Bourgeoisie and Proletariat." The basic portrait was of a three-class society, with the "center" dwindling in numbers and importance. The classes were the grande bourgeoisie (the owners of the major means of production), the petite bourgeoisie or lower-middle class (owners of smaller enterprises), and the proletariat (wageworkers). The fall of the petty bourgeoisie into the proletariat would change the numerical relationship, enlarging the latter's numbers. The disappearance of the middle category would produce a society facing a sharp polar confrontation. The relationship, clearly, would be asymmetrical with a small, wealthy, powerful class of owners opposed by the proletariat, by the "immense majority." Revolution would inevitably follow.

Bernstein and a small group of other revisionists challenged those basic claims. On the basis of a growing body of evidence, they put forward a series of alternative conclusions, ones that significantly changed both the theory and its derived practical imperatives. The principal revised conclusions were as follows:

1. A growing bourgeoisie: The concentration of the means of production predicted by Marx and Engels would mean a decline in the size of the grande bourgeoisie. With big business regularly driving out its competitors, the number of owners would decline. After a review of available British, French, and German evidence, Bernstein concluded that it was "quite wrong to suppose that the present development shows a relative or indeed absolute decrease in the number of property-owners. The number of property-owners increases absolutely *and* relatively."[5]

2. Petty bourgeois persistence, farm enterprises: Making use of census data, Bernstein showed an unexpected persistence of the independent farm populations. That evidence, he wrote, "apparently contradicts everything that the socialistic theory has hitherto advanced." As opposed to concentration, in agriculture he found "a standing-still or a direct retrogression in regard to the size of holdings." That was, of course, the experience at the end of the nineteenth century.

3. Petty bourgeois persistence, nonfarm enterprises: In opposition to the Marxian expectation that the small firms, the artisans, producers, and proprietors, would be driven out by competition with more efficient giant firms (the ex-proprietors then being forced into the proletariat), Bernstein showed this class continuing to have a significant numerical presence at the turn of the century. "Centralisation of businesses," he showed, was a fact in many branches of industry. But it was also "a no less well-established fact that in a whole series of branches of industry small and medium-sized undertakings appear quite capable of existing beside the large industries."[6]

4. Growth of the salariat: The revisionists argued the importance of a class not included in the original nomenclature. Drawing on census data, they pointed to the rapid growth of the salaried white-collar employees, the hundreds of thousands employed in the growing bureaucracies of private businesses and government. Those people were not owners, hence were not part of the bourgeoisie. They were different from the proletariat in that, typically, they had better pay, greater job security, and greater chances for advancement. They also, ordinarily, had more frequent contact with their employers than did the wageworkers. All of these differences of social condition, it was thought, would lead them to differ also in their politics. They would hold moderate or centrist political views. This new class has generally been referred to as the "new middle class."[7]

5. Relative decline of the proletariat: Given the stability of the old-middle-class segments and the growth of the new or salaried middle class, it followed that the working class would experience a relative decline. Contrary to a central Marx–Engels prediction, the proletariat was not growing. It would not become the "immense majority."

As opposed to the Marxian prediction, that of polarization and a general simplification of class relations, the revisionists saw the emergence of a modified three-class arrangement, one that would not involve a "confrontation of opposites." As Bernstein put it, "If the collapse of modern society depends on the disappearance of the middle ranks between the apex and the base of the social pyramid, if it depends on the absorption of these middle ranks by the extremes above and below them, then its realisation is no nearer in England, France, and Germany today than at any earlier time in the nineteenth century." The old-middle-class persistence and the new-middle-class growth meant that the anticipated asymmetric development of bourgeoisie and proletariat was not happening. Three developments, the persistence of the old middle class, the growth of the new middle class, and the appearance of affluent workers, stood in the way of the direct revolutionary confrontation.[8]

6. Growing affluence: The advanced capitalist societies were becoming richer. As noted in the previous chapter, real living standards

were increasing. This brought an important transformation within the working class; by the turn of the century, the signs were unmistakable. The development was most obvious among the skilled workers. They were able to adopt a middle-class living standard. Their real conditions were no longer adequately described with the phrase from the *Manifesto*—"they have nothing to lose but their chains." The argument, put simply, was that those "affluent" workers would adopt reformist or centrist outlooks. The basic lesson was clear: The base of support for the revolutionary option was declining. With growing real incomes, support for revolution within the working class would, at best, be restricted to an ever-smaller segment, the poorly paid semiskilled and unskilled workers.[9]

7. Correlates of class, relative satisfaction: Improved real living standards would bring a shift in outlooks, creating relatively satisfied workers. Class differences would continue to exist but their importance would be attenuated.

8. Correlates of class, political moderation: The satisfied workers would become moderate or reformist in outlook, abandoning the revolutionary option. Given the general well-being of the new middle class, they too would be moderate or centrist in outlook. Bernstein saw the new middle class as open to a reformist, democratic socialist option.[10]

9. Social mobility: The basic Marxian prediction was one of downward mobility. The lower middle class would lose out; its members would "fall into the proletariat." The revisionist argument challenged that claim. The persistence of the two old-middle-class segments and the growth of the new middle class meant a change in direction; more people would move up into the middle class than down into the working class. An important correlate: The net upward mobility would also, presumably, bring greater satisfaction and more moderate outlooks.

10. Reformist policy: The principal conclusion, a prescriptive judgment, followed from these empirical findings: It was the need for a reformist policy. The revisionist arguments were addressed to Europe's socialist parties, beginning with the German Social Democrats. The majority of voters in modern societies, so it was argued, were destined to be reformist in outlook. To gain the votes of that majority, of the working-class and new-middle-class moderates, socialist parties would have to develop reformist programs.

To appreciate the importance of the revisionist critique, one must know something of the context. The Social Democrats first officially adopted a Marxist program in 1891 at the Erfurt Congress. The statement opens with a claim about the development of bourgeois society leading with natural necessity to the destruction of small firms. The means of production, it stated, would increasingly be monopolized by capitalists and large landholders. The proletarian numbers would be ever larger, all of this leading to a sharp opposition of exploiters and exploited. Those pages, the "theoretical" statement, were written by Karl Kautsky, the party's leading theorist and defender of "orthodox" Marxism. Bernstein wrote the "immediate" program, a set of practical legislative demands: universal suffrage, reapportionment of districts after every census, election days as legal holidays, the eight-hour workday, prohibition of child labor, and so on.

The subsequent revisionist critique challenged, with evidence, the fundamentals of the Erfurt theoretical statement. The party had announced the "truth" of modern societies and their development. The critique, in effect, declared that the party, its leaders, intellectuals, and the approving party congress, were mistaken on all major points. The party dealt with the challenge politically. Revisionism was rejected, by overwhelming majorities, in subsequent party congresses. The SPD continued with the radical rhetoric for some three score years while in day-to-day activity its practice was increasingly reformist. The "contradiction" was resolved only in 1959, when the SPD adopted the moderate—that is, revisionist—Godesberg Program.[11]

The revisionist analysis of class transformations provided the basis for much social-science discussion and analysis in Germany of the interwar period. Many of those analyses were empirically based, especially those dealing with the growth or decline of the various class categories. An active, growing social science generated that information out of census materials. But the claims with respect to outlooks and political choices remained largely a matter of speculation. Prior to the appearance and use of polls and surveys, the provision of compelling systematic evidence on those questions was next to impossible. As a result, discussion of these questions remained on the level of guesswork. Conclusions were often boldly stated, but those forceful pronouncements hid or obscured a simple fact: They amounted to little more than "armchair speculation."[12]

Those lines of analysis were eclipsed by the events of subsequent decades. World War I transformed all of the then current analyses. The 1920s saw the rise of Fascism in Italy. In 1922, a paramilitary organization replaced a democratic government in a mock coup d'état, the March on Rome. Several years later, between 1928 and 1932, the National Socialists made spectacular gains in German elections. In January 1933, Hitler was named as Chancellor and his forces quickly dismantled another democratic regime. Fascist parties had appeared, in one form or another, in all nations of Europe (apart from the Soviet Union). The worldwide depression also posed problems for a theory predicting general improvement. Another theory was fashioned to account for the developments of the 1920s and 1930s. It combined elements of Marxism and of revisionism to account for these unforeseen events.

The argument began with a single, exclusive reading of the outlooks of the lower middle class. The development of capitalism, it was said, imposed strains on the members of that class and led them to favor "restorationist" solutions. This "explanation" originally appeared some eighty years earlier in a famous line of the *Communist Manifesto*: "They are reactionary, for they try to roll back the wheel of history." In the new formulation, the line was applied to old-middle-class (petty bourgeoisie) and new-middle-class segments alike. The latter, it was said, were "losing position" relative to the workers. In another formulation, they were "being proletarianized" and, as a result, sought desperately to restore their former status. The fascist parties gained their support, it was said, by promising such a restoration. The argument gained considerable currency and, for a half-century, was easily the leading explanation for the coming of fascism. But the claim turned out to be groundless. No evidence had been presented to show the alleged lower-middle-class support for fascism. The notion proved to be a social construction, a belief that was widely accepted within intellectual circles but one based on group dynamics rather than on an examination of appropriate evidence.[13]

In the postwar period, the affluent 1950s, revisionism, now detached from its Marxist origins, had its greatest impact. The framework provided the terms of analysis for the general affluence that appeared in the United States, Canada, Britain, France, Germany, Italy, and the smaller democracies of Europe. Shareholding became more widespread, this being termed "people's capitalism." The pattern of income distribution changed, going from a broadbased pyramid to a diamond shape as more and more families moved into middle-income categories. The suburban explosion meant that many previously deprived groups were becoming homeowners. With their high and increasing incomes, workers could now achieve a middle-class standard of consumption. Away from the job, it was said, working-class and middle-class lifestyles were indistinguishable. In contrast to the sharp categorical opposition of classes, a key phrase in the new reading assumed a convergence or commonality of condition. A "blurring of class lines" had occurred.

Quite apart from the questions of income and lifestyles was the central underlying fact; namely, a change in occupational structure. Readily available evidence showed a decisive transformation: These societies, it was said, now had middle-class majorities. The number of persons employed in nonmanual (or white-collar, or middle-class) occupations was now greater than those employed in the manual or blue-collar ranks. This change, the shift in quantitative dominance, it was argued, meant a definitive rejection of a central Marxian prediction, the proletariat as immense majority. A major structural change in contemporary capitalist societies had made the proletariat a minority, one destined to become ever smaller.

These two developments, the general affluence and the structural change, had definitively reduced the base for leftist political initiatives. A sizable affluence and the worker literature appeared in the 1950s, detailing the changes and arguing the consequences. Much of the analysis was based on a simple motivational assumption, one summed up in the phrase, "more money, more conservative."

That conclusion seemed amply confirmed by the larger events of the age. Moderate conservative parties either came to power or remained in power throughout Western Europe and North America. The Conservatives were returned to power in Britain in 1951. A year later, in the United States, the Republicans, led by a moderate candidate, Dwight Eisenhower, regained the presidency and secured a majority in both houses of Congress. Germany's moderate Christian Democrats increased their following throughout the decade, in 1957 gaining an absolute majority, the first freely elected parliamentary majority in German history. Italy's Christian Democrats were not quite as successful, but still showed remarkable durability. In 1957, the Progressive Conservatives formed a minority government in Canada; in 1958 they won a majority of seats. The Labour Party had come to power in Australia at the end of the war, but in 1949 they were displaced by a Liberal–Country Party coalition, one that was to remain in office for twenty-three years. The lesson seemed unassailable: The history of the world would be one of growing affluence and political moderation. Any party of the left that did not heed the lesson would be small and destined to decline.[14]

ASSESSMENT

The next task is to provide an assessment of the revisionist hypotheses. With one exception, those claims will be considered in the order of the initial exposition.

1. A growing bourgeoisie: The standard definition of the key term, "bourgeoisie," proves to be problematic in several ways. In the routine formulation, bourgeoisie refers to "owners of the means of production." The expression is treated as if it had a clear and unambiguous meaning.[15] A first problem involves coverage, since judging by usage more than production is intended. In addition to textile manufacturing, coal mines, steel mills, and oil refineries, the term is applied also to services, to banking, finance, insurance, and transportation. This

problem could be easily solved by altering the definition to include those other business activities.

A second problem arises with respect to the meaning of "owner." In most instances, again judging by usage, the term refers to shareholders, to those in possession of common (or voting) stock. That could mean ownership of all outstanding shares, a rare, pointless, and unwise accomplishment. It could mean ownership of a majority of the shares, or, a more practical option, of a controlling minority. It could also refer to small fractional shareholders, those persons owning five or ten shares of General Motors stock. Those small holders would constitute by far the largest number of owners but, as will be seen, they possess only a small fraction of common stock. This points up the need for specification.

Going again by general Marxist usage, bourgeoisie refers to major owners. It is big businessmen (or the monopoly capitalists) who are being discussed in the unqualified formulations. Because of concentration, Marx argued, the number of major holders would decline. Bernstein, citing sketchy ownership figures, disputed the claim and argued an absolute increase. To address the issue, one must define terms: What is a major holder? At minimum, a cutting line is required, one allowing a distinction between major holders and those with only minor participation. An important lesson appears in this connection: If the dividing line has not been specified, it follows that the question has not been researched.

The categorical treatment, owner versus nonowner, presents a third problem, that of combinations. One could be both new middle class and bourgeois, as, for example, in the case of an employee who at some time bought some shares of IBM. A corporation seeking commitment from its employees through a stock-purchase plan, another possibility, might create blue-collar workers who were simultaneously owners. This problem again points to the need for further definition.

A fourth problem stems from the limited focus. Shareholding is only one form of ownership. An exclusive focus on the corporate form overlooks other possibilities; specifically, single-person proprietorships and partnerships. Although generally smaller than corporations, there are some obvious exceptions. At one extreme, an individual (or family) might own outright a large manufacturing establishment with several thousand workers. The giant law firm with several hundred lawyers and an even larger support staff is owned by a handful of partners. At the other extreme, there are the small establishments, the family-owned neighborhood convenience store and Al's Body Shop.

In addition, we have some not-so-obvious ownership arrangements. An owner (or an owning family) might find it advantageous to incorporate. The former owner is then "hired" to serve as the chief execu-

tive of the new enterprise. U.S. census procedures define that executive as a salaried manager. That owner would now be counted with
the new middle class.[16]

Voluntary associations, charitable efforts, philanthropic societies, and
advocacy groups are not normally counted as private businesses. But
the person who founds an association, creates the board of trustees,
heads the board, and who also arranges for his or her own employment as chief executive is, in effect, the owner of a private enterprise.
In census and social-science reports, these persons are also listed as
salaried, in this case, as officials. In fact, however, they are entrepreneurs; they are in the voluntary-association business.[17] These problems too are difficult to handle. The implication, however, is clear:
The number of "owners" present in the United States is larger than
one would ordinarily expect.

A fifth problem arises with respect to the persons involved. Most
discussions of the owners focus on individuals and/or families. But
in recent decades there has been a significant growth of institutional
investment, of ownership by other corporate entities. Retirement funds
have become important stockholders. The California Public Employees' Retirement System is one of the nation's largest owners, with
shareholdings, at year end 1997, valued at $128 billion. The Teachers
Insurance and Annuity Association–College Retirement Equities Fund,
familiarly known as TIAA–CREF, had $200 billion in assets in 1997.
All participating professors might, therefore, be classified as "objec-
tively" bourgeois, as appropriators of "surplus value" produced by
millions of workers. All together, in October 1997, private and public
pension funds held $3 trillion in U.S. equities, amounting to 26.6 per-
cent of the U.S. corporate total.[18]

Mutual funds are a second important variety of indirect ownership.
These funds experienced an extraordinary takeoff in recent decades,
the assets in equity funds coming to $2.98 trillion in 1998. Individuals
buy shares in such funds and those organizations, in turn, buy shares
in corporations (as well as other capital goods). Should those individuals be counted as owners of the means of production?[19]

Institutional holdings of all kinds have increased considerably over
the past five decades. In 1950, institutions held 7.2 percent of U.S. corporate equities; in 1996, they held almost half, 49.6 percent.[20]

Bernstein began his 1899 discussion by pointing up the limitations
of the available evidence: "Unfortunately there is a general lack of
statistical evidence for the actual distribution of the original shares,
preference shares, etc. of the joint-stock companies . . . because in most
countries [England excepted] they are anonymous. . . . The compila-
tion of more exact statistics of shareholders is a gigantic task on which
no one has yet ventured. We can only make a rough estimate of their
number." The problem is still with us more than ninety years later.[21]

The gap between the bold declarations about owners and capitalists and actual evidence on the subject is enormous. The slogans and clichés that dominate discussions in this area point up the problem. Research begins with precise operational definitions. The absence of such definition means that, with rare exceptions, the necessary research is still to be done. Definition is one problem, the absence of appropriate information is another. Much of the information needed to answer the "who owns" question is not in the public record.

Another consideration should be noted in this connection: A person could have immense wealth but by the Marxian definition not be bourgeois. Mrs. Horace Dodge Sr. put her entire fortune, $56 million, in tax-exempt bonds and thus was not an owner as defined here. Bondholders and holders of preferred shares have preferential rights of payment, their returns coming before any dividends on the common stock. But they do not have ownership rights—that is, the voting rights coming with common stock ownership—and thus, strictly speaking, are not members of the bourgeoisie.[22]

The New York Stock Exchange has undertaken a dozen surveys of individual stock ownership within the U.S. population beginning in 1952. The surveys show that the number of American shareowners increased enormously from 6.5 million in 1952 to nearly 31 million in 1970. A decline of some 5 million was indicated in 1975, small investors having withdrawn in the troubled OPEC years. But the numbers increased again, reaching a high of 51 million in 1992. The definition used covers those with stock in mutual funds, who account for about one-sixth of the total. Direct stock ownership increased from 4.2 percent of the population in 1952 to 19.3 percent in 1992. Not surprisingly, the percentages among older segments of the population are considerably higher. The studies also touch on some of the problems just discussed. In 1992, approximately 8 million blue-collar workers were shareowners.[23]

Most stockholders had very modest participation; 32.2 percent of them in 1992 reported a portfolio valued at less than $5,000. At the other extreme, approximately one-sixth of stockowners reported a portfolio of $100,000 and more. A portfolio worth $100,000 might mean 2,000 shares, each valued as $50. Two thousand shares would be a tiny fraction of 1 percent in most major corporations, which means that cutting line is clearly a modest one. If taken as the standard, some 4.6 million individuals would be classified as members of the bourgeoisie. Adding family members would produce a bourgeoisie of some 10 to 15 million persons. Shifting the cutting line upward, taking a million-dollar portfolio as the lower limit, would obviously reduce the size of the bourgeoisie by a considerable margin.[24]

Has the bourgeoisie decreased in size? Has the absolute number of persons declined because of concentrated ownership? Or has this class increased in number as a result of the extended general affluence? The research required to answer this question does not appear to have been conducted. One would have to define the key term, "major stock-holder." That definition must then be adjusted so as to have approximately the same meaning at each point of inquiry. One might take, for example, a million-dollar portfolio in 1900 as the initial standard and, adjusting for price changes, find the equivalent figures for 1940, 1970, and 1990. Lacking that research, one cannot establish the conclusion of more (or less, or the same as) versus some previous point in time. The appropriate conclusion therefore is "don't know."

One may always speculate. It is very likely that the number of persons with million-dollar stock portfolios has increased. It is likely that the absolute number and the percentage of such persons in the total population both increased in the 20th century. The increased general affluence means more money for investment, common stocks being one recommended option.

Although a central and repeated concern for both Marxists and revisionists, one possibility is that the answer is of no great importance. Consider the following hypothetical possibilities: first, that the American bourgeoisie numbered 250,000 persons in 1900 and declined to 100,000 in 1990, and second, that the bourgeoisie in 1900 numbered 250,000 persons and increased to 1,000,000 in 1990. Would the consequences be significantly different? Would workers be more (or less) revolutionary in the latter case? If the change is not seen or appreciated by the workers (the social sciences having failed to establish either claim), how would such information move them?

The terms of the analysis, in short, are poorly defined, rarely going beyond the vague slogan. We have not been provided with usable definitions for any of the key terms, for "bourgeoisie," for "big" (or *grande*), or for "means of production." The intellectual *Praxis* of Marxist scholars carries with it an obvious lesson: The precise size of the bourgeoisie and the trend, whether growth, stability, or decline, are not important concerns.[25]

The bourgeoisie, the large owners, might conceivably form a minuscule 1 percent of the total population. The remainder of this assessment will be concerned with the other 99 percent, beginning with the farm sector, the subject of the second of the previously listed claims. The aim here is to find and report data which match, as closely as possible, the categories used in both the Marxist and revisionist analyses, so as to allow assessment of their claims.

The initial discussions in the following pages deal with the number of persons within various categories and with their relative proportions. This discussion deals with body counts as opposed to questions of consciousness. One should not, therefore, assign any specific meanings to those findings. Actual outlooks will be considered later in this chapter.

None of the definitions and none of the procedures used here are in any sense final. Every one of them involves elements of judgment and of approximation. The manual–nonmanual distinction involves a sorting of 12,741 occupational titles into two comprehensive categories.[26] It is, however, a rare occupation that is exclusively mental or physical. The mail carrier must be literate, able to sort out names and addresses, and must carry out and deliver large quantities of material to the ultimate recipients. Another problem is posed by the categorical reading. Some people are classified as farmers, others as nonfarm blue-collar workers. But people could easily be both, holding two jobs simultaneously or doing each in an appropriate season. Another possibility is that a person could be in the labor force, employed as a blue-collar worker, and, at the same time, be a student at a prestigious university and be from an upper-middle-class family (the parents thought work was good for character).

2. Petty bourgeois persistence, farm enterprises: In the first half-century of its existence, the United States was overwhelmingly rural, the vast majority of its population living on farms. The date of the transformation to the nonfarm majority is not precisely known, the first serious statistical account coming in 1880, at which point 43.8 percent of the population was still "on the farm." The percentages fell regularly thereafter in every census. In 1990, the farm population formed 1.9 percent of the total (Table 3.1).

Much of the discussion of farms and farmers in the United States, by Marxists and non-Marxists alike, could be put under a one-word heading: decline. In 1882, Marx and Engels wrote a brief preface for the Russian edition of the *Manifesto* pointing to this fact. Commenting on the United States, they declared, "Step by step the small and middle landownership of the farmers, the basis of the whole political constitution, is succumbing to the competition of giant farms."[27]

From one perspective, that conclusion is accurate: The history has been one of continuous *relative* decline. But the focus on relative standing—farmers (and farm population) as a percentage of the total—is misleading. In absolute numbers the farm population increased with every census through to 1910. The slight downturn that came in the next decade was probably due to a decline in the size of the average farm family. The number of farms actually increased, reaching the all-time high, 6,454,000, in 1920. The subsequent downward movement was initially a rather gradual one, the total falling by 159,000 farms in 1930, and by

Table 3.1
Farms, Farm Proprietors, and Farm Population

Year	Farms (1,000s)	Farmers and Farm Managers (1,000s)	As Percentage of Civilian Labor Force	Farm Population[a] (1,000s)	Farm Population (%)
1850	1,449				
1860	2,044				
1870	2,660				
1880	4,009			21,973	43.8
1890	4,565			24,771	42.3
1900	5,740	5,763	19.8	29,875	41.9
1910	6,366	6,163	16.1	32,077	34.9
1920	6,454	6,442	15.5	31,974	30.1
1930	6,295	6,032	12.4	30,529	24.9
1940	6,102	5,362	10.1	30,547	23.2
1950	5,388	4,375	6.9	23,048	15.3
1960	3,962	2,528[b]	3.5	15,635	8.7
1970	2,954	1,428	1.7	9,712	4.8
1980	2,440[c]	1,485	1.4	6,051[c]	2.8
1990	2,140[c]	1,250[d]	1.0	4,591[c]	1.9

Sources: U.S. Bureau of Census, *Historical Statistics of the United States: Colonial Times to 1970*, part 1 (Washington, D.C.: U.S. Government Printing Office, 1975), 126–127, 139, 457; *Residents of Farms and Rural Areas: 1991*, Current Population Reports (Washington, D.C.: U.S. Government Printing Office, 1993), 20–472; Bureau of Statistics, U.S. Department of Treasury, *Statistical Abstract of the United States* (Washington, D.C.: U.S. Government Printing Office, 1981), 379, 395–398, 401–404, 657, 660; 1992, 394.

[a]Total of males and females.
[b]1970 classification.
[c]New definition in 1974.
[d]This is for 1991.

another 193,000 in 1940. The precipitous fall came in the next decade, basically after World War II, with 714,000 farms disappearing by 1950, another 1.4 million by 1960, and still another million by 1970.

In summary, the number of farms increased until 1920. The number was over 6 million at all points from 1910 to 1940. The farm population numbered just over 30 million in that same period, showing only slight declines. The "succumbing" that Marx and Engels announced in 1882 was not to come for another three score years. Their claim about the growth in size is also not supported. In 1850, the average farm in the United States had 203 acres. The trend in subsequent decades was downward, the average in 1880 being only 134 acres. The increase thereafter was gradual, the 200-acre average not being reached again until 1949. Rapid growth came after that point.[28]

From at least the beginning of the 20th century, a majority of those engaged in farming were owners or managers. In 1900, a large proportion, just under half, were tenants or farm laborers, but that proportion declined in all subsequent decades. A large part of both segments or, more likely, their children, left the farm and took up blue-collar jobs in the city. For farm owners, that might have meant a "fall" into the proletariat, thus confirming a Marxian hypothesis. But, as indicated in the previous chapter, it is not clear how such moves should be interpreted. It is possible too that the new job was a distinct improvement. Some evidence on this point will be reviewed later.

A persistent bias appears in the literature: Farmers are regularly portrayed as victims. In the romantic versions, the sheriff's foreclosure sale figures prominently, as, for example, in John Steinbeck's novel *The Grapes of Wrath* or in the film *The Asphalt Jungle*. But there is another easy option: The children left the farm in search of better opportunities. They wanted a better life, less onerous work, more income, greater security, and more attractive leisure-time options.[29]

The dramatic absolute decline of the farm population, as noted, came after 1940. The number had fallen below 15 million as of 1960 and was halved again by 1980. This period of significant losses, after 1940, was also one of unusual affluence; that is, of exceptional opportunities in the nonfarm sector. Relatively few, at that point, lost their properties through bankruptcy followed by a sheriff's auction. Farms were "lost"—were sold—in the course of postwar suburban development. For those farmers, the land boom paid off with greater rewards than were ever dreamed in the course of the Oklahoma land rush.

Suburbanization did not begin in 1950. Most of the territory of any modern metropolis was farmland at the beginning of the 19th century. Any farmer with land in the path of urban development was likely to make major gains. The twenty-two-acre Gramercy Farm in Manhattan (between 19th and 23rd Streets and between Broadway and Second Avenue) was purchased for development in 1831. It was divided into 108 city lots, 42 of them being used for a private park. Brooklyn in 1810 was "occupied mostly by farms," its population less than 5,000. With the coming of the ferry, "Brooklyn the Beautiful" became an option for persons working in Manhattan. By the end of the century, the farms were gone; Brooklyn was the fourth largest city in

the nation.[30] Discussions of farmers, in short, need some minimal specification. Farmers whose properties lie in the path of urban development were likely to be major winners; those located in depopulating
rural areas were likely to be major losers.

One other consideration deserves attention: The minuscule farm
sector of the 1990s, less than 2 percent of total employment, generated
the largest quantity of food ever produced in the United States. It also
produced large quantities of cotton and wool. As opposed to the standard romantic silliness, the portrait of the modern world as a history
of unending loss, most people would view this productivity as an
unambiguous gain; that is, as a good thing.[31]

The United Kingdom, Marx's prime case, was also the unique case.
There, the decline of farming came a century earlier, both relatively
and absolutely. In 1841, only 28 percent of employed males were in
agriculture, horticulture, and forestry. The absolute number peaked
in 1851, moving slowly but steadily downward in every subsequent
decade. Elsewhere, the experience is similar to that of the United States.
In Germany, the percentage of persons in farming, forestry, and fish-
eries (including all proprietors, family members, and laborers) declined
steadily between 1882 and 1939, falling from 43.4 percent to 25 percent. But the absolute number increased through to 1907. The number
declined somewhat in later years, but even in 1939, it was larger, by
700,000, than the farm population of 1882. In 1950, within the Federal
Republic of Germany, 22.1 percent were engaged in farm occupations.
The rapid decline came after that point, to 13.3 percent in 1960 and to
8.9 percent in 1970.

In France, the percentage of the economically active population in
agriculture fell steadily from 51.5 percent in 1856 to 35.2 percent in
1936. But again, the absolute numbers tell a different story. There were
7,275,000 persons in agriculture in 1856, a figure that increased in subsequent decades to over 8,000,000 at the turn of the century and then
peaked at 8,951,000 in 1921. Even as late as 1946, the number was still
high, at 7,484,000. The precipitous decline came thereafter. Almost
3,000,000 had disappeared from agriculture as of 1959.[32] Marx and
Engels, in short, were seriously mistaken in their claims about the timing of this process.

The changes in the nonfarm labor force will be considered next. Most
discussions in both the Marxist and revisionist traditions center on
the manual–nonmanual distinction, on the division between blue-collar
and white-collar workers or, expressed still another way, between
working class and middle class. For convenience of the exposition, we
begin with the fifth of the listed claims, the key revisionist proposition: the relative decline of the working class. That will be followed by
consideration of the two middle-class segments, the old and new
middle classes.

The revisionists argued, with evidence, that the middle class had shown relative growth, rather than, as in Marxism, experiencing a pronounced decline. The obvious correlate was that the working class (or blue-collar or manual rank) had shown an equivalent relative decline. A half-century later, following the same lines of argument, the 1950s revisionists put forward the claim of a class shift, that the middle class had become (or was soon to be) the majority. The immediate task here is to address those claims about the changing manual–nonmanual proportions.[33]

To deal with the 12,741 occupations in the labor force, some categorization is required. Every country, accordingly, has developed procedures for simplifying an otherwise impossible complexity. The resulting categories vary in their usefulness; that is, in the degree to which they allow adaptation for testing of theoretical claims. Early in the present century, a U.S. census employee, Alba Edwards, developed categories that, with some important modifications in 1980, have been used ever since. Four of those categories have routinely been grouped to form the middle class or nonmanual rank. These are professionals, technical, and kindred; managers, officials, and proprietors; clerical and kindred; and sales. Three categories have routinely been grouped together as the manual or blue-collar segment. These are craftsmen, foremen, and kindred; operatives and kindred; and laborers. The latter approximate the common distinction into skilled, semi-skilled, and unskilled workers. Two other categories have often been treated separately, their location being somewhat problematic: private household workers and service workers. Since they generally match the blue-collar workers in terms of income, education, and status, they have been classified in the tables within this chapter with the manual workers.[34]

This initial exploration, it should be emphasized, is necessarily rather approximate. These occupational categories are a poor match for the categories found in Marxism and revisionism. The self-employed, as will be seen, appear in many of the Edwards categories and are not easily separated for analytic purposes. Some independents, basically artisans, appear in various blue-collar categories. A small collection of salarieds, the foremen, are classified with the skilled workers. Appropriate adjustments will be considered in later discussion.[35]

Looking first at the totals, one may see the shifting proportions. Beginning as a sizable majority, 72 percent in 1900, the manual (or working-class) segment has decreased in relative size throughout the century (Table 3.2). In this series, the 50-percent point was reached around 1970 and the decline continued such that the workers amounted to only two-fifths of the total in 1995. With this conceptualization and this procedure, the Marxian hypothesis—a growing proletariat—is rejected and the revisionist claim confirmed. It is important, however, to consider some details. While these do not change the basic lesson, that of

Table 3.2
Occupational Distribution: 1900–1995, Nonfarm Males and Females

Year	Total		Males		Females		Nonfarm Labor Force	Female Percentage of Nonfarm Labor Force
	Nonmanual	Manual	Nonmanual	Manual	Nonmanual	Manual		
1900	28	72	30	70	22	78	18,142	23.8
1910	31	69	31	69	31	69	25,758	24.3
1920	34	66	31	69	45	55	30,816	24.2
1930	37	63	34	66	48	52	38,363	25.7
1940	38	62	34	66	47	53	42,747	28.2
1950[a]	42	58	36	64	54	46	52,372	30.4
1960[b]	45	55	38	62	57	43	63,858	34.3
1970[c]	49	51	41	59	61	39	77,354	38.9
1980	54	46	44	56	66	34	96,562	43.1
1990	59	41	48	52	72	28	114,141	46.3
1995	60	40	49	51	72	28	121,444	46.8

Sources: U.S. Bureau of the Census, Historical Statistics of the United States: Colonial Times to 1957 (Washington, D.C.: U.S. Government Printing Office, 1960), 74; Bureau of Statistics, U.S. Department of Treasury, Statistical Abstract of the United States (Washington D.C.: U.S. Government Printing Office, 1984), 417; (1996), 405–407; idem., Employment and Earnings (Washington, D.C.: U.S. Government Printing Office), May 1990, 35. Data for 1900–1950 are for "Experienced Civilian Labor Force"; those for 1960–1995 are for "Employed Civilian Labor Force."

[a]1960 classification.

[b]1970 classification.

[c]Persons sixteen years old and older.

a relative decline, they point to the need for specification with respect to definition, process, and timing.

The labor force involvements of men and women differ considerably. Because of those differences, and because the processes and rates of change differ, separate consideration is appropriate. The class shift occurred first on the female side of the labor force in the 1940s. There is no mystery about this process: It stemmed from the creation of opportunities in the white-collar ranks, especially in clerical jobs. At one time, almost all clerks were men. But with the growth of bureaucracy, men were moved upward into supervisory positions and the routine clerical jobs were opened to women. There was also, as may be seen in Table 3.2 (in the column at the right), a significant growth of women's participation in the labor force. The combined result, as seen, put the transition at around 1970. But the class shift proceeded much more slowly on the male side of the labor force (which contained most of the main earners). The working-class percentage among males fell to 51 percent in 1995. This turning point, in short, came some five decades after that of the equivalent females.

The procedure used to this point draws on readily available U.S. government data and depends on two central definitions, the labor force and class as based on conventional combinations of the Edwards categories. The procedure, however, is problematic in several respects. The first of the difficulties stems from the definition of the labor force. The civilian labor force consists of all persons who, during the reference week, were either at work, on temporary leave, or looking for work. It includes unpaid workers in a family enterprise who put in a minimum of fifteen hours. It also includes part-time employees, specifically those who put in a minimum of an hour's work. Being "in the labor force," in short, has a wide range of meanings.[36] It might mean a full-time commitment, as is normally required for sustaining a family. Or it might mean a limited commitment, providing modest supplemental earnings for a son or daughter still in high school. Most discussions of class assume influences that have powerful determining impacts. A part-time job, however, might be a peripheral event, a minor determinant of outlooks and behaviors.

Part-time job holders are more likely than the full-time employed to be in blue-collar or service occupations. Part-timers, especially among males, are just starting out on their careers and, consequently, have limited skills. Some of them are from middle-class families. Although found mowing lawns, stocking shelves in the supermarket, or employed in fast-food shops, counting them as working class might be inappropriate since, for many, those jobs do not reflect either their class of origin or their likely subsequent employment. One way of dealing with these problems is to exclude them and to focus only on the full-time employed.

A second problem appears in this connection: As noted, some persons classified as blue-collar workers in the relevant Edwards categories are independents. They are sellers of goods and/or services rather than wageworkers. Accordingly, to be consistent with the Marxist and revisionist concepts, they should be counted with the petty bourgeoisie as members of the old middle class.

The definition of the labor force, a third problem, focuses on individuals and as such gives no consideration to family status. The nuclear family, the traditional form, consists of a husband, a wife, and dependent children. Until recently, the husband was customarily defined as the head of the household. In most cases, he was the family's main earner or, another handed-down term, its breadwinner. For that reason, a social-science tradition developed according to which the class of the family was defined by the occupation of the husband. The procedure was appropriate for earlier experience and, on the whole, with some modification, still seems useful. To do otherwise, to focus on individuals, disaggregates families and, in many cases, would put its members in different classes. The banker's son who earns money mowing suburban lawns would be classified as working class. The machinist's wife employed part time in a neighborhood convenience store would be counted as middle class.[37]

Such misplacement is a serious problem in presentations that focus on individuals. The most serious difficulty is that many wives with middle-class occupations have husbands in working-class occupations. Should the wives (or the employed daughters) in those families be classified as middle class or as working class? Some part of the class shift found on the female side of the labor force in Table 3.2, therefore, provides ambiguous evidence for the claim of a class shift. Given the working-class backgrounds and political socialization of those wives and daughters, one would anticipate similar outlooks within the family; for example, in party preferences, political issues, and class identifications. This is in fact the case. Sizable majorities of working-class wives, for example, regardless of their own occupational status, identify themselves as working class. For further discussion and evidence, see the Appendix.

The National Opinion Research Center's (NORC) annual General Social Surveys (GSS) allow investigation of several questions raised here.[38] The annual surveys have been merged to produce four combinations, 1975–1979, 1980–1984, 1985–1989, and 1990–1994. The aims are to provide larger base numbers and to show possible trends. The first approach to these questions focuses on all nonfarm full-time employed persons. The self-employed blue-collar workers have been classified with the old middle class. Foremen, the "first line of management," have been classified with the new middle class. The results have been presented separately for men and women, since, as indicated, their employment patterns differ.

This procedure suggests that the class shift among males came in the early 1970s. Just over half (53%) of the full-time employed males in 1975–1979 were in middle-class occupations. The working-class decline continued over the twenty-year period. For women, clearly, the middle-class majority arrived much earlier. Only a third of the full-time employed women had working-class jobs in the late 1970s. That fell to less than a quarter in the early 1990s.

In later analysis, satisfactions, political outlooks, and mobility patterns will be examined by class. Presenting results separately for males and females would entail considerable complication, doubling the size of tables and more than doubling the amount of text required. To simplify matters, a combination will be used, one that follows the logic just spelled out. The procedure takes, first, married men employed full time in nonfarm occupations. They are classified by their own occupations. Second, all married women are included, full- and part-time employed plus housewives, and have been classified by their husbands' occupations. Third, it includes all other full-time employed men and women (including the single, separated, divorced, and widowed). They have been classified by their own occupations. Several categories have been omitted, namely, not-married part-timers, unemployed, and retirees. Various complications arise in the placement of these categories, hence the choice to omit them.

The classification of wives by husband's occupation, as noted, has been the source of much controversy. The key question is this: If located in different classes, do those wives match their husbands in class identifications and political outlooks or do they match others in their own class? Examination of several appropriate GSS questions showed a close correspondence of husband–wife attitudes, which is to say that family solidarity (or cohesion) was considerably stronger than individual class ties or loyalties. That being the case, the combination used here appears justified (see Appendix).[39]

This combination, shown in Table 3.3, yields results comparable to those just reported. The working class shows continuous decline, a total of 10 percentage points, in this two-decade span. The shift to the middle-class majority would have occurred at some point before 1975, probably around 1970.

3. Petty bourgeois persistence, nonfarm enterprises: As noted, many researchers and commentators define the manual and nonmanual categories through use of basic U.S. census categories.

Table 3.3
The Size of the Classes (NORC–GSS: Four Merged Sets)

	1975-1979	1980-1984	1985-1989	1990-1994
Class: All Full-Time Employed Males				
Old Middle	11 %	15 %	14 %	15 %
New Middle	42	44	46	46
Working	47	42	40	39
N =	(1,583)	(1,510)	(2,008)	(1,940)
Class: All Full-Time Employed Females				
Old Middle	6 %	7 %	9 %	8 %
New Middle	62	69	68	69
Working	32	24	23	23
N =	(1,047)	(1,240)	(1,571)	(1,764)
Class: Combination[a]				
Old Middle	11 %	13 %	14 %	14 %
New Middle	44	47	49	51
Working	45	40	37	35
N =	(3,441)	(3,383)	(4,184)	(4,195)

[a]See Appendix for the procedure used.

While having the advantage of ease and simplicity, the procedure is problematic in that some groups are misplaced. The resulting middle class would include a part of the bourgeoisie (a tiny segment, any major shareholders who were in the labor force) and most but not all of the petty bourgeoisie. Some independent proprietors, as noted, are classified with the blue-collar categories, the conventional procedure thus treating them as working class. Most of the salarieds are included within this broad middle class, but some, the foremen and supervisors, a group often described as the first line of management, are classified with the "crafts" and thus are also treated as blue-collar workers.[40] Appropriate readjustments have been made using the National Opinion Research Center's General Social Surveys.

In the 1980s, approximately one-seventh of the full-time employed males in the nonfarm civilian labor force were self-employed independents (Table 3.3). Seen from another perspective, the old-middle-class segment forms approximately one-fourth of the middle class. Old-middle-class employment of women is considerably less frequent, approximately half that of men. It too shows a slight but irregular increase. The combination (just explained) shows a result similar to that for the full-time employed males. The basic finding then is slight growth of the old middle class. Contrary to the long-standing Marxian claim, the old middle class has been increasing in size, both relatively and absolutely.[41]

The old middle class, it should be noted, is very diverse. It includes those employing hundreds of workers and those employing only a couple of family members. It includes independent professionals, doctors, lawyers, tax consultants, poets, artists, musicians, and freelance journalists, as well as self-employed artisans or craftsmen. Given that diversity of condition, common outlooks and political orientations would be a very unlikely assumption.

In what was probably the most important English-language presentation on this subject, C. Wright Mills provided figures showing the decline of the old middle class. It fell from 85 percent of the middle-class total in 1870 to 44 percent in 1940. But almost all of that decline was accounted for by the farm proprietors, who fell from 62 percent to 23 percent. The businessmen fell by a mere two points, from 21 percent to 19 percent, in the same period. That could be read as decline but, as a test of the competing Marxian and revisionist claims, one would, on first sight, have to count this evidence as favoring the latter. Given the increase in the size of the nation's population and labor force in that period, it is obvious that the modest relative decline would mask a considerable increase in the absolute numbers of nonfarm proprietors. Mills's figures, moreover, depend to a great extent on judgment, inference, and estimation. As he put it, in an appendix dealing with sources, his reclassification of "free enterprisers" was "mainly determined by projecting 1940 information in regard to 'class of work' . . . to earlier years."[42]

Harold Kerbo's social-stratification text, the most popular in the field, contains only a few fragments of information on the old middle class. One comment declares that "these self-employed workers are hardly significant in the economy." The "concentration of the means of production, greater technical complexity of production, and increased size of production units," he declares, "have reduced the ranks of the old middle class relative to other occupations." That sentence continues with a parenthetical recognition of a "slight increase" of the old middle class in the 1970s and 1980s. Mills's work is discussed in this connection. While generally approving, Kerbo criticizes Mills for his "overly positive view" of the old middle class.[43]

Although the petty bourgeoisie or old middle class figures prominently in both the Marxist and revisionist traditions, it is odd that until recently little relevant evidence has been presented on the subject.

If, following Marx, one expected the old middle class (or petty bourgeoisie) to have declined almost to disappearance, that expectation is
mistaken. The recent experience, in the United States and elsewhere,
points in an opposite direction, with modest growth indicated.

4. Growth of the salariat: The data problems noted with respect to
the nonfarm independents appear also with respect to the equivalent
salarieds. Mills's key table showed a considerable growth of the new
middle class between 1870 and 1940, an increase from 15 percent to 56
percent, but that result is again contaminated by the inclusion of farm
proprietors and the undifferentiated mix of male and female occupations. Kerbo's social-stratification text contains a table showing occupational distributions from 1900 to 1990. While offering more detail
than Mills, the same problems appear there. Moreover, his use of the
Edwards categories does not allow precise separation of the old and
new middle classes.[44]

Data for the last two decades (see Table 3.3) show 46 percent of the
full-time employed nonfarm males and 69 percent of the equivalent
females in new-middle-class occupations. Both figures are somewhat
higher than in the late 1970s, and both show continued although modest increase. The combination shows the same growth. These figures
show the new middle class as a majority in the early 1990s.

That new middle class, obviously, is also very heterogeneous. It includes school teachers and corporate managers, dental assistants and
union leaders, scientists and government officials. As opposed to the
assumption of some compelling classwide effects, considerable diversity in outlooks and behaviors should be anticipated.

One line of division within this class, curiously, has received little
attention in the stratification literature: Few accounts systematically
distinguish between the new-middle-class segments in the public and
private sectors. C. Wright Mills's book contains one brief index reference: "Government, bureaucracy in, 78–81." But even there the distinction is blurred and no serious analysis is provided. It should make
a difference, presumably, whether one is employed by General Motors, the State of Michigan, Wayne County, the City of Detroit, or the
Detroit School Board.[45]

5. Relative decline of the proletariat: The decline of the proletariat
is clear and unambiguous. As seen in Table 3.3, the working class is a
minority, forming two-fifths of the full-time males and less than one-

quarter among the equivalent females. In the combination, the working class forms roughly one-third of the total.

6. Growing affluence: Toward the end of the 19th century, real-income growth was evident in all advanced capitalist nations. Defenders of capitalism made much of the achievement. Bernstein and the other revisionists focused on the implications for the working classes and for their political agencies, the socialist parties. The general tendency was much disrupted in the three decades after 1914 and, not too surprisingly, this particular claim fell into abeyance. After World War II, however, the sustained economic growth beginning in the early 1950s led to a resurgence of attention to this theme and the "affluent society" became a dominant theme in popular discussion, in the social sciences, and in political practice. In the early 1970s, in the midst of the Vietnam War, the aura seemed to have disappeared. Family income levels were stagnant; in many years losses were registered. For some groups, notably blue-collar workers in heavy industry, the losses appeared to be both serious and permanent. In this period, accordingly, the exuberant analyses of affluence and its correlates disappeared again from public discussion. The new analyses dealt with more somber topics: deskilling, deindustrialization, and job loss. For entire generations, for the "baby boomers," the prediction was one of a "retreat," of lower living standards.

Evidence showing stagnation since 1970 is readily available. Median household income in 1970, as expressed in 1993 dollars, was $31,341. The equivalent figure for 1994 was $32,264. That suggests very modest growth but for some years in this period the median was below the 1970 level. As for income distribution, the trend, beginning in the 1980s, was inequalitarian, a tendency continuing into the 1990s. It seemed clear that major segments of the population were losing position and many were experiencing absolute losses.[46]

Although a plausible and widely shared position, those conclusions are mistaken. In the mid-1980s, Ben Wattenberg criticized and assessed many of those pessimistic views, including the notion that real living standards were declining. For one part of his critique, Wattenberg reviewed the *Statistical Abstract of the United States*, looking for evidence on consumption patterns. He found dramatic increases in well-being in a wide range of areas from 1970 to the early 1980s. These included many leisure-time activities: attendance at various sporting events (for example, professional football and basketball), video-game use, golfing and boating, and symphony concert-going. Total recreational spending increased from $41 billion to $141 billion. Even after correction for inflation, that meant a 35-percent increase (versus a 14% increase in population). He also found significant increases in foreign travel (not included in the cited figures), the number of telephones, cable television subscriptions, videocassette recorders, and restaurant dining. The increase of car purchases was well ahead of the increase in the adult population. All these things were happening, moreover, at a time when more people were attending college. The two claims, stable (or declining) income and markedly increased spending, are incompatible.[47]

The paradox, Wattenberg shows, has an easy explanation. The series used at the beginning of this discussion was based on household income. And households during this period were declining in size. A roughly constant household income combined with declining unit size means increased per capita income. Wattenberg reviewed two studies providing per capita figures. One found an increase of 35 percent between 1970 and 1984. A second study, operating with somewhat different assumptions, found an increase of 16 percent between 1970 and 1980, and an estimate of "no more than 20 percent" for the 1970–1984 span. A later source, one reviewing the experience of twenty-five years, 1964 to 1989, reports the increase of real per capita disposable income to be 72 percent.[48]

A summary picture showing household size and consumption expenditure over four decades, 1950 to 1990, is provided in Table 3.4. There was, as shown in the third column, a steady decline in household size over the period, most of this occurring after 1965, the ending of the baby boom. Per capita consumption expenditure (measured in constant 1987 dollars) showed a steady and significant increase over the same period. These figures also show a considerable increase in consumption expenditure per household. The increases in per capita living standards during the 1950s and 1960s are readily seen here, the 1970 level being 53 percent above that of 1950. Contrary to the argument of subsequent stagnation, the 1990 figure is 48 percent above the 1970 level. These results are entirely in line with Wattenberg's findings published more than a decade ago.[49]

One may pursue the logic of the case with another line of evidence. From approximately 1940 onward—that is, for half a century—the United States has experienced a generally upward course with respect to economic performance. There have been, to be sure, periods of modest recession, some episodes of setback, but no extended crises to match the 1930s. Most people living in the early 1990s would know of this sustained improvement through personal experience. When asked about their own lives, accordingly, one would expect responses reflecting that improvement. This is in fact the case. In February 1991, a Gallup survey asked the appropriate question: "Comparing your present family circumstances with those when you were a child, would you say you are better off, or worse off, than your parents were then?"

Table 3.4
Measures of Well-Being: 1950–1990

Year	Total Personal Consumption Expenditure[a]	Average Size of Household	Adjusted per Capita Consumption Expenditure[b]	Adjusted Consumption Expenditure per Household[c]
1950	$ 191.0	3.37	$ 5,764	$ 19,424
1955	254.4	3.33	6,335	21,096
1960	325.2	3.33	6,698	22,304
1965	432.8	3.31	7,703	25,497
1970	616.7	3.14	8,842	27,764
1975	973.0	2.94	9,711	28,550
1980	1,748.1	2.76	10,746	29,659
1985	2,667.4	2.69	12,015	32,320
1990	3,748.4	2.63	13,044	34,324

Sources: Bureau of Statistics, U.S. Department of Treasury, *Statistical Abstract of the United States* (Washington, D.C.: U.S. Government Printing Office, 1971), 36, 306; (1977), 429; (1988), 407; (1993), 55, 442, 445.

[a]Current dollars in billions. Defined as "goods and services purchased by persons resident in the United States," in *National Income and Product: Accounts of the United States*, vol. 2, *1959–1988* (Washington, D.C.: U.S. Government Printing Office, 1992), M-6.

[b]1987 constant dollars.

[c]Multiplication of average size of household and adjusted per capita consumption expenditure.

Seventy-eight percent reported they were better off. One in eight said "worse off" and roughly one in ten volunteered a "no difference" response. The latter, incidentally, were spread fairly evenly across the income spectrum. Some, in other words, indicated they were well-off both then and now.[50]

The most comprehensive analysis of the longterm trend, by Richard A. Easterlin and his coworkers, finds little support for the prevailing pessimistic judgments. Their findings are based on the U.S. Census Current Population Surveys, probably the best available source for addressing these questions. Their conclusions are as follows: "The evidence clearly belies the notion that on average the baby boomers are doing less well than their parents." The earnings of males in the "boomer" cohort "were 30 percent greater than for their parents; total family income, about 50 percent greater." The popular press, these authors report, "created the impression" of considerably lower savings among the boomers, but again the best available data do not support that claim. The boomers were doing less well with respect to home ownership, the single unambiguous instance of intergenerational loss. But the "overriding reason" was the exceptionally high mortgage rates prevailing in the early 1980s, just as this group was entering the housing market. It is entirely possible, the authors note, that the boomers would "make up for some or all of this shortfall" at a later point when much lower interest rates prevailed. Home ownership rates did eventually move upward again, reaching new highs in the mid-1990s.

The amount of advantage experienced by the boomer generation varies with income level. Given the inequalitarian trend of the 1980s, the highest earners obviously showed the greatest advances over the equivalent categories in the parental cohorts. For the lowest-income segment, "It remains true that those in the baby boom generation are currently doing better than their counterparts in the parental generation," but the percentage advantage "is much less than for the upper income group." The low earners among the younger boomers, the "trailing edge," those born in 1961–1965, show the least advantage. The authors offer a tentative judgment here: "Unless there is a turnaround in the recent growth of inequality, it seems possible that the lowest income segment of the trailing edge boomers may end up worse off than their counterparts in the parental generation."[51]

The remarkable growth of affluence and the increase of real incomes experienced in the postwar years did not end somewhere around 1970. For most people, for the vast majority, the favorable trend has continued to the present. That upward movement, moreover, did not begin in the early 1950s. It began with the war, effectively in the early 1940s. The sustained growth has been with us now for approximately a half-century. Most members of the working class, as defined here, would be among the gainers. In the Gallup data, three-quarters of those in the lowest-income category reported they are better off than when growing up. That would include most persons who, by the official definition, are classified as poor.[52]

To this point, we have concentrated on the distinction of old- versus new-middle-class segments. Another important distinction, one regularly invoked, is that of upper-middle class versus lower-middle class. Most such discussions are categorical in format, as if there were a sharp distinction between the two. The dichotomous treatment, however, is merely a convenience, a usage that bypasses the actual differences that are matters of degree. For the sake of that convenience, as a first approach to some of the issues raised in the revisionist tradition, that convention, the dichotomous treatment, will be maintained here.

The General Social Surveys contain a rating of occupational prestige based on public assessments, the rankings extending from 1 to 100. Taking the nonmanual populations, persons with scores of 56 or more were classified as upper-middle class, those with 55 or below as lower-middle class. Using the combination described earlier and the merged NORC–GSS from 1990–1994, we have the following result: upper-middle class, 20 percent; lower-middle class, 45 percent; working class, 35 percent (N = 4,195). The upper-middle class falls into two very unequal segments, new middle, 17 percent, and old middle, 3 percent. The respective figures for the lower-middle class are new middle, 34 percent; old middle, 11 percent. All this is for the nonfarm labor force. The upper-middles have considerably higher incomes than the lower-middles, although there is much overlap. The upper-middles also have considerably higher levels of educational achievement (for details, see Appendix).[53]

This use of occupational-prestige scores to delineate the classes is intended as a rule-of-thumb procedure. In a previous work, *Class and Politics*, I divided the upper- and lower-middle class segments on the basis of family income, again an arbitrary break in a continuum. But a given income has markedly different implications depending on the community and region (in Tunica County, Mississippi, for example, versus San Mateo County, California). It would be very difficult, next to impossible, to separate upper- and lower-middle classes in the parental generation on the basis of income. Occupational prestige is more likely to have similar meaning in the diverse contexts.

One might assume that the upper-middle-class independents, that tiny 3 percent, are owners of manufacturing enterprises or of major businesses. But the assumption is mistaken: It is a diverse category, including accountants and auditors, management analysts, architects, physicians, psychologists, lawyers, and authors. There is, clearly, a large representation of professionals. The lower-middle-class independents are much more likely to be businessmen (including independent craftsmen). Few independent professionals appear in this category.

The upper segment of the new middle class contains accountants and auditors, a wide variety of engineers, computer system analysts, elementary and secondary school teachers, and administrators and managers in educational and medical institutions. All professors fall into this category. The equivalent lower-middle class contains supervisors, sales representatives, cashiers, clerks, secretaries, receptionists, and bookkeepers.

C. Wright Mills, as noted, overlooked an important dividing line within the new middle class, that separating persons in public and private employment. A question from the General Social Surveys of 1985 and 1986 allows investigation of this issue. Of the full-time employed married males, the percentages working for the government are upper-middle class, 43 (79); lower-middle class, 13 (168); and working class, 14 (208). The figures for comparable females are, respectively, 60 (53), 16 (140), and 10 (63). The salaried upper-middle class is clearly very disproportionately government workers. While one might think of clerks and civil servants in this connection, it should be remembered that a large majority of teachers and professors are also employed by public agencies.

7. Correlates of class, relative satisfaction: Spelling out class categories is one thing; establishing the importance of those distinctions with regard to attitudes or behavior is another. Class might have a powerful impact, but prior to investigation the possibilities also include "minor difference" and "no difference." Some appropriate measures—reported happiness, job satisfaction, and financial satisfaction—are shown in Table 3.5.

The differences in reported happiness are not large. Although many sociologists assign considerable importance to class, this summary measure of impact suggests, at best, rather modest effects. Workers, as expected, have the lowest overall level of reported happiness, but the differences vis-à-vis the two new-middle-class segments are very small. Although we are regularly told of the problematic condition of lower-middle-class independent businessmen, an above-average percentage report themselves to be "very happy." The upper-middle segment of the old middle class, largely professionals, it will be remembered, stand out as by far the happiest of the five segments. These results, it should be remembered, include the responses of wives who are part-time employees and/or homemakers.

In response to a question on job satisfaction, all segments have substantial majorities reporting positive assessments. The working-class reports less satisfaction (as was seen earlier in Table 2.2), but in this connection there is only a modest 5-percent difference between them and the lower-new-middle-class segment. Again, the two old-middle-class segments, basically the professionals and the smaller independent businessmen, stand out in their positive assessments. Lower-middle-class independents are often portrayed as "threatened," a distressed category, facing competition, uncertainty, marginal profits, and so forth. That imagery is not sustained here; they are very positive about their jobs.[54] Job satisfaction varies with class level among the dependent jobholders, the salary- and wageworkers, but again the differences are modest. From high to low, upper-middle, lower-middle, and working class, the percentages saying "very satisfied" are, respectively, 53, 45, and 40.

In regard to financial satisfaction, the upper segment of the old middle class, predominantly professionals, has the highest percent-

Table 3.5
Happiness, Work Satisfaction, and Financial Satisfaction by Class
(NORC–GSS: 1990–1994)

	Class					
	Upper Middle		Lower Middle			
	New	Old	New	Old	Working	Total
Happiness						
Very Happy	37 %	53 %	32 %	36 %	29 %	33 %
Pretty Happy	57	46	58	55	62	59
Not Too Happy	6	1	9	9	9	8
N =	(701)	(116)	(1,421)	(458)	(1,476)	(4,172)
Respondents' Job Satisfaction (Includes Homemakers)						
Very Satisfied	53 %	69 %	45 %	57 %	40 %	47 %
Moderately Satisfied	37	25	42	34	45	41
A Little Dissatisfied	7	6	9	7	12	9
Very Dissatisfied	3	1	4	2	4	3
N =	(685)	(109)	(1,405)	(451)	(1,451)	(4,101)
Financial Satisfaction						
Pretty Well Satisfied	33 %	43 %	25 %	32 %	20 %	26 %
More or Less Satisfied	51	36	49	45	50	49
Not Satisfied	16	21	26	23	29	25
N =	(704)	(116)	(1,424)	(456)	(1,478)	(4,178)

See Appendix for details of class combinations.

age of positive reports. They are followed, at a slight remove, by two
other middle-class segments. The lower-middle-class salaried employees report the lowest levels of satisfaction of the four middle-class categories. The least satisfaction is reported in the working class. Although
in the expected direction, the higher-status segments being more satisfied, the differences again, on the whole, are rather small. For the
three dependent categories, from top to bottom, we have 33, 25, and
20 percent saying they are "pretty well satisfied."

The summary conclusions are as follows: First, the old-middle-class
segments give more positive reports than their new-middle-class peers.
On balance, going by these assessments, they are the best-off segments
in the society. The differences between the three dependent groups,

the white-collar and blue-collar categories, with respect to happiness and the two satisfaction questions are in the expected direction. At the same time, however, the differences are rather small.

8. Correlates of class, political moderation. The General Social Surveys ask about class identifications; that is, whether the respondents consider themselves to be upper, middle, working, or lower class (Table 3.6). This question has a long history in American sociology, going back to a 1945 study by Richard Centers. The question ordinarily yields some of the largest differences by class to be found in the entire stratification literature. Sixty-eight percent of the working-class respondents defined themselves as working class versus 27 percent of the upper-new-middle-class segment, a 41-percentage point difference.

This result might be seen as strong support for a key Marxist assumption, two-thirds of the workers recognizing their class position. But other evidence shows that is not the case. The responses differ significantly depending on the categories provided. The earliest class identification studies provided three options, upper, middle, and lower class, and they, in the 1930s, regularly yielded a substantial middle-class majority. Richard Centers first added working class to the options, a change that brought a working-class majority. Use of the term "laboring" (as opposed to "working") also produced a middle-class majority. The Marxian notion assumes ownership is the decisive factor in class placement. One investigation, however, found that husband's income was most salient to Americans' class identifications. Husband's ownership appeared as a distant seventh-ranked determinant of class identification.[55]

An important finding appears in the identifications of the lower-middle class. This segment, it is said, is strongly attached to its middle-class status, struggling to prevent the threat of "proletarianization." But substantial minorities, 48 and 40 percent, respectively, of the new- and old-middle-class segments, do not conform to that image: They choose the working-class identification. Similar findings have appeared from the time of the original Centers study. Many social scientists still, nevertheless, argue the original position.[56]

The recent American experience does not allow exploration of one central revisionist concern; that is, support for radical or reformist directions within a Socialist Party.[57] The Democratic Party, as indicated earlier, is a left-liberal party, one favoring an ample welfare state, support for the "underdog," and equality of opportunity. Following the logic of economic interest, the Democrats, possibly the best of the available options, should be strongly favored by the workers. The suppos-

Table 3.6
Class Identification, Party Identification, and Political Views by Class
(NORC–GSS: 1990–1994)

	Class					
	Upper Middle		Lower Middle		Working Class	Total
	New	Old	New	Old		
Class Identification						
Upper	4 %	22 %	2 %	7 %	1 %	3 %
Middle	68	65	48	52	28	45
Working	27	14	48	40	68	50
Lower	1	-	2	2	4	2
N =	(701)	(116)	(1,423)	(457)	(1,478)	(4,175)
Party Identification[a]						
Democrat	45 %	37 %	43 %	36 %	47 %	44 %
Independent	9	8	11	13	14	12
Republican	46	55	46	51	38	44
N =	(700)	(115)	(1,422)	(456)	(1,473)	(4,166)
Political Views[b]						
Liberal	32 %	36 %	28 %	24 %	27 %	28 %
Moderate	29	24	36	35	40	36
Conservative	38	40	36	40	33	36
N =	(698)	(113)	(1,403)	(450)	(1,434)	(4,098)

See Appendix for details of class combinations.

[a]Democrat (Republican) combines strong, not very strong, and independent close to Democrat (Republican).

[b]Liberal (conservative) combines extremely through slightly liberal (conservative).

edly conservative upper-middle class should provide strong support for the Republicans.

Again, as with the patterns of satisfaction, the prediction with regard to direction is supported but the expectation with regard to strength (or weight) is not. In the early 1990s, 47 percent of the workers (the combined category) identified as Democrats, not quite a majority, since 38 percent were Republican identifiers, the rest being

Independents. That Democratic percentage is the highest percentage of all five segments. But again, the most striking findings are the small differences vis-à-vis the two salaried middle-class segments. The old-middle-class segments are the most conservative of the five, with both showing slight Republican majorities. The lesson is that class, as here defined, is not strongly related to party identifications.

Similar results appear with respect to political views; that is, whether respondents see themselves as liberal, moderate, or conservative. This measure shows very small class differences. The liberal percentages for the salaried and wage categories are, high to low, 32, 28, and 27, just the opposite of what might be expected. One might expect the upper segment of the old middle class to be predominantly conservative, but that also is not the case: They divide almost equally, 40 percent conservative and 36 percent liberal. The rest indicated they were moderates. The working class, by a small margin, is most likely to choose the moderate option.

9. Social mobility: For this purpose, we examine the patterns of intergenerational mobility, looking first at the occupations of fathers and sons. The fathers' occupations have been divided into four categories: upper-middle class, lower-middle class, working class, and farm (see Table 3.7). Nonmanuals were divided according to the occupational prestige rating (as previously outlined). The distributions of the fathers' and sons' occupations may be seen for the merged General Social Surveys of 1990 to 1994.

The most important single observation to be made about the result is the large overall quantity of mobility. One may note, first of all, that roughly one-seventh of the upper-middle-class sons are found in working-class occupations and two-fifths are in lower-middle-class positions. As opposed to the image of a privileged class able to retain its position across generations, these data show a remarkable incidence of "failure," that being the majority experience. Some of those who retained position, moreover, would have done so on the basis of demonstrated talents or abilities. In terms of the liberal theory, that would be justified "status retention."

Roughly three-tenths of the lower-middle-class sons fell into the working class, one-fifth advanced to the upper-middle class, and the remaining half retained their original position. As opposed to the Marxian expectation of no advance for the workers, one-seventh of the sons arrived in the upper-middle class and roughly two-fifths were in lower-middle-class positions. Roughly half remained in their class of origin. Looking at those of nonfarm origin who later crossed over

Table 3.7
Intergenerational Mobility: Males and Females (NORC–GSS: 1990–1994)

| Respondent's Class | Class of Origin | | | | |
	Upper Middle	Lower Middle	Working	Farm	Total
Males					
Upper Middle	45 %	21 %	14 %	10 %	20 %
Lower Middle	40	50	38	32	59
Working Class	15	28	48	42	36
Farm	-	1	-	16	2
N =	(199)	(586)	(646)	(185)	(1,616)
Data as above with rows adding to 100 %					**N**
Upper Middle	28 %	38 %	28 %	6 %	(320)
Lower Middle	12	43	36	9	(682)
Working Class	5	29	53	13	(581)
Farm	-	12	-	88	(33)
Percentages Across	12	36	40	11	= 99 %
Females					
Upper Middle	33 %	22 %	19 %	20 %	22 %
Lower Middle	50	60	54	49	55
Working Class	16	18	27	31	23
Farm	1	-	*	1	*
N =	(201)	(539)	(538)	(153)	(1,431)
Data as above with rows adding to 100 %					**N**
Upper Middle	21 %	37 %	32 %	9 %	(318)
Lower Middle	13	41	37	10	(787)
Working Class	10	30	46	15	(323)
Farm	33	-	33	33	(3)
Percentages Across	14	38	38	11	= 101 %

*Less than 0.5 percent.

the manual–nonmanual division, it will be noted that there was considerably more upward than downward mobility.

Most of those currently engaged in farming are sons of farmers. The overwhelming majority of those sons, however, 84 percent of the total, are in nonfarm occupations. They divide in two equal parts, half in the middle class, half in the working class. That result, to be sure, combines diverse experience; namely, the sons of farm proprietors and those of farm laborers. The former were more successful, and larger percentages are currently active as farm proprietors, in the nonfarm middle class, and in the upper-middle segment.[58]

One other finding deserves attention. The daughters of upper-middle-class fathers are slightly more likely to be downwardly mobile than are the sons. The three other segments are more likely to either retain position or to experience upward mobility. Almost three-quarters of the full-time employed daughters of working-class fathers are in middle-class occupations.

How should these results be assessed? Is it an occasion for congratulation, that "the system" rewarded one-seventh of the working-class sons with an upper-middle-class position? The "pure" equality option would reward one-fifth of the sons from each class with an upper-middle-class position. That would mean a six-point deficit for those of working-class origins (this refers to the 20% marginal, versus the 14% achievement). But that conclusion assumes an original random distribution of talents, as if all classes, from the outset, had an identical distribution of talents and expended equal effort. That is not likely, of course, unless one assumes an equalitarian cosmology.[59]

One may consider the same data from another perspective, that of class composition. The basic question in this case is the origins of the current members. Given the relatively large size of the working class in the parental generation, a small proportion, the one-seventh of upwardly mobile working-class sons, constitutes a large part, 28 percent, of the contemporary upper-middle class. A comparable result holds for those of lower-middle-class origins. The one-fifth who moved upward form a considerable portion of the upper-middle class, 38 percent of the total. A majority of the upper-middle class, in short, consists of newcomers, of persons from working-class and lower-middle-class origins. The stable upper-middle class, the inheritors, are a smallish minority, 28 percent, within "their" class. This circumstance poses a serious problem for the standard assimilation hypothesis, the assumption that upwardly mobile persons will seek to adopt upper-middle-class values. It assumes that the newly arrived majority would seek out and emulate the ways of that second-generation minority. Quite apart from the question of concern or interest, the possibility of establishing contact with those to be emulated would not be an easy task.

Some consideration of the satisfactions and dissatisfactions associated with mobility is appropriate. The standard hypotheses assume that those who have achieved a higher position would show gratification. They would be happier and, as a result, would be moderate in their politics or even conservative. They would be "defenders of the status quo." Those who moved downward would be frustrated, feel dissatisfaction, and, somehow or other, be more disposed to some political insurgency. They might strive to retrieve their lost position. Or, another possibility, they might assimilate with other workers and favor either radical or left-liberal positions. Most discussion of these questions comes without benefit of evidence.

The responses to the general happiness question show limited support for those standard hypotheses. The working-class sons who "made it" into the upper-middle class reported roughly the same level of happiness as the "indigenous" members of the class and differed only slightly from those they left behind. Thirty-nine percent of the upwardly mobile said they were "very happy" (N = 89) versus 33 percent of the nonmobile workers (N = 308). With respect to work satisfaction, the differences were somewhat larger, the respective figures being 57 percent (89) and 41 percent (308). A "gratification effect" is there, but on the whole proves rather limited.

The downwardly mobile men of lower-middle-class origins, those who have fallen into the proletariat, differ little in terms of happiness from those who retained their positions, the respective figures being 29 percent (N = 161) and 35 percent (N = 287). A larger difference in the anticipated direction appears with respect to work satisfaction, the respective figures being 34 percent (N = 160) and 52 percent (N = 286).

Overall, those of farm origin who are now workers differed little from other workers in reported happiness. They were the most likely of all the working-class segments to report being "very satisfied" with their jobs: 47 percent (N = 79) versus 40 percent overall (see Table 3.5). The majority of those making the farm to working-class move are sons of farm proprietors, persons who presumably have lost position. A comparison of those downwardly mobile workers with the current farm proprietors did not support the inference of loss. The two segments differed little in their reported happiness and in their reported work satisfaction. In the NORC–GSS 1990–1994 merge, manual workers of farm origin gave more positive responses to both questions than did the current farm proprietors. Three-quarters of those who fell identified themselves as working class, somewhat more than the class as a whole. One other finding should be noted: Two-thirds of the farm proprietors also described themselves as working class. One possible hypothesis: they see themselves as hard-working, doing a lot of physical labor.

These findings point to an alternative interpretation of the farm-to-city movement. For some it might be a lateral move, a shift from one onerous job to another. For others it might mean improvement, they had moved up to better jobs.[60]

A recent survey question allows some investigation of the latter possibility. This comes from the 1987 General Social Survey: "Please think of your present job (or your last one if you don't have one now). If you compare this job with the job your father had when you were 16, would you say that the level or status of *your* job is (or was) [higher, the same, or lower]"? Overall, the responses were distributed as follows: much higher than the father's job, 21 percent; higher, 29.4 percent; about equal, 25.2 percent; lower, 16 percent; and much lower than the father's job, 8.3 percent (N = 1,141). Roughly half, in other words, reported a job that was higher than the father's, a fourth said "equal to," and another fourth said lower. This result is consonant with the revisionist argument; it goes strongly against Kautsky's (and Mills's) "saving" revisionism. The result, in general, goes strikingly against the claim of a general skill degradation.

The same question allows direct investigation of the responses to downward mobility, the presumed fall into the working class. The respondents of lower-middle-class origin who were now working class (N = 33) gave the following responses: Two-fifths described their jobs as better than the fathers' jobs; another quarter said the jobs were "about equal." Among those who had left the farm, including sons of owners and farm laborers (N = 22), 95 percent said they were better off.[61]

The heavy emphasis regularly placed on class seems unjustified. This is shown in two ways, in the happiness and job satisfaction associated with their present class positions and the same reports seen in conjunction with mobility. Those moves should give rise to expressions of gratification or grievance. Those expectations are generally supported but the effects are modest.

10. Reformist policy: Socialist and Communist Parties throughout Western Europe eventually adopted the revisionist policies. They abandoned the near-exclusive focus on the working class and made appeals to other groups in the society. They abandoned the demand for total or exclusive power and joined in coalition governments. They also abandoned the maximalist program and agreed instead to a wide range of reformist efforts. Most eventually gave up the demand for "socialization of the means of production," the experience in the Second and Third Worlds generally proving not very salutary. In effect, the parties transformed themselves and became left-liberal in orientation. They favored extension of the welfare state and, in general, offered aid to the underprivileged. Exceptions test the rule: In the 1970s, the British Labour Party turned to the left and suffered electoral losses as a result. The Mitterand regime in France instituted socialist measures. These were generally unsuccessful and voter disenchantment followed.[62]

Conclusions

How do the original revisionist hypotheses stand up? Does the evidence presented here support those claims? Does it run contrary to them? Or is some other conclusion appropriate?

1. A growing bourgeoisie: Uncertainty. The appropriate tasks, definition of key terms and subsequent research, do not seem to have been undertaken. The appropriate conclusion, therefore, is "don't know."

That means, specifically, we do not know whether the absolute number of owners, that is, of *major* stockholders, has increased, remained the same, or decreased. As indicated, the answer to that specific question does not appear to be of any great importance, either to the Marxist original or to the revisionist variant.

There has been an unambiguous increase in the number of small stockholders, a development that would, at minimum, complicate the arrangement of classes. Put differently, it would stand in the way of the polar confrontation predicted by orthodox Marxists. In recent decades, another development has occurred: the considerable growth of institutional investment, principally of pension plans and mutual funds. This too provides some complication, something that could not have been anticipated at the turn of the century or even a half-century later. The new developments should lead to new lines of theorizing (or at least speculation). Within academic sociology, that does not appear to have been the case.

2. Petty bourgeois persistence, farm entrepreneurs: Mixed. Some specification is needed. Orthodox Marxists predicted decline. The revisionists pointed to persistence. The evidence from the United States shows a relative decline throughout the nation's history. In absolute numbers, however, the number of farms increased through to 1920. That was followed by a gradual decline over the subsequent three decades. The precipitous decline began in the early 1940s. This segment of the petty bourgeoisie, in short, showed an unexpected persistence, something not recognized in orthodox formulations. The decline in absolute numbers had been advanced by several score years, a conclusion not justified by then-available statistics.

The dwindling of the farm sector, whether coming early or late, is routinely portrayed as involving loss; it is said to represent a fall into the proletariat. That judgment, as indicated, derives from an unresearched logic. Some evidence presented later in this chapter indicated that most of those who made that move saw it differently. They saw it as a step up.

3. Petty bourgeois persistence, nonfarm entrepreneurs: Mixed. Again, we are faced with a lack of appropriate evidence; that is, an absence of a series for most of this century. As with the *grande bourgeoisie*, there are also serious problems of definition, many independents being classified by the census with salaried employees. Our best conclusion, based on recent surveys, is one of modest growth. This means, for the recent period, a rejection of the claim. Some 15 percent of full-time nonfarm employed men are self-employed. They form approximately one-quarter of the nonmanual or middle-class rank.

4. Growth of the salariat: Confirmed. The salaried category has shown considerable growth. As with the independents, obtaining precise data for earlier decades proved unexpectedly difficult. But recent

evidence shows a sizable presence and continued growth. In the early 1990s, 46 percent of the full-time employed nonfarm males had new middle-class occupations. For comparable females the percentage was 69. The new middle class at this point was larger than the working class. On this specific point, the quantitative growth of the salaried class, the revisionist argument is clearly confirmed.

5. Decline of the proletariat: Confirmed. The relative decline of the working class is clear and unambiguous. Given the long-term development, that class is not destined to become the immense majority. The persistence and growth of the nonfarm old middle class and the significant growth of the new middle class has produced a middle-class majority.

6. Growing affluence: Confirmed. As opposed to the Marxist claim of inevitable crises, the revisionists argued relatively stable growth. The periodic cycles continued, but the general course was unmistakably upward as measured in real living standards. The general collapse of the 1930s shook the previous confident expectations. Many commentators anticipated continued difficulties after World War II, but the first postwar decades brought what was probably the longest and most substantial economic growth in recorded history.

Some commentators claim that growth ended early in the 1970s, the subsequent years being viewed as ones of stagnation or decline. The latter conclusion, as seen, is mistaken. The substantial economic growth has continued now for a half-century. A sizable majority of the U.S. population report their conditions, their jobs and incomes, to be better than that of their parents, a conclusion that holds for all age categories. On this point too, the revisionist argument is clearly confirmed.

7. Correlates of class, relative satisfaction: Confirmed. The working class proves to be relatively satisfied, certainly with respect to incomes and jobs. The long-standing expectation, satisfaction increasing with class level, is confirmed. The class differences, however, are very small. There is little justification in these findings for the central importance regularly assigned this variable.

8. Correlates of class, political moderation: Mixed results. The American working class is, on the whole, generally moderate or reformist in political outlook. There are few signs of support for a revolutionary option. That moderation, however, did not bring mass support for a reformed socialism. Support for the Socialist Party, never very strong in the United States, declined to minuscule levels by the 1930s.[63] From at least that time, American workers have tended, by smallish margins, to favor the left-liberal Democratic Party. Workers in most European countries with free elections have generally supported moderate socialist parties, this being the case in the United Kingdom, France, Germany, and elsewhere. The "immoder-

ate" working-class parties, the communists, facing serious losses, eventually shifted and adopted the reformist position. Bernstein expected new-middle-class support for a reformist socialist option but, in the United States, that clearly has not been the case. In West European countries the moderate socialist parties have received fair-sized support from middle-class populations. Class identifications are strongly related to class (as seen in Table 3.6), but they do not appear to have any great importance.

9. Social mobility: Confirmed. The revisionist argument, especially as put forth in the 1950s, anticipated significantly more upward than downward mobility. Evidence supporting this conclusion has now been in the literature for some decades. The basic Marxian prediction was one of downward mobility, a fall of the lower-middle class. That argument, obviously, is rejected. The notion of rigidity, of class reproduction and high levels of intergenerational transmission of position, is very misleading.

10. Reformist policy: Confirmed. This argument, as indicated, has a different character, involving prescription rather than empirical scientific judgment. For what it is worth, the major left parties, socialist and communist, did eventually move in the recommended direction and adopted reformist policies. Going beyond the Bernstein recommendation, they abandoned the demand for socialization of the means of production.

COMMENTARY

Bernstein made a major contribution. He reviewed census materials (and whatever other evidence he could find) and brought evidence to bear on the long-standing claims about the classes and their development. He demonstrated that the direction of development was not as predicted and that a significant change in the theory was needed. Later investigations were undertaken in the Weimar period by academics working within the revisionist framework. Emil Lederer, Jakob Marschak, Hans Speier, and Theodor Geiger, four leaders in this effort, provided additional documentation and detail, important contributions to the analysis of stratification in advanced capitalist societies.

That said, it is important to note what was missed; that is, what was not researched. The evidence available from the census allowed a statement of the quantities involved. It allowed a "body count": How many workers? How many old middle class? How many new middle class? But prior to the appearance and use of polls and surveys, no systematic evidence was available on the "consciousness" of those classes. Theodor Geiger's important book, *Die Soziale Schichtung des deutschen Volkes*, published in 1932, contained the most detailed portrait of the size and changes in the class structure yet produced. But his comments about the outlooks of those classes were entirely speculative; it was guesswork. Geiger laid out four possible political directions that the new middle class might follow, leaving the empirical question open.

Some twenty years later, C. Wright Mills introduced the subject matter to a North American audience and reproduced the same four possibilities. Presenting no evidence, bypassing the survey evidence then available, he offered an array of disdainful conclusions: "They do not know where to go. So now they waver. They hesitate, confused and vacillating in their opinions, unfocused and discontinuous in their actions. They are worried and distrustful. . . . On the political market-place of American society, the new middle classes are up for sale; whoever seems respectable enough, strong enough, can probably have them."[64]

A serious methodological failure is indicated in this performance, one which, regrettably, was repeated all too frequently in subsequent decades. Polls and surveys made their appearance, for all practical purposes, beginning in the early 1950s. Prior to that time, researchers and commentators had very limited options with respect to evidence on class outlooks and consciousness. But with the coming of the polls, and with the regular improvement in their quality, it was possible to address those "ancient" questions with evidence. But then, oddly, many commentators neglected that evidence and continued to provide gratuitous conclusions with regard to all class segments.

Serious surveys appeared in West Germany beginning in the early 1950s. A major secondary analysis of several surveys, undertaken by Juan J. Linz in 1959, investigated many of the questions discussed in this chapter. As opposed to the simplicity typical of "armchair speculation," one regular result was complexity. The salaried white-collar employees, so it was said, were "conservative," generally supporting traditional middle-class parties. But among the employed men in that category, one-third supported the Social Democrats and 44 percent supported the Christian Democrats, leaving only about one in five supporting bourgeois parties. Almost half of that new-middle-class group was of working-class origin and they provided that strong Social Democratic support, their level being almost twice that of others in the class. Those men who had achieved middle-class status did not appear to have rejected their origins. Many of them appear to have transplanted their political preferences, bringing them along into this new class position.

Linz's investigation pointed up another fact: the importance of religion, a regularly neglected communal factor. Supposedly long-since gone, a matter of little or no importance, it was a constant presence. Most workers who did not vote Social Democratic voted for the Christian Democrats. Religion, in effect, was somehow the principal explanation for "false consciousness." Many commentators have difficulty facing up to the implications of such evidence.[65]

Weak support for the class argument should ordinarily give rise to some alternative lines of theorizing and to exploration of other causal factors. One must develop some explanation for the exceptions, for the 45 percent of the upper-middle-class salarieds who identify as Democrats and for the three-eighths of the working class who identify as Republican (Table 3.6). Something more is needed than the catchphrase "false consciousness." That is no explanation; it is simply another way of saying "an exception."

One could begin anew, rethinking matters either "from scratch" or from some other theoretical framework. Party identifications, it is said, are learned in the family; that is, are the result of some original political socialization. Families tend to cluster together in local communities that provide support for their traditional views. These causal factors have long been noted in studies of mass political behavior, ones showing that Protestants, Catholics, and Jews of a given class have different political preferences.[66]

Overall, in the 1990–1994 GSS merge, 48 percent of the upper-middle class identified themselves as Republicans. That class is composed of, in order of size, the following communities: Protestants, Catholics, "no religion," Jews (all of those categories being white), and a small black minority. The Republican percentages for those five groups are, respectively, 60, 45, 25, 30, and 15. The same overall percentage of the lower-middle class identified as Republican. The equivalent figures for those same communities within that class were 58, 48, 28, 30, and 13. The working class is similarly divided. The overall figure, 39-percent Republican, combines results for the diverse communities, the equivalent figures being 47, 39, 35, 43, and 13. The modal class positions, in short, are averages of very diverse tendencies (Table 3.8). The implication, clearly, is that much more attention should be paid to those communal factors.[67]

In summary, the revisionists were correct in their conclusions about the development of the classes, about the changing quantitative relationships and the failure of the polarization hypothesis. They were correct also in their predictions of moderation as the dominant and most frequent political choice.[68] They appear to have been mistaken in their assumption of class-specific responses, in this case being misled by their theoretical convictions. The dominance of class in their thinking led them to avoid other factors entirely or, alternatively, to give little weight to those factors.

For orthodox Marxists, the revisionist findings posed considerable problems. The persistence or growth of the middle-class segments blocked the "final conflict," forestalling the polar confrontation of bour-

Table 3.8
Party Identification by Race, Religion, and Class (NORC–GSS: 1990–1994)

	White				Black	Total
	Protestant	Catholic	None	Jewish		
Upper-Middle Class						
Party Identification						
Democrat	32 %	46 %	61 %	64 %	80 %	44 %
Independent	7	9	13	3	5	8
Republican	60	45	25	30	15	48
N =	(402)	(177)	(75)	(33)	(60)	(747)
Lower-Middle Class						
Party Identification						
Democrat	33 %	40 %	48 %	64 %	78 %	41 %
Independent	17	12	24	6	9	11
Republican	58	48	28	30	13	48
N =	(934)	(477)	(152)	(47)	(142)	(1,752)
Working Class						
Party Identification						
Democrat	38 %	49 %	41 %	43 %	76 %	47 %
Independent	14	13	25	14	11	14
Republican	47	39	35	43	13	39
N =	(726)	(304)	(106)	(7)	(236)	(1,379)

geoisie and proletariat. The proportionate increase of the middle class challenged the claim of the proletariat as "immense majority." The increased well-being of the working class, especially of the more affluent skilled ranks, reduced the support for revolutionary insurgency. Those unwilling to accept the implications of those findings had, somehow or other, to revise revisionism.

Bernstein's most vociferous opponent, Karl Kautsky, had a ready answer to the claim of middle-class growth. Granting the point, which was hardly disputable, he argued that the entire class had "lost position," that it had "come down in the world." Earlier in the 19th century, supposedly, clerks and shopkeepers were relatively well-off, having incomes and lifestyles that put them at a considerable distance from the workers. But in the course of subsequent decades, they lost that distinctiveness. Their incomes were no longer markedly different; their ability to maintain a separate status, accordingly, was now seriously diminished. Those on the lower margins of the class, the lower-middle class, both the old- and new-middle-class segments, were being "proletarianized."[69] This line of argument has been a staple of left or orthodox Marxist thought up to the present. The claim also found its way into academic social science, initially in that of Weimar Germany, where the lower-middle-class "status panic," it was said, led the lower-middle class to support Adolf Hitler and his party. There too, a very important communal factor, religion, was neglected (Protestants generally favoring, Catholics generally opposed). In most cities, support for Hitler and his party varied directly with class, relatively low in working-class districts, highest in the upper- and upper-middle-class areas.[70]

Bernstein's claims, on the whole, are better supported than the Marxist originals. The man, in short, made an important, serious contribution to the understanding of 19th- and 20th-century social developments. Nevertheless, he is, curiously, treated rather deprecatingly in the literature. That is, perhaps, understandable in the heavily partisan literature of the left. But a similar tendency, somewhat more restrained, is found in scholarly sources. George Lichtheim described the two leading contenders as follows: "If Kautsky was not really a theorist of the first rank, Bernstein was no theorist at all, but rather an erudite publicist with a talent for simplifying complex matters—sometimes to a dangerous extent. This made it comparatively easy for Kautsky to demolish him." Since few academics nowadays read either man, such judgments might easily be taken at face value. But Kautsky's works are modest, slogan-filled, simplistic, largely undocumented defenses of Marxist orthodoxy. It would be difficult for any serious reader to defend their intellectual merit.[71]

Marx and Engels provided a vast sweep of comment, some of which touched on colonialism. Bernstein wrote on the subject, most of that coming later, but it was not central to the revisionist controversy.[72] The principal determinants of the then-current developments were seen as internal to the capitalist societies. Lenin's analysis shifted the focus dramatically by making the colonies central to those internal developments. Imperialism was the key to the stabilization of capitalism and the general affluence. That is the subject of the next chapter.

NOTES

1. For accounts of the SPD in this period, see Gerhard A. Ritter, *Die Arbeiterbewegung im Wilhelminischen Reich: Die sozialdemokratische Partei und die freien Gewerkschaften 1890–1900* (Berlin: Colloquium Verlag, 1963); W. L. Guttsman, *The German Social Democratic Party, 1875–1933: From Ghetto to Gov-*

ernment (London: George Allen and Unwin, 1981); Gary P. Steenson, *Karl Kautsky, 1854–1938: Marxism in the Classical Years* (Pittsburgh: University of Pittsburgh Press, 1978); Gary P. Steenson, *After Marx, before Lenin: Marxism and Socialist Working-Class Parties in Europe, 1884-1914* (Pittsburgh: University of Pittsburgh Press, 1991); Donald Sasson, *One Hundred Years of Socialism: The West European Left in the Twentieth Century* (New York: New Press, 1996); and Manfred B. Steger, *The Quest for Evolutionary Socialism: Eduard Bernstein and Social Democracy* (New York: Cambridge University Press, 1997). Additional references may be found in Steger, *Quest*, 1–7. For an account of the SPD's influence within the International, see Robert Michels, "Die deutsche Sozialdemokratie im internationalen Verbande: Eine kritische Untersuchung," *Archiv für Sozialwissenschaft und Sozialpolitik* 25 (1907): 148–231.

    2. See Peter Gay, *The Dilemma of Democratic Socialism: Eduard Bernstein's Challenge to Marx* (New York: Columbia University Press, 1952); Francis Ludwig Carsten, *Eduard Bernstein, 1850–1932: Eine politische Biographie* (Munich: C. H. Beck, 1993); and Steger, *Quest*. For a brief account, see Roger Fletcher, "The Life and Work of Eduard Bernstein," in *Bernstein to Brandt: A Short History of German Social Democracy*, ed. Roger Fletcher (London: Edward Arnold, 1987); and, for a wealth of material, see Roger Fletcher, *Revisionism and Empire: Socialist Imperialism in Germany, 1897–1914* (London: George Allen and Unwin, 1984). For an overview and for an array of texts, see Henry Tudor and J. M. Tudor, eds. and trans., *Marxism and Social Democracy: The Revisionist Debate, 1896–1898* (Cambridge: Cambridge University Press, 1988).

    Eduard Bernstein's major work is *Die Voraussetzungen des Sozialismus und die Aufgaben der Sozialdemokratie* (Stuttgart: Dietz, 1899). That title may be translated as *The Preconditions of Socialism and the Tasks of Social Democracy*. The original English-language version appeared under the title *Evolutionary Socialism: A Criticism and Affirmation*, trans. Edith C. Harvey (New York: B. W. Huebsch, 1909). It has been reprinted on several occasions (for example, New York: Schocken, 1961). Although not indicated as such, this was an abridged edition, an entire chapter and much of Bernstein's documentation having been omitted. For a complete scholarly edition, see Bernstein, *The Preconditions of Socialism*, ed. and trans. Henry Tudor (Cambridge: Cambridge University Press, 1993). This edition is used throughout the present chapter.

    Although most often identified with the revisionist controversy, Bernstein's intellectual interests were wide-ranging. Among other things, he produced studies of the English Civil War, the 1848 revolution in France, and the 1918 revolution in Germany. For a list of his many books, see Steger, *Quest*, 263–264.

    3. For doubts about the claim that Weber's effort was directed against Marxism, see Richard F. Hamilton, *The Social Misconstruction of Reality: Validity and Verification in the Scholarly Community* (New Haven: Yale University Press, 1996), 104–106.

    4. Max Weber, *From Max Weber, Essays in Sociology*, ed. and trans. H. H. Gerth and C. Wright Mills (London: Routledge and Kegan Paul, 1948); C. Wright Mills, *White Collar: The American Middle Classes* (New York: Oxford University Press, 1951); Seymour Martin Lipset, *Political Man: The Social Bases of Politics* (Garden City, N.Y.: Doubleday, 1960). On the Gerth–Mills relationship, see Irving Louis Horowitz, *C. Wright Mills: An American Utopian* (New York: Free Press, 1983), 48–54.

A few brief pages cannot do justice to this complex intellectual history. An American sociologist, W. Lloyd Warner, made an important contribution to the discussion and legitimation of class, this with a series of books collectively entitled the "Yankee City Series." The first of these was W. Lloyd Warner and Paul S. Lunt, *The Social Life of a Modern Community* (New Haven: Yale University Press, 1941). The framework was not Marxian. The classes depicted there were, in Max Weber's terms, basically status groups. Warner's work had considerable influence in the 1940s and 1950s. In the 1960s, that influence dwindled, almost entirely disappearing. For a brief overview, see Harold R. Kerbo, *Social Stratification and Inequality: Class Conflict in Historical and Comparative Perspective*, 3d ed. (New York: McGraw-Hill, 1996), 117, 130.

Studies of social mobility necessarily involve some class categories and, in one way or another, also address the competing claims of liberalism and Marxism. For three compendious studies, see Pitirim Sorokin, *Social Mobility* (New York: Harper, 1927); Seymour Martin Lipset and Reinhard Bendix, *Social Mobility in Industrial Society* (Berkeley and Los Angeles: University of California Press, 1959); and Robert Erikson and John H. Goldthorpe, *The Constant Flux: A Study of Class Mobility in Industrial Societies* (Oxford: Clarendon Press, 1992).

5. Bernstein, *Preconditions*, 56–66. The quotation is from p. 61. Gay's work reviews this point (and the subsequent ones) at greater length, covering prior and later discussions and citing relevant literature. See Gay, *Dilemma*, 166–174. Bernstein first quotes a passage from *Capital* in which Marx states that "the number of capitalists grows to a greater or less extent." Bernstein then cites a passage, also from *Capital*, where Marx reports the "constantly diminishing number of the magnates of capital." See Bernstein, *Preconditions*, 57–58, 168, n. hh. The passages as quoted here are from *Capital*, MECW, 35: 620, 750. Bernstein's paragraphs reporting this contradiction do not appear in Harvey's translation; that is, in *Evolutionary Socialism*.

6. Bernstein, *Preconditions*, 73–78 (for the farmers), 66–73 (for the nonfarm proprietors). See also Gay, *Dilemma*, 198–204, 204–219.

7. The new middle class received only passing mention in Bernstein, *Preconditions*, 72–73, 106–107. It took on greater importance in Bernstein's later essays. In the Weimar period, it was a major theme in German sociology. See Gay, *Dilemma*, 210–219.

8. Bernstein, *Preconditons*, 78.

9. Gay, *Dilemma*, 121–130.

10. Bernstein, *Preconditions*, ch. 4; Gay, *Dilemma*, ch. 8. The notion of middle-class socialism goes very much against the insistent belief that the middle class is conservative or, as in the *Manifesto*, that it is reactionary. But readily available evidence from the turn of the century made it clear that the Social Democrats had a significant middle-class following. See R. Blank, "Die soziale Zusammensetzung der sozialdemokratischen Wählerschaft Deutschlands," *Archiv für Sozialwissenschaft und Sozialpolitik* 20 (1905): 507–550; and Robert Michels, "Die deutsche Sozialdemokratie. I. Parteimitgliedschaft und soziale Zusammensetzung," *Archiv für Sozialwissenschaft und Sozialpolitik* 23 (1906): 471–556. Blank's study, however, greatly exaggerates the middle-class presence among the SPD voters. See the critique by Gerhart A. Ritter, *Die Arbeiterbewegung im Wilhelmischen Reich: Die sozialdemokratische Partei und die freien Gewerkschaften 1890–1900* (Berlin: Colloquium, 1963), 77–78. Late in his

career, Engels wrote a study of Bismarck's role in Germany. He announced that some of the petty bourgeoisie "drew close to the Social Democrats, some virtually joining the labour movement." See Engels, *Role of Force in History* (New York: International Publishers, 1968), 93.

11. On the revisionist struggle and its outcome prior to 1914, see Gay, *Dilemma*, ch. 9. See also George Lichtheim, *Marxism: An Historical and Critical Study* (New York: Praeger, 1961), 259–300; Leszek Kolakowski, *Main Currents of Marxism*, vol. 2, trans. P. S. Falla (Oxford: Clarendon Press, 1978), chs. 2, 4; David McLellan, *Marxism after Marx: An Introduction* (New York: Harper & Row, 1979), ch. 2; Gary P. Steenson, *Karl Kautsky, 1854–1938: Marxism in the Classical Years* (Pittsburgh: University of Pittsburgh Press, 1978), ch. 4; Massimo Salvadori, *Karl Kautsky and the Socialist Revolution, 1880–1938*, trans. Jon Rothschild (London: NLB, 1979); and Ingrid Gilcher-Holtey, *Das Mandat des Intellektuellen: Karl Kautsky und die Sozialdemokratie* (Berlin: Siedler, 1986), part 4. On the joint authorship of the Erfurt Program, see Tudor and Tudor, *Marxism*, 7; and Steenson, *Kautsky*, 15. Steenson's account, unfortunately, does not do justice to Bernstein or to revisionism.

For the transformation of the SPD after 1945, see Theo Pirker, *Die SPD nach Hitler: Die Geschichte der Sozialdemokratischen Partei Deutschlands 1945–1964* (Munich: Rütten and Loening, 1965); Harold Kent Schellenger Jr., *The SPD in the Bonn Republic: A Socialist Party Modernizes* (The Hague: Martinus Nijhoff, 1968); and Kurt Klotzbach, *Der Weg zur Staatspartei: Programmatik, praktische Politik und Organisation der deutschen Sozialdemokratie 1945 bis 1965* (Berlin/Bonn: Dietz, 1982).

12. That armchair speculation, moreover, was (and is) typically categorical. Entire classes do things, are moved to action, or respond to events. Public-opinion polls and surveys rarely support such sweeping conclusions. With much greater frequency, they indicate differentiated responses and relatively small differences between classes. That may be seen in Julian Linz's comprehensive analysis of surveys from the early postwar period in the Federal Republic of Germany, one addressing many of the themes discussed here. See Linz, "The Social Bases of West German Politics" (Ph.D. diss., Columbia University, 1959), especially chs. 4, 14–19.

13. See Richard F. Hamilton, *Who Voted for Hitler?* (Princeton: Princeton University Press, 1982); and Richard F. Hamilton, *The Social Misconstruction of Reality: Validity and Verification in the Scholarly Community* (New Haven: Yale University Press, 1996), chs. 4, 5.

For a comprehensive analysis of the voting patterns in Weimar Germany, see Jürgen W. Falter, *Hitlers Wähler* (Munich: C. H. Beck, 1991). Many commentators argued, without any serious supporting evidence, that both old- and new-middle-class segments provided general support for Hitler and his party. Falter found strong support in the Protestant old middle class but no distinctive tendency among equivalent Catholics. He found no exceptional support in the new middle class. Many commentators declared the tendency to be most pronounced in the lower, impoverished, or threatened segments of those classes. In rural areas, among Protestants, an opposite tendency was found, the small farm areas being least affected. Many commentators declared that the unemployed turned to the National Socialists. Falter shows that they turned to the communists. For a brief summary of this important work, see Richard F. Hamilton, review of *Hitlers Wähler* by Jürgen W. Falter, *Contemporary Sociology* 22 (1993): 543–546.

14. A major work, one that defined the era, was John Kenneth Galbraith, *The Affluent Society* (Boston: Houghton Mifflin, 1958). Two influential popular accounts from that period were Russell W. Davenport, and the Editors of *Fortune, U.S.A.: The Permanent Revolution* (New York: Prentice Hall, 1951); and Frederick Lewis Allen, *The Big Change: America Transforms Itself, 1900–1950* (New York: Harper, 1952).

The revisionist themes were discussed throughout Western Europe in this period. Among others, we have Mark Abrams and Richard Rose, *Must Labour Lose?* (Harmonsworth, U.K.: Penguin, 1960); Marianne Feuersenger, ed., *Gibt es noch ein Proletariat?* (Frankfurt/Main: Europäische Verlagsanstalt, 1962); Horst Krüger, ed., *Was ist Heute Links?* (Munich: Paul List Verlag, 1963); and Roger Garaudy, *Peut-on être communiste aujourd'hui?* (Paris: Bernard Grasset, 1968).

Later on, a fair-sized research literature developed that challenged many of the sweeping and largely impressionistic claims of this 1950s revisionism. On the United States, France, and Germany, respectively, see Richard F. Hamilton, *Class and Politics in the United States* (New York: Wiley, 1972), especially ch. 10; *Affluence and the French Worker in the Fourth Republic* (Princeton: Princeton University Press, 1967); "Affluence and the Worker: The West German Case," *American Journal of Sociology* 71 (1965): 144–152; and "Einkommen und Klassenstruktur: Der Fall der Bundesrepublik," *Kölner Zeitschrift für Soziologie und Sozialpsychologie* 20 (1967): 250–287. On the United Kingdom, see John H. Goldthorpe et al., *The Affluent Worker: Industrial Attitudes and Behaviour* (Cambridge: Cambridge University Press, 1968); *The Affluent Worker: Political Attitudes and Behaviour* (Cambridge: Cambridge University Press, 1968); and *The Affluent Worker in the Class Structure* (Cambridge: Cambridge University Press, 1969). Michael Harrington challenged another aspect of the 1950s "world view" in Harrington, *The Other America: Poverty in the United States* (New York: Macmillan, 1962).

15. Engels provided two definitions. From 1847, we have, "The class of big capitalists who already now in all civilised countries almost exclusively own all the means of subsistence and the raw materials and instruments (machinery, factories, etc.), needed for the production of those means of subsistence," from his "Principles of Communism" (*MECW*, 6: 342); and from 1888, a note appended to the English edition of the *Communist Manifesto*: "By bourgeoisie is meant the class of modern Capitalists, owners of the means of social production and employers of wage-labour" (*MECW*, 6: 482).

Much research in recent decades has used the language of class but in fact deals with business executives and corporate directors. While those groups overlap with the owners, they are by no means coterminous. Analyses of the top leaders in corporate hierarchies are actually elite studies. Those elites, numbering perhaps a hundred persons in a given firm, would constitute only a tiny fraction of the stockholders. It is not necessary that those elites be major shareholders or even that they hold any shares at all. It is not "in the cards" either that those elites would represent the interests of the major holders. For a study that argues class, explicitly rejects the elite concept, but then depends on studies of corporate elites rather than of owners, see Tom Bottomore and Robert J. Brym, eds., *The Capitalist Class: An International Study* (New York: Harvester Wheatsheaf, 1989), especially chs. 1, 8. Bottomore's definition of "bourgeoisie" (p. 4) is no better than the Marx–Engels originals; the persistent difficulties are clearly evident in his note 5.

16. See John E. Bregger, "Self-Employment in the United States, 1948–62," *Monthly Labor Review* 86, 1 (1963): 37–43; Robert N. Ray, "A Report on Self-Employed Americans in 1973," *Monthly Labor Review* 98, 1 (1975): 49–54; T. Scott Fain, "Self-Employed Americans: Their Number Has Increased," *Monthly Labor Review* 103, 11 (1980): 3–8; Eugene H. Becker, "Self-Employed Workers: An Update to 1983," *Monthly Labor Review* 107, 7 (1984): 14–18; Sheldon E. Haber, Enrique J. Lamas, and Jules H. Lichtenstein, "On Their Own: The Self-Employed and Others in Private Business," *Monthly Labor Review* 110, 5 (1987): 17–23; and "Industrial Districts: The Road to Success for Small Businesses," *Monthly Labor Review* 115, 2 (1992): 46–47. The last article tells of the "remarkable success of the small enterprise. . . . The trend toward centralization of production and employment in Europe has been on the wane for the last 15 years. In France, for example, between 1976 and 1988, the proportion of employment in small firms grew from 43.3 percent of all employment to 52.5 percent." See also John E. Bregger, "Measuring Self-Employment in the United States," *Monthly Labor Review* 119, 1 (1996): 3–9.

For discussion of incorporation and its implications, for the owner as salaried employee, see Ray, "A Report," 49; Fain, "Self-Employed Americans," 7; Becker, "Self-Employed Workers," 14; and Haber, Lamas, and Lichtenstein, "On Their Own," 17. Two questions are used for this classification, one on self-employment, the other on incorporation, put in that order. If a person declared self-employment and incorporation, the procedure stipulated classification as salaried. In 1976, according to the census procedure, the United States had 5,689,000 nonagricultural self-employed persons. In March of that year, an additional 1.5 million reported themselves as self-employed but, because incorporated, were classified by the Census Bureau as salarieds. Incorporations grew rapidly in the following years. In 1979, the equivalent figures were 6,652,000 and 2.1 million. Some people reported themselves initially as wage and salary employees but were actually incorporated self-employeds. "There is no way," Fain reports, "to determine how large this group might be or to know whether it has grown larger or smaller over time" (p. 7). For information on later procedural revisions, see Bregger, "Measuring Self-Employment."

17. On persons in the voluntary association business, see Richard F. Hamilton, *Restraining Myths: Critical Studies of U.S. Social Structure and Politics* (New York: Sage–Halsted–Wiley, 1975), ch. 7.

18. New York Stock Exchange, *Fact Book for the Year 1995* (New York: New York Stock Exchange, 1996), 57. The 1997 figures are from "Pension Assets Grow," *Pensions & Investments*, 20 January 1997, pp. 3, 96; and "Big Public Funds Reap Gains," *Pensions & Investments*, 9 March 1998, pp. 2, 68. On TIAA–CREF, described as the "world's biggest pension system," see Reed Abelson, "A Teacher's Pet Is Facing the Hounds," *New York Times*, 27 July 1997, sec. 3, p. 1.

19. Jeffrey M. Laderman, *1991 Business Week's Annual Guide to Mutual Funds* (New York: McGraw-Hill, 1991), ch. 1; New York Stock Exchange, *Fact Book for*

the Year 1998 (New York: New York Stock Exchange, 1999), 60; Investment Company Institute, *1999 Mutual Fund Fact Book*, 39th ed. (Washington, D.C.: Investment Company Institute, 1999), ch. 2.

20. New York Stock Exchange, *Fact Book, 1998*, 60.

21. Bernstein, *Preconditions*, 58. A similar concern was expressed, some seventy years later, by Philip H. Burch Jr. In the United States, he observed, "there has been little reliable stock ownership or other evidence presented since the days of the depression." See Burch, *Managerial Revolution* (Lexington, Mass.: D. C. Heath, 1972), 9.

Two important exceptions, studies that do address the who-owns question, are Maurice Zeitlin, "Corporate Ownership and Control: The Large Corporation and the Capitalist Class," *American Journal of Sociology* 79 (1974): 1073–1119; Maurice Zeitlin, *The Large Corporation and Contemporary Classes* (Cambridge: Polity Press, 1989), especially chs. 1, 5; and Thomas R. Dye, "Who Owns America: Strategic Ownership Positions in Industrial Corporations," *Social Science Quarterly* 64 (1983): 863–870. On the limitations of the available information on ownership, see Zeitlin, *Large Corporation*, 14–19.

Erik Olin Wright has reformulated the Marxian categories and undertaken research within several variant frameworks. See Wright, *Class, Crisis and the State* (New York: Schocken, 1978); *Classes* (London: Verso, 1985); and *Class Counts: Comparative Studies in Class Analysis* (Cambridge: Cambridge University Press, 1997). In *Classes*, he defined the "bourgeoisie" as consisting of self-employed persons with ten or more employees.

Applying that framework to a cross-sectional survey in Britain, Gordon Marshall and his coworkers found twenty-six persons, a bourgeoisie which formed 2 percent of the total. But on further examination they discovered an odd assortment, none of them owners of major firms. The lesson was that the bourgeoisie will not ordinarily appear in cross-sectional samples. For an extended, empirically based critique of Wright's categories, see Gordon Marshall et al., *Social Class in Modern Britain* (London: Hutchinson, 1988), especially ch. 3.

22. Philip M. Stern, *The Great Treasury Raid* (New York: Signet, 1965), 22.

23. See New York Stock Exchange, *Shareownership 1990* (New York: New York Stock Exchange, 1991); and *Fact Book for the Year 1995*, 53–55. The 8-million figure is my calculation based on 1990 census figures for the adult population. The same procedure was used for the estimates in the following paragraph.

24. New York Stock Exchange, *Shareownership 1990*, 15, 17 (with my recalculations).

This entire discussion is clearly hypothetical. The purpose is to point up a lesson: Little research has been done on this central theme of the Marxist theory.

25. The absolute size of the bourgeoisie would, however, be a factor facilitating or hindering the development of class consciousness or class action. A larger bourgeoisie would be more diverse in terms of backgrounds, attitudes, and interests. Organizing a class of 250,000 would be easier than doing the same for a class of 1,000,000.

Another important problem is that the bourgeoisie might own the means of production, but not control them. This refers to the argument of a managerial revolution. The number of stockholders, it is said, is so large, the typical holding so small, and the interests so diverse, that control by the "owners" would be infrequent. De facto control of most corporations, accordingly, falls to the managers, those with a detailed knowledge of the firm's everyday operations. This is an important argument, one that gained ever-greater attention beginning in the 1930s. It was not part of the original revisionist repertory. For discussion and a critique, see Zeitlin, *Large Corporation*, 76–84, 156–161. See also the important study by Myles L. Mace, *Directors: Myth and Reality* (1971; reprint, Boston: Harvard Business School Press, 1986). In a striking case, one that might signal an important new role for the institutional investors, TIAA–CREF ousted the entire board of a poorly performing corporation. See "Give and Take," *Chronicle of Higher Education*, 12 June 1998, p. A37.

26. U.S. Department of Labor, *Dictionary of Occupational Titles*, 4th rev. ed. (Washington, D.C.: U.S. Government Printing Office, 1991). See also Ann R. Miller et al., eds., *Work, Jobs, and Occupations: A Critical Review of the Dictionary of Occupational Titles* (Washington, D.C.: National Academy Press, 1980).

27. *MECW*, 24: 425–426.

28. Laarni T. Dacquel and Donald C. Dahmann, *Residents of Farms and Rural Areas: 1991*, U.S. Bureau of the Census, Current Population Reports, P20-472 (Washington, D.C.: U.S. Government Printing Office, 1993); and, U.S. Bureau of the Census, *Historical Statistics of the United States, Colonial Times to 1970*, part 1 (Washington, D.C.: U.S. Government Printing Office, 1976), 126–127, 457.

29. Among males in farming, owners and managers constituted 55.2 percent of the total in 1900, 61.3 percent in 1930, and 66.5 percent in 1950. The number of proprietors increased by 281,000 between 1910 and 1920. The number of farm laborers and foremen decreased by 420,000 in the same period. From Bureau of the Census, *Historical Statistics*, 139. It is easy to see farm proprietorship and farm labor as permanent positions held over the entire adult lifespan. But mobility could occur here also. An owner's son might begin as a farm laborer, later buying or inheriting land. For a useful corrective vis-à-vis the romantic imagery, see Richard Hofstadter, *The Age of Reform: From Bryan to F.D.R.* (New York: Vintage Books, 1955), ch. 1.

30. See Kenneth T. Jackson, *Crabgrass Frontier: The Suburbanization of the United States* (New York: Oxford University Press, 1985), 22, 27–29.

31. For an overview of the recent history, see Daniel B. Suits, "Agriculture," in *The Structure of American Industry*, ed. Walter Adams, 8th ed. (New York: Macmillan, 1990). For figures on the total farm output (in 1992 dollars, carried through to 1996), see U.S. Bureau of the Census, *Statistical Abstract of the United States, 1998* (Washington, D.C.: U.S. Government Printing Office, 1998), Table 1109.

32. From B. R. Mitchell, *Abstract of British Historical Statistics* (Cambridge: Cambridge University Press, 1962), 60; Statistisches Bundesamt, *Bevölkerung und Wirtschaft: 1872–1972* (Stuttgart: Kohlhammer, 1972), 142; and J.-C. Toutain, *La Population de la France de 1700 à 1959*, supplement no. 133 (Paris: Cahiers de l'institut de science économique appliquée, 1963), Tables 57, 60. The declines continued in subsequent decades. The German farm population numbered 1,191,000 in 1994, 3.3 percent of the labor force. The French farm population, in 1993, numbered 1,101,000, 5 percent of the total. See United Nations, *Statistical Yearbook*, 42d ed. (New York: United Nations, 1997), 256.

33. The agreement on the importance of the manual–nonmanual distinction is striking. It is central to Marxism and revisionism. It is built into the

basic occupational categories of all major nations. For a review of the considerations underlying this distinction, see Seymour Martin Lipset and Reinhard Bendix, *Social Mobility in Industrial Society* (Berkeley and Los Angeles: University of California Press, 1959), 13–17; and Hamilton, *Class and Politics*, ch. 4.

34. See Alba M. Edwards, "Social–Economic Groups of the United States," *American Statistical Association Quarterly* 15 (1917): 643–661; and James Scoville, "The Development and Relevance of U.S. Occupational Data," *Industrial and Labor Relations Review* 19 (1965): 70–79. On the placement of the service workers, see Hamilton, *Class and Politics*, 154–155.

The 1980 revised occupational categories are executive, administrative, and managerial; professional specialty; technicians and related support; sales; and administrative support, including clerical. These are counted here as nonmanuals or middle class. The manual or working-class occupations are precision production, craft, and repair; machine operators, assemblers, and inspectors; transportation and material-moving occupations; handlers, equipment cleaners, helpers, and laborers; private household occupations; and protective-service occupations. Farm occupations appear as farming, forestry, and fishing occupations. For further details, see U.S. Bureau of the Census, *The Relationship between the 1970 and 1980 Industry and Occupation Classification Systems*, Technical Paper 59 (Washington, D.C.: U.S. Government Printing Office, 1989).

35. There is no definitive classification procedure. Officials in the economically advanced nations began, early in the 19th century, with some crude categories. Then, in response to the growth in the number of jobs and changes in the kinds of jobs, they made modifications of those original categories. For the theoretical purposes under discussion here, some categorizations are better than others. The categories developed in France and Germany make the distinction between old- and new-middle-class occupations. They also allow easy separation of the salaried white-collar employees into public and private segments. These distinctions are not possible with the basic or modified Edwards categories reviewed here.

36. For an easily accessible definition of the labor force, see U.S. Bureau of the Census, *Statistical Abstract, 1998*, 400.

37. For an earlier discussion, references, and evidence on these points, see Hamilton, *Class and Politics*, ch. 5. For more recent discussion of some of the issues raised, see John H. Goldthorpe, "Women and Class Analysis: In Defence of the Conventional View," *Sociology* 17 (1983): 465–488. For further comment, see Michelle Stanworth, "Women and Class Analysis: A Reply to John Goldthorpe," *Sociology* 18 (1984): 159–170; and Goldthorpe, "Women and Class Analysis: Replies to the Replies," *Sociology* 11 (1984): 491–499. See also Annemette Sørensen, "Women, Family and Class," *Annual Review of Sociology* 20 (1994): 27–47.

The use of the traditional definition is intended to facilitate research and understanding. No normative judgment, either for or against the traditional family, is intended, that being a separate question. Readily available evidence does, however, show many benefits associated with the nuclear family. See the summary by David Popenoe, "American Family Decline, 1960–1990: A Review and Appraisal," *Journal of Marriage and the Family* 55 (1993): 527–555.

38. For a description of the samples, see Chapter 2, note 45.

39. For discussion and evidence on the outlooks of working-class wives, see Hamilton, *Class and Politics*, 211–212. There is a sizable literature on the subject. For a recent overview, see Nancy J. Davis and Robert V. Robinson, "Do Wives Matter? Class Identities of Wives and Husbands in the United States, 1974–1994," *Social Forces* 76 (1998): 1063–1086.

40. William Form, "Self-Employed Manual Workers: Petty Bourgeois or Working Class?" *Social Forces* 60 (1982): 1050–1069. The information on foremen comes from the General Social Surveys, the 1990–1994 merge. Of the full-time employed males in the crafts category, 14 percent were foremen and 15 percent were self-employed (N = 373). Among the remaining male workers (operatives, laborers, service), 6 percent (N = 532) were self-employed.

41. The slight increase has also been reported in Carl J. Cuneo, "Has the Traditional Petite Bourgeoisie Persisted?" *Canadian Journal of Sociology* 9 (1984): 269–301; F. Bechhofer and B. Elliott, "The Petite Bourgeoisie in Late Capitalism," *Annual Review of Sociology* 11 (1985): 181–207; George Steinmetz and Erik Olin Wright, "The Fall and Rise of the Petty Bourgeoisie: Changing Patterns of Self-Employment in the Postwar United States," *American Journal of Sociology* 94 (1989): 973–1018; commentary by Marc Linder and John Houghton, *American Journal of Sociology* 96 (1990): 727–735; reply by Steinmetz and Wright, idem: 736–740. See also, for a later version, Wright, *Class Counts*, ch. 4. Bregger, "Measuring Self-Employment," 4, shows a very slight increase of self-employment in nonagricultural industries between 1967 and 1993, but that result excludes self-employed persons who incorporated (and were classified as salaried), a choice that increased considerably in that period.

42. C. Wright Mills, *White Collar: The American Middle Classes* (New York: Oxford University Press, 1951), 65, 358–359.

43. Kerbo, *Social Stratification*, 220–223. Mills's account of the old middle class is actually extremely negative, one of the most hostile portraits in the entire social-science literature. See Mills, *White Collar*, especially 28–33, his account of "The Lumpen-Bourgeoisie." Kerbo's description of the self-employed as "hardly significant" is based on the work of Erik Olin Wright, who has a minimal definition of the petty bourgeoisie, one stipulating no employees (Steinmetz and Wright, "Fall and Rise," 979–980). Thus, by definition, his research would show a diminutive class.

For a later discussion, see Wright, *Classes*. There, due to an ambiguity in the questionnaire, the petty bourgeoisie is defined differently, including those with, possibly, one employee (p. 150). For another recent discussion, see Erik Olin Wright and Bill Martin, "The Transformation of the American Class Structure, 1960–1980," *American Journal of Sociology* 93 (1987): 1–29. Wright and Martin report the "petty bourgeois" to be 4.3 percent of the currently employed workforce in 1980. Another 5 percent are "small employers" (p. 13). See also Marshall et al., *Social Class*, ch. 3.

44. Kerbo, *Social Stratification*, 222.

45. French and German sociologists are much more likely to make the public–private distinction. For more than a century, the distinction has been built into the census occupational categories: *fonctionnaires* and *employées, Beamte* and *Angestellte*.

Kerbo's brief discussion of the new middle class (*Social Stratification*, 222–223) is based largely on Mills. Kerbo, incidentally, makes no reference to the outstanding work of Jürgen Kocka, *White Collar Workers in America, 1890–1940: A Social–Political History in International Perspective*, trans. Maura Kealey (Beverly Hills, Calif.: Sage, 1980). See also for a useful commentary, Axel van den Berg, "Creeping Embourgeoisement? Some Comments on the Marxist Discovery of the New Middle Class," *Research in Social Stratification and Mobility* 12 (1993): 295–328.

46. U.S. Bureau of the Census, *Statistical Abstract of the United States, 1996* (Washington, D.C.: U.S. Government Printing Office, 1996), Tables 710 and 719.

47. Ben J. Wattenberg, *The Good News Is the Bad News Is Wrong*, rev. ed. (New York: Simon & Schuster, Touchstone, 1985), 130–135.

48. Ibid., 136–147. He also spells out a range of other important demographic considerations having directional implications. The same result, incidentally, would obviously obtain were one to focus on families rather than on households. The recent source mentioned in the text is Council of Economic Advisers, *Economic Report of the President* (Washington, D.C.: U.S. Government Printing Office, 1993), 355. In his 1994 State of the Union message, President Clinton declared that for twenty years "the wages of working people have been stagnant or declining." See *New York Times*, 27 January 1994, A10. For a comprehensive review of the subject of real income changes, with extensive documentation, see Richard B. McKenzie, *What Went Right in the 1980s* (San Francisco: Pacific Research Institute for Public Policy, 1994), chs. 4, 5.

49. Another series, this showing per capita personal consumption expenditures extending from 1960 to 1997, shows the same result. See U.S. Bureau of the Census, *Statistical Abstract, 1998*, Table 722.

50. *Gallup Poll Monthly* 307 (April 1991): 39.

51. Richard A. Easterlin, Christine M Schaeffer, and Diane J. Macunovich, "Will the Baby Boomers Be Less Well Off Than Their Parents? Income, Wealth, and Family Circumstances Over the Life Cycle in the United States," *Population and Development Review* 19 (1993): 497–522. The article explores and comments on the impacts of a range of demographic changes among the smaller families. While of considerable importance, those findings, unfortunately, cannot be reviewed here.

Women entered the labor force in large numbers in recent decades, their efforts adding significantly to per capita family incomes. Those contributions, however, do not fully account for the upward trend. The real earnings of male baby boomers were 30 percent greater than for their parents. See Easterlin et al., "Baby boomers," 502–504.

52. For evidence showing the improvements in the condition of the American poor, see Heritage Foundation, "How 'Poor' Are America's Poor?" *Backgrounder*, no. 791, 21 September 1990; and "The Myth of Widespread American Poverty," *Backgrounder*, no. 1221, 18 September 1998. In the mid-1990s, 41 percent of those defined by the Census Bureau as "poor" were homeowners (median value, $65,200). Seventy percent of poor households owned a car or truck; 27 percent owned two or more vehicles. Two-thirds of those households had air conditioning. Almost all had color television. Almost three-quarters had VCRs. More than half had stereo equipment.

53. For a description of the prestige scales, see Davis and Smith, *General Social Surveys*, Appendix G. For a key discussion, see Robert W. Hodge, Paul M. Siegel, and Peter H. Rossi, "Occupational Prestige in the United States, 1925–1963," in *Class, Status, and Power*, ed. Reinhard Bendix and Seymour Martin Lipset, 2d ed. (New York: Free Press, 1966). For a recent investigation and commentary, see Robert M. Houser and John Robert Warren, "Socioeconomic Indexes for Occupations: A Review, Update, and Critique," *Sociological Methodology* 27 (1997): 177–298.

54. For his portrait of both old and new middle classes, Kerbo depends on Mills's *White Collar*, which, he announces, "continues to be the best sociology has to offer." "The alienation of the new middle class," he writes, "is no doubt less than Mills described, while times were often hard for the old middle class" (Kerbo, *Social Stratification*, 275). Mills's 1951 account of that middle-class "alienation" was not supported by any evidence nor, four decades later, are Kerbo's judgments. The outlooks of these classes were analyzed, with evidence, in Hamilton, *Restraining Myths*, ch. 2, "The Politics of Independent Business," and ch. 3 "The Salaried Middle Class: Some Reconsiderations."

55. Richard Centers, *The Psychology of Social Classes* (Princeton: Princeton University Press, 1949), 138–139; and Hamilton, *Class and Politics*, 100–102. The investigation of the salient factors, income versus ownership, is reported in Davis and Robinson, "Do Wives Matter?" See also Kerbo, *Social Stratification*, 147–150.

56. Hamilton, *Restraining Myths*, 68–69, 104–108, 127–131.

57. As opposed to a "no-adequate-test" argument, this fact points to another failed prediction. Karl Kautsky, writing in 1902, declared, "America shows us our future, in so far as one country can reveal it at all to another." August Bebel, in a 1907 interview, stated, "You Americans will be the first to usher in a Socialist Republic." See Seymour Martin Lipset, "Why No Socialism in the United States?" in *Sources of Contemporary Radicalism*, ed. Seweryn Bialer and Sophia Sluzar (Boulder, Colo.: Westview, 1977), 49.

58. Only a small number of farm-labor fathers appeared in the 1990–1994 GSS merge, the percentage of sons of farm proprietors in the working class was 40 (N = 171). For sons of farm laborers the equivalent figure was 74 (N = 14). Looking at the sons of farm owners and managers (in the 1985–1989 GSS merge), we find 13 percent upper-middle class, 32 percent lower-middle class, 37 percent working class, and 18 percent continuing as farm proprietors (N = 189). Among the sons of farm laborers, we have 2 percent upper-middle class, 25 percent lower-middle class, 65 percent working class, and 8 percent farm proprietors (N = 63).

59. The key assumptions are rarely discussed by sociologists. Intelligence is, in part, a function of genetics and, in part, a function of environment. Do the children of all classes, upper, middle, working, and lower, have an identical aggregate genetic character at birth? If one wishes to argue the affirmative, some explanation is required. How does it happen that despite mobility and intermarriage the gene pools would remain identical in each generation?

For consideration of these factors, see Bruce Eckland, "Genetics and Sociology: A Reconsideration," *American Sociological Review* 32 (1967): 173–194; Otis Dudley Duncan, "Ability and Achievement," *Eugenics Quarterly* 15 (1968): 1–

11; and Sandra Scarr and Richard A. Weinberg, "The Influence of 'Family Back-ground' on Intellectual Attainment," *American Sociological Review* 43 (1978): 674–692.

60. My father, Delmer Vernon Hamilton, first brought this hypothesis to my attention. I once asked him why his father, Richard Hamilton, sold the farm that had been in the family for three generations. His immediate response was, "We wanted to better ourselves." In "the city," my grandfather and his sons worked as carpenters in home construction.

61. Davis and Smith, *General Social Surveys*, 601. The last two findings, it will be noted, are based on a small number of cases. That limited evidence, however, is preferable to the standard readings that typically provide no system-atic evidence. For another study offering evidence on these questions, see Alain Girard and Henri Bastide, "Niveau de vie et répartition professionelle," *Popula-tion* 12 (1957): 37–70, especially pp. 60–63. They found a significant minority, 17 percent, of small businessmen recommending blue-collar jobs for a son.

62. On the initial nationalization efforts in Britain, see Henry Pelling, *The Labour Governments, 1945–51* (London: Macmillan, 1984), ch. 5. See also Ken-neth O. Morgan, *Labour in Power, 1945–1951* (Oxford: Clarendon Press, 1984), ch. 3; and Peter Hennessy, *Never Again: Britain, 1945–1951* (New York: Pan-theon, 1993). For the later shift to the left, see Ian Bradley, *Breaking the Mould? The Birth and Prospects of the Social Democratic Party* (Oxford: Martin Robertson, 1981); and Paul Whiteley, *The Labour Party in Crisis* (London: Methuen, 1983). For the French experience, see George Ross, Stanley Hoffmann and Sylvia Malzacher, eds., *The Mitterrand Experiment: Continuity and Change in Modern France* (Cambridge: Polity Press, 1987). For general overviews, see Adam Przeworski, *Capitalism and Social Democracy* (Cambridge: Cambridge Univer-sity Press, 1985); Stephen Padgett and William E. Paterson, *A History of Social Democracy in Postwar Europe* (London: Longman, 1991); Christiane Lemke and Gary Marks, eds., *The Crisis of Socialism in Europe* (Durham, N.C.: Duke Uni-versity Press, 1992); and Herbert Kitschelt, *The Transformation of European So-cial Democracy* (Cambridge: Cambridge University Press, 1994). See also Lipset, "No Third Way: A Comparative Perspective on the Left," in *The Crisis of Leninism and the Decline of the Left: The Revolutions of 1989*, ed. Daniel Chirot (Seattle: University of Washington Press, 1991).

63. Marxism and revisionism are general theories. The processes described operate, presumably, in all advanced capitalist nations. The absence of social-ism in the United States, revolutionary or reformist, accordingly is evidence against both positions. The American exception does pose an important ana-lytical problem. See Lipset, "Why No Socialism."

64. Geiger laid out the four options in an important article, "Panik im Mittelstand," *Die Arbeit* 7 (1930): 637–654. For Mills's discussion, see *White Collar*, 137–138, 290–291. Mills's only Ph.D. student, William H. Form, re-searched and wrote on the topic, but his findings do not appear in Mills's volume. See Form, "The Sociology of a White-Collar Suburb: Greenbelt, Mary-land" (Ph.D. diss., University of Maryland, 1944), and his later account, "Mills at Maryland," *American Sociologist* 26 (1995): 40–67. For other examples of per-sistent data indifference with respect to class outlooks, see Hamilton, *Social Misconstruction*, ch. 5.

65. Linz, "Social Bases," 527, 531. For discussion and evidence on class and religion, see his ch. 4. For evidence from the United States, see the many discussions in Bernard R. Berelson, Paul F. Lazarsfeld, and William N. McPhee, *Voting: A Study of Opinion Formation in a Presidential Campaign* (Chicago: University of Chicago Press, 1954); Hamilton, *Class and Politics*; and Hamilton, *Restraining Myths*. For recent accounts, see Kenneth D. Wald, *Religion and Politics in the United States*, 3d ed. (Washington, D.C.: CQ Press, 1992); and David C. Leege and Lyman A. Kellstedt, *Rediscovering the Religious Factor in American Politics* (Armonk, N.Y.: M. E. Sharpe, 1993).

66. Berelson, Lazarsfeld, and McPhee, *Voting*, chs. 4, 6; Hamilton, *Class and Politics*, ch. 5. Some recent research found the influence of both class and religion declining; some other research has disputed those claims. See Chapter 5, n. 19, for a brief discussion and references.

67. For a brief review of the political correlates of class, see Kerbo, *Social Stratification*, 236–239. There is no index reference to religion. Despite its manifest importance, the subject is given only fleeting attention, on pp. 62–63 and 377. Two of Erik Olin Wright's books, *Classes* and *Class Counts*, contain no index references to religion.

68. Many discussions assume, without evidence, that the workers have changed from radicalism at some time in the past to this present moderation. That too, in most formulations, comes as an unsubstantiated trend statement. There is an easy alternative, that the workers were moderate, reformist, and concerned with bread-and-butter issues at all times. It is possible, as one writer has suggested, that we are dealing with a myth. See Ralph Miliband, "Socialism and the Myth of the Golden Past," in *The Socialist Register: 1964*, ed. Ralph Miliband and John Saville (New York: Monthly Review Press, 1964), 92–103.

Large numbers of workers, in many contexts, have voted for socialist parties. Were those workers voting for socialism? Or were they voting for the party's immediate program for the so-called bread-and-butter options? The British Labour Party was voted into office on July 1, 1945. A Gallup Poll had asked about the "most important issues" during the campaign. Forty-one percent said housing; 6 percent mentioned "nationalisation of industry." See Hennessy, *Never Again*, 85.

69. Karl Kautsky, *Bernstein und das sozialdemokratische Programm Eine Antikritik* (Stuttgart: Dietz, 1899), 128–135.

70. For criticism and evidence on this point, see Hamilton, *Who Voted*, ch. 4, and *Social Misconstruction*, chs. 4, 5.

With the coming of the depression in Germany, it is said, the middle class in Germany "turned to the Nazis" because of their economic losses. William Sheridan Allen, in a 1965 publication, presented evidence showing real gains for the middle class as the depression worsened. See Allen, *The Nazi Seizure of Power*, rev. ed. (New York: Franklin Watts, 1984), 13–14, 24, 73, 108–109, 140. For a review of national evidence on the same point, see Hamilton, *Who Voted*, 376–377, 605, n. 45, and *Social Misconstruction*, 135.

71. Lichtheim, *Marxism*, 273; see also Steenson, *Kautsky*, 177; and Ritter, *Arbeiterbewegung*, 196–204. One article in a scholarly journal is remarkably free in its denigration of revisionists and moderates. Ignaz Auer is described as "the bland mainstay of the reformists in the executive committee." Friedrich

Ebert and Otto Braun "were opportunists." Georg von Vollmar was "the eminent Bavarian opportunist." See Harry Marks, "The Sources of Reformism in the Social Democratic Party of Germany, 1890–1914," *Journal of Modern History* 11 (1939): 334–356. Four decades later, the same journal published a review article which offered a very positive assessment. See David W. Morgan, "The Father of Revisionism Revisited: Eduard Bernstein," *Journal of Modern History* 51 (1979): 525–532. In 1964, Carlo Schmid, the noted Social Democratic parlamentarian and intellectual, declared, "Bernstein has triumphed all along the line!" (p. 526). See also Charles F. Elliott, "Quis custodiet sacra? Problems of Marxist Revisionism," *Journal of the History of Ideas* 28 (1993): 71–86.

Those unfamiliar with Kautsky's work might look at the following: Karl Kautsky, *The Social Revolution*, trans. A. M. Simons and May Wood Simons (Chicago: Charles H. Kerr, 1912); *Das Erfurter Programm*, 13th ed., translated, abridged, as *The Class Struggle [Erfurter Programm])*, trans. William E. Bohn (Chicago: C. H. Kerr, 1910), and *The Road to Power*, trans. A. M. Simons (Chicago: S. A. Bloch, 1909). The *Erfurter Programm*, Steenson writes, was Kautsky's "most famous and most translated work." Robert Tucker called it "one of the minor classics of Marxist thought" (Steenson, *Kautsky*, 99–100). Those observations, it should be noted, say nothing about its intellectual merit.

See also Kautsky, *The Dictatorship of the Proletariat*, trans. H. J. Stenning (1964; reprint, Westport, Conn.: Greenwood Press, 1981). This edition contains a useful introduction by a grandson, John H. Kautsky, reviewing Kautsky's later conflict with V. I. Lenin.

72. Fletcher, *Revisionism and Empire*, chs. 7, 8.

CHAPTER 4

Leninism:
The Argument of Imperialism

Like Bernstein, Vladimir Ilyich Lenin also dealt with the range of developments not anticipated in the original Marx–Engels theory. There were the problems posed by the improvements of working-class living standards, the appearance of trade unions, the growing socialist parties, and the reality of social reform within capitalism. The most important problem, of course, was the absence of the proletarian revolution. Writing in the midst of World War I, Lenin also provided an explanation for that conflagration (war was notably absent in Bernstein's account).

Lenin's major claim was that capitalism had been "saved" through imperialism. He predicted a shift in the immediate location of the struggle: The revolution would occur first in the colonies. This position was developed in Lenin's most important monograph, *Imperialism: The Highest Stage of Capitalism: A Popular Outline.*[1]

EXPLICATION

Lenin's argument focuses on the export of capital. The investment of capital in backward countries yielded high profits, "superprofits," which were returned to the home country where they were used to bribe the "labor aristocracy." The exploitation of colonies was the source of the working-class affluence and its consequent political moderation. The result was a temporary stabilization of capitalism. The colonies now became the pivotal centers of capitalist exploitation and, accordingly, the initial revolutionary struggles would be fought there. The victories of the national liberation movements would end the flow of superprofits. The leading capitalist nations would then again face the fundamental economic crisis that would lead to the "final conflict."

Lenin's argument stands in sharp contrast to the Marx–Engels position on colonies and imperialism. Their judgment, on balance, was favorable to such domination. British rule in India was breaking up a centuries-old heritage of ignorance and small-minded feudal rule. Engels approved of the American takeover of California. The "industrious Yankees" would do more with that territory than the "lazy Mexicans." Marx and Engels condemned specific outrages, the behavior of British troops in India and of French troops in Algeria, but they approved the end result, counting it as both inevitable and, in its way, progressive. The extension of capitalism, the breakdown of backward states, and their integration into the world market would advance the historical movement and accelerate the revolution.

Lenin's reading reversed that assessment, making colonialism a bad thing. It was now regressive, the key to the capitalist persistence. Unlike Bernstein, who was willing to signal an error in the work of his mentors, Lenin carefully preserved the sanctity of the original. Toward the end of the 19th century, he argued, capitalism had changed from a competitive to a monopolistic form. With this change, he argued, imperialism became regressive and hence, from then on, was to be opposed.[2]

Lenin's revision of the original Marxism became the official ideology of the Soviet Union and, after World War II, of several East European satellite states. With some additional modifications, his position was also adopted in China. Lenin's position appeared in the many collections of Marx–Engels writings that originated in Moscow, ones that either blurred or hid the differences between Marxism and Leninism. For many Marxists in the First, Second, and Third Worlds, Lenin's reading of things was Marxism. Many of those Marxists appear to have been unaware of the transformation.

In general usage, especially prior to 1945, the term imperialism referred to direct takeovers, to political control and domination of "backward areas." This usage is made unambiguously in Lenin's text. While acknowledging the possibility of decisive influence over nominally independent states, he declared that "finance capital finds it most 'convenient,' and is able to extract the greatest profit from a subordination which involves the loss of the political independence of the subjected countries and peoples" (81). The point is reiterated in several variations. "Colonial possession alone," he wrote, "gives complete guarantee of success to the monopolies against all the risks of the struggle with competitors" (82). Touching on the question of raw materials, he wrote that "finance capital strives to seize the largest possible amount of land of all kinds and in any place it can, and by any means, counting on the possibilities of finding raw materials there, and fearing to be left behind" (84). Returning to his main theme, he declared, "The necessity of exporting capital also gives an impetus to the conquest of colonies, for in the colonial market it is easier to eliminate competition, to make sure of orders, to strengthen the necessary 'connections,' etc., by monopolist methods (and sometimes it is the only possible way)" (84).

In addition to the argument of direct rule, three other themes are broached in these passages: investment (Lenin's central concern), trade (markets for goods), and raw materials. The four subject matters are separate and distinct, each requiring independent analysis. One can have trade without rule; one can invest for the purpose of manufacturing but care little or not at all about available raw materials. Given still other sources of diversity—the colonies differing in market size, average incomes, location, ease of transport, skill levels of the labor force, and the specific raw materials available (oil versus coffee, for example)—the range of combinations is very large. That fact should cast some doubt at the outset about one aspect of Lenin's intellectual enterprise, his formulation of a *general* theory of imperialism.

One minor phrase points up a serious difficulty in Lenin's analysis: The finance capitalists will strive, "by every means," to seize all that land. The statement is curiously indifferent to the question of economic costs. There is no hint of a cost–benefit analysis, that it might require, say, £20,000,000 to take, hold, and maintain Colony A for ten years, at the end of which the return could be only £20,000, or worse, nothing. The question of "returns" was signaled more than a century earlier when Voltaire, in *Candide*, commented on the costs of the Seven Years' War, the goal of which, he said, was *quelques arpents de neige* (a few acres of snow), a reference to France's North American colony. Lenin's "economic determinism" is peculiarly one-sided in that the finance capitalists (or the politicians serving their interests) do not appear to be constrained by cost factors.

Lenin's central argument does not appear until Chapter 4 of his monograph. Chapter 1 deals with "Concentration of Production and Monopolies." He provided data on the ongoing tendency toward concentration. In effect, he extended and supported a key Marxian argument (discussed in Chapter 2, Proposition 4). Lenin saw this as a basic transformation. Capitalism had moved from its early competitive form to the new "monopolist" variety, the result being "immense progress in the socialisation of production" (25). For each nation discussed, Lenin's evidence shows a dramatic decline in the number of producers. Moving from the established fact, oligopoly, he simply declared the next point, that of collusion, which for his purposes amounts to monopoly. The result, concentration together with capitalist "planning," was welcomed as the antecedent to the coming socialist economy.

Those processes of concentration occur entirely within the major capitalist nations. An isolated sentence appears in the midst of this discussion which announces, "Capitalism has been transformed into imperialism" (22). In that context the statement is a non sequitur, since no logic or argument is provided to explain the linkage of concentration and imperialism. A fugitive comment appears later, dealing with the possibility of the cartels capturing "all the sources of raw materials, or at least, the most important of them" (27). And still later another such comment tells of "the prodigious increase of capital, which overflows the brim, as it were, [and] flows abroad" (29).

Lenin's second chapter deals with "The Banks and their New Role," introducing the argument of *Finanzkapital*. The conclusion is, "Thus, the beginning of the twentieth century marks the turning point from the old capitalism to the new, from the domination of capital in general to the domination of finance capital" (46). The data presented show a remarkable growth of the major banks. Going far beyond his data, Lenin offers a comprehensive claim of domination: "We find that a handful of monopolists control all the operations, both commercial and industrial, of the whole of capitalist society" (35). This chapter contains nothing on imperialism.

Chapter 3 deals with "Finance Capital and the Financial Oligarchy." It too makes sweeping claims about the ability of the major capitalists to control firms, the economy, and the entire society. Two kinds of claims appear here, those dealing with the growth and resources of the monopolists and those dealing with their control. Lenin provides some evidence on the former; the latter claims are, for the most part, unsupported declarations. At the end of the chapter Lenin presents data on "financial securities," showing massive growth since 1871 and also a remarkable concentration in four countries: Great Britain, the United States, France, and Germany. Moving from numbers to alleged control, he announces that, in one way or another, "nearly the whole of the rest of the world is more or less the debtor to and tributary of these four international banker countries, the four 'pillars' of world finance capital" (61). It is again, clearly, a non sequitur.

In Lenin's account, in his extended discussion of control, the capitalists never lose. Their planning, presumably, is flawless. A monopoly, he writes, "inevitably penetrates into *every* sphere of public life, regardless of the form of government" (58). Chapter 5 opens with this declaration: "Monopolist capitalist combines—cartels, syndicates, trusts—divide among themselves, first of all, the whole internal market of a country, and impose their control, more or less completely, upon the industry of that country" (68). Also, as has been indicated, colonial possession alone "gives complete guarantee of success to the monopolies against all the risks of the struggle with competitors" (82).

The focus on imperialism begins with Chapter 4, which deals with "The Export of Capital." It is useful to present the argument in terms of its key propositions.

1. Capital export: "Under the old capitalism," Lenin wrote, "when free competition prevailed, the export of *goods* was the most typical feature. Under modern capitalism, when monopolies prevail, the export of *capital* has become the typical feature" (62). The new arrangement produces an enormous "superabundance of capital" which will be exported abroad to "the backward countries." There "profits are usually high, for capital is scarce, the price of land is relatively low, wages are low, raw materials are cheap" (63). This "necessity for exporting capital" also stems from conditions in the capitalist nations themselves: "Capitalism has become 'overripe' [and] cannot find 'profitable' investment" in the home country (63).

2. Superprofits: This is a key concept, especially in the later Marxist–Leninist discussions. This much-used term, however, has only a fleeting presence in Lenin's monograph. It appears in a parenthesis late in the text (107), that being its only appearance in the entire work. Most subsequent commentators have read that as meaning a "high rate of return," suggesting that capitalists receive perhaps 30 percent or more on colonial investments as opposed to only 5 percent at home. The expression appears again later in Lenin's 1920 preface, where it is given a different meaning: The superprofits "are obtained over and above the profits which capitalists squeeze out of the workers of their 'home' country" (13). It is no longer a "rate of return" but rather some "in addition to" that is being discussed. The disparity is not signaled and, of course, is not resolved.

3. The labor aristocrats: The profits from foreign investment are returned to the home country, and some part of those returns are used to reward a segment of the working class and its leaders. Lenin's formulation in the 1920 Preface reports that out of those superprofits, "it is quite *possible to bribe* the labour leaders and the upper stratum of the labour aristocracy. And the capitalists of the 'advanced' countries are bribing them; they bribe them in a thousand different ways, direct and indirect, overt and covert" (13–14). It is Lenin's explanation for the improvement of working-class living standards and for the consequent moderation of their political outlooks.

4. The political dynamics: If Lenin's argument was accurate, it follows that the "monopoly capitalists" would recognize the necessity of imperialism and would seek to further it on every possible occasion. Imperialism, after all, would be a "life-and-death" matter for advanced

capitalism. It follows also that those politicians serving the capitalist interests must carry through in response to those demands. Substantial evidence on these points, on the capitalists' "consciousness," on their efforts of influence, and on the politicians' response, should be readily available in the massive array of documents made public over the last 100-plus years.

5. National liberation struggles: With the most serious exploitation now occurring in the colonies, the location of the class struggle is changed. It now becomes a struggle between the "proletarian nations" and their imperial oppressors. With the success of those national liberation struggles and the denial of the superprofits, the location of the class struggle will again shift. The final conflict will then take place in the leading capitalist nations.

The work had a formidable impact. Etherington, writing in 1984, reports that Lenin's *Imperialism* "has been enshrined as a classic of socialist thought by the Revolution that made him famous. It has been lovingly edited by Soviet scholars, translated into every major language, read and studied by millions of people who know no other book on imperialism."[3]

ASSESSMENT

1. Capital export: Lenin supported his claim about the centrality of overseas investment with two tables, one showing "Capital Invested Abroad" (63), the other showing "Distribution (Approximate) of Foreign Capital in Different Parts of the Globe (circa 1910)" (64). His first table shows a remarkable growth of foreign investment by Britain, France, and Germany. Britain went from 3.6 (in billions of francs) in 1862 to 75–100 in 1914. The figures provided are rather sparse, rounded, and in two instances wide ranges are indicated. For France, beginning in 1869, we have 10, then 15, 20, 27–37, and 60 (in 1914). The data for Germany are incomplete, 12.5 in 1902 and 44 in 1914. Although listed among the four pillars of world finance capital, Lenin presented no data for the United States. The latter was distinctive in the period prior to World War I, since it was a net receiver of investment capital. In 1897, American private investors had approximately $700 million invested abroad. At that point, foreign investors had placed $3.4 billion in the United States. As of 1908, the respective figures were $2.5 and $6.4 billion. Lenin, obviously, had misrepresented the American case. That pattern reversed only in 1919.[4]

Three problems should be noted with respect to this presentation. First, some comparable figures are needed, those showing capital invested at home. Without that information, one cannot assess the "lack of domestic opportunity" claim, nor can one judge the extent of that foreign involvement. With all three European capitalist economies experiencing considerable growth, it is possible that the foreign investment amounted to, say, 20 percent of the total at all times. Second, one must consider the more basic problem of the validity of the figures as given. For the reasons indicated, those figures ought to be viewed with some skepticism. Lenin appended a supporting footnote which lists ten sources, beginning with "Hobson, *Imperialism*, London, 1902, p. 58." These figures and sources will be discussed later. Third, one must ask, did the exported capital go to that country's colonies or did it go somewhere else?

Lenin's second table is even more problematic. Since the data presented in that table are central to his argument, effectively the cornerstone for the entire position, it is reproduced here in its entirety (Table 4.1).

We have, first of all, an "approximate" distribution of "exported" capital. No trend data are given. The parenthesis—figures are for "about 1910"—signals some further imprecision. The unit of currency has been changed from francs to marks. The location of that foreign investment is given, somewhat vaguely, by continent: Europe, America, and a composite (Asia, Africa, and Australia). If that composite is supposed to represent the "backward nations," Lenin's own data do not support his claim: One-fifth of German foreign investment went there along with a slightly larger share, 23 percent, of French investment. Britain is Lenin's "best case," but even there the share was roughly two-fifths. Over half of Britain's foreign investment, according to Lenin's own figures, was in "America" (a term that probably refers to the Western hemisphere, including Canada and Latin America). His figures also indicate diverse patterns: The majority of French and Ger-

Table 4.1
Distribution (Approximate) of Foreign Capital in Different Parts of the Globe (circa 1910)

	Great Britain	France	Germany	Total
Europe	4	23	18	45
America	37	4	10	51
Asia, Africa, and Australia	29	8	7	44
Total	70	35	35	140

Sources: V. I. Lenin, *Imperialism: The Highest Stage of Capitalism* (New York: International Publishers, 1939), 64; in *Collected Works* (Moscow: Progress Publishers, 1964), 243.

man foreign investment was in Europe. Britain put only 4 percent of its total in Europe.

If one accepted the figures as given, the most appropriate conclusion would be that the claim is not supported. We have not been told how much of total investment was invested abroad; less than half of the foreign investment went to that vague three-continent composite; since the investment in "America" would have included the United States, Canada, and some "backward" nations, more information is needed; no trend data are provided; and one does not know whether the investment went into the respective "empires."

The difficulties were clearly recognized by Lenin. In the paragraph following the table, he wrote of the differences: Britain with "enormous exports of capital" to its "enormous colonies"; French capital exports mainly in Europe, "particularly in Russia"; and since the German colonies were "inconsiderable," her foreign investments were "divided fairly evenly between Europe and America" (65). Undaunted by the implications of his own evidence, Lenin argued, from the subtitle onward, that "imperialism" was the key to the modern experience. In his 1920 preface to the German and French editions, overlooking the findings of his table and text, he offered this major conclusion: "Capitalism has grown into a world system of colonial oppression and of the financial strangulation of the overwhelming majority of the people of the world by a handful of 'advanced' countries" (10–11).

The scholarly literature on foreign investment is enormous. In 1916, as indicated, Lenin was able to cite ten sources on the subject. The literature has grown considerably since then; the findings have been refined with the availability of better data and more advanced statistical techniques. It is useful, however, to begin with an early work, one published in 1930, Herbert Feis's, *Europe the World's Banker: 1870–1914*. Appearing only thirteen years after Lenin's monograph, there is understandably a considerable reliance on the same sources.[5] The differences in the two readings are instructive. The trend figures for Great Britain presented by Lenin and Feis are presented in Table 4.2.

British Investment

Lenin's data show a clear and unambiguous linear pattern, one of steady growth. Feis's data show broad cyclical swings. His summary reads,

Plainly the movement of British capital into the outer world was no regular and uninterrupted trend. Resting, as it did, upon individual calculation, it rose and fell, was active or inactive, according to the multitude of conditions which determined the investors' judgment. The movement of interest rates, the state of business at home and abroad, the financial condition of borrowing

Table 4.2
British Foreign Investment: Lenin and Feis Compared

Lenin		Feis	
Capital Invested Abroad (in billions of francs)		**British Foreign Investment (in millions of pounds)**	
			Annual Average of Period
1862	3.6		
1872	15.0	1870-1874	61.0
		1875-1879	1.7
1882	22.0	1880-1884	23.9
		1885-1889	61.1
1893	42.0	1890-1894	45.6
		1894-1899	26.8
1902	62.0	1900-1904	21.3
		1904-1909	109.5
1914	75-100	1910-1913	185.0

Sources: V. I. Lenin, *Imperialism: The Highest Stage of Capitalism* (New York: International Publishers, 1939), 64; in *Collected Works* (Moscow: Progress Publishers, 1964), 63; Herbert Feis, *Europe the World's Banker, 1870–1914* (1930; reprint New York: Norton, 1965), 11. The overlapping dates, 1894 and 1904, are as given in Feis.

governments, the shock of losses experienced, the lure of newly discovered opportunities abroad, wars and rumors of war—these are but a few of the matters which decided the volume of investment abroad at any one time.

Of special note, given Lenin's focus on the transformation of capitalism, is the steady decline of foreign investment for the twenty-year span from the late 1880s to the early 1900s. To give the image of capitalism's steady outward expansion, Lenin made a very artful selection of dates.[6]

One factor on Feis's list of determinants deserves special attention: "the shock of losses." Lenin, as noted, gave no indication of this possibility. But it was a factor that could hardly be missed. Feis reports

[The] fortune-making effort of the United States collapsed into the panic of 1893, and half of the American railroad system was in bankruptcy. The Argentine Government was forced to suspend payment on its huge foreign debt which was mainly held in Great Britain; many of the other Latin-American governments either went into default or seemingly faced that prospect. On the continent, the Portuguese and Greek governments reduced their interest payments; the finances of Spain and Serbia wavered. Drought in Australia brought heavy loss to the land and development companies; many of the South African mining companies were not fulfilling the promises of their promoters.

Feis added a footnote to this comment: "*Economist*, March 23, 1895, calculated, for example that the securities of North and South America listed on the London Stock Exchange had depreciated 125.3 million pounds sterling during the preceding five years." The *Economist* was, and is, a leading source on the world's financial affairs. Marx and Engels made regular use of the magazine, which undoubtedly was available in Zurich for Lenin's use.[7]

Feis also provided detailed figures on the location of British foreign investment in a table bearing the title, "Long-Term Publicly Issued British Capital Investment in Other Lands." This was based on a 1914 publication which showed £1,780 million invested in British colonies against 1,983 million invested elsewhere. The investments within the empire were concentrated in four settings: Canada and Newfoundland, 514.9; Australia and New Zealand, 416.4; India and Ceylon, 378.8; and South Africa, 370.1. The remainder of the empire received 100 million.[8]

Outside the empire, the prime "target" for investment was the United States. From the times of Queen Elizabeth, Feis reports, English investment in the American colonies and later in the United States had been substantial. Despite all of the turbulence in British–United States relations, "the volume of British capital invested in this country was probably never greater than 1913—well over a third of the whole British investment outside the empire." The three-quarters of a billion pounds, he reports, was "scattered over the United States, invested in our municipal and state bonds, in our largest railway systems, industrial plants, and public utility enterprises. The earlier investments in the land and cattle companies of Texas, Arkansas, Dakotas, and the rest of our earlier frontier regions had been mainly liquidated. . . . The largest holdings were in the·railway systems and the United States Steel Corporation." After the United States, the largest investments outside of the empire, in millions of pounds, were in Argentina, 319.6; Brazil, 148.0; Russia, 110.0; and Mexico, 99.0. Blaug provides a useful summary:

Outside the Empire the United States and Argentina took the lion's share of British capital. Instead of capital flowing to densely populated China or India, where capital was scarce and labor cheap, two-thirds of Britain's overseas investment in the years 1870–1914 went to the so-called regions of recent settlement, stimulated and complemented by the migration of something like 60 million people. The unique element of capital movements in the classic era of imperialism was just this: capital and labor flowed together from the Old World to the New, a striking fact completely ignored in the Marxist literature.[9]

Of the four leading capitalist nations considered by Lenin, Britain provides the best case for his imperialism thesis. Even there, however, the limited involvement in the empire is striking. Britain's investors clearly favored four of the nation's vast colonial holdings and proved remarkably indifferent to the rest. Two of the four were areas with considerable British settlement and a third, South Africa, had a fair-sized minority of European settlers, the Boers. "India and Ceylon" best fits the picture of exploitation of "backward areas," and India, of course, was distinctive in having the largest population in the entire empire. Lenin made passing reference to Western involvement in China, but investment there (£43.9 million) was less than in Chile (£61.0 million). British investors at that point saw more opportunity in Japan (£62.8 million).[10]

French Investment

Lenin's data for France showed a steady increase in foreign investment in the period from 1869 to 1914, the amounts indicated for those dates being 10 and 60 billion francs, respectively. France was an exuberant lender during most of this period. The rates of return at home were relatively low, and the opportunities for domestic investment, relative to other capitalist nations, rather limited. Feis gives a 45 billion figure for 1914, 25 percent below Lenin's; otherwise, the two series show general agreement.

Feis's account indicates that Lenin had again, as with the British experience, "constructed" a clear linear pattern through selective reporting of evidence. "In the decades of the fifties and sixties," he writes, "France had been a venturesome foreign investor on a large scale. The sovereigns of Italy, Spain, Austria, Hungary, and Portugal, among others, went into debt to the French people. Stimulated by the example of the British, French contractors, engineers, bankers, and diplomats, had united their efforts to construct railways in these lands. De Lesseps had started the Suez Canal in 1859 and completed it in 1869." But that effort came to an abrupt end with the Franco–Prussian War. France's defeat brought a massive indemnity which, for several years, required a considerable effort of financial mobilization, "all available liquid capital" being needed for that purpose. French government securities went to 6 percent, well above earlier levels, and previously acquired foreign securities were sold. In 1873, a major financial crisis began that affected all countries. As a result, very little foreign investment occurred in the period 1871–1875. Feis also reports "none or very little" such investment in the period 1881–1885. Lenin dropped these cyclical fluctuations from his account, hiding the possibility of capitalist losses while suggesting the "inevitability" of the development.[11]

The next issue is that of location: Where was that French capital invested? Feis opens his discussion with some straightforward, uncomplicated summary statements: "France, as it always has done, lived and traded primarily within Europe and along the Mediterranean shores. . . . Europe remained up to the war the chief field of employment of French capital abroad, despite the acquisition of a large colonial domain, the opening up of fertile continents, and the extension of French commerce and political interest throughout Asia." Feis provides a detailed table showing the geographic distribution of French foreign long-term investment in 1900 and in 1914. Russian investment led the list at both times with one-quarter of the total. The French colonies received 5 percent of the total in 1900 and 9 percent in 1914. Lenin's claim about the importance of colonies receives no serious support from this evidence.[12]

Lenin portrays the "monopoly capitalists" as informed, knowledgeable, and astute, as sovereign calculators of advantage. They see their advantage in "backward areas" and accordingly invest there, unmoved by any sentimental concerns. French investment, however, Feis points out, was moved by an entirely different set of determinants:

French foreign lending was not dominated by careful, objective measurement of economic opportunity. Guided and often controlled by government and the opinions of the financial institutions, it was swayed by antipathies and sympathies, traditional, emotional, political. These bound it to the countries of the Latins and Slavs. To retrace the history of French foreign lending would be . . . almost equivalent to writing the history of French political sympathies, rapprochements, vague dreams of influence, alliances in arms.[13]

The "loans to the Russian Government and the private investments made within that country," Feis writes, "grew unceasingly from the formation of the Alliance." Emphasizing the role of political determinants, he notes that Russia had been temporarily deprived of British and German support. As a result, after 1887, Russia "not only met all its current needs in Paris, but converted at lower rates issues outstanding elsewhere. The government and the banks threw their combined effort behind the successive flotations, defended Russian credit, and made place for Russian securities second only to . . . those of the French Government."[14] This immense Russian investment will be discussed at greater length.

The two arguments, about the role of government and the role of historic sentiments, receive convincing support in Feis's key table. British investors saw considerable opportunities for profits in English-speaking countries (the United States, Canada, and Australia), and responded accordingly. In sharp contrast, the total French investment in those three Anglo-Saxon nations, as of 1914, was 2 billion francs, less than was put in Austria-Hungary, less than in the Balkans, and roughly half of that placed in Spain and Portugal. Very little, apparently, was invested in Britain.

Investment in railroads and mining in the French colonies was restricted, by law, to French investors. But investment there, as indicated, was limited, with two-thirds of this small flow going to Algeria, Tunisia, and Morocco, and most of the remainder to Indochina. A range of "diverse conditions," Feis reports, discouraged investment:

The colonial governments were fumbling in their efforts to develop their domains. The home government was preoccupied with continental plans and politics. Railroad construction went forward less vigorously than in the corresponding British areas. French private enterprise suffered many losses in their early ventures and grew afraid. Even into the North African colonies the French migration was small, and into the other colonies it was almost negligible. The colonists took mainly to farming; they organized few enterprises of large enough dimension to win the attention of the financial syndicates of Paris. In the tropical regions, curiously enough, little capital was engaged in the production of raw materials. The concession *régime* in the French Congo worked poorly, and in Indo-China the private enterprises which undertook raw material production were comparatively few.[15]

German Investment

Feis begins his discussion of Germany with a consideration of the trend in foreign investment. In the early 1870s and middle 1880s, "more than one-tenth, perhaps as much as one-fifth of the savings in the country" was invested abroad. In subsequent years, however, that proportion declined, just the opposite of Lenin's claim: "From 1900 to 1914 less than one-tenth . . . of current saving went abroad despite the appeal of undeveloped lands, the exertion of the Government in behalf of foreign enterprise, [and] the great growth of the overseas banking system and commerce."[16] Lenin, it will be remembered, gave information on "capital invested abroad" for only two points: 12.5 billion francs in 1902 and 44 in 1914. His presentation, clearly, was very misleading.

A cyclical pattern was also found in Germany, although the "waves" did not, indeed could not, parallel those of French investment. An economic boom followed the victory in the Franco–Prussian War, stimulated by German unification, the French indemnity, and the adoption of the gold standard. An exuberant episode of foreign investment came at that time, with investors "attracted to the securities of the Austro-Hungarian, Russian, Turkish, Greek, Roumanian, and Portuguese governments," and to those of American railways, especially those in the west and northwest. The 1873 crash ended that movement for the remainder of the decade.

Foreign investment picked up again in the 1880s, Feis reports, in part stimulated by political decisions: "The rate of interest on German government loans was reduced, the German railroads were nationalized." Investors seeking higher returns again purchased, through the banks, Feis reports, securities "issued by the Balkan states, by Turkey, Russia, Spain, and Portugal," many of these being of "doubtful quality." Bismarck expressed his alarm, but the flow continued, the "high tide" for foreign investment coming between 1887 and 1890. The outreach now was greater than in the early 1870s: "Heavy purchases of Argentine securities were made. At Bismarck's behest financial assistance was repeatedly extended to the Italian Government. The Deutsche Bank earned the Anatolian Railway Concession by a loan to the Turkish Government. The securities of the Venezuelan and Mexican governments made their first appearance in the German market. In Berlin there was flushed speculation in the shares of gold mines and the Panama Canal." Contrary to Lenin's insistent claims of immense profits and control, Feis reports a "harvest of disappointment." German investors were involved in all the subsequent defaults, among the most serious of which were "the numerous failures of the American railways; that of the Northern Pacific was particularly felt." According to Schmoller's estimate, Feis reports, "German losses in foreign investment between 1885 and 1893 could not have fallen far short of a billion marks—about one tenth of the total investment."[17]

Foreign investment picked up again in the 1890s, this time with some greater caution, the new chemical and electrical industries providing the basis for a "fresh impulse." On balance, however, "the outward movement of capital was not very large." In the 1900s—in fact, up to 1914—the demand for capital (and the rates of return) within Germany discouraged foreign investment. The aggregate sum did increase, as Lenin reported, but its importance within total economic activity declined. Foreign investment, Feis states, "remained but a minor fraction of total German wealth, growing in about the same proportion as the total and representing in 1914 in the neighborhood of one-fifteenth of the total German wealth." In the 1900s, he estimates that less than 3 percent of the national total income went to foreign investment. After 1911, when domestic investment became "more urgent," the foreign contribution was "certainly no more than 2 per cent" of the total. Lenin's argument centers on the earnings returned from abroad. Feis reports that the "income received from these foreign employments of capital made up between 3 per cent and 4 per cent of the total national income up to 1900; thereafter it tended to fall to about 3 per cent."[18]

Where was German foreign investment placed? To the end of the 19th century, Feis reports, "It moved mainly toward near-by states, especially those on its eastern frontiers. The governments of these countries were bound to Germany by friendly alliance or by fear." With the shift in one key alliance with Russia, the capital flows changed accordingly. German investment declined and was replaced, as seen, by a massive inflow of French funds. As of 1914, most German capital was invested in Europe, with Austria-Hungary leading the list and four other nations (or a group thereof) following with roughly equal shares: Russia, Turkey, the Balkan countries, and Spain and Portugal. The largest share of overseas investment was roughly equally divided between North and South America. Some went to railways in the United States and Canada. German firms also built branch plants there in industries where they were preeminent, notably "establishments to utilize chemical and metallurgical patents and formulas." In Latin America, investment was largely in government bonds, both national and municipal, especially in Argentina, Brazil, Mexico, Chile, and Venezuela. German investors showed little interest in Asia, only China being described as "of importance." Investors participated in general loans to the Chinese government. Some went directly to the German concession in China, to Shantung. Germany had four colonies in Africa. More African investment, however, was made outside than inside the colonies. The principal interest was in South African gold mines and in railways. Investment in the German colonies prior to 1907 was largely "in trading and plantation companies, some of which possessed imperial charters." Heavy losses were suffered and "the German Government and Great Banks had to come to their rescue repeatedly." Investors showed greater interest between 1906 and 1914, when railroad building was pushed "vigorously" with government aid and mining investment was also doing somewhat better.[19]

Lenin's account, in summary, grossly misrepresents Germany's involvement as of 1914. He presented only the two figures, aggregate foreign investment for 1902 and 1914, but provided no information on foreign investment as a percentage of total investment. With total foreign investment producing about 3 percent of national income, the German colonies themselves could have produced, at best, only a fragment of a percent. The German empire was a modest and unpromising undertaking, four territories in Africa acquired between 1883 and 1885—German Southwest Africa, Cameroons, Togo, and German East Africa, plus some Pacific islands and a China concession acquired later. In 1871, when considering the Franco–Prussian War settlement, Bismarck had rejected the possible annexation of French colonies. His position on the subject was clear and unambiguous; colonies were a useless luxury. The sudden shifts of policy in the mid-1880s, first to take those African territories, then to halt further expansion, has been a problem for historians ever since.[20]

Much of Germany's foreign investment was lost between 1914 and 1919. Confiscations occurred in all of the nations allied against Germany. The African colonies and those in the Pacific were lost, first in the war and then, permanently, in the Versailles settlement. The German concession in China, Shantung, was given to Japan by the Versailles negotiators. Any investments in Russia not confiscated in 1914 were lost in the general repudiation following the revolution.[21]

The focus in the previous pages has been on the foreign investments of three major capitalist nations, their location, and their returns in order to address the main points of Lenin's argument. That argument, as was seen, began with the assumption of dwindling investment opportunities at home, an assumption that was bypassed and never documented. Given the fluctuations, the waves of outward movement and, in the downswings, of capital repatriation, a general conclusion would, at the outset, seem unlikely. One series for the United Kingdom shows gross domestic fixed-capital formation as a percentage of gross national product (at constant prices). It shows an increase from 6.4 to 10.2 percent between 1870 and 1876, a decline to 5.8 percent in 1887, an increase to 11.1 percent in 1903, and a decline to 7.9 percent in 1913. It was followed, in the 1920s, by another upswing.[22]

The economic history reviewed to this point is very limited, treating only three nations and covering a relatively short time span, roughly a half-century. That span, however, proves to be exceptional. Some unique events occurred then, events that could not be repeated. A more extended review of modern economic history is therefore appropriate.

An important study of the British experience by A. K. Cairncross provides some apparent support for Lenin's claim about the importance of foreign investment. In the forty years between 1875 and 1914, capital at home, exclusive of land, increased by more than 80 percent to £9.2 billion. In the same period, aggregate foreign investment rose by some 250 percent to approximately £4 billion. In the peak year, 1913, he reported, "foreign investment took over half the total of British savings." Cairncross's initial summary, however, undercuts Lenin's claim about the superprofits, since "only about one-tenth of her national income came . . . as interest on foreign investments." Much of that, moreover, would have been investment in other capitalist nations, not in colonies.[23]

Where Lenin (and many followers) portrayed that growth of foreign investment as an inherent requirement of advanced capitalism, Cairncross reports that the "forty or fifty years before 1914 were clearly an exceptional period in economic history." Those conditions, he added, "can hardly recur." To match the British experience of 1913, he indicates, the United States, in 1951, would require overseas investments of at least $600 billion at a point when private investment did not exceed $1 billion per year. To equal Britain's 1913 achievement, the United States would require an investment flow some thirty times larger or, put differently, "the entire Marshall Plan would have to be carried out twice a year."[24]

Cairncross provided some basic information on the uses of capital in 1875, that base determining the possibilities in the subsequent decades. From the 1840s to the 1870s, he states, "the main investment effort in Britain had been concentrated on railways, but by 1875 most of the main-line railways were already in being, and from then on railway-building normally absorbed smaller amounts of capital." At the same time, "fixed capital in manufacturing industry was less in 1875 than the capital of the railways. It was transport and commerce that used large amounts of capital, not industry."[25]

Only one of the countries discussed by Lenin, the United Kingdom, placed a majority of its current investment outside the nation and, even then, only in a single year, 1913. None of the three countries placed so much as half of its foreign investment capital in the nation's colonies. The proportion going to the colonies differed considerably, being high in the British case but very low for France and Germany. For Lenin's theory, investment in the colonies is the decisive claim. But the bulk of French investment at this time was in Europe. Cairncross summarizes the point in a footnote: "In 1914, 60 percent of all French foreign investment was in European countries—chiefly in government bonds." That last clause says that it was indirect investment—someone else was the prime or direct exploiter. It also leaves open a key question: How much of the remaining 40 percent went to the colonies? Herbert Feis provided a relevant figure: In 1914, 8.9 percent of French long-term foreign investment went to French colonies. The overwhelming majority of French foreign investment, in short, was *not* going to France's colonies. It went elsewhere.[26]

2. Superprofits: Lenin, as noted, was unexpectedly ambiguous on this point, giving two different definitions and suggesting an enormous rate. His formulations on this theme prove rather tepid, for example, in his statement that "profits are usually high" in these backward countries (63). If evidence showing striking differences in profit margins at home and in the colonies had been available, he would certainly have presented it. The crucial evidence, clearly, is missing.

Mark Blaug summarizes one small part of the investment experience as follows: "The average annual income from the entire British investment from nearly a thousand firms in Latin America rarely rose above five or six percent of the par value of the investment; these rates are quite comparable to British stock yields during the past century. Latin American government bonds were bringing as much as 8 percent but almost half of these were in default by the close of the century."[27]

Cairncross's discussion of one important capital flow provides further evidence on the subject. "By 1914," he writes, "France had embarked close to £500 [million] in Russian bonds bearing 4 and 5%." Those returns would not strike most readers as excessive or as superprofits. Given the flimsy state of Russian finances, Cairncross writes, a war or revolution "would bring certain default." That did happen, of course: "The loans were repudiated outright and not a penny of the whole £500 m. has ever been recovered." Cairncross reports that the "loans which France had made, with equal craziness, to Turkey, Greece, Austria-Hungary, the Balkans and South America, were also repudiated. In all, France lost two-thirds of the net total of her foreign investments, or about six times the amount of the German indemnity of 1870."[28]

Lenin assumed a transparency about the entire arrangement, one that made the capitalists highly rational decision makers. But the Russian experience points up the difficulty with that unexplored assumption. The French investors, Cairncross reports, did not know, for example, that "the Russian government was spending half of its borrowings on armaments." They did not know that it "was relying to an increasing extent upon profits from the sale of alcohol in order to meet its ordinary expenses." Where Lenin invites his readers to think in terms of direct investment, foreign-owned factories, and the exploitation of wage earners, the actual dynamics were quite different. The Russian government proved to be the leading exploiter, not through direct appropriation of surplus value, but through the taxes on a specific consumer "good": The "alcohol monopoly brought in a third of the ordinary revenue, and the consumption of alcohol per head increased by a third in the years 1902–10." The Russian government, in fact, had been "more or less on the verge of bankruptcy ever since the nineties."[29]

Why would the French investor not see the problem? Cairncross's answer is that the individual investor did not have "the information on which to base a sound judgement." The problem, basically, was one of corrupt or interested sources:

The financial columns of the large dailies were leased to financial writers privileged to conduct their columns with complete liberty. It was estimated that only 25 out of 186 financial journals had any claim to independence, and only two or three of these could be said to be thoroughly honest in their comments on new issues. Misrepresentation was carried to extraordinary lengths both in the press and in prospectuses; there was no legal requirement that the statements made should be accurate.

The basic problem was that these "tipsters" recommended "the issues that were most profitable to themselves."[30]

3. Labor aristocracy: The superprofits taken from the colonies, Lenin argued, allowed the bourgeoisie to "bribe" the labor leaders and the upper stratum of the working class in the advanced capitalist nations. He was addressing the problem considered earlier by the revisionists: working-class affluence. Lenin was clearly agreeing with them, both about the fact, increased real incomes, and the presumed consequence, political moderation (the rejection of the revolutionary option). The key assumption here is that a significant part of the profits gained in the colonies would be transferred to some segment of the working class in the home country.

Assessment of this claim requires demonstration of the large flow of profits out of the colonies. Most of those returns would go directly to the capitalists. Another part, presumably, was diverted for this bribery of workers and their leaders. The latter flow had to be considerable: In addition to providing for some hundreds or thousands of labor leaders, the economic condition of the "upper stratum of the labour aristocracy" was being bettered. For the major capitalist nations, the number of persons involved would be enormous, some millions or tens of millions. Lenin's discussion of this central point was very limited. It consisted of a single unsubstantiated allegation: The capitalists "bribe them in a thousand different ways, direct and indirect, overt and covert" (193–194).

Lacking specifics on the "thousand different ways," assessment of this claim poses some difficulty. One may begin first with a consideration of the logic of this argument. Much of that investment, we have seen, was in the form of loans, specifically bonds, securities having a fixed rate of interest. Those well-publicized rates allow a test of the superprofits claim. The Russian 4- and 5-percent bonds provide some measure of the profit-making opportunities. One would expect a higher average rate of return from direct investments there, that is, from outright purchase of an enterprise or purchase of shares, but that was an infrequent choice. If the average rate of return on direct investment was significantly higher, such as would justify the superprofits claim, investors would have had little incentive to buy the bonds.

Much of the income from those foreign investments, whether from stocks or bonds, was doubtlessly returned "home" to the individual investors. In the familiar image (or caricature), we might be dealing with *rentiers*, the "coupon clippers." Lacking evidence, however, we should not exclude other possibilities: investment-banking houses, full-time employed capitalists, civil servants, or small investors. Two problems appear in this connection. First, there is the question of plausibility: What would move any of those investors to give some part of their earnings to labor leaders or to the broad ranks of the skilled workers? Second, if they were disposed to do so, how was that transfer accomplished? One must imagine, for example, an English landlord or country squire who has invested in South American railroads and who later received his annual returns. Did he somehow transfer a part of that income to British labor leaders? Did some part of that income go to, say, skilled workers employed by British railways? The argument seems unlikely. If it actually happened, some documentary evidence should be available attesting to that fact.

While perhaps not available to Lenin at the time (and under the circumstances, wartime Zurich), such evidence should have become available in subsequent decades through the diligent efforts of the world's social historians and other scholars. Lenin's vague reference to the "thousand" overt and covert ways means he had no substantial evidence on this point. If he had had even one well-documented instance in which that influence had been exerted, he would certainty have revealed it in the 1920 Preface.

Both logic and evidence go strongly against Lenin's major claim, that profits derived from the colonies enabled the enrichment of working classes in the major capitalist nations. First, the aggregate flows were not sufficient for the task. Second, no evidence has been presented showing *rentier* incentives and responses. Finally, evidence showing transfers of funds from rentiers to workers is entirely absent.[31]

4. Political dynamics: Recognizing the urgent needs of capitalism in this, the "highest stage," business leaders, particularly those heading the major banks, should have been at the forefront of the imperialist effort. Lenin's argument on this point is no more than a simple allegation. If capitalism "required" imperialism, a documentary record should be available showing that major capitalists supported such initiatives and directed political leaders to undertake the necessary steps of implementation.

If Lenin was correct, imperialism in the United Kingdom should have been supported by the party of the capitalists; that is, by the Liberals. In fact, however, in the last quarter of the 19th century the

Liberals generally opposed the expansion of the empire. The imperialist efforts were most frequently undertaken by Conservatives, the party of the landed aristocracy. Early in his career, Benjamin Disraeli, the Conservative leader, opposed imperialism as a foolish and costly policy. The colonies, he said, were "a millstone round our necks." But later, in the 1870s, as the leader of what seemed a permanent minority party, he needed a winning issue, one that would allow him to enlarge his base of support, and imperialism seemed a useful option. Joseph Schumpeter writes, "In this predicament Disraeli struck a new note. The election campaign of 1874—or, to fix the date exactly, Disraeli's speech in the Crystal Palace in 1872—marked the birth of imperialism as a catch phrase of domestic policy." The new imperialism was not rooted, as Lenin held, in the imperatives of advanced capitalism. The renewed interest in imperialism had political origins.[32]

In the two decades between 1885 to 1906, when the "scramble for Africa" occurred, the nation was ruled, apart from two brief Gladstone governments, by the Conservatives. Gladstone, keeping with liberal traditions, opposed the imperialist tide. The prime minister during much of this period was a Conservative, Lord Salisbury. He was succeeded in 1902 by his nephew, Arthur Balfour. Robinson and Gallagher report, "Throughout the partition of Africa, the Foreign Secretaries were all peers and great landowners. Foreign policy, of which African policy was part, was still made at house parties, not by the man in the street or the man in the Stock Exchange." Cecil Rhodes, an exuberant entrepreneur and possibly the leading imperialist, carved a state out of Africa which was then named Rhodesia and whose capital city was named for the Conservative prime minister. One leading imperialist, Joseph Chamberlain, was a very successful manufacturer of wood screws. Originally a Liberal, he broke with Gladstone over Irish home rule. As leader of the Unionist faction, he joined with Salisbury, in whose cabinet he served as minister of colonies. It would be a mistake, however, to see imperialism solely in terms of these either/or dichotomies—political or economic, Liberal or Conservative. Some younger Liberals, Rosebery, Asquith, Grey, and Haldane, moving with the tide, rejected their party's traditional stance and declared themselves to be Liberal-Imperialists (or "Lib-Imps," or "Limps"). In 1899, Cecil Rhodes said, "They are tumbling over each other, Liberals and Conservatives, to show which side are the greatest and most enthusiastic Imperialists."[33]

Two separate and distinct questions are involved here: Who led the "scramble"? And why; what were their motives or purposes? Robinson and Gallagher's work, based on their extensive review of British government papers, addresses the latter question. Their conclusion is as follows:

If the papers left by the policy-makers are to be believed, they moved into Africa, not to build a new African empire, but to protect the old empire in India. . . . A century and more of accumulated experience confirmed one precept: that Britain's strength depended upon the possession of India and preponderance in the East, almost as much as it did upon the British Isles. Therefore, her position in the world hung above all upon safe communications between the two. This was a supreme interest of Victorian policy: it set the order of priorities in the Middle East and Asia, no less than in Africa. . . . At the first level of analysis, the decisive motive behind late-Victorian strategy in Africa was to protect the all-important stakes in India and the East.[34]

Given what was said earlier about British trade and investment, this claim about India's centrality may seem puzzling. But a near-exclusive focus on trade and investment is misleading, overlooking a key component of the imperial enterprise: military power. India's growing trade and revenues, Robinson and Gallagher report,

nourished the military forces of the Indian government; and this force in turn secured and promoted trade and investment throughout India, south-east Asia, and the Far East. This reciprocal action of power and trade depended on dominion in India. The *ultima ratio* of that rule was the army of India. But it also had another function. The Indian army provided the means of over-awing and, in the last resort, of crushing the resistance of Asiatic rulers who obstructed British influence and trade.

They list twelve such interventions from 1839 to 1896. It was a very convenient arrangement: "Not only did the Indian taxpayer bear the cost of his own occupation, but something like half the British Army was billetted upon him. The Indian empire thus provided a uniquely self-financing army, which allowed Victorian governments to exert power in the Far and Near East without always having to foot the whole bill." The arrangement also gave "relative freedom from Parliamentary scrutiny and Treasury control."[35]

Intellectual contributions played some role, some written for the intelligentsia and some for the masses. A Cambridge history professor, Sir John Seeley, published *The Expansion of England* in 1883, a work that "awoke countless Britons to their imperial greatness." Two quality newspapers took up the cause of empire: In 1883, W. T. Stead became editor of the *Pall Mall Gazette* and, in 1888, W. E. Hanley founded the *National Observer*. In 1899, the *Daily Mail*, the first of the sensationalist dailies, carried the imperial message out to its half-million readers. G. A. Henty published some eighty adventure books for boys, including many exuberant tales of empire: *With Clive in India, With Wolfe in Canada, Through the Afghan Passes, The Dash for Khartoum*, and *With Roberts to Pretoria*. John Buchan, a generation after Henty, also wrote novels dealing with the imperial experience. Two later ideological contributions were provided by Karl Pearson, the foremost Social Darwinist, and by the poet–novelist, Rudyard Kipling.[36]

Voluntary associations also played some role. The Imperial Federation League, formed in 1885, wished to see a closer union among the dominions. The United Empire Trade League was formed in 1891 to campaign for neomercantilist ideas of imperial trade. This effort was followed, a decade later, by Joseph Chamberlain's campaign for imperial tariffs, one that brought defeat for the Conservatives. These organizational efforts, it will be noted, point to imperfections in the imperial system. It was by no means the purposeful integrated system Lenin imagined.

Eventually, Britain had thousands of civil servants, commissioners, informal advisors, army officers, and tradesmen scattered throughout the world. Their leaders were referred to as the men "on the spot." In outlook, they were tough, headstrong, and resourceful. Many were schooled in the "truths" of empire, including, among others, the belief in white supremacy. Operating "in the field" some thousands of miles from London, many of them took action without orders or any previous consultation with the Colonial Office. Prior to the establishment of cable connections, it took months for the news of their accomplishments to reach London. Some time for decision making (or dithering) would follow. News of the government's reactions then took months to reach the men on the spot.[37] This decentralized process, it will be noted, differs markedly from Lenin's portrait of finance capitalists directing operations from The City.

The acquiescence of the Colonial Office to those actions taken in the field may seem puzzling. To reject a fait accompli was viewed as impossible; such a decision, it was thought, would challenge public opinion overwhelmingly favorable to expansion. Schumpeter reviewed a minor episode involving the Ionian Islands. A protectorate from 1815, the nation's foreign secretaries saw the possession as "meaningless and untenable" but, nevertheless, "none dared surrender it." The "only thing to do was to insist that Corfu was a military base of the highest importance which must be retained." Later, with the spread of cable connections and still later with wireless transmission, the governments of the imperialist powers could respond quickly and directly to those distant events. One result was that the men on the spot lost influence.[38]

Robinson and Gallagher's account, as noted, is based on the "papers left by the policy-makers." Those authors report almost nothing on finance capitalists and their initiatives. They assign no weight to the imperialist literature. The policy-makers reacted to events "in the field," not to domestic pressures. Public reactions, in general, came after the fact, after the intervention or the catastrophe. Those authors assign no weight to the voluntary associations. The men on the spot

were a source of continuous difficulty, the Jameson raid in Transvaal
being the most problematic of the lot.

Lenin's monograph begins with the following sentence: "During the
last fifteen or twenty years, especially since the Spanish–American War
(1898) and the Anglo–Boer War (1899–1902), the economic and also
the political literature of the two hemispheres has more and more often adopted the term 'imperialism' in order to describe the present
era" (15). Those two wars, however, provide lessons about the political dynamics that differ markedly from those advanced by Lenin.

In April 1898, the United States declared war on Spain, ostensibly
coming to the aid of oppressed Cubans fighting for their independence.
In the first action, Dewey's squadron destroyed a Spanish fleet in the
Philippines. Several months later, demoralized Spanish troops were
defeated in Cuba in a few limited engagements near Santiago. Another Spanish fleet, trying desperately to escape, was destroyed there.
In the settlement, the United States annexed Puerto Rico, the Philippines, and Guam. In separate moves, Hawaii was annexed and a year
later Wake Island was taken. The U.S. Senate, in April 1898, expressly
forbade the annexation of Cuba. But in the aftermath, the United States
occupied the island until 1902, during which time an informal empire
was established, with an assured "right" of intervention.

Hobson declared that the war was stimulated by the major capitalists and that they profited from it. "It was Messrs. Rockefeller, Pierpont
Morgan, Hanna, Schwab and their associates who need Imperialism
and who are fastening it upon the shoulders of the great Republic of
the West. They need Imperialism because they desire to use the public
resources of their country to find profitable employment for their capital which otherwise would be superfluous."[39] Hobson provided no
documentation to support those claims. If valid, they would provide
important support for Lenin's position.

In the spring of 1898, many American observers agreed on one key
point; namely, that "big business" *opposed* the nation's involvement in
any war. The "jingoes" endlessly denounced Wall Street because of
this obvious reluctance. Within a couple of decades, however, some
commentators had turned that history around and, like Hobson, declared that "big business" was prowar and in favor of the "large policy."
Julius W. Pratt, in an important 1936 study, reviewed the evidence
then available and sustained the original reading. Pratt writes, "That
business sentiment, especially in the East, was strongly anti-war at
the close of 1897 and in the opening months of 1898, is hardly open to
doubt. . . . So marked, indeed, was the anti-war solidarity of the finan-

cial interests and their spokesmen that the jingoes fell to charging Wall Street with want of patriotism."[40]

Subsequent biographies and business histories have provided strong and consistent support for Pratt's conclusion. John Pierpont Morgan was the nation's leading finance capitalist. As head of the "House of Morgan" he had reorganized railroads, sold American securities throughout Europe, and rescued the nation's finances during the Panic of 1893. A comprehensive history of the Morgan firm by Vincent P. Carosso gives only a single page to the war: "Like many other Wall Street bankers, Morgan had hoped that the conflict might be avoided. He considered it pointless." Morgan and two other firms made offers to handle a $200-million war loan. But, providing some evidence of their power, the offers were rejected and the loan was "sold to the public, with small individual and institutional buyers taking most of it." A second history of the firm, by Ron Chernow, has only a brief paragraph on the Spanish–American War. The attitude toward the war is described in a single sentence: "The Morgans had opposed the war, and Jack [the banker's son] . . . lamented the 'needless waste of life & property.'" The war clearly did not figure prominently in the affairs of the firm.[41]

The major biographies of John D. Rockefeller appearing subsequent to Pratt's book contain, at best, only fugitive references to the war with Spain. This is most striking in Allen Nevin's extensive, detailed accounts in his original two-volume study of 1940 and revised account of 1953. Rockefeller had "various investments in iron mines" in Cuba, some 4,000 acres, plus a costly railroad and dock—but he also owned the Mesabi field in Minnesota. The Cuban investment and/or market possibilities did not appear of sufficient importance as to justify any further comment. A comprehensive history of the Standard Oil Company reports the presence of a refinery in Havana from 1881 and another in Puerto Rico begun in 1890. But it makes no mention of the Cuban revolution or of the Spanish–American War. Chernow's biography of Rockefeller has three index references to the war. These are best described as fugitive—one deals with hookworms, another with yellow fever. There is no indication of imperial ambitions.[42]

Andrew Carnegie, head of the nation's largest steel company, was out of the country in the months prior to the war. The response to the prospect of war fell to his second-in-command, Henry Clay Frick. Early in 1898, Frick "was writing anxious letters to senators and congressmen, urging them to support McKinley's attempts to avoid war with Spain." When war came, late in April, "Frick and other conservative businessmen, who feared the effects of war on business conditions, blamed McKinley for yielding to the popular clamor." "A stronger man," Frick wrote to Carnegie, "would have held the Jingoes in check, and avoided war, at least until there was a good cause for one."[43]

Carnegie was a leading figure in the international peace movement and was well-known for his pacifist sentiments. His support for the war, therefore, came as something of a surprise. That support was based on his understanding of the war's purposes, on "McKinley's assurances that it was a war only to give Cuba its independence and to drive one more European nation completely out of the Western Hemisphere."[44]

When Carnegie saw that McKinley had changed his position and was yielding to expansionist demands with respect to the Philippines, he indicated unambiguous opposition to this new direction. Perhaps recognizing the imminent possibility, even when approving the war to make *Cuba libre*, he had provided generous financial support to the New England Anti-Imperialist League, an organization formed in the early spring of 1898 by Edward Atkinson, a Boston manufacturer. In August, Carnegie published an article in the *North American Review* entitled "Distant Possessions—The Parting of the Ways." Joseph Frazier Wall, his most recent biographer, describes it as a "bitter, unequivocal attack upon American Imperialism." Later, on hearing that the United States was offering Spain $20 million as a settlement for the Philippines, Carnegie offered McKinley "the same amount to purchase them from the United States in order to give them their independence." Having failed in this, he embarked on an extensive campaign with the clear purpose of "thwarting imperialism."[45]

The United States faced immediate opposition in the Philippines in the form of a national liberation movement. The movement was eventually defeated, but the costs were high. For the United States, the losses were more than 4,000 killed and 2,800 wounded. The Filipinos suffered much more: "About 18,000 of their soldiers were killed and between 100,000 and 200,000 noncombatants died on the sidelines in torched villages and famine in Spanish-style reconcentration camps, and from war-related diseases. Further souring the taste of America's imperial apple were shocking and all-too-true reports of widespread U.S. atrocities against both soldiers and civilians."[46]

This development, more than any other, "proved" the anti-imperialist case, an impact seen in subsequent policy making. With the death of McKinley in September 1901, Theodore Roosevelt, an ardent expansionist, assumed the presidency. Yet as Ernest R. May put it, "The United States did not continue a career as an imperial power." In Roosevelt's seven years of office, the only acquisition was the Panama Canal Zone, a ten-mile-wide strip across the isthmus. The nation's expansion as a colonial power, May writes, "effectively came to an end as of 1899 or 1900. . . . Imperialism as a current in American public opinion appeared to be dead."[47]

In 1946, the Philippines were granted independence. Those arguing that "powerful economic interests" are the driving force behind the imperialist efforts routinely overlook the opposite process: decolonization. The countermovement began when free trade was established between the United States and the colony in 1913. This stimulated the formation of a new anti-imperialist coalition when "American sugar, cotton, and dairy producers insisted on building protective walls against Philippine sugar and coconut oil imports." "It was not the American Anti-Imperialist League," Beisner writes, "but such organizations as the Beet Growers' Association, the Oklahoma Cottonseed Crushers' Association, and the American Farm Bureau Federation which finally helped rid the United States of her Far Eastern empire."[48]

The second imperialist conflict mentioned in Lenin's opening sentence was the Anglo–Boer War. The Boers, settlers of Dutch origin and Calvinist beliefs, had occupied lands on the southern tip of Africa in the 17th century and, among other things, enslaved the native populations. In 1808, in the midst of the Napoleonic wars, the British seized the Cape Colony to protect their sea lanes to India. Slavery was outlawed in the empire in 1834 and, shortly thereafter, the Boers began the Great Trek to the north, where they founded three independent states, Transvaal, the Orange Free State, and Natal. The latter was taken by the British in 1842. In 1877, Transvaal was annexed but the Boers fought back, successfully, and again achieved self-government. The discovery of gold and diamonds brought aggressive British settlers to the region, 44,000 of them by 1896, but they were a minority vis-à-vis the Boers, who in turn were a minority vis-à-vis the black population. Some of the British, interested in having things their way, took measures to achieve hegemony throughout the entire region, the plan being to bring the various states together in a Union of South Africa which would, of course, become part of the empire.

A first effort, the Jameson raid, was a dismal failure, discrediting its leader and a behind-the-scenes sponsor, Cecil Rhodes. A second effort of intervention was carried through by Alfred Milner, the High Commissioner to South Africa, the man on the spot, and by Joseph Chamberlain, an ardent imperialist, the Colonial Secretary in the British government. Rhodes was also very much involved in this effort. Salisbury and his cabinet, at a hastily called meeting, gave approval for the dispatch of troops on the basis of deficient and misleading information provided by the perpetrators. The persons driving the effort, it will be noted, were a key cabinet official, a colonial administrator, some British businessmen in South Africa, and some other settlers in the field. British bankers, the finance capitalists, do not appear as central figures in this effort.

The largest force since the Crimean War was dispatched. The takeover was expected to be brief and without difficulty, since the Boers had no organized military. But the Boers' irregular forces provided serious and stubborn resistance and the war lasted two and a half years. Some 400,000 British troops were required—against 60,000 Boers. Concentration camps were used to contain civilian populations, and some 20,000 died there. British foreign relations suffered when most of the rest of the world showed undisguised sympathy for the Boers. The latter ultimately surrendered on the basis of a promise that they would receive self-governing dominion status. Given the "whites only" suffrage, that would mean Boer dominance in subsequent elections. The Union of South Africa was formed in 1910, with dominion status, and Boer dominance followed.[49]

Chamberlain subsequently sought to create a unified empire with consultative institutions and coordinated defense arrangements. Most important, abandoning Britain's long-standing free-trade policy, he worked for a new tariff arrangement, one providing for "imperial preference." This became a central issue in the 1906 election campaign. The Liberal and Labor opposition countered with a very effective slogan, that the tariff was a "bread tax," and the Conservatives suffered a serious defeat.

The imperialist drive that had been building for centuries was stopped. The sudden, unexpected high costs of the Anglo–Boer War (the costs of lives, money, and national reputation) were the key factor. Alfred Cobban, in an essay on "The New Imperialism," summarized as follows:

The Boer War proved to be rather more than the military picnic so light-heartedly anticipated. It was not a masterpiece of political or military art, and it delivered a shock to the public conscience from which jingoism never really recovered. It was difficult to represent the victory of a great Empire over a tiny nation as a glorious triumph. The strong vein of humanitarianism in the country made any permanent acceptance of the doctrine of blood and iron impossible.[50]

Those high costs brought a definitive halt to Britain's "forward movement." From then on, from the Boer War to World War II, the empire is perhaps best described as a holding operation. The British Empire did increase by some 1,900,000 square miles in 1920. This resulted from the transfer of Germany's African colonies to Britain as League of Nation mandates.[51]

The Italian experience also revealed the costs of imperialism. The first attempt to take Ethiopia, in 1896, led to disaster. Facing many difficulties, Prime Minister Crispi needed a success to divert the public. The military felt the army "would become demoralized" without a war. General Baratieri, who was "both rash and incompetent," marched his troops to Adowa where, "with no accurate maps, with thoroughly ineffective intelligence, he led six thousand men to their deaths in a heroic but hopeless engagement. In one single day, March 1, 1896, as many Italians lost their lives as in all the wars of the *risorgimento* put together." Italy retained Eritrea, but it "was unsuitable as a colony of settlement because of its climate, and instead of paying for itself it would devour money through the costs of administration. Despite all the absurd nationalist propaganda, colonialism was materially a dead loss."[52]

The Italian government moved "forward" again in Libya in 1911–1912, an effort intended "to last a few weeks at a negligible cost [but which] dragged out . . . for over a year and seriously depleted Italian strength." The Italian involvement in World War I also aimed for imperial gains, but again the costs were heavy and the returns modest. Under Mussolini, Italy tried again, this time with a military success in Abyssinia. In 1939, with little difficulty, he conquered a very poor neighbor, Albania. His next venture, the invasion of Greece in 1940, proved disastrous.[53]

5. National liberation: As of 1900, Britain, France, and the United States, as indicated, had stopped their forward policies. Three other nations, three late developers, Germany, Japan, and Italy, continued their forward movement. Lenin could have observed the continued expansion of Japan, and he argued the imperial ambitions of Germany which, subsequently, in 1918, were clearly revealed in the Treaty of Brest-Litovsk. Germany lost her overseas colonies in 1919 with the Versailles settlement, but that did not prove the disaster Lenin had predicted.[54] Then, in 1944 and 1945, Germany lost most of "the east" (the contiguous territories acquired over several centuries), and that too, as the experience of subsequent decades showed, was no disaster. All three of the late developers were to pay heavy costs in the 1940s because of their imperialist efforts. After defeat and forced decolonization, all three experienced unprecedented economic growth. For the early imperialist nations—Britain, France, Belgium, and The Netherlands—the early postwar period, basically from 1945 to 1960, brought a sweeping decolonization. For them too, the correlate was unprecedented economic growth.[55]

Lenin's propositions may be assessed as follows:

1. Capital export: Rejected. The actual investment flows did not proceed in the directions Lenin predicted. The noteworthy fact is the relatively small share of foreign investment going to backward countries in the years reviewed by Lenin. In later decades, underdeveloped countries have faced a persistent opposite problem: Domestic savings accumulated there tend to flow outward to the advanced capitalist nations.

2. Superprofits: Rejected. Most foreign investment went elsewhere, not to the colonies. The rates of return from backward nations were often high, but that signaled a problem Lenin left unmentioned: the risk of default or, in the extreme case, the risk of repudiation.

3. Labor aristocrats: Rejected. The profits drawn from colonial investments, even if turned over to the workers or the aristocrats among them, were not sufficient for the task. No evidence was provided to document this alleged transfer of funds. If the concern were to "bribe" labor leaders, the relatively small sums required could easily have been drawn from domestic sources. But there too, no serious evidence was provided to support the claim.

4. Political dynamics: Rejected. If imperialism was required for the maintenance of capitalism, business leaders, fully conscious of their interests, would provide unambiguous support for the imperialist efforts. No support for this claim was provided in the original monograph. On the whole, business appears to have opposed imperialist efforts. This was evident from the outset, when British liberals denounced the Empire as "a vast system of poor relief" for the aristocracy. American business leaders opposed the Cuban involvement and the war with Spain.

5. National liberation struggles: Rejected. Liberation of the colonies would deny the superprofits to the former colonial powers. The class struggle would then be brought "back home" and the long-postponed proletarian revolution would follow. In fact, decolonization was followed by substantial, sustained, long-term economic growth. As conventionally measured, that growth has continued for a half-century.

COMMENTARY

Lenin's pamphlet dates from 1917, Feis's work from 1930. Both were published when the British Empire was intact. Cairncross published in 1953 when the empire was in dissolution. The literature on the subject has increased enormously since then. Two leading experts, P. J. Cain and A. G. Hopkins, began a 1980 article with a comment on the shift from certainties about British imperialism to "a debate so diverse and voluminous as to defy ready comprehension."[56]

One unambiguous fact about the late capitalist period is the exceptional character of the most visible of the empires; that is, the British case. One expert sums up as follows:

The expansion of British investment abroad from 1860 to 1914 was paralleled by expansions of trade, migration, culture and political sovereignty. Of the earth's land area, 10 per cent was added to the British empire. By 1914, with nearly a quarter of the earth's population and land mass the empire was the largest the world had known. The amounts of new territory taken in each half of the hundred years between 1815 and 1914 were roughly equal; many historians have given the last quarter of the nineteenth century the title, "the age of high imperialism" but this overemphasises the extent of the territory acquired in that period.[57]

Lenin's analysis, from the title onward, was of imperialism, the common or general process of advanced capitalism. But the asymmetries are much more striking. As of 1910, shortly before Lenin's writing, the four empires, British, French, German, and American, were markedly different in their size and resources. The British Empire, the largest in the history of the world, had a population of more than 350,000,000. Towering above the others, its population was seven times larger than the French Empire, the next largest contender. Most of the territory of the French Empire, it should be noted, was Saharan desert. The 1910 populations of the four empires, British, French, German, and American, were (in millions): 352, 52, 15, and 9. Britain's advantages, its opportunities for exploitation were presumably enormous. The differences after World War I were even more striking. Germany's empire was reduced to zero; Britain had gained more than 50,000,000 persons in its colonies. The 1925 populations of the British, French, and American empires were (in millions): 405, 56, and 12 (Table 4.3).

In 1910, Britain had twenty-three times as many colonials as Germany from whom it could "extract surplus value." British economic growth, accordingly, should have been outstanding. The differences in size of the colonial empires allow a test of Lenin's basic claim that colonies were key to the well-being of the leading capitalist nations. An examination of economic growth in three periods, 1880–1899, 1900–1913, and 1920–1929, allows some tests of Lenin's claim. The measure used is per capita growth of gross national product.

Following Lenin's assumptions, Britain should have been the unquestioned leader in all comparisons. In fact, of the eight comparisons, Britain led in only one, over France in the earliest period. In the five comparisons of 20th-century experience, the three other imperialist nations have rates of growth that are twice (or more) those of Britain (Table 4.4).

The British Empire was obviously unique. By far the largest of the imperialist undertakings, it differed also in that, for a while at least, it had a strong free-trade commitment. All the other leading capitalist nations, especially after the 1870s, operated behind serious tariff barriers. Britain, France, Germany, and the United States followed strikingly different colonial paths. Russia, also a major "player," had an empire that stretched across Asia and into North America. Italy, as seen, made repeated moves in Africa. And Japan, in some ways the

Table 4.3
Four Empires Compared: 1910 and 1925

	United Kingdom	France	Germany	United States
Year	1909-1910	1909	1910	1910
Population of the Nation	45,469,564	39,376,000	64,903,423	91,972,266[a]
Population of the Empire[b]	351,791,945	41,653,650	14,546,000	8,963,988
Territory of the Empire (sq. miles)[b]	11,333,471	4,776,126	1,027,820	138,187
Year	1921	1921	1919	1920
Population of the Nation	44,200,000	39,209,766[c]	59,857,283[c]	105,710,620[a]
Population of the Empire[b]	405,383,000	53,583,905	0	11,940,271
Territory of the Empire (sq. miles)[b]	13,260,793[d]	5,119,138[d]	0	125,182

Sources: J. S. Keltie, ed., *Statesman's Yearbook 1911* (London: Macmillan, 1911), U.K., p. xxxiv; France, pp. 751, 786; Germany, pp. 829, 862; U.S., pp. 359, 553, 555, 589, 561; J. S. Keltie and M. Epstein, eds., *Statesman's Yearbook 1922* (London: Macmillan, 1922), France, p. 864; Germany, p. 940; J. S. Keltie and M. Epstein, eds., *Statesman's Yearbook 1926* (London: Macmillan, 1926), U.K., p. xvii; U.S., p. 440.

[a]Continental United States without Alaska (64,356 in 1910 and 55,036 in 1920).

[b]Excludes population and territory of the imperial powers.

[c]Alsace and Lorraine (Rhin-Bas, Rhin-Haut, and Moselle) returned to France in 1919. Wartime losses of 1.4 million in France and 1.8 million in Germany.

[d]Includes territories mandated under the League of Nations.

boldest of all, defeated imperial Russia and later sought hegemony in China and in the colonial holdings of the United States, Britain, France, and The Netherlands.[58]

The kinds of controls used by the imperialist powers also differed, with important subsequent consequences. "One of the most widely recognized and powerful determinants of the likelihood of democracy among the new nations of the developing world is . . . whether or not the nation has been ruled by Britain."[59] A general theory, in short, one applicable to all advanced capitalist nations, seems inappropriate.

Two fundamental economic truths need consideration. First, with other things equal, the opportunities for profit, through trade or investment, are greater in rich nations than in poor ones. For European capitalists in the 19th and early 20th centuries, the greatest incentives

Table 4.4
Average Annual Per Capita Growth of National Product

	United Kingdom[a]	France[b]	Germany	United States[c]
1880	54	652	456	774
1899	65	720	660	1,000
Percentage Annual Average Change	0.9	0.5	1.6	1.2
1900	63	63	647	1,011
1913	68	83	769	1,351
Percentage Annual Average Change	0.6	1.9	1.2	1.9
1920	110	70		1,315
1929	124	111		1,671
Percentage Annual Average Change	1.2	4.1		2.4

[a]With the exception of France for the period 1880 to 1899 and the United States, the national income is from B. R. Mitchell, *European Historical Statistics 1750–1970* (Cambridge: Cambridge University Press, 1975). The French and British figures are based on gross national product, while German figures used net national product. The per capita incomes are denominated in that nation's currency and the price is standardized as follows: United Kingdom = 1,900 pounds; France = 1,938 francs; Germany = 1,913 marks. In order to derive the per capita income figures, the national income was divided by the estimated population for the years noted. The population was estimated using the two censuses that were nearest to the beginning and the end of the period examined. The average annual growth rate was then calculated. Using the nearest census as the base, the national population was estimated for the year cited. For example, the British 1880 per capita income figure used the 1881 census population as the base year, and the estimated growth rate for 1881–1901 was subtracted from the base year to obtain an estimate of the 1880 population. For the 1913 per capita income figure, the 1911 census was the base year and the average annual growth for the 1901–1911 period was added to the base year. With the exception of the United States, all per capita figures were estimated using this method. The census population figures were also obtained from Mitchell, *European Historical Statistics*.

[b]The per capita income estimates for France for the years 1880 and 1899 are based on the median of four national income estimates in *The Cambridge Economic History of Europe*, vol. 7, part 1, 289.

[c]The per capita GNP for the United States was obtained from the U.S. Bureau of the Census, *Historical Statistics of the United States: Colonial Times to 1970*, part 1 (Washington, D.C.: U.S. Bureau of the Census, 1976). The figures reflect the 1958 price of the dollar.

would be for trade and/or investment in other European nations or, later, in the United States. This conclusion is supported even in Lenin's crude figures.[60] Second, all economic patterns change with time; there are no constants in either the national or international arrangements. This is merely a special application of Heraclitus's general rule: All is flux. This is not to argue indeterminacy, but rather that the character of support for (and opposition to) expansionist efforts would change with the transformations of any economy.

Following the first of these rules, Britain would ordinarily have invested in and traded with the European continent. But from an early point, the United Kingdom's entrepreneurs faced serious difficulties: The continental nations blocked that "normal" route. Little was possible during the quarter-century of the French Revolution and the Napoleonic wars. Thereafter, national tariffs, again a political factor, blocked entry of British goods. Even before the coming of free trade, with the repeal of the Corn Laws in 1846, the "national liberal" tendencies on the continent involved larger trade territories, with modest barriers against outsiders. The most familiar of these was the Prussian Customs Union of 1834. In the late 1870s, tariff rates were increased all across Europe, from France to Russia. The United States operated similarly, erecting high tariff barriers to protect its infant industries. With access to continental markets restricted, Britain, more than any other nation, was motivated to turn outward; that is, to link its economy with those of societies elsewhere, some of them colonies, some "informally" linked, and some independent. "Expansion abroad," Cain and Hopkins write, "provided compensation for weakness in Europe."[61]

On the second point, altered circumstances, the incentives for British producers, investors, and supporters of empire changed over time. At one point, the concern was with tea, coffee, sugar, and spices; basically, a range of luxury goods. Later, the concern was with cotton, the raw material and outlets for manufactured products. Another episode involved railroad building and investments. And still later there was the development of the chemical and electrical industries. Each of these episodes had a different group of supporters, each with differing incentives.

In each of the episodes, it is important to recognize the assymetries as well as the parallels. Each nation built railroads, but those activities differed in timing and significance. The main trunk lines came early in Britain. The subsequent opportunities in that field were limited, basically to smaller branch lines that ordinarily brought more modest returns. The later opportunities in railroads had to be elsewhere, on the European continent, in North America, and, still later, in South America and in Asia. In a small country, other things equal, railroads count for less than in a large one. Two railroad magnates, the

Vanderbilts, father and son, were the richest men in the United States. Toward the turn of the century, still other railroad magnates—Hill, Harriman, and Huntington—gained wealth and importance. But no equivalent magnates or fortunes appeared in Britain, France, Germany, Belgium, or The Netherlands. The later major railroad-building efforts were to come in Anatolia, the Berlin-to-Bagdad line, in Russia with the Trans-Siberian route, and in China. That shift to overseas investment was "in the cards" and also was limited in time; it too was effectively an episode. Later investment in electrical and chemical industries was again largely domestic, as was, still later, investment in aircraft and in electronic data processing.[62]

An adequate theory of imperialism must recognize the diverse "support groups" behind the expansionist efforts. Among those driving the movement we have clergy, missionaries, the military (army and navy), settlers of all kinds (plantation owners, small holders), civil service (especially in the colonies), those supplying services to the colonies, men on the spot (economic–political entrepreneurs), and some groups of intellectuals. One should recognize also the importance of combinations. A key linkage in many settings (Algeria, Indochina, Angola) was the settler–military combinations, sometimes aided by men on the spot. Settlers and armed forces were natural allies in the original creation of offshore colonies. The same combination appears decisively in the decolonization phase where, as in Algeria and Indochina, they provided the determined last-ditch opposition to the efforts of the anti-imperialist forces in the metropolis.[63]

An adequate theory must also recognize the diverse range of groups opposed to imperialism. Policy outcomes would, in effect, be the results of a continuously changing "dialectical struggle." The composition of the pro and anti coalitions, as seen in the British and American experience at the turn of the century, obviously changed over time. One key dynamic element in all such contentions, of course, is the cost factor. Some pro groups, those who anticipated easy gains, shifted to opposition when the costs—money, reputation, and deaths—escalated. The suggestion, clearly, is that another theoretical framework is appropriate, basically that of pluralism, the argument of diverse power holders. That approach has the virtue of realism—consonance with evidence—as opposed to the unsupported claim, that the *haute bourgeoisie*, or *Finanzkapital*, alone was (or is) the decisive agency.

It is instructive to see what Lenin did with Hobson's original argument. Hobson put forth a thoughtful criticism of Britain's late 19th-century imperialism. He considered, and rejected, a range of causes. Reviewing trade figures, he showed that the new colonies provided no significant outlet for British products. He rejected also the claim that the new possessions provided an outlet for population. A small proportion of the nation's emigrants settled in British possessions and "an infinitesimally small fraction settled in the countries acquired under the new Imperialism."[64]

The crux of Hobson's argument appears in a chapter entitled "Economic Parasites of Imperialism." The expansionist effort, he held, was irrational for the nation; it was, however, rational "from the standpoint of certain classes in the nation." He provided a long list of beneficiaries, those receiving public monies for "ships, guns, military and naval equipment and stores," and those floating new public loans. There were "more posts for soldiers and sailors and [those] in the diplomatic and consular services," benefits for some classes of exports and for some manufacturers, and, finally, "employment for engineers, missionaries, speculative miners, ranchers, and other emigrants." His review, which covers several pages, also mentions those in the shipping trade as having "a very definite interest" in imperialism. He then returns to the military services, for whom the "itch for glory and adventure among military officers" has been "a most prolific source of expansion in India." Seconding the influence of the services is the "less organised but powerful sympathetic support on the part of the aristocracy and the wealthy classes, who seek in the services careers for their sons." Every expansion of the empire gave these same classes "new openings for their sons as ranchers, planters, engineers, or missionaries." Hobson concluded, "These influences, primarily economic, though not unmixed with other sentimental motives, are particularly operative in military, clerical, academic, and Civil Service circles, and furnish an interested bias towards Imperialism throughout the educated circles." Hobson added a famous quotation at this point, one he attributed to James Mill, namely that the colonies are "a vast system of outdoor relief for the upper classes."[65]

Hobson proceeded then to his pivotal argument: "By far the most important economic factor in Imperialism is the influence relating to investment." Every advanced industrial nation, he stated, "is tending to place a larger share of its capital . . . in foreign countries, or in colonies, and to draw a growing income from this source." He indicated, appropriately, that "no exact or even approximate estimate of the total amount of the income of the British nation derived from foreign investment is possible." He did, however, offer some indirect evidence based on income tax assessments that showed a near doubling of income from foreign sources between 1884 and 1903, and they, he sensed, understated the actual quantities. From this weak empirical base, Hobson offered his principal conclusion: "The modern foreign policy of Great Britain is primarily a struggle for profitable markets of investment." The conclusion is repeated with many variations and applied also to the foreign policy of France, Germany, and the United States.[66]

This argument was taken over by Lenin and made the cornerstone for his entire case. It is important to note the defects in Hobson's case. First, the evidence on the returns from invested capital is very weak; it is based on a poorly described indirect measure. Second, his figures do not indicate what part of those profits came from the colonies and what part from other nations. And third, his conclusion with regard to weight—"By far the most important economic factor in Imperialism is the influence relating to investments"—is merely asserted, not supported. His subsequent claims about the influence of "finance" are also unsubstantiated assertions. The city, he asserts, "notoriously exercises a subtle and abiding influence upon leading London newspapers, and through them upon the body of the provincial Press." Hobson's argument on this point is on a par with Lenin's claim of influence exercised in "a thousand different ways."[67]

Hobson and Lenin built very different conclusions on this cornerstone. Lenin's was an argument of necessity. Colonial expansion was something the capitalists had to do in order to survive. Hobson argued a mistaken choice: It was the "fallacy of the supposed inevitability of imperial expansion." Imperialism, he declared, was detrimental to the nation. It threatened the benefits of Britain's long-standing free-trade policy. It stimulated enormous armaments expenditures and brought the threat of major conflict. It brought enormous charges in the form of colonial administration. All these costs were incurred for the benefit of a collection of "parasites."

In a closely related argument, Hobson offered an underconsumption theory, this too allowing a choice. The upper classes were generating profits, not spending them, and thus accumulating significant savings that then required some investment opportunity. The working class and poor did not have sufficient earnings to purchase the goods produced in Britain, hence the regular recessions. Those savings were invested abroad and the nation as a whole suffered. Redistribution, he argued, would create a healthy economy without recourse to the "wreaking policy of Imperialism."[68] These contrasting claims would be put to a test after 1945, when decolonization, after some muddling and some armed struggle, became the new reality.

Lenin's original formulation of the imperialism theory is rarely cited in the contemporary social-science literature. Some of the specific claims, however, have been carried over and incorporated in subsequent theorizing, the most important of these being the arguments of capital export and exploitation of "the periphery." The carryover is most clearly seen in the influential "world-system theory" of Immanuel Wallerstein and his school. The principal difference vis-à-vis Lenin is the rejection of the "new imperialism" claim, with Wallerstein arguing that the pattern of exploitation has existed for centuries. Chirot and Hall, in a review article, summarize the position as follows: "Latin America, most of Asia, and later, Africa . . . were forced into different paths of development by Western powers. [England] proceeded only with the aid of the surplus it extorted from the societies it exploited." The critique of Lenin's work contained in this chapter would of course apply also to the world-systems position. The main point is that exploitation of the periphery was of peripheral importance for the development of the major capitalist nations.[69]

The second major difference vis-à-vis Lenin is the abandonment of the "formal" empire stipulation. The argument of "informal empire" has a long history, one long antedating the recent controversies. Britain, in the late 19th century, had formal control over the largest empire in the world's history. Robinson and Gallagher, providing ample documentation, report the British leaders actually preferred the informal style—it was less costly. This was their procedure in several nominally independent states of Latin America (Argentina, Brazil, and Peru).[70] Decolonization in 1945–1960 undermined Lenin's argument of formal empire (or direct rule) as the "ideal form." The economic takeoff that occurred in the major capitalist nations in this period severely damaged his claim about the necessity of imperialism and, on the surface at least, sustained Hobson's main argument that imperialism was a mistake that hindered development. To sustain the imperialism argument after 1960, a reversion to the informal empire argument was necessary. Decolonization, it was claimed, merely changed the appearances.

Most of the latter-day arguments of informal empire involve hypotheses about process and the ways in which imperial powers (or core nations) direct the affairs of smaller or weaker nations. Another option, one more easily assessed, is to focus on outcomes. A default (or a repudiation) is an indication of the failure of the informal controls. Another outcome, nationalization of foreign holdings, even more decisively attests to the failure of such controls.

A review of some cases is useful. British and American oil companies, in the early decades of this century, had significant investments in Mexico. All of that ended in 1938, when Mexico's president signed a decree which nationalized the holdings of seventeen companies. The British firms declared their loss at $250 million, the American firms reported a loss of $200 million. In the final settlement, the firms received a total of $24 million. The U.S. government did not intervene to alter this result. Dutch Shell and Standard Oil of New Jersey organized an extensive punitive campaign, but that effort collapsed with the onset of World War II.[71]

In 1960–1961, Cuba "unceremoniously liberated a billion dollars" in American fixed assets (p. 13). In 1968, Chile nationalized Anaconda's copper mines, promising $500 million in indemnification. The International Petroleum Corporation was nationalized by Peru, Occidental Petroleum by Libya, and Roan Selection by Zambia. The biggest event of all was the "repatriation" of oil properties by an assortment of Arab nations, followed by the formation of OPEC.[72] The most forceful response to these various actions was the boycott of Cuba organized by the U.S. government. The OPEC revolution had the most far-reaching consequences, but that problem was ultimately resolved, basically by market forces. The cartel was not able to maintain its control over world oil prices. In the 1990s, the real cost of gasoline for the American consumer was less than that paid in the 1950s.

None of these nationalizations, addressing Lenin's point, produced serious lasting damage to the American economy. All of them, addressing the subsequent argument, demonstrate the ineffectiveness of any prior informal controls. The limited response—or nonresponse—by the U.S. government indicates either an unwillingness to undertake more forceful measures, a perceived inability to do so, or, possibly, a sense that such measures were not necessary or appropriate. Regardless of the motives involved, the fact is that the informal controls failed and, apart from Cuba, little or nothing was done to rectify the problem.

Dependency theory is another development having some links with the Lenin original. Focusing on economic "penetration" by the major capitalist nations, it differs strikingly, however, in that its concern is with the effects on the exploited nations of the periphery. Their persistent underdevelopment and consequent poverty stems from colonial experience and the continuing impacts of that heritage. The experience of the Pacific rim "tiger" nations—South Korea, Taiwan, Malaysia, and Indonesia—at least up to the mid-1990s economic troubles, provides a serious challenge to the central arguments of this position. The recent experience of China also provides a challenge. Two recent research studies have dealt a serious blow to the underlying empirical claims of this position.[73]

As noted earlier, few experts give credence to Lenin's imperialism argument. That conclusion holds for diplomatic historians, economic historians, and the overwhelming majority of economists. Support for the claims continues within various pockets of academia—among the adherents of the Monthly Review school, among those of the world-systems school, those arguing the dependency theory, and, here and there, on the margins of sociology. That loyalty appears to depend on continued use of Lenin's method, the neglect of readily available evidence.[74]

NOTES

1. All references here are to the readily available "Little Lenin Library" edition (New York: International Publishers, 1939), vol 15. Page references appear in the text in parentheses. The monograph appears also in V. I. Lenin, *Collected*

Works, vol. 22 (Moscow: Progress Publishers, 1964), 185–304. I checked all passages quoted here against that version but found no significant differences.

The monograph was written in Zurich in 1916. Lenin's preface is dated April 26, 1917. The Russian language edition gives the date of publication as April 1917. The English edition gives September 1917. For some history and commentary, see Louis Fischer, *The Life of Lenin* (New York: Harper & Row, 1964), 95–107; Robert Service, *Lenin: A Political Life*, vol. 2, *Worlds in Collision* (Bloomington: Indiana University Press, 1991), 113–118; and Dmitri Volkogonov, *Lenin: A New Biography*, trans. Harold Shukman (New York: Free Press, 1994), 103–104. For more detail, see Neil Harding, *Lenin's Political Thought*, vol. 2, *Theory and Practice in the Socialist Revolution* (London: Macmillan, 1981), ch. 3.

For overviews, comment, and critique, see George Lichtheim, *Imperialism* (New York: Praeger, 1971), chs. 7–9; Wolfgang J. Mommsen, *Theories of Imperialism*, trans. P. S. Falla (New York: Random House, 1980); V. G. Kiernan, *Marxism and Imperialism* (London: Edward Arnold, 1974), ch. 1; Bill Warren, *Imperialism: Pioneer of Capitalism*, ed. John Sender (London: NLB, 1980); Norman Etherington, *Theories of Imperialism: War, Conquest and Capital* (London: Croom Helm, 1984); and Anthony Brewer, *Marxist Theories of Imperialism: A Critical Survey*, 2d ed. (London: Routledge, 1990).

Although regularly referred to as Lenin's theory, elements of this position appeared earlier in the work of Kautsky, Luxemburg, and Bukharin. See Kiernan, *Marxism*, 8–36; and Brynjolf J. Hovde, "Socialistic Theories of Imperialism Prior to the Great War," *Journal of Political Economy* 38 (1928): 569–591.

2. Lenin's difficulties with this change are reviewed in Bertram D. Wolfe, *Marxism: One Hundred Years in the Life of a Doctrine* (New York: Dial, 1965), 88–97. Lenin was most emphatic on this point: "In 1891 no imperialism existed at all (I have tried to show in my pamphlet that it was born in 1898–1900, not earlier)." See V. I. Lenin, letter to Inessa Armand, 25 December 1916, in *Collected Works*, vol. 35 (Moscow: Progress Publishers, 1966), 268.

3. Etherington, *Theories of Imperialism*, 131. Three influential English-language works in the Leninist tradition are Paul A. Baran, *The Political Economy of Growth* (New York: Monthly Review Press, 1957); Paul A. Baran and Paul M. Sweezy, *Monopoly Capital: An Essay on the American Economic and Social Order* (New York: Monthly Review Press, 1966); and Harry Magdoff, *The Age of Imperialism: The Economics of U.S. Foreign Policy* (New York: Monthly Review Press, 1969). For a thorough and well-documented critique of their work, see S. M. Miller and Roy Bennett, "A New-Imperialism Critique: Do the Rich Nations Need the Poor?" New York University, *Center for International Studies Policy Papers* 4, 1 (1971). Eric Hobsbawm, the noted British historian, describes Lenin's argument about the "new phase of capitalism" as "undoubtedly right in principle, though not necessarily in the details of its theoretical model." See Hobsbawm, *The Age of Empire, 1875–1914* (New York: Pantheon, 1987), 72.

4. U.S. Bureau of the Census, *Historical Statistics of the United States, Colonial Times to 1970* (Washington, D.C.: U.S. Government Printing Office, 1975), series U26-39.

5. Herbert Feis, *Europe the World's Banker, 1870–1914* (1930; reprint New York: Norton, 1965). Some other works covering the same ground, a small sample from a very large literature, are A. K. Cairncross, *Home and Foreign*

Investment, 1870–1913: Studies in Capital Accumulation (Cambridge: Cambridge University Press, 1953); D. K. Fieldhouse, *Economics and Empire, 1830–1914* (London: Weidenfeld and Nicolson, 1973); P. L. Cottrell, *British Overseas Investment in the Nineteenth Century* (London: Macmillan, 1975); P. J. Cain, *Economic Foundations of British Overseas Expansion 1815–1914* (London: Macmillan, 1980); Michael Edelstein, *Overseas Investment in the Age of High Imperialism: The United Kingdom, 1850–1914* (New York: Columbia University Press, 1982); D.C.M. Platt, *Britain's Investment Overseas on the Eve of the First World War: The Use and Abuse of Numbers* (London: Macmillan, 1986); and P. J. Cain and A. G. Hopkins, *British Imperialism: Innovation and Expansion, 1688–1914* (London: Longman, 1993). A very important work dealing with the political aspects is William L. Langer, *The Diplomacy of Imperialism, 1890–1902*, 2d ed. (1951; reprint New York: Knopf, 1972).

6. Feis, *Europe*, 11. Feis gives his source as C. K. Hobson, *The Export of Capital* (London: Constable, 1914), 204. The dramatic fluctuations are clearly indicated in the series contained there. The cyclical character of overseas investment has of course been repeatedly confirmed. Much of the later scholarship has focused on the sources of the fluctuations. For a brief overview covering the same period, see Cottrell, *British Overseas Investment*.

Lenin's key source was John A. Hobson, *Imperialism: A Study* (Edinburgh: Ballantyne, Hanson, 1902). This edition is the one cited by Lenin. A second and revised edition, the one cited by Feis, appeared in 1905 (London: Archibald Constable). In 1938, Hobson published a third edition, basically a reissue of the second with added appendices (London: George Allen and Unwin). The latter has been reprinted several times. The fourth edition used here is a reprint of the third (Ann Arbor: University of Michigan Press, 1965). For comprehensive reviews and comment, see D. K. Fieldhouse, "'Imperialism': An Historiographical Revision," *Economic History Review*, 2d ser., 14 (1961): 187–209; and P. J. Cain, "J. A. Hobson, Cobdenism, and the Radical Theory of Economic Imperialism, 1898–1914," *Economic History Review*, 2d ser., 31 (1978): 565–584. Cain shows that Hobson's *Imperialism* was "an interim statement," one that was "modified drastically" in his later writing. See also William L. Langer, "A Critique of Imperialism," *Foreign Affairs* 14 (1935): 102–119; and David S. Landes, "Some Thoughts on the Nature of Economic Imperialism," *Journal of Economic History* 21 (1961): 496–512.

Most accounts of Hobson's argument focus, understandably, on business, capitalists, bankers, and so forth. At one point, a strong anti-Semitic emphasis appears: Hobson intimated that it was Jewish financiers who, "situated in the very heart of the business capital of every State . . . are in a unique position to manipulate the policy of nations" (pp. 56–57). This argument is assessed, with evidence, by Fritz Stern, *Gold and Iron: Bismarck, Bleichröder, and the Building of the German Empire* (New York: Knopf, 1977), 395, 416–418.

7. Feis, *Europe*, 12. Argentina's foreign debt, Feis reports, was "mainly held" in Britain. Lenin classified Argentina among the "Countries Financially Dependent on Germany" (291).

8. Ibid., 23. Feis's figures were adopted from a work by Paish, one of Lenin's sources. Lenin, however, did not cite that specific source, which perhaps was not available to him in Zurich.

Mark Blaug notes that "even within the Empire, Canada, Australia, and New Zealand—hardly outstanding examples of the ruinous effect of imperialism—accounted for one-half of British investment, and more was invested in Australia and New Zealand alone than in India and the whole of Africa." See Blaug, "Economic Imperialism Revisited," *Yale Review* 50 (1960): 335–347. The quote is from p. 341.

9. Feis, *Europe*, 23, 25; and Blaug, "Economic Imperialism," 341–342. See also Leland H. Jenks, "Britain and American Railway Development," *Journal of Economic History* 4 (1951): 375–388; and Dorothy R. Adler, *British Investment in American Railways, 1834–1898* (Charlottesville: University Press of Virginia, 1970). Much of the literature on British foreign investment depends, directly or indirectly, on estimates generated by George Paish, the first and most significant of these appearing in 1909. These have been subjected to criticism by Platt, *Britain's Investment Overseas*. The long-standing convention, based on Paish, holds that the "stock" (total) of Britain's overseas investment placed between 1870 and 1913 amounted to £4 billion, which produced a return of £200 million (or 5%). Platt argues that some of the £4 billion was held by other nationals and that some had been repatriated. He concludes that the total was £3.1 billion (pp. 8, 59). Some commentators have challenged Platt's conclusion. For an overview of the subsequent discussion, see Cain and Hopkins, *British Imperialism*, 173–176.

Platt also argues that the focus on the total placed in the entire period neglects the question of flows—the amounts placed annually—and thus overlooks changes in the overall pattern. In the period 1908 to 1913, Canada had become the leading receiver of British investment funds, which was followed at some distance by the United States. In third place was Argentina. In this period more was invested in Brazil than in India and Ceylon (*Britain's Investment Overseas*, 89).

10. Feis, *Europe*, 23. Blaug, "Economic Imperialism," 344, reports that "more European capital flowed to Japan in the years 1890–1914 than to all the rest of Asia."

11. Feis, *Europe*, 43–49. Spain, Italy, Austria, and so on were not, of course, colonies of France. The objects of this investment, moreover—railroads and canals, infrastructure—were not those ordinarily focused on by Lenin—raw materials and production. Because of the size, infrastructure ventures are ordinarily initiated and directed by governments and by politicians, not by capitalists. And the ordinary form of investment, accordingly, is bonds. Lenin recognized the problem, touching on it in two brief sentences: "The possibility of exporting capital is created by the fact that numerous backward countries have been drawn into international capitalist intercourse; main railways have either been built or are being built there; the elementary conditions for industrial development have been created" (63).

12. Feis, *Europe*, 49–51. Platt presents a table showing seventeen estimates of French overseas investment in the years prior to World War I. Paish, one of Lenin's sources, estimates £1.7 billion. Sixteen of the estimates range between £1.2 billion (the earliest figure, for 1901) and £1.8 billion. Lenin's figure, the outlier, is £2.4 billion. See Platt, *Britain's Investment Overseas*, 132.

13. Feis, *Europe*, 50.

14. Ibid., 51–52.

15. Ibid., 55–56.

16. Ibid., 61–62.

17. Ibid., 69–70. On the Northern Pacific, see Sig Mickelson, *The Northern Pacific Railroad and the Selling of the West: A Nineteenth Century Public Relations Venture* (Sioux Falls, S.D.: Center for Western Studies/Pine Hill Press, 1993).

18. Ibid., 72, 73.

19. Ibid., 73–78.

20. For further discussion of the German case, see Prosser Gifford and William Roger Louis, eds., *Britain and Germany in Africa: Imperial Rivalry and Colonial Rule* (New Haven: Yale University Press, 1967); Hartmut Pogge von Strandmann, "Domestic Origins of Germany's Colonial Expansion under Bismarck," *Past and Present* 42 (1969): 140–159; Hans-Ulrich Wehler, *Bismarck und der Imperialismus* (Cologne: Kiepenheuer and Witsch, 1969); Helmut Böhme, "Thesen zur Beurteilung der gesellschaftlichen, wirtschaftlichen und politischen Ursachen des deutschen Imperialismus," in *Der moderne Imperialismus*, ed. Wolfgang J. Mommsen (Stuttgart: Kohlhammer, 1971); Wolfgang J. Mommsen, *Der europäische Imperialismus* (Göttingen: Vandenhoeck and Ruprecht, 1979), ch. 3; and Stern, *Gold and Iron*, ch. 15. See also W. O. Henderson, "British Economic Activity in the German Colonies, 1884–1914," *Economic History Review* 15 (1945): 56–66. Henderson reports that there "was no attempt to secure for the mother country a monopoly of colonial trade by means of tariff preferences. German and foreign merchants paid the same rate of duties" (p. 58). See also W. O. Henderson, *The German Colonial Empire, 1884–1919* (London: Cass, 1993).

The risks and losses appear frequently in these works. Stern reports that between 1854 and 1875 the Ottoman Empire had contracted a foreign debt of £200 million. In 1875, the Ottoman government "reduced the interest rate on the outstanding debt by half; a year later it suspended payments altogether" (Stern, *Gold and Iron*, 419). For a portrait of Germany's leading imperialist, a "man on the spot," see Martin Reuss, "The Disgrace and Fall of Carl Peters: Morality, Politics and Staatsräson in the Time of Wilhelm II," *Central European History* 14 (1981): 110–141.

21. On German aspirations in World War I, see Gerald D. Feldman, ed., *German Imperialism, 1914–1918: The Development of a Historical Debate* (New York: Wiley, 1972). Also important in this connection is Lamar Cecil, *Albert Ballin: Business and Politics in Imperial Germany, 1888–1918* (Princeton: Princeton University Press, 1967). Ballin was the managing director of the Hamburg–American Line, the world's largest steamship company. The company suffered heavy losses in August 1914, either through confiscation or through internment of ships in neutral ports.

22. C. H. Feinstein, *National Income, Expenditure and Output of the United Kingdom, 1855–1965* (Cambridge: Cambridge University Press, 1972), Table 19.

23. Cairncross, *Home and Foreign Investment*, 4, 2, 3. Those returns, it should be noted, are based on Paish's estimates. For some comment and criticism, see Platt, *Britain's Investment Overseas*, 80–81.

24. Cairncross, *Home and Foreign Investment*, 3.

25. Ibid., 8–9. Marx was mistaken with his insistent focus on "industry" and the "means of production." The cotton industry looms large in popular accounts of the period. It was Britain's largest manufacturing industry, em-

ploying a half-million workers and providing a third of its exports. But the amount of capital involved in 1875, £100 million, was less than that involved in railways. Employment in the cotton industry increased in later decades, but the capital needs were modest.

One other comment by Cairncross deserves attention: "It would be a serious error to study investment fifty years ago as if we knew, or ever could know, all the facts. We are ignorant enough in 1952 of many of the most elementary facts about *current* investment, for all that our curiosity on the subject is so much sharper and our statistical dossier so much bulkier" (p. 10). Feis too alerts his readers, at many points, to the inadequacies of the evidence at his disposal. These statements must be taken in conjunction with Lenin's comment about "irrefutable bourgeois statistics" (9). See also D.C.M. Platt, *Britain's Investment Overseas*; and D.C.M. Platt, *Mickey Mouse Numbers in World History: A Short View* (London: Macmillan, 1989).

26. Cairncross, *Home and Foreign Investment*, 225; Feis, *Europe*, 51.

27. Blaug, "Economic Imperialism," 340. See also Platt, *Britain's Investment Overseas*, 82–83.

Many accounts are one-sided in their reporting of the flows, focusing exclusively, for example, on the profits returned to Britain from elsewhere. But investors from other economically advanced countries had holdings in Britain and they too were returning profits to their home countries. But this flow, typically, goes unreported. It is another example of the benefits-without-costs approach to economics. A considerable part of the investment in the Manchester cotton industry was of German origin. Friedrich Engels's family was directly involved there. The Souchays, one branch of Max Weber's family, were major investors. See Stanley Chapman, *Merchant Enterprise in Britain: From the Industrial Revolution to World War I* (Cambridge: Cambridge University Press, 1992), 91, 145; Guenther Roth, "Weber the Would-Be Englishman: Anglophilia and Family History," in *Weber's Protestant Ethic, Origins, Evidence, Contexts*, ed. Hartmut Lehmann and Guenther Roth (Cambridge: Cambridge University Press: 1993), 83–121; and Guenther Roth, "Heidelberg–London–Manchester: Zu Max Webers deutsch–englischer Familiengeschichte," in *Heidelberg im Schnittpunkt intellektueller Kreise*, ed. Hubert Treiber and Karol Sauerland (Opladen: Westdeutscher Verlag, 1995), 184–209.

28. Cairncross, *Home and Foreign Investment*, 223–224. Cottrell, *British Overseas Investment*, 55, states that in Britain, from 1911 to 1913, "the return on domestic physical capital was 10.7 per cent, while on foreign bonds it was only 4.7 per cent." The former, he notes, was primarily private equity capital, the latter, obviously, loans. There was, he states, "some bias of the market in favour of foreign issues." For more detail, see D. N. McCloskey, "Did Victorian Britain Fail?" *Economic History Review*, 2d ser., 23 (1970): 446–459; and the response by W. P. Kennedy, "Foreign Investment, Trade and Growth in the United Kingdom, 1873–1913," *Explorations in Economic History* 11 (1974): 415–444. Cottrell, *British Overseas Investment*, 21, incidentally, touches on another cluster of losing investments; that is, "the partial or complete default of Arkansas, Illinois, Indiana, Mississippi, Louisiana, Maryland, Michigan, Pennsylvania and Florida in the 1840s."

29. Cairncross, *Home and Foreign Investment*, 225.

30. Ibid., 224. Feis also commented on the quality of information available to investors, noting some differences between nations. Individual investors in Germany, he wrote, "retained more independence of judgment than in France. The financial journals were better informed and more honest." German investment leadership, he said, "was more informed, vigorous, and conscientious than the French, more dominant, but also more circumscribed than the British." Later, "French capital was more freely and cheaply available for European borrowers; French savers showed less anxiety regarding the solvency of badly governed states." See Feis, *Europe*, 67–68, 73.

31. In 1909, August Bebel accused the business manager and editors of the *Sozialistische Monatshefte* of seeking funds from certain "bourgeois politicians in Frankfurt." The allegation must have been a flimsy one, since the controversy "did not even stir up a breeze and was soon forgotten." William Harvey Maehl, *August Bebel: Shadow Emperor of the German Workers* (Philadelphia: American Philosophical Society, 1980), 452.

The *Monatshefte* was edited by Joseph Bloch, described by Rudolf Hilferding as the true "impresario of German revisionism." Dr. Leo Arons, a socialist and a *Privatdozent* in physics at the University of Berlin, was the journal's principal financial supporter. Arons was the son-in-law of liberal banker Julius Bleichröder, whose brother, Gerson, was Bismarck's banker. See Fritz Stern, *Gold and Iron*, 543; and Roger Fletcher, *Revisionism and Empire: Socialist Imperialism in Germany, 1897–1914* (London: George Allen and Unwin, 1984), ch. 2. The journal, it should be noted, supported imperialism.

Gerald D. Feldman reports that in the early 1920s the journal received "substantial financial assistance from certain big business circles." See Feldman, "The Social and Economic Policies of German Big Business, 1918–1929," *American Historical Review* 75 (1969): 48. This could be taken as an instance of bribery or, more precisely, as manipulation designed to insure moderate outlooks on the part of Germany's workers. This fact, however, does not save Lenin's argument about the necessity of imperialism. The sums involved, as a share of annual corporate profits, would have been modest, something that could have come out of the "small change" account of any major firm.

A cautionary note: The validity of the revisionist claims reviewed in the previous chapter must stand or fall on the basis of evidence. Sponsorship—who "paid the piper"—is a separate question.

32. Joseph Schumpeter, "Imperialism," in *Imperialism and Social Classes*, ed. Paul M. Sweezy (New York: A. M. Kelley, 1951), 12. Schumpeter argues further that for Disraeli, the term remained a catch phrase. It was not followed by new policy initiatives (pp. 13–16). See also Robert Blake, *Disraeli* (1967; reprint New York: Carrol and Graf, 1987), 523–524, 760; Sarah Bradford, *Disraeli* (New York: Stein and Day, 1982), 295, 303–304, 363–369; and Stanley Weintraub, *Disraeli: A Biography* (New York: Truman Talley/Dutton, 1993), 503–505. For a more extensive review, see Richard Koebner and Helmut Dan Schmidt, *Imperialism: The Story and Significance of a Political Word, 1840–1960* (Cambridge: Cambridge University Press, 1964).

Richard Cobden and John Bright, perhaps the two leading liberal intellectual activists of the century, were both strong opponents of empire and imperialism and, more generally, of all foreign political involvement. See Wendy

Hinde, *Richard Cobden: A Victorian Outsider* (New Haven: Yale University Press, 1987), 16–20, 26–27; and James L. Sturgis, *John Bright and the Empire* (London: Athlone, 1969). For a sample of Cobden's views, see Cobden, *England, Ireland, and America*, ed, Richard Ned Lebow (1835, reprint Philadelphia: Institute for the Study of Human Issues, 1980), 24–25, 34, 36, 85, 104.

33. Ronald Robinson, John Gallagher, and Alice Denny, *Africa and the Victorians: The Climax of Imperialism* (New York: St. Martin's, 1961), 23.

For accounts of the chief actors and decision making, see A. L. Kennedy, *Salisbury, 1830–1903: Portrait of a Statesman* (London: John Murray, 1953), chs. 19, 20; Denis Judd, *Radical Joe: A Life of Joseph Chamberlain* (London: Hamish Hamilton, 1977), chs. 10, 11; Richard Jay, *Joseph Chamberlain: A Political Study* (Oxford: Clarendon Press, 1981), chs. 8, 9; Robert I. Rotberg, *The Founder: Cecil Rhodes and the Pursuit of Power* (New York: Oxford University Press, 1988); John Marlowe, *Milner: Apostle of Empire* (London: Hamish Hamilton, 1976); and Terence H. O'Brien, *Milner: Viscount Milner of St. James's and Cape Town, 1854–1925* (London: Constable, 1979). For the "limps," see H.C.G. Matthew, *The Liberal Imperialists: The Ideas and Politics of a Post-Gladstonian Elite* (London: Oxford University Press, 1973).

34. Robinson and Gallagher, *Africa*, 464. At this point there were two lines of communication with India, through Suez and around the Cape.

35. Ibid., 11–13.

36. This paragraph and the one that follows summarize the description contained in Clayton Roberts and David Roberts, *A History of England*, 3d ed., vol. 2 (Englewood Cliffs, N.J.: Prentice Hall, 1991), 683–684. For more details, see A. P. Thornton, *The Imperial Idea and Its Enemies: A Study in British Power* (London: Macmillan, 1959), chs. 1, 2 (for a discussion of Henty, see pp. 92–94); and C. J. Lowe, *The Reluctant Imperialists: British Foreign Policy, 1878–1902* (New York: Macmillan, 1969). See also the brief account of Henty in Patrick A. Dunae, *Dictionary of Literary Biography*, vol. 18, *Victorian Novelists after 1885*, ed. Ira B. Nadel and William E. Freedman (Detroit: Gale Research, 1983), 142–148. In the early 1890s, Henty's "books were selling 150,000 copies annually in Britain and between 25,000 and 50,000 copies in Canada and the United States. His books were also in great demand in elementary schools." Many commentators see Kipling as the leading literary advocate of the imperial mission. It is likely that Henty's influence was much greater. See also Guy Arnold, *Held Fast for England: G. A. Henty, Imperialist Boys' Writer* (London: Hamish Hamilton, 1980), ch. 2. For a brief overview of this genre, see Patrick A. Dunae, "Boys' Literature and the Idea of Empire, 1870–1914," *Victorian Studies* 24 (1980): 105–121.

37. Roberts and Roberts, *History*, 686. For more detail on the dynamics involved, see John S. Galbraith, "The 'Turbulent Frontier' as a Factor in British Expansion," *Comparative Studies in Society and History* 2 (1960): 150–168; Robert A. Huttenback, *The British Imperial Experience* (New York: Harper & Row, 1966), ch. 5; and Roger D. Long, ed., *The Man on the Spot: Essays in British Imperial History* (Westport, Conn.: Greenwood Press, 1995).

38. Schumpeter, "Imperialism," 15–16. The government in this case, it will be noted, was anticipating a "public opinion." For a study of one important episode, see Richard Price, *An Imperial War and the British Working Class: Working-Class Attitudes and Reactions to the Boer War, 1899–1902* (London: Routledge

and Kegan Paul, 1972). See also, Landes, "Some Thoughts," 506–512. For discussion of cable communications, see James A. Field, Jr., "American Imperialism: The Worst Chapter in Almost Any Book," *American Historical Review* 83 (1978): 644–668, especially, 660–663.

39. Hobson, *Imperialism*, 83. The United States comes in for much attention on his pp. 77–85.

40. Julius W. Pratt, *The Expansionists of 1898: The Acquisition of Hawaii and the Spanish Islands* (1936; reprint Chicago: Quadrangle, 1964), ch. 7. The quotations are from pp. 234–235.

41. Vincent P. Carosso, *The Morgans: Private International Bankers, 1854–1913* (Cambridge: Harvard University Press, 1987), 349; and Ron Chernow, *The House of Morgan: An American Banking Dynasty and the Rise of Modern Finance* (New York: Atlantic Monthly Press, 1990), 80. A recent biography of the financier concurs on all points, see Jean Strouse, *Morgan: American Financier* (New York: Random House, 1999), 369–371. The leading biography of George W. Perkins, Morgan's principal executive in this period, contains no index reference to Cuba, Spain, or the war. See John A. Garraty, *Right-Hand Man: The Life of George W. Perkins* (New York: Harper, 1960).

42. Allen Nevins, *John D. Rockefeller: The Heroic Age of American Enterprise*, vol. 1 (New York: Scribner, 1940), 359, 368, 377, 412; and Allen Nevins, *John D. Rockefeller: A Study in Power*, 2 vols. (New York: Scribner, 1953). For the history of Standard Oil, see Ralph W. Hidy and Muriel E. Hidy, *Pioneering in Big Business, 1882–1911* (New York: Harper, 1955), 128; see also Ron Chernow, *Titan: The Life of John D. Rockefeller, Sr.* (New York: Random House, 1998), 388, 487, 569. Two other accounts containing no mention of the war are Peter Collier and David Horowitz, *The Rockefellers: An American Dynasty* (New York: Holt, Rinehart, and Winston, 1976); and John Ensor Harr and Peter J. Johnson, *The Rockefeller Century* (New York: Scribner, 1988).

43. Joseph Frazier Wall, *Andrew Carnegie* (1970; reprint Pittsburgh: University of Pittsburgh Press, 1989), 690.

44. Ibid., 691. For another account of Carnegie's reactions which points up some significant contradictions in his position, see Robert L. Beisner, *Twelve against Empire: The Anti-Imperialists, 1898–1900* (1968; reprint Chicago: Imprint Publications, 1992), ch. 8. Carnegie "reconciled himself" to a possible annexation of Cuba. He favored, for strategic reasons, the taking of Puerto Rico and Hawaii (p. 176).

45. Wall, *Carnegie*, 695–713. Hobson passed over Carnegie, instead putting Charles M. Schwab, the president of Carnegie Steel, on his list of presumed imperialists. A biography contains nothing on his attitude toward imperialism and the war. Some discussion of the price of armor plate for warships appears, but that is another issue. See Robert Hessen, *Steel Titan: The Life of Charles M. Schwab* (New York: Oxford University Press, 1975). Hobson also listed Mark Hanna as an imperialist, but he was opposed to the war. See Thomas Beer, *Hanna* (New York: Knopf, 1929), 197–198, 206.

46. Robert L. Beisner, *From the Old Diplomacy to the New: 1865–1900*, 2d ed. (Arlington Heights, Ill.: Harlan Davidson, 1986), 140–141. See also Stanley Karnow, *In Our Image: America's Empire in the Philippines* (New York: Random House, 1989), chs. 6, 7.

47. Ernest R. May, *American Imperialism: A Speculative Essay* (New York: Atheneum, 1968), 12–15.

48. Beisner, *Twelve against Empire*, 106. America's university students would not be prepared to assess either Hobson's or Lenin's reading of business, the war, and the resulting expansion. I reviewed seven American history textbooks. Only one cited Pratt's *Expansionists*. None of them provided a clear statement of Pratt's findings

49. Robinson and Gallagher, *Africa*, ch. 14; Thomas Pakenham, *The Scramble for Africa, 1876–1912* (New York: Random House, 1991), chs. 27, 31; Thomas Pakenham, *The Boer War* (London: Weidenfeld and Nicolson, 1979); and Byron Farwell, *The Great Anglo–Boer War* (Toronto: Fitzhenry and Whiteside, 1976). See also the sources cited in note 33.

50. Alfred Cobban, *France Since the Revolution and Other Aspects of Modern History* (London: Jonathan Cape, 1970), 164–172. The quotation is from p. 171.

51. On the disposition of the German colonies, see William Roger Louis, *Great Britain and Germany's Lost Colonies, 1914–1919* (Oxford: Clarendon Press, 1967). It is a complicated history. The German overseas empire, Louis reports, never ran a profit; in 1913, the deficit amounted to over £6 million. The transfer of the colonies, in effect, amounted to a transfer of losing enterprises, most to Britain, some to France, and some to Japan. Much of the discussion in 1919 argued strategic concerns as opposed to economic advantages. The most vociferous demands came from British dominions. South Africa was given the mandate for German Southwest Africa, Australia was given the Bismarck Archipelago, and New Zealand was given Samoa.

52. See Denis Mack Smith, *Italy: A Modern History*, rev. ed. (Ann Arbor: University of Michigan Press, 1969), 182–187. The quotations are from p. 185. See also pp. 272–273; and Langer, *Diplomacy of Imperialism*, 271–282.

Still another demonstration of the rising costs occurred in the summer of 1900, when, in the previously subdued territory of Peking, the Boxers rose in arms. This struggle required an eight-nation expedition led by British, American, Russian, and Japanese units to restore the "peace." For a brief account, see John King Fairbank, Edwin O. Reischauer, and Albert M. Craig, *East Asia: The Modern Transformation* (Boston: Houghton Mifflin, 1965), 394–404. See also Chester T. Tan, *The Boxer Catastrophe* (New York: Columbia University Press, 1955); Victor Purcell, *The Boxer Uprising: A Background Study* (Cambridge: Cambridge University Press, 1963); and Joseph Esherick, *The Origins of the Boxer Uprising* (Berkeley and Los Angeles: University of California Press, 1987).

53. Mack Smith, *Italy*, 272–281 (Libya), 282–337 (World War I), 446–453 (Abyssinia), 465–466 (Albania), 477–479 (Greece).

54. Post–World War I Germany faced many serious problems. In addition to the loss of colonies, the nation was obliged to pay large sums for reparations and experienced the ruinous inflation culminating in 1923. The reparations costs were countered, beginning in 1924, by sizable short-term American investments. Most commentators see the years from 1924 to 1929 as ones of substantial economic growth. Those were the Weimar republic's "good years." From Lenin's perspective, lacking any colonies, Germany should have had no good years.

55. Henri Grimal, *Decolonization: The British, French, Dutch and Belgian Empires 1919–1963*, trans. Stephan De Vos (1965; reprint Boulder, Colo.: Westview,

1978); Michael Barratt Brown, *After Imperialism*, rev. ed. (New York: Humanities Press, 1970); Miles Kahler, *Decolonization in Britain and France: The Domestic Consequences of International Relations* (Princeton: Princeton University Press, 1984); Raymond F. Betts, *France and Decolonisation, 1900–1960* (New York: St. Martin's, 1991). On The Netherlands, see H. L. Wesseling, "Post-Imperial Holland," *Journal of Contemporary History* 15 (1980): 125–142; and H. L. Wesseling, *Imperialism and Colonialism: Essays on the History of European Expansion* (Westport, Conn.: Greenwood Press, 1997), especially chs. 4, 6, 8, 10. In the late 1940s, there was a widespread "fear of total ruin if the colonies were lost." In fact, however, the Dutch economy showed "spectacular growth," the rate for 1950–1970 being seven times that of the first forty years of the century (Wesseling, "Post-Imperial Holland," 126, 128). On Belgium, see Jean-Philippe Peemans, "Imperial Hangovers: Belgium—The Economics of Decolonization," *Journal of Contemporary History* 15 (1980): 257–286. Peemans reports that "the decolonization process had no economic consequences for Belgium" (p. 157).

56. P. J. Cain and A. G. Hopkins, "The Political Economy of British Expansion Overseas, 1750–1914," *Economic History Review*, 2d ser., 33 (1980): 463–490.

57. Michael Edelstein, "Imperialism: Cost and Benefit," in *The Economic History of Britain since 1700*, ed. Roderick Floud and Donald McCloskey, 2d ed., vol. 2 (Cambridge: Cambridge University Press, 1994), 197.

58. For the dynamics of Japanese imperialism, an important borrowing from the West, see Fairbank, Reischauer, and Craig, *East Asia*, chs. 3, 4, 7. An interesting discussion of Marxism in Japan appears there on pp. 549–554. "In the development of theory and in the volume of scholarly Marxism produced [in the early 1930s] Japan was probably ahead of all countries except Russia and Germany" (p. 551). A rapid rise of Marxism occurred also after World War II. "In China and other Asian areas where Communism became identified with nationalism, it was the anti-imperialist dogma that was crucial. But in Japan, which was more sinner than sinned against, Lenin's theory of imperialism had only a secondary appeal" (p. 553). Langer, "Critique of Imperialism," 113, writes, "In the case of Japan, as in the case of many other countries, it is easier to show that the military and official classes are a driving force behind the movement for expansion than to show that a clique of nefarious bankers or industrialists is the determining factor."

59. Larry Diamond and Seymour Martin Lipset, "Colonialism," *Encyclopedia of Democracy*, vol. 1 (Washington, D.C.: Congressional Quarterly, 1995), 262–267.

60. George Paish, P. J. Cain reports, demonstrated that British "capital exports had . . . gone mainly to other advanced or rapidly developing countries and flowed in the same direction as trade, to which they were a stimulant." This demonstration helped Hobson, Cain adds, to change his position, now accepting foreign investment "as a normal feature of international economic life, building up interconnexions between nations and helping them on their road to progress." See Cain, "Hobson, Cobdenism," 581–582. The reference is to Paish, "Great Britain's Investments in Other Lands," *Journal of the Royal Statistical Society* 72 (1909): 456–480; and "Great Britain's Capital Investments in Individual Colonial and Foreign Countries," *Journal of the Royal Statistical Society* 74 (1911): 167–200. The latter is cited by Lenin.

61. Cain and Hopkins, "Political Economy," 468.

62. On the shifting character of the empire and its supporters, and the underlying incentives, see P. J. Cain and A. G. Hopkins, "Gentlemanly Capitalism and British Expansion Overseas. I: The Old Colonial System, 1688–1850," *Economic History Review* 2d ser., 39 (1986): 501–525; and "Gentlemanly Capitalism and British Expansion Overseas. II: New Imperialism, 1850–1945," *Economic History Review* 2d ser., 40 (1987): 1–26.

63. See, especially, Ian S. Lustick, *Unsettled States, Disputed Lands: Britain and Ireland, France and Algeria, Israel and the West Bank–Gaza* (Ithaca: Cornell University Press, 1993).

64. Hobson, *Imperialism*, chs. 2, 3. The number and titles of the chapters are identical in the three editions. The quotation given here is from the first edition (1902), p. 48, that used by Lenin. Substantial support for Hobson's findings with respect to population, trade, and the costs of colonies appears in Grover Clark, *The Balance Sheets of Imperialism: Facts and Figures on Colonies* (New York: Columbia University Press, 1936).

Hobson's findings with respect to trade and empire which rejected the then-standard claim—capitalists searching for markets—forced Lenin to change direction and focus on the poorly documented argument about the requirements of investment. Subsequent writers, on occasion, have returned to the market-search argument, pointing to some unquestionable "Western" presence. It is important to distinguish the two issues, system requirements (Lenin's theme) and individual (or firm) advantage. Coca-Cola can make money in poor countries, but that does not support an argument about the needs of "American capitalism."

65. Hobson, *Imperialism*, ch. 4. The quotations are also taken from the 1902 edition, pp. 52, 53, 55, 56.

A slightly different version and different author of the "outdoor relief" quotation appears elsewhere. John Bright, in a speech commenting on the maintenance of large overseas establishments, said, "This regard for the liberties of Europe, this care at one time for the Protestant interest, this excessive love for the balance of power, is neither more nor less than a gigantic system of outdoor relief for the aristocracy of Great Britain." See Robert Stewart, ed., *Dictionary of Political Quotations* (London: Europa Publications, 1984), 22. In both versions, eminent liberal spokesmen were denouncing "empire" as a parasitic effort, one serving the needs of a (presumably) declining class as opposed to those of capitalism. Although Hobson clearly agrees with the conclusion, Lenin hid that fact and passed over the argument entirely.

66. Hobson, *Imperialism*, 1902, 56–57, 60.

67. Ibid., 56, 67.

68. Ibid., 91 (versus inevitability) and 95 (wreaking policy).

69. Daniel Chirot and Thomas D. Hall, "World-System Theory," *Annual Review of Sociology* 8 (1982): 81–106. The quotation is from p. 83, but see also pp. 85, 86, 88–89. For the original statement, see Immanuel Wallerstein, *The Modern World System*, 3 vols. (New York: Academic Press, 1974, 1980, 1988). For a brief statement, see Immanuel Wallerstein, "The Collapse of Liberalism," in *Socialist Register 1992*, ed. Ralph Miliband and Leo Panitch (London: Merlin, 1992), 96–110. See also the compendium by Christopher Chase-Dunn, *Global Formation: Structures of the World-Economy* (Oxford: Basil Blackwell, 1989). For

a critique, see Patrick O'Brien, "European Economic Development: The Contribution of the Periphery," *Economic History Review*, 2d ser., 35 (1982): 1–18. See also the findings in Paul Bairoch, *Economics and World History: Myths and Paradoxes* (Chicago: University of Chicago Press, 1993).

70. For an early statement, see John Gallagher and Ronald Robinson, "The Imperialism of Free Trade," *Economic History Review*, 2d ser., 6 (1953): 1–15. For their extended statement, see Robinson and Gallagher, *Africa*. For comment, see D.C.M. Platt, "The Imperialism of Free Trade: Some Reservations," *Economic History Review*, 2d ser., 21 (1968): 296–306; and "Further Objections to an 'Imperialism of Free Trade', 1830–60," *Economic History Review*, 2d ser., 26 (1973): 77–91. See also, W. M. Mathew, "The Imperialism of Free Trade: Peru, 1820–70," *Economic History Review*, 2d ser., 21 (1968): 562–579; and H. S. Ferns, "Britain's Informal Empire in Argentina, 1806–1914," *Past and Present* 4 (1953): 60–75. For discussion of the various issues involved, see William Roger Louis, ed., *Imperialism: The Robinson and Gallagher Controversy* (New York: New Viewpoints, 1976).

Lenin, as seen, argued formal empire with a trade and investment monopoly, his image being one of total control. Some imperial ventures, however, were open from the beginning. Bismarck did what he could to encourage German activity in the nation's African colonies, but "most of the trade remained in British hands." Even in "so closed a colony as the Dutch East Indies, more than half the investment in extraction and refining came from Britain and France" (Landes, "Thoughts," 503–505). On Vietnam under the French, see Bernard B. Fall, *The Two Viet-Nams: A Political and Military Analysis*, 2d rev. ed. (New York: Praeger, 1967), 27–29.

Cain and Hopkins provide summary overviews of the British experience. For a brief statement of their position, see Cain and Hopkins, "Political Economy," 463–490. For extended statements, see P. J. Cain, *Economic Foundations of British Expansion Overseas, 1815–1914* (London: Macmillan, 1980); P. J. Cain and A. G. Hopkins, *British Imperialism: Innovation and Expansion, 1688–1914* (London: Longman, 1993), and *British Imperialism: Crisis and Deconstruction, 1914–1990* (London: Longman, 1993).

71. See Michael C. Meyer and William L. Sherman, *The Course of Mexican History*, 5th ed. (New York: Oxford University Press, 1995), 603–605. See also Merrill Rippy, "The Economic Repercussions of Expropriation: A Case Study: Mexican Oil," *Inter-American Economic Affairs* 5 (1951): 52–72, and *Oil and the Mexican Revolution* (Leiden, The Netherlands: Brill, 1972).

72. Miller and Bennett, "New-Imperialism Critique," 13–14.

73. For a statement of the dependency theory, see Andre Gunder Frank, *Capitalism and Underdevelopment in Latin America* (New York: Monthly Review Press, 1969). For recent critiques, see Glenn Firebaugh, "Growth Effects of Foreign and Domestic Investment," *American Journal of Sociology* 98 (1992): 105–130; and Glenn Firebaugh and Frank D. Beck, "Does Economic Growth Benefit the Masses?" *American Sociological Review* 59 (1994): 631–653.

74. The three most important works of the Monthly Review school are those cited in note 3. All three were still in print in 1996, a rare achievement for any scholarly publication. The Miller and Bennett critique of those works has been unavailable for more than two decades and, moreover, is seldom referred to

in the academic literature. For an enthusiastic supportive statement from the field of sociology, see James W. Russell, *Introduction to Macrosociology*, 2d ed. (Upper Saddle River, N.J.: Prentice Hall, 1996), 99–105. Russell provides no references to critiques of Lenin's position.

The collapse of the Soviet Union had a dramatic effect on Lenin's "citation count." The *Arts and Humanities Citation Index* (Philadelphia: Institute for Scientific Information) for January–June 1989 contained four columns of citations. Lenin was the most cited 20th-century author at that time (the second most cited was Sigmund Freud). The *Index* for January–June 1997 contained only a single column of citations. The *Social Science Citation Index*, the annual for 1989, gave Lenin approximately five columns of citations (five columns to a page). The 1997 edition showed only a little more than one column. At both points most of that citation was in East European sources.

CHAPTER 5

Some Conclusions

The central concern with respect to the three theoretical positions as- sessed here is that of empirical adequacy. The basic questions are these: Which propositions are supported? Which are not? And where is the evidence equivocal?

ON MARXISM

The Marxist theory has had an unusual history. The original formu- lation, provided in the work of Karl Marx and Friedrich Engels, ap- peared in the 19th century, basically in a fifty-year span from the 1840s to the 1890s. The theory analyzes events within the leading capitalist nations and predicts imminent revolution there. The central prediction was that the working classes in the advanced capitalist nations would overthrow the bourgeoisie and take power. The proletarian revolu- tion would end the bourgeois epoch and initiate a new historical era.

The most striking aspect of this theory is the failure of its central argument: The proletarian revolutions did not appear as predicted. No revolutionary takeover has occurred in any of the leading capitalist nations, now 150 years after the confident predictions of the *Manifesto*. Despite the failure, however, the Marxian theory, in many diverse revi- sions, continues to be presented by some authors as viable, as somehow presenting a useful contribution to the analysis of the "modern world." Robert G. Wesson, one of the few authors to address this curious ten- dency, described it as "The Continuing Success of a Failed Theory."[1]

The assessment of the fifteen propositions reviewed here yielded six rejections and nine mixed conclusions. The rejections include the decisive prediction, that of a proletarian revolution. The mixed conclusions provide food for thought, but obviously need rethinking and reformulation. In each case, the directions taken are different, more complex, and associated with consequences differing from those of the original prediction. That reworking has been undertaken in subsequent literature, which, on the whole, provides a far better guide to the modern world than the imperfect originals.

The most appropriate practical strategy is to consign the Marxian theory to intellectual history courses. It is something that was taught, accepted, and believed by various intellectuals and political leaders in a given period. It had enormous practical impact in the 20th century. In some circles, the theory is still thought to be viable (some of those efforts will be reviewed later). But apart from the wish to know intellectual history, the key question needing attention is that of the sources of belief: Why did a failed theory have such a widespread and persistent following?

ON REVISIONISM

The Marxian theory is distinctive in that it is known largely through its derivatives, through the many variations intended to save elements of the original. The first of these variants, revisionist Marxism, appeared roughly a century ago, within the context of German Social Democracy. The key aims were to explain the absence of the revolution and to argue the need for a new strategy. Socialism was to be achieved by way of elections and through the use of a moderate program. This option, in its most influential formulation, was termed *evolutionary socialism*.

Although rejected by Germany's Social Democrats and by later orthodox Marxists, this depiction has more to be said for it than either the original version or most of the later derivatives. For the ten propositions, we have six confirmations, three mixed results, and one uncertainty. The revisionist analysis of the class structure, with some emendation to be sure, has proved more accurate than orthodox Marxist readings. The working class has declined relative to others. There has been an unexpected persistence and growth of the nonfarm segment of the old middle class. There has been considerable growth of the new middle class. And there has been a general increase in real living standards. No obvious increase in revolutionary working-class consciousness has occurred. The revisionist account is accurate also in its depiction of socialist parties coming to power in many "advanced capitalist" nations through the electoral route.

Either before gaining power or after, however, socialist parties throughout the world dropped the major practical offering: They abandoned socialism. One way or another, they recognized that "socialization of the means of production" was not a feasible goal. Put differently, the various attempts did not prove "good for the workers" (or for most other groups). With this transformation, those parties became left-liberal in orientation, defenders of the welfare state, supporters of the underprivileged, and defenders of minority rights. In their new appearance, they were close cousins to America's Democrats and to the New Deal liberals.[2]

ON LENINISM

The Leninist variant is perhaps the best known of the positions assessed here. Most contemporaries, as seen, equate this view with Marxism per se, the differences between the original and this copy having been submerged in many contemporary accounts. Rejection is indicated for all five of the propositions reviewed. Rich nations invest in rich nations. A nation might, on occasion, extract superprofits from a colony, but that comes with serious risks, including the possibility of default, repudiation, or nationalization. Investors, on the whole, do not share their earnings with "labor aristocrats." The claim about the political dynamics, that big businessmen (or finance capital) would be the principal instigators of imperialist ventures, was not supported. And finally, the liberation of the colonial nations in the decades after World War II did not bring the collapse of advanced capitalism. One major correlate is that the rate of economic growth in the major capitalist nations accelerated with the loss of the colonial burden.

ON THE SUPPORT FOR FAILED THEORIES

Theories, as noted in the Introduction, are like maps. They provide simplified depictions of complicated territories. A map is ordinarily judged by its usefulness: Does it help us achieve our goals? Does it allow us to get quickly to some location, or to get somewhere by a scenic route, or to find things (hotels, restaurants, museums, mineral deposits, soil characteristics, or average temperatures)? If the map does not serve our purposes, we would normally look for a better map. Implicit in the procedure is a scientific concern, that the map provides an accurate depiction of the territory.

Karl Marx regularly signaled his commitment to a scientific outlook. His theoretical position was labeled scientific socialism. At an early point, Marx and Engels stated explicitly the need for empirical verification.[3] That scientific commitment may be seen also in his personal motto—*de omnibus dubitandum*—"doubt everything." In his actual practice, however, Marx showed no such skepticism. His intellectual effort involved what might be called "willful mapmaking." Every one of the *Manifesto* propositions reviewed here involves what might be called "accelerators," social processes that would further the ultimate working-class revolution. Alternative hypotheses, ones involving decelerators, inhibiting, or immobilizing processes, are routinely overlooked or discounted.

For Marx, Engels, and many others, evidence showing the map to be faulty did not lead to discarding but rather to a reconstitution. Faced with evidence of inadequacy, the persistent tendency has been revision and alteration of key elements so as to "save" the theory. Three years after Marx's death, Engels brought out the first English-language edition of *Capital*. His Preface vouches for the work, commending it to his readers. Faced, however, with an obvious difficulty, he ended his brief comments with a new and unexpected prediction: Marx had been "led to the conclusion that, at least in Europe, England is the only country where the inevitable social revolution might be effected entirely by peaceful and legal means." The odds for a successful prediction were thereby doubled.[4]

A significant omission provides further evidence that this was meant to be a "saving" option. Engels introduced this new claim with high praise for the author and his work. Marx was "a man whose whole theory is the result of a lifelong study of the economic history and condition of England," and that lifelong study led him to the new conclusion. But Engels does not indicate where Marx stated the new conclusion. Nor does he indicate where the logic or evidence for it might be found. Significantly, the editors of the *Collected Works*, normally very diligent in such matters, also provided no appropriate citations or references. Engels's Preface ends with still another prediction: Marx "never forgot to add that he hardly expected the English ruling classes to submit [without a rebellion] to this peaceful and legal revolution." Again, Engels is having it both ways: Yes, a peaceful revolution will occur, and yes, a significant counterrevolutionary struggle will occur. Again, no specific source is given.

Almost sixty years later, the British Labour Party was voted into office and proceeded to socialize several major industries. No rebellion occurred; the nation had a "peaceful revolution." Nationalization was carried through with little fuss. Managers, in the steel industry, for example, did not fight. Most of them simply retired. The anticipation of rebellion is another failed prediction.[5]

It is important to consider the sources of the misplaced efforts. These may be categorized under three headings: psychological, social psychological, and social organizational.

As opposed to the matter-of-fact empirical orientation found with regard to maps, a persistent cathexis (psychological attachment) appears with regard to theories. Many people "bond with" the framework that in some way has served them. They then expend energy in its defense. The amount of energy expended varies of course, ranging from that of the zealot—the defender of the faith, one who would use fire and sword—to that of the mild skeptic—one who has doubts but reserves judgment pending the appearance of more compelling evidence. In regard to Marxism, for example, we have seen a refusal to recognize the failure of the key prediction. The response, for those maintaining the revolutionary faith, was the provision of supplementary arguments to explain the postponement and/or relocation of the key historical event. One easy option was not considered, that the original assumption was invalid or, put differently, that the revolution was not "in the cards."

Marx and Engels protected some important aspects of their theory in another way. In a brilliant rhetorical move, they put a range of hypotheses beyond the test. Their effort, it was announced, was scientific. They were analyzing the dynamics of capitalist society, charting the course of ongoing events. But the character or dynamics of that next epoch, of that socialist society, were unknowable. No evidence was yet available to allow scientific empirical analysis. That being the case, no conclusions at all could be offered with respect to that epoch. There was an inconsistency here. The claim that the revolution would usher in a beneficent classless society was unjustified. The revolution could just as easily bring a disaster. Prior to the event, there was no way one could know.

With the Russian Revolution, a range of evidence came into view. One could now examine the operations of "real, existent socialism." But here too, very quickly, protective orientations made their appearance. Lincoln Steffens, the noted journalist, wrote his widely disseminated "conclusion": "I have seen the future and it works," *prior* to his visit to the Soviet Union. When Max Eastman, another influential intellectual, wrote critically of what he had seen in the Soviet Union, Steffens organized the effort to undermine his influence. Nothing, Steffens wrote, "must jar our perfect loyalty to the party and its leaders."[6]

Subsequent revolutions, or takeovers, in Eastern Europe in 1945, China in 1949, and Korea, Vietnam, Cuba, and various Marxist regimes in Africa, allowed further investigation of the dynamics of the new regimes. The reports on this subject, in much of the scholarly world, were poor and/or misleading. The principal lessons, First World economic success, Second World failure, and the disastrous failure of socialism in the Third World, have only a fugitive appearance in some of the social sciences. Although easily one of the most important institutional changes in the world after 1945, socialism is a minor entry in most current sociology textbooks. When the world was providing the lesson of socialist failure, academic sociology "discovered" Marxism. Many leading textbooks routinely continued to present "Marxism" as a viable theory for analysis of modern societies.[7]

The second constraint limiting one's freedom with respect to theories is best termed *social psychological*. The psychological constraints just discussed involve the propensities of the individual psyche. But individuals operate in groups and, to one degree or another, they are dependent of those group ties. This means that "knowledge," in this case theoretical preferences, will depend to some degree on group dynamics. To some extent at least, the preferred outlooks will be a function of primary socialization (people being taught various theories) and subsequent reinforcements (people being rewarded or punished for their loyalties).

One important element in these processes is conformity. That term refers to a disposition to follow cues provided by "significant others." Put differently, it refers to an unwillingness or an inability to stand alone, to make autonomous judgments. The linkage of intellectual life and conformity may seem paradoxical, but that feeling stems from a self-image provided by intellectuals themselves, a depiction that portrays "the intellectual" as independent and autonomous. The Lincoln Steffens experience just discussed points up the social-psychological component of at least one pocket of intellectual life. For some, he was an authority figure providing direction. The other side of the relationship involves persons disposed and willing to accept direction. Steffens's cues and the conformist responses, apparently, successfully reduced Eastman's influence. The evidence Eastman presented, in short, was bypassed. The outcome was determined by group dynamics.[8]

The third constraint has been referred to as *organizational*. Knowledge, including here both theories and fact, flows from producers to consumers. The producers might be freelance intellectuals or salaried professionals, academics, applied technicians, journalists, and so on. The consumers, or users, might be other elites (business, political, military, religious, voluntary association leaders), the educated public, or members of the general public. The producer–consumer relationship is necessarily indirect or mediated. Within the many diverse mediating organizations—universities, book publishers, journals, magazines, news-gathering agencies—various "gatekeepers" sift and winnow a massive quantity of material, making decisions about what information will flow from source to receiver.

Here is a commonplace example: Because of the extent of the task, universities have divided their activities among several faculties and many departments. Within those departments, groups of specialists produce knowledge and disseminate it directly in classes and indirectly in specialized publications. The lessons disseminated and vouched for may on occasion differ significantly from one department to the next. The discussions of Marx and Marxism in sociology textbooks, for example, are generally extensive and hortatory, commending both the author and the theory. They typically lack serious assessment and fail to provide references to such assessments. Unless dealt with in classrooms by the professors, students would receive no serious understanding of the usefulness or empirical adequacy of the theory. Students of economics typically receive an entirely different reading. Gregory Mankiw's *Principles of Microeconomics*, for example, widely used in American universities, gives three paragraphs to Marx and socialism. Following a mention of the ideal, the classless society, it states that the experience was one of general failure: "Planning is just too difficult."[9]

The differences in orientation between sociology and economics textbooks probably stems from market demands, the orientations or preferences of professors in those fields differing significantly. In a 1984 survey of the nation's professors, 30 percent of the sociologists described themselves as "left," and another 49 percent said "liberal." The left-plus-liberal total was 79 percent. The respective percentages for economists were 6 and 22, for a total of 28 percent.[10]

The academic division of labor is a necessary arrangement, there being no other feasible way to organize this massive and growing intellectual enterprise. An implicit assumption (or hope) is that the knowledge produced in any given department will be disseminated to other appropriate users. But as seen, that is often not the case. Sociologists routinely vouch for the "Weber thesis," for the "Protestant ethic." Economic historians, persons who have researched the origins of capitalism and the "rise of the West," with rare exception, see no merit in the argument.[11]

For assessment of Marxism, Leninism, or the Weber thesis, the most likely academic specialists would be economic historians. Their number is relatively small. The key professional group in the United States, the Economic History Association, had a total of 713 American members in 1998 (and 306 elsewhere in the world). The United States has more than 2,200 four-year institutions of higher learning. The larger institutions typically have several resident experts (Ohio State University, for example, currently has three). That means the majority of universities and colleges do not have a single such expert in residence. Many faculty members, in short, cannot inform themselves through a local telephone call or a casual visit with a colleague.[12]

One could read the works of those economic historians, either their journal articles or their book-length publications. Those journals and books allow a wider audience to have contact with the producers and disseminators of expert knowledge in these areas. The leading economic history journals have small circulations. The *Journal of Economic History*, for example, is received by 2,088 college and university libraries at home and abroad. Some college libraries clearly do not subscribe. Some issues, moreover, might be in the libraries but have few readers; some might just "sit on the shelf."

The knowledge produced by specialized experts, in short, is likely to remain within the "compartment" that produced it. The problem is one of limited transmission. In recent years, universities have made much of interdisciplinary efforts, but a sizable gap exists between the aspiration and the achievement.

A separate and largely independent "transmission belt" is provided by the "quality" news sources. An assortment of public-affairs journals and "prestige" newspapers offer information and opinion for the attentive public. On a given topic of actual or potential interest, the media decision makers would, presumably, reach out to appropriate experts. They would obtain the findings, observations, and judgments of those experts and would distill and transmit those results to readers, listeners, viewers, and so on. There is an extensive literature on the subject, including studies of "gatekeepers," audiences, and impacts.

An instructive case study of knowledge transmitted through quality news sources appeared in 1998, provided by the 150th anniversary of the publication of the *Communist Manifesto*. The first of many commentaries appeared in January 1998 in *The New Yorker*. The author, John Cassidy, reported a discussion with an old friend, an unnamed source, who was working for a Wall Street investment bank. Much to his surprise, the friend announced his conviction that "Marx was right." That conclusion was based on a handful of quotations from the *Manifesto*, ones that presumably, with unique insight, anticipated subsequent developments. Marx and Engels wrote that the need for new markets "chases the bourgeoisie over the whole surface of the globe." This meant that all "old-established national industries have been destroyed or are daily being destroyed." These statements, it was claimed, anticipated present-day globalization. Cassidy's final comment is that Marx's "books will be worth reading as long as capitalism endures."[13]

The *New York Times Book Review* gave an entire page to the subject in a contribution by Steven Marcus entitled "Marx's Masterpiece at 150." Apart from one sentence, it is a work of unrestrained celebration. In unusually vaporous prose, Marcus reported that the *Manifesto*

was and is a work of immense, autonomous historical importance . . . [which] continues to yield itself to our readings in the new light that its enduring insights into social existence generate. . . . [It] emerges ever more distinctly as an unsurpassed dramatic representation, diagnosis and prophetic array of visionary judgments on the modern world. . . . The detonating power and conceptual fullness of [its] utterances constitute a species of dramatic performance . . . a singular kind of action writing . . . [and] possess a structural complexity and a denseness of thematic play. . . . [Its] trains of metaphoric figures and images are part of the dense local entwinements that constitute the microstructure of [its] linguistic fabric and argument. The macrostructure is equally complex and tightly interwoven.[14]

Two-thirds of the way through, Marcus, in a parallel to Cassidy's procedure, points to an important prediction. Nothing, he writes, is more "striking and pertinent" than Marx and Engels's "vision of capitalism's triumphant globalization: 'Modern industry has established the world market, for which the discovery of America paved the way.'" Several other "achievements" are their recognition of "steam navigation, railways, electric telegraphs, [and] the canalization of rivers."

The problem, for both authors, is that those statements do not provide unique prescient insights. For more than two centuries prior to this "vision," Portuguese, Spanish, Dutch, French, and English trading companies had been pushing their trade outward to the antipodes. And Adam Smith, along with many others, had advocated worldwide free trade, which, more than two centuries later, would be termed "globalization." Any defender of capitalism in the 1840s would have pointed to the steam engines, railways, and canals. Cassidy and Marcus are crediting the two latecomers for their recognition of a patently obvious reality. The rhetorical difficulty is indicated in their choices of "successful" claims. Of all the hypotheses contained in the *Manifesto*, those chosen for celebration are best described as commonplace.

Marcus touches on the fundamental failure only in a brief final paragraph: "There is much of importance the Manifesto did not get right: the revolution it hailed was not successful; the proletariat did not become the gravediggers of the bourgeoisie; the ever-deeper pauperization of the working class" did not occur. Undaunted by the problem, Marcus announces that the Manifesto "got certain things right as no other work of its time, or any other time." It "remains a classic expression of the society . . . whose doom it prematurely announced."[15]

The two organizational settings discussed here, universities and publishers, have only loose and tenuous connections. Academic specialists rarely intervene in "the mass media" to correct views they know to be inadequate or false. The subsequent issues of the *New York Times Book Review* contained no responses to Marcus's account.

The central underlying principle of scientific effort is that conclusions should be based on evidence. Put differently, the expectation is that conclusions should, in one way or another, be "constrained" by evidence. But that expectation was not fulfilled in these anniversary reports, both showing what might be termed evidence-averse tendencies. If conclusions do not reflect readily available evidence, a consideration of those other constraints—psychological, social psychological, and organizational—is appropriate.

Exploration of these varieties of constraints present serious methodological difficulties. Evidential lessons may be assessed with relative ease. Evidence is (or is not) presented; it may be assessed as adequate, borderline, or unsatisfactory. The study of those other constraints and their possible impacts, however, poses no end of difficulties. Did a given judgment, a theoretical emphasis, for example, stem from personal psychological commitment? Or did it stem from conformity, from some group dynamics? Or was it due to compartmentalization; the author simply did not know what other academics had done? Or was it some combination of these factors?

Sociologists have a subspecialty called the sociology of knowledge. Basically, it explores the social-structural determinants of knowledge and understanding. It might, for example, explore the organizational constraints discussed here. Many sociologists, however, disapprove of and recommend the exclusion of individual psychological factors, one methodological principle cautioning against "psychological reductionism." But that exclusion, that "response set," which is reinforced by interpersonal pressures, yields a distorted understanding. Paranoia is a "fact of life," something present in many social settings. But social-science practitioners guided by that exclusionary "principle" would not be inclined to recognize or to analyze the problem.[16]

SOME COUNTERMEASURES

The consideration of the constraints, of the unexpected "stickiness" in theoretical matters, points up the need for consideration of remedies. The basic need is for procedures that allow or require one to overcome those ever-present social and psychological influences. Put differently, the need is for procedures that give greater weight to evidence. Put still another way, the need is for procedures that will make evidence-aversion strategies more costly. Five procedural recommendations follow.

First, there is a need for consideration of alternative hypotheses. As opposed to the exclusive focus on a single hypothesis, frequently a favorite, one should search for, develop, and justify plausible alternatives. This methodological recommendation was put forward by T. C. Chamberlin in an article published in *Science* in 1890. It has been republished there on four subsequent occasions.[17]

Here is an illustration drawn from earlier discussion. We have the hypothesis that class is a powerful determinant of political attitudes. The easiest alternative hypothesis is the null hypothesis, that there is no relationship between class and those attitudes. A second alternative would involve partitive options, that the direction of the relationship is as predicted but the linkage is weak or only moderate in strength. A third alternative, actually a set of them, would involve substantive options, namely that some other factors, political socialization, religion, ethnicity, or the like, are more important. Tests for the entire range of options should force more appropriate intellectual behavior.

We routinely assume that evidence will force an appropriate intellectual response. But one finds repeated instances in which the logic of favored paradigms takes precedence over readily available contrary evidence. A compendious review of evidence on electoral behavior in fifteen countries, provided by Richard Rose in 1974, found that in nine of them religion was a better predictor of partisanship than occupation. Neither factor predicted partisanship in Ireland. The religious factor was not measured in the Danish study. The role of occupation was strongest in the four religiously homogeneous Scandinavian countries (and there the role of religion was negligible). Elsewhere, occupation had a modest impact. In the United States and Great Britain, for example, it explained 3.0 and 3.3 percent of the variance, respectively. A brief final chapter by Philip E. Converse provided recommendations for subsequent research. One of these reads, "If party location alone was at stake as a dependent variable, we might move religion into the front rank of determinants."[18]

Ronald Inglehart's *Silent Revolution*, from 1977, contains a similar review which also includes "parents' party," a measure of family political socialization. This evidence also challenged the routine assignment of class as the most powerful determinant. With one exception, parents' party, the political-socialization factor, appeared as the strongest predictor, followed by a measure of religion. Those and similar findings appear in the specialized social-science literature. In the "popular" social sciences textbooks, for example, they are rarely signaled.[19]

A recent study by Jeff Manza and Clem Brooks provides evidence on the importance of the various cleavages in the United States and on the trends over a forty-year period from 1952 to 1992. They summarize as follows: "Far from approaching the point of insignificance predicted by the 'declining cleavage' thesis, the religious cleavage appears to be nearly twice the magnitude of the more widely debated class cleavage. . . . Not only is the magnitude of the religious cleavage considerable, the results of the current study . . . suggest little reason to believe that it is likely to experience a major decline in future elections."[20]

A second recommendation is that we undertake repeated systematic testing of central hypotheses. Put differently, the concern here is with replication. Although routinely approved in research-methods courses, in practice replication is an infrequent occurrence. Again, some illustrative cases demonstrating the need appear in earlier discussions. For decades, leading commentators have provided ungrounded statements with respect to the outlooks of various classes. Polls and surveys made their first appearance in the United States in the 1930s. An explosion of polling activity began in the 1950s. Originally located only in private archives, the studies became widely available to the academic community and to the interested public beginning in the 1970s. If anyone, in 1999, wished to know about the values of the old middle class and make comparison with the equivalent new middle class, it could be done twenty-one times with the National Opinion Research Center's General Social Surveys. If any doubt remained, one could undertake further replication using more than twenty National Election Studies.[21]

Surveys are one of many available research procedures. We also have direct observational studies, sometimes called qualitative or field studies. These studies, it has been noted, are rich in detail, providing a wide range of observations and insights. The principal difficulty with such studies is the question of typicality. Is the study site, Community A, Workplace B, or Street Gang C, typical of the larger universe of experience? Or does it "stand alone," a unique exception to all rules? Ideally, one should join these efforts, linking findings of the observational studies and the surveys.

Before discussing this option further, we should consider a fourth desideratum. Researcher theorists should know and make use of a large repertory of theories. This point is obviously linked to the first recommendation, the need for alternative hypotheses. Those alternative theories will ordinarily contain a range of readings, ones involving useful hypotheses that also need assessment.

Horace Miner wrote an insightful community study entitled *St. Denis*. It describes and analyzes social processes in a small farming community in Quebec in the mid-1930s.[22] The monograph was based on research and observations made during a one-year stay there. The account is written within the framework of a conventional academic sociology. This means that the orientations and outlooks of the St. Denis citizenry were formed through interpersonal influences, mainly those of family, community, and church. That trinity of factors, that cluster of social bases, was said to explain, in great measure, the local orientations and outlooks.

Reaching beyond those interpersonal influences, Miner added some observations about demographic determinants and borrowed some elements from the mass society theory. Population growth within a fixed quantity of land stimulated emigration to larger cities, either in Quebec or in New England. Although not encouraged by family, community, or church, the land–resources relationship was such as to force the process. In the last chapters, Miner reached out in another direction and noted some mass-media impacts (radio and motion pictures) that brought new and different values into the community. Some propertyless persons lived on the edge of the community, this too pointing to some emergence of the "mass society." Miner, in short, had organized his observations in terms of the sociological position and, intelligently and creatively, extended that framework through the use of observations drawn from population and the mass society theories.

Because all theories are partial, when writing or reading a research report one should consider what has been left out or, put differently, what might be gained through use of another theory. Use of the Marxian theory would have led Miner to a markedly different set of initial questions. The principal concern would have been with class and class relationships. Those small farmers (independent proprietors) would be identified as "petty bourgeois," as members of the lower-middle class. That class, presumably, faced competition from larger, more efficient, capital-intensive units. Its members, who were destined to lose out in the competitive struggle, would then fall into the proletariat. St. Denis would appear to provide an ideal setting for study of this process, especially given the timing, the mid-1930s, in the midst of the worst economic crisis of the modern era.

Miner's account, however, says little about farm prices. The book contains little information on the markets for St. Denis produce. Little is said about buyers or middlemen; there is next to nothing on farm indebtedness, banks, foreclosures, or forced sales of properties. These are topics, it will be noted, that dominated the literature on farms and farmers of the period, whether in Schleswig-Holstein, Saskatchewan, or Oklahoma.[23]

It is possible that Miner overlooked this option. Another possibility, of course, is that those dynamics were not present in St. Denis at that point. In any event, nothing would have been lost by explicit consideration of the Marxian hypotheses and something might have been gained. If, for example, those farmers were not in debt, they might have been able to weather the depression with little loss. If that were the case, some specification of the original general claim about the farmers would be appropriate.

The relationship between theories and research should be reciprocal; it should be a two-way street. Theories inform (provide enlightenment for) research. And research provides findings that should lead to improved theories.[24] In this example, Miner has indicated the basic movement: the petty bourgeoisie falling into the proletariat. Many children of St. Denis moved off to the cities and, because of the poor and inappropriate education they had received, most ended up in working-class jobs. Miner presented evidence showing the movement out of St. Denis as having demographic sources. The changing population–land ratio forced the search for alternative employment. That represents a second hypothesis as to the causes of the movement, the first being the Marxist claim. In subsequent research, one should inquire as to the relative frequencies: How much movement stemmed from competitive failure? How much from demographic pressures? How much from combinations? How much from other causes?

The St. Denis experience would allow exploration of a range of attitudinal questions. Were those "threatened" lower-middle-class farmers reactionary? Did they, as Marx and Engels claimed, "try to roll back the wheel of history?" Were they, to borrow the language of a later era, latent fascists? And what happened to those "precipitated" into the proletariat? Did they abandon their previous traditional outlooks and become members of a radical working class? It is not at all clear that the St. Denis outmigrants saw themselves as experiencing downward mobility; that is, a "fall." Of the two leading options, staying home or leaving, outmigration appeared preferable. If so, it might have been experienced as improvement, as a move upward. One should not beg the question; it should be seen as an open issue, a problem to be added to an appropriate research agenda.

From fragments of evidence scattered throughout the book, the Marxian predictions do not appear to be supported. Most farmers were either Liberals or Conservatives, these orientations following family traditions (again supporting the sociological position). Those who left St. Denis for Drummondville, Sherbrooke, Montreal, or New England appear to have maintained their original outlooks with only little change. While unexpected from both the Marxian and the mass society perspectives, Miner's account provides a plausible explanation. In those new settings, their associates (kin, neighbors, coworkers) were people very much like themselves; that is, family members and others from their home community, or people from farm villages elsewhere in Quebec. Many new influences were undoubtedly present—say, in Holyoke, Massachusetts or Manchester, New Hampshire—these including employers, textile mills, labor unions, schools, different mass-media content, a different dominant language, and different ethnic groups. But many influences within their lives, it seems, showed unexpected continuity.[25]

This fragmentary evidence allows a very modest test of some Marxian claims and, as indicated, provides an alternative hypothesis for the understanding of working-class outlooks. The persistent failure of the key claim, that of the working-class revolution, as seen, posed a major task for the theory's defenders. The most-frequently offered explanation is "false consciousness." Actually no more than a label, the phrase merely restates the problem: Workers are not thinking and behaving as the theory predicted. Miner's work, however, allows a positive explanation: original socialization and subsequent interpersonal supports. It explains how one segment of workers came to think the way they did and why they persisted in that tendency.[26]

A second research monograph offers some parallel lessons. William Foote Whyte, working at about the same time as Miner, produced a justly famous volume entitled *Street Corner Society*.[27] The book focused on young men in the North End of Boston and detailed their activities on the street, in recreation (bowling, gambling), in a settlement house, and in politics. The study provides a detailed account of the men's interpersonal activities and their links to some of the neighborhood institutions. The "corner boys" were of Italian background and the book accordingly also has an ethnic dimension (the subtitle is "The Social Structure of an Italian Slum"). The underlying theory in this case would again be the sociological position. Essentially, it charts and documents the importance of interpersonal influences.

One might again raise the "what if" question: What if Whyte had approached his subject with a different theory? If he had begun with the Marxian theory, the corner boys would be seen as unemployed workers, victims of the worldwide depression. Their class position would be detailed, together perhaps with that of their fathers (or older brothers). The character of the crisis would be elaborated. And the next topic, presumably, would be attitudinal responses; that is, the outlooks of workers facing the collapse of the capitalist economy. The street corner boys, Whyte reports, were bowling, hanging around the settlement house, and linked up with the local Democratic Party organization. It might not be a satisfying account of "why the revolution failed," but it would be an empirically documented one.

There are other gaps. Whyte was fully aware of these, providing a list of the omitted subjects: family, church, and school. In theory and in research, one cannot cover everything, that being the lesson of an ancient cliché. But one can note the gaps and think through the implications. The three omitted contexts would probably also involve conservative or traditional influences. That is, of course, only hypothesis, again something for a subsequent research agenda. Whyte's book, it has been noted, focuses almost exclusively on men. Women, whether mothers, sisters, girlfriends, or wives, hardly make any appearance. The female "half" of this working-class segment is missing, along with all its possible impacts. In this respect, it should be noted, the focus of *Street Corner Society* is identical with that of the Marxian theory, which is a theory about men, their employment (or lack thereof), and their political actions.[28]

As a useful supplement, one may consider a third research monograph, Michael Young and Peter Wilmott's *Family and Kinship in East London*.[29] This study focuses on a London working-class community,

Bethnal Green, which in many respects would resemble Boston's North End. This study also focuses on social networks and on supports. It is again in the basic sociological tradition. The specific focus, however, differs significantly from Whyte's, in that its concern is with family and kinship. The research focuses on activities in the home, as opposed to those on the street. And it is concerned, for the most part, with the women of the community. The community proved to be matrilocal (and to some extent matriarchal), with much of the account centering on "mum" and her daughters. The mothers, it appears, were a source of cultural conservatism. They passed on a wide range of handed-down "folk wisdom" to daughters and granddaughters. In contrast to most Marxist accounts, jobs, employers, factories, unions, working-class parties, and the "dynamics of advanced capitalism" are almost completely absent. Those facts were doubtlessly present, all somewhere to be seen in and around Bethnal Green, but the authors provided little information on those topics.[30]

The fifth recommendation is that one should synthesize: Elements drawn from disparate sources should be brought together to create a more adequate theory. Or, a related possibility, one might elaborate and develop a given theory, adding elements and enriching the initial or received framework. Here we have reviewed three studies that dealt in some way with working-class life. All three placed an emphasis on patterns of interpersonal influence, suggesting that those patterns were decisive in the formation and maintenance of attitudes and behavior. The implication is that we need a theory, a simplifying scheme, that gives prominence to those interpersonal influences.

Theories are ordering devices. A given theory, among other things, is a system for filing information. For the thinking person, a theory helps to retain information; it is a data-management device. The more theories known, the more "places" for storage of information. Conversely, if there is no place for a range of fact, it will ordinarily be neglected and ultimately will be forgotten. The chances of retaining information depend on knowing many theories. One should know the theories well, so as to be able to see their implications for any given research. And one should recognize where research findings have implications for given theoretical claims.

Theories should be seen as tools to help one's understanding. The task is to think about them and assess them from that perspective. Neutral inquiry is recommended, inquiry that asks, what may I learn from Theories M, N, and O? Some people, unfortunately, treat theories as articles of faith. Instead of neutral assessment, their task is advocacy: "Theory A is championed and some opposed Theory B is defeated. One slays the Marxist dragon and raises the colors of Democratic Pluralism."[31] But the effort should not be seen as an either/or question, of Theory A *versus* Theory B. And the acceptance of or defense of a theory should rest on evidence, on empirical adequacy.

These comments may be summarized in a set of recommendations. One should be willing to make partitive judgments; that is, to pick and choose the valid and useful elements from the theories that have been discussed. One should attempt to synthesize those useful elements into a new and better framework. And one should be willing to discard theories and elements that are not useful.

NOTES

1. Robert G. Wesson, *Why Marxism? The Continuing Success of a Failed Theory* (New York: Basic Books, 1976).

2. For a comprehensive review, see Seymour Martin Lipset, "No Third Way: A Comparative Perspective on the Left," in *The Crisis of Leninism and the Decline of the Left: The Revolutions of 1989*, ed. Daniel Chirot (Seattle: University of Washington Press, 1991).

3. See the passage quoted in Chapter 2, note 9.

4. *MECW*, 35: 36. The quotations in the following paragraph of the text appear on the same page.

5. On the British experience, see Arnold A. Rogow, *The Labour Government and British Industry, 1945–1951* (Ithaca: Cornell University Press, 1955); Reuben Kelf-Cohen, *British Nationalisation, 1945–1973* (London: Macmillan, 1973); and Peter Hennessy, *Never Again: Britain, 1945–1951* (New York: Pantheon, 1993).

6. William L. O'Neill, *The Last Romantic: A Life of Max Eastman* (New York: Oxford University Press, 1978), 108–109. On Steffens's famous quotation, see John M. Thompson, *Russia, Bolshevism, and the Versailles Peace* (Princeton: Princeton University Press, 1966), 175–176, 162.

7. Although socialism is a major institutional development in the 20th century, most sociology textbooks provide little information on the subject. One gives three paragraphs to the subject and no sources are provided. See Neil Smelser, *Sociology*, 5th ed. (Englewood Cliffs, N.J.: Prentice Hall, 1995), 335–336.

One leading sociologist, Gerhard Lenski, has written on the subject, providing an important exception to what might be called the "rule of neglect." See Lenski, "Marxist Experiments in Destratification: An Appraisal," *Social Forces* 57 (1978): 364–383; and "New Light on Old Issues: The Relevance of 'Really Existing Socialist Societies' for Stratification Theory," in *Social Stratification: Class, Race, and Gender in Sociological Perspective*, ed. David B. Grusky (Boulder, Colo.: Westview, 1994), 55–61. But Lenski's work, in turn, has been neglected, as indicated by subsequent citation. From publication through to 1996, *The Social Science Citation Index* (Philadelphia: Institute for Scientific Information, all appropriate years) reports a total of seven citations of Lenski's "Marxist Experiments" article.

8. With conformity, as with cathexis, we are ordinarily dealing with degrees or tendencies rather than with sharply opposite kinds of behavior. Some degree of conformity (or easy acceptance) is inherent in social life: We cannot "check out" every assertion that comes our way. Many of them, most in fact,

must be taken "on faith." See Richard F. Hamilton, *The Social Misconstruction of Reality: Validity and Verification in the Scholarly Community* (New Haven: Yale University Press, 1996), 9–15, ch. 7.

9. The current best-selling textbook in sociology is John J. Macionis, *Sociology*, 7th ed. (Upper Saddle River, N.J.: Prentice Hall, 1999). For his discussion of Marx and Marxism, see pp. 14, 102–107, 248–252, 408–412, 631, 639. The economics textbook is N. Gregory Mankiw, *Principles of Microeconomics* (Fort Worth: Dryden, 1998), 228–229. This text also, like those of sociology, comes without references to supporting evidence.

10. See Richard F. Hamilton and Lowell L. Hargens, "The Politics of the Professors: Self-Identifications, 1969–1984," *Social Forces* 71 (1993): 603–627.

11. Hamilton, *Social Misconstruction*, ch. 3. Illustrating the problem, we have the following conclusion: "Though a few writers have expressed doubts about aspects of the Weberian thesis concerning Western rationality, most of the major sociological commentators have accepted his views." See Jack Goody, *The East in the West* (Cambridge: Cambridge University Press, 1996), 45. Nothing is said there about the grounds for doubt and no critical sources are given. The statement about the agreement of those sociological commentators is probably accurate, but a consensus by itself tells nothing about the evidence bearing on the claim.

12. Li Liang of the Economic History Association provided the membership figures. There were 2,244 four-year colleges in the United States in 1995. See U.S. Bureau of the Census, *Statistical Abstract of the United States, 1998* (Washington, D.C.: U.S. Government Printing Office, 1998), 191. One might, to be sure, consult with other historians; for example, those with a detailed knowledge of Britain, France, or Germany, or specialists in the colonial affairs of India, South Africa, Latin America, and so forth.

13. John Cassidy, "The Next Thinker: The Return of Karl Marx," *The New Yorker*, 12 January 1998, 248–259.

14. Steven Marcus, "Marx's Masterpiece at 150," *New York Times Book Review*, 26 April 1998, 39.

15. Ibid.

16. Social psychology is alright; that is to say, it is socially approved. The taboo applies to the consideration of individual psychological traits. For some sense of the losses resulting from such exclusion, see Herbert E. Krugman, "The Role of Hostility in the Appeal of Communism in the United States," *Psychiatry* 16 (1953): 253–261; Robert S. Robins, ed., *Psychopathology and Political Leadership* (New Orleans: Tulane Studies in Political Science, 1977); and Robert S. Robins and Jerrold M. Post, *Political Paranoia: The Psychopolitics of Hatred* (New Haven: Yale University Press, 1997).

17. T. C. Chamberlin, "The Method of Multiple Working Hypotheses," *Science* 148 (1965): 754–759. For an example of the difficulties associated with a single working hypothesis, see Richard Sennett and Jonathan Cobb, *The Hidden Injuries of Class* (New York: Knopf, 1973). The work is based on poorly described casual sampling procedures (pp. 40–41). The authors report that they reworked the comments of those respondents. In a few instances, for example, "we have put words in people's mouths, words they were strug-

gling for, we felt, but couldn't find." They hope the respondents "will forgive [them] for pushing the presentation . . . so close to the boundaries of fiction." They then proceed to explain why "some measure of artful freedom has been necessary" (pp. 42–43).

18. Richard Rose, ed., *Electoral Behavior: A Comparative Handbook* (New York: Free Press, 1974), 17, and, for Converse, 733–735.

19. Ronald Inglehart, *The Silent Revolution: Changing Values and Political Styles among Western Publics* (Princeton: Princeton University Press, 1977), 246–249; and *Culture Shift in Advanced Industrial Society* (Princeton: Princeton University Press, 1990), 309.

The religious factor is considered at length in specialized studies. See, for example, Hans Daalder, ed., *Party Systems in Denmark, Austria, Switzerland, The Netherlands, and Belgium* (London: Frances Pinter, 1987); and Mark N. Franklin, Thomas T. Mackie, and Henry Valen, *Electoral Change: Responses to Evolving Social and Attitudinal Structures in Western Countries* (Cambridge: Cambridge University Press, 1992).

The best-selling social-stratification textbook provides a brief summary of studies dealing with "Political Values and Behavior." The description of class and voting is restricted to the United States, the relationship being twice described as "strong." See Harold R. Kerbo, *Social Stratification and Inequality: Class Conflict in Historical and Comparative Perspective*, 3d ed. (New York: McGraw-Hill, 1996), 236–239. Although obviously relevant, the sweeping comparative studies of Rose and Inglehart are not cited. Kerbo's book has many index references to class, gender, and race, but none to religion.

20. Jeff Manza and Clem Brooks, "The Religious Factor in U.S. Presidential Elections, 1960–1992," *American Journal of Sociology* 103 (1997): 38–81. The quotations are from p. 73. For their analyses of the importance of class, described as "still robust," see Clem Brooks and Jeff Manza, "Class Politics and Political Change in the United States, 1952–1992," *Social Forces* 76 (1997): 379–408; and Jeff Manza and Clem Brooks, "Does Class Analysis Still Have Anything to Contribute to the Study of Politics?" *Theory and Society* 25 (1996): 717–724. Their many important findings cannot be summarized here. Basically, they find diverse trends for subgroups within the broad manual–nonmanual aggregates. The same conclusion, diverse patterns, was found for various religious groups. For a comparative analysis, see Jeff Manza, Michael Hout, and Clem Brooks, "Class Voting in Capitalist Democracies: Dealignment, Realignment, or Trendless Fluctuation, *Annual Review of Sociology* 21 (1995): 137–163.

The centrality of political socialization, family tradition, and religious communities was demonstrated earlier in an important study of Bernard F. Berelson, Paul F. Lazarsfeld, and William N. McPhee, *Voting: Study of Opinion Formation in a Presidential Campaign* (Chicago: University of Chicago Press, 1954), ch. 4; and Gerhard Lenski, *The Religious Factor* (Garden City, N.Y.: Doubleday, 1961). See also the compendious listing of relevant sources in Manza and Brooks, "Religious Factor."

In Germany, in the early 1930s, religion was easily the strongest predictor of Nazi voting, with Protestant support very high and Catholic support very low. In subsequent analysis, however, the religion factor was neglected or at best given only passing mention. Instead, commentators focused on class, and the never-demonstrated propensities of the lower-middle class. See Hamilton, *Social Misconstruction*, chs. 4, 5.

21. These problems are discussed in Hamilton, *Social Misconstruction*, chs. 6, 7. On the problems with replication, see pp. 205–206, 219–221.

22. Horace Miner, *St. Denis: A French-Canadian Parish* (1939; reprint Chicago: University of Chicago Press, 1967).

23. Rudolf Heberle, *From Democracy to Nazism: A Regional Case Study on Political Parties in Germany* (Baton Rouge: Louisiana State University Press, 1945); and *Landbevölkerung und Nationalsozialismus: Eine soziologische Untersuchung der politischen Willensbildung in Schleswig-Holstein 1918 bis 1932* (Stuttgart: Deutsche Verlags-Anstalt, 1963); Seymour Martin Lipset, *Agrarian Socialism: The Cooperative Commonwealth Federation in Saskatchewan* (Berkeley and Los Angeles: University of California Press, 1950); and John Steinbeck, *The Grapes of Wrath* (New York: Viking, 1939). Although put in the past tense, the study of debt and foreclosures in Quebec in the 1930s could still be done today.

24. Robert K. Merton, *Social Theory and Social Structure*, rev. ed. (Glencoe, Ill.: Free Press, 1957), ch. 2, "The Bearing of Sociological Theory on Empirical Research," and ch. 3, "The Bearing of Empirical Research on Sociological Theory."

25. Kenneth Underwood, *Protestant and Catholic: Religious and Social Interaction in an Industrial Community* (Boston: Beacon, 1957); Tamara K. Hareven and Randolph Langenbach, *Amoskeag: Life and Work in an American Factory-City* (New York: Pantheon, 1978); and Tamara K. Hareven, *Family Time and Industrial Time: The Relationship between the Family and Work in a New England Industrial Community* (Cambridge: Cambridge University Press, 1982). See the comments in Chapter 1, note 29.

26. The affirmation of Thesis B, here the social-bases theory, says nothing about the validity of Thesis A, in this case that it was (or is) in the cards that workers will revolt. There is another obvious possibility, that they would not revolt. It is possible that the original hypothesis was mistaken.

27. William Foote Whyte, *Street Corner Society*, enl. ed. (1943; reprint Chicago: University of Chicago Press, 1955). Another study that focuses on the same community is Walter Firey's *Land Use in Central Boston* (Cambridge: Harvard University Press, 1947), ch. 5. Herbert Gans has a study of another Italian community in Boston in the South End. See Gans, *The Urban Villagers: Group and Class in the Life of Italian-Americans* (New York: Free Press, 1962). These works begin with different theoretical concerns, but all three contain information that helps to explain the absence of class consciousness.

28. One may also make use of insights gained from literary sources. Ernst Toller, the noted German dramatist, has a play set in the early 1920s. In one scene, workers in a tavern are conversing, discussing the curiosities of their lives. One describes the misery of his home, the concerns of his wife and her unending labors, and his bedraggled children. The hopelessness of it drives him to the tavern. He points up an irony of their situation. Men are partly responsible, he says. In every meeting, "we talk to strangers about the new truthful life." But, he adds, "with one's own wife we bring not a word over our lips." In translation, socialism is a program for men, one addressing men's

problems. See Ernst Toller, *Hinkemann: Eine Tragödie* (Potsdam: Kiepenheuer, 1924), 23. Decades later, this fact became a central theme in feminist writing. See, for example, Heidi Hartmann, "The Unhappy Marriage of Marxism and Feminism," in *Women and Revolution*, ed. L. Sargent (Boston: South End Press, 1981), 15–29.

29. Michael Young and Peter Willmott, *Family and Kinship in East London* (Harmondsworth, U.K.: Penguin, 1957).

30. On the centrality of mothers in the socialization of children, both male and female, see Marion J. Levy Jr., *Our Mother-Tempers* (Berkeley and Los Angeles: University of California Press, 1989).

31. Richard F. Hamilton, *Class and Politics in the United States* (New York: Wiley, 1972), 22.

The Class Categories

The class categories used here require some further explanation and justification. The principal task is to define the categories so as to match the conceptualizations set forth in the Marxist and revisionist discussions.

Generally speaking, a person's economic circumstances will depend on one of three main determinants. First, they could depend largely on earnings gained through full-time employment. Second, they could depend largely on the earnings of another family member's full-time employment, as in the case of housewives and dependent children. And third, they could depend principally on transfer payments, from Social Security or some other pension or support system. For some, a small minority, their economic circumstances depend on the returns from a substantial fortune.

Analyses of class typically focus on employment and labor-force status. Because "occupation" and its correlates are no longer the decisive immediate determinants for the retired population, those persons have been omitted here. Another option, of course, would be to classify them by their previous occupations, that being the procedure used in my earlier work, *Class and Politics in the United States*. The present procedure recognizes the new range of determinants, the immediate life chances depending on pension arrangements versus the previous conditions of employment.

Analyses of class in Marxist and revisionist discussions typically pay little attention to either marital status or the family and its circumstances. The basic procedure used throughout most of the modern era, implicitly or explicitly, has been to classify wives and dependent children (even if in the labor force) by the occupation of the "head of the house" (or principal earner), which ordinarily refers to husbands and/or fathers.

Two major developments occurred in the second half of the 20th century to force reconsideration of that procedure. First, women entered the labor force in large numbers, many of them in full-time employment (some of them, of course, earning more than their husbands). Second, many women from working-class families, those with husbands or fathers in blue-collar employment, came to be employed in white-collar jobs. The key question is this: Should they be classified as working class or middle class?

In Chapter 3, those wives have been classified by their husbands' occupations. The reason, put simply, is that they match the husbands in outlooks; for example, in class identifications and political-party identifications. Put differently, family solidarity is stronger, by a considerable margin, than class solidarity. This procedure allows considerable economy in presentation, reducing tables and text by at least half. Some evidence supporting these claims appears in Chapter 3. Some additional evidence on the condition of the classes as delineated is presented here.

The circumstances of married men will be considered first (Table A.1). They have been classified into the five categories delineated in the text. The two upper-middle segments are strongly represented in professional occupations; they report very high family incomes. The smaller old-middle-class segment is by far the most advantaged. People in both categories recognize their advantage, with majorities reporting their incomes as above average. They also have, by far, the highest educational levels (again with the old-middle segment leading). In all these respects, the two upper-middle segments are, on the whole, very privileged categories.

Majorities of both lower-middle-class segments are employed in the "managers, sales, administration" occupational category. Some middle-class persons, it will be noted, appear in blue-collar census categories (crafts, operatives, and service). As indicated in the text, they are independent proprietors and supervisors, persons counted in both Marxist and revisionist accounts as middle class. The family incomes are high to middling. The old-middle segment shows more dispersion, more persons falling to both extremes. The two are middling also in education, with majorities reporting twelve to fifteen years.

The working class, not surprisingly, reports the lowest incomes of the five. There is general recognition of these differences. Taking the three salary/wage segments, upper-middle, lower-middle, and working class, the respective percentages reporting above-average incomes are 55, 38, and 18. The educational differences are also striking. The percentages reporting sixteen or more years are, respectively, 75, 43, and 6.[1]

Table A.1
Occupation, Income, Relative Financial Status, and Education by Class:
Nonfarm, Full-Time-Employed, Married Males (NORC–GSS: 1990–1994)

	Class					
	Upper Middle		Lower Middle			
	New	Old	New	Old	Working	Total
Occupation (Census Categories)						
Professional, Technical	78 %	76 %	11 %	3 %	-	19 %
Manager, Sales, Administrative	22	20	56	56	-	28
Clerical	-	-	23	2	-	7
Crafts	-	4	10	25	36 %	20
Operatives, Laborers	-	-	1	9	47	19
Service	-	-	-	6	17	7
N =	(204)	(46)	(347)	(163)	(471)	(1,231)
Family Income						
$ 75,000 or Over	33 %	54 %	21 %	28 %	5 %	19 %
$ 50,000 - $ 74,999	35	17	32	19	21	26
$ 35,000 - $ 49,999	21	11	24	24	32	26
$ 22,500 - $ 34,999	9	11	19	15	27	19
Less Than $ 22,500	1	6	5	14	15	9
N =	(160)	(35)	(259)	(120)	(358)	(932)
Relative Financial Status						
Above Average	55 %	67 %	38 %	43 %	18 %	35 %
Average	34	22	50	41	61	49
Below Average	11	11	12	16	21	16
N =	(204)	(46)	(342)	(163)	(464)	(1,219)
Education						
17 Years or More	50 %	61 %	15 %	9 %	1 %	17 %
16 Years	25	24	28	23	5	18
12 - 15 Years	24	13	53	58	70	54
0 - 11 Years	2	2	4	10	24	12
N =	(204)	(46)	(347)	(163)	(468)	(1,228)

The occupations of full-time employed wives differ somewhat from those of the husbands (Table A.2). The upper-middle-class wives are less likely to be in professional occupations. The most striking difference, one repeatedly signaled, is that a majority of working-class wives are in middle-class occupations.

Not shown in Table A.2 are the percentages of those with part-time employment or working as housekeepers. The differences by class are generally small and irregular, but one result stands out. Overall, 27 percent of the wives are housekeepers. For the wives of the upper-middle old-middle-class segment, the figure is 47 percent, well above

Table A.2
Occupation, Income, Relative Financial Status, and Education by
Husband's Class: Females with Nonfarm, Full-Time-Employed Husbands
(NORC–GSS: 1990–1994)

	Husband's Class					
	Upper Middle		Lower Middle			
	New	Old	New	Old	Working	Total
Wife's Occupation[a] (Census Categories)						
Professional, Technical	38 %	63 %	23 %	18 %	16 %	23 %
Manager, Sales, Administrative	25	19	26	43	16	25
Clerical	26	19	32	22	30	29
Crafts	1	-	3	3	2	2
Operatives, Laborers	3	-	8	5	17	10
Service	8	-	8	9	19	12
N =	(104)	(16)	(218)	(100)	(248)	(686)
Family Income						
$ 75,000 or Over	32 %	50 %	22 %	23 %	3 %	18 %
$ 50,000 - $ 74,999	40	32	29	31	19	27
$ 35,000 - $ 49,999	19	9	23	18	30	24
$ 22,500 - $ 34,999	6	6	19	15	26	19
Less Than $ 22,500	3	3	8	13	23	11
N =	(172)	(34)	(302)	(131)	(377)	(1,016)
Relative Financial Status						
Above Average	47 %	57 %	29 %	33 %	11 %	27 %
Average	46	28	57	53	64	56
Below Average	7	15	14	14	25	17
N =	(221)	(46)	(395)	(181)	(497)	(1,340)
Wife's Education						
17 Years or More	23 %	34 %	12 %	9 %	3 %	11 %
16 Years	30	34	19	19	6	17
12 - 15 Years	44	32	62	61	67	61
0 - 11 Years	3	-	7	11	20	12
N =	(222)	(47)	(397)	(181)	(499)	(1,346)

[a]Full-time employed women only.

the other categories. That class, in short, is uniquely privileged. Its
families are much more likely to achieve their exceptionally high incomes through the efforts of a single earner. It should also be noted
that those upper-middle-class men work more than the men of the
other classes, putting in a median of fifty-four hours per week. This
compares to forty-five-hour workweeks for the two new-middle-class
segments and forty hours for working-class men.

The reported incomes and assessments of relative financial status
provided by the married women are, understandably, very close to

Table A.3
Class Identification and Party Identification: Working-Class Husbands
and Their Wives by Wife's Employment Status (NORC–GSS: 1990–1994)

	Wife's Employment					
	Full-Time Employed		Part-Time Employed		House Keeping	Total
	Blue Collar	White Collar	Blue Collar	White Collar		
Class Identification	Percentage Middle and Upper Class					
Husbands	27 %	37 %	24 %	32 %	30 %	32 %
N =	(70)	(166)	(25)	(50)	(134)	(445)
Wives	25	42	25	30	34	34
N =	(84)	(162)	(36)	(44)	(138)	(464)
Party Identification	Percentage Republican[a]					
Husbands	40 %	40 %	36 %	39 %	43 %	41 %
N =	(70)	(167)	(25)	(51)	(132)	(445)
Wives	41	40	29	43	37	39
N =	(84)	(163)	(35)	(44)	(137)	(463)

Note: Excludes wives who are "temporarily not at work," "unemployed," "retired,"
or "at school."

[a]Other categories are "Democratic" and "Independent."

those given by the married men. Except for the workers, their levels of
education are lower than those reported by married men. The most
striking differences appear in the upper-middle-class segments, where
husbands are far better educated than wives.

The outlooks of working-class wives, broken down by their own
occupational status, are shown in Table A.3. Overall, the husbands
and wives differ little in their class identifications, the wives showing
only a 2-percent edge in middle-class identifications. The most striking finding for the present purpose is that only one-third of the working-class wives count themselves as middle class. The wives who are
employed full time in white-collar positions are most likely to identify as middle class, but even there it is a minority choice (42%). Their
husbands also, it should be noted, have the highest level of middle-
class identifications of the five segments.

The same table shows a similarly small overall difference in regard
to party identifications. A "gender gap" appears here. Overall, women
are less likely to be Republican identifiers, but the difference among
the marrieds is minuscule, only 2 percentage points. There does not
appear to be any serious class effect with regard to party identification among working-class wives. That is to say, those wives with full-
time middle-class jobs do not differ at all from their working-class

Table A.4
Class Identification and Party Identification: Husbands and Wives by
Husband's Class (NORC–GSS: 1990–1994)

	Husband's Class					
	Upper Middle		Lower Middle			
	New	Old	New	Old	Working	Total
Class Identification	Percentage Middle and Upper Class					
Husbands	81 %	91 %	62 %	60 %	31 %	55 %
N =	(204)	(46)	(347)	(158)	(467)	(1,222)
Wives	78	89	58	64	33	55
N =	(221)	(47)	(396)	(177)	(497)	(1,338)
Party Identification	Percentage Republican[a]					
Husbands	49 %	61 %	58 %	57 %	41 %	50 %
N =	(204)	(46)	(346)	(157)	(467)	(1,220)
Wives	46	55	47	50	39	45
N =	(222)	(47)	(396)	(177)	(496)	(1,338)

Nonfarm, full-time employed males; wives married to same.

[a]Other categories are "Democratic" and "Independent."

husbands and they differ little from the other categories of working-
class wives.

Looking now at the entire spectrum, we see that class identifications
vary strikingly by class (as seen in Table 3.6). The husband–wife differences within the classes, however, are minuscule, not worth discussing
(Table A.4). As for party identifications, as seen earlier, the differences by
class are small and irregular. Somewhat larger gender gaps appear with
respect to party identifications, these being largest, 11 and 7 percent,
for the new-lower-middle and old-lower-middle segments.

One must also consider the large numbers of nonmarried adults.
Approximately one-quarter of the full-time employed males are not
married or, more precisely, are not part of a current intact marriage.
They are either single, by far the largest segment, or are separated,
divorced, or widowed. The possibilities here are rather complicated.
Single persons, male and female, might be living at home with their
original family. Or they might be "on their own," with full-time employment, or they could be unemployed, or students, or with part-
time employment, or with combinations of these options. The options
for the separated, divorced, and widowed are even more complicated.
In some respects, however, all four segments have less attractive life
circumstances. The singles, overwhelmingly, are young, persons just

starting out on careers. The separated and divorced are also relatively young and are coping with damaged or broken marriages, with the many attendant costs. The widowed are, of course, older. Since we are dealing with full-time employed persons, the latter is a relatively small category (the majority of widowed being both older and retired).

To simplify matters, the four have been combined for the following discussion. We have taken only those with full-time employment, and they have been classified by their own occupations. Some "slippage" doubtlessly appears in this process, but, again, the aim is economy of presentation as opposed to ultimate precision.

The occupational distributions of the nonmarried men, on the whole, are similar to those of married men (Table A.5). The most important difference is the very limited presence of the nonmarried in the old upper-middle class. That level of independence is ordinarily achieved at a somewhat more advanced age. The incomes of the nonmarried are considerably lower than those of the comparable married segments, which holds for all categories. Despite the manifest disadvantage, the upper-new-middle-class segment made relatively favorable assessments of their financial situation, reflecting, perhaps, satisfaction with the achievement at what is an early point in their careers. The other segments, appropriately, gave less positive assessments than the comparable marrieds.

The nonmarried women with full-time employment show some similarities and some strikingly different patterns vis-à-vis comparable males (Table A.6). In terms of occupation, there is relatively strong representation in the upper-new-middle-class rank, overwhelmingly among the professionals. This distribution differs sharply from the employment pattern of comparable middle-class wives.

Representation in both old-middle-class segments is very limited. Those in the lower-new-middle class are heavily represented in the clerical category, forming a modest majority there, the highest level for any of the groups considered here. And the working class segment is, by definition, entirely working class (in contrast to the wives with working-class husbands). Unlike other working-class categories, a majority are found in service occupations.

The income levels for all these categories are very low; more than two in five reported earnings of less than $22,500. One might expect high earnings for upper-new-middle-class professionals, but that is not the case. Only one in seven reported earnings of $50,000 or more, which compares with roughly three in ten for the comparable males and two in three for the comparable marrieds. A majority of this upper-middle-class segment, accordingly, described its earnings as "average."

To guard against possible misinterpretation, it should be noted that *ceteris paribus* is definitely not the case. We are considering different

Table A.5
Occupation, Income, Relative Financial Status, and Education by Class:
Nonfarm, Full-Time-Employed Males, Single, Separated, Widowed, and
Divorced Combined (NORC–GSS: 1990–1994)

| | Respondent's Class | | | | | |
| | Upper Middle | | Lower Middle | | | |
	New	Old	New	Old	Working	Total
Occupation						
Professional, Technical	75 %	44 %	18 %	10 %	-	18 %
Manager, Sales, Administrative	25	56	49	51	-	25
Clerical	-	-	25	1	-	8
Crafts	-	-	9	27	32 %	19
Operatives, Laborer	-	-	-	10	47	20
Service	-	-	-	3	22	9
N =	(105)	(9)	(227)	(74)	(293)	(708)
Family Income						
$ 75,000 or Over	13 %	-	5 %	9 %	2 %	5 %
$ 50,000 - $ 74,999	18	43 %	15	16	7	13
$ 35,000 - $ 49,999	23	43	27	21	15	21
$ 22,500 - $ 34,999	33	14	28	25	30	29
Less Than $ 22,499	12	-	25	29	46	32
N =	(82)	(7)	(174)	(56)	(221)	(540)
Relative Financial Status						
Above Average	52 %	67 %	30 %	28 %	13 %	27 %
Average	38	33	48	47	58	50
Below Average	10	-	22	25	30	23
N =	(105)	(9)	(225)	(72)	(291)	(702)
Education						
17 Years or More	39 %	11 %	14 %	8 %	2 %	12 %
16 Years	33	56	24	22	4	17
12 - 15 Years	27	33	54	57	73	58
0 - 11 Years	1	-	8	14	21	13
N =	(105)	(9)	(226)	(74)	(291)	(705)

professions—basically, teaching, primary and secondary, versus engineering. There are, of course, many other confounding factors.

The nonmarrieds differ from the marrieds in a couple of other respects. Fair-sized differences in class identification appear in the two new-middle-class segments (Table A.7). Almost half of these upper-middle-class women do *not* identify as middle class. Only about half of the lower-middle-class men identify as middle class. Among the lower-new-middle-class women, only 35 percent do so.

Table A.6
Occupation, Income, Relative Financial Status, and Education by Class:
Nonfarm, Full-Time-Employed Females, Single, Separated, Widowed, and
Divorced Combined (General Social Survey: 1990–1994)

| | Respondent's Class | | | | | |
| | Upper Middle | | Lower Middle | | | |
	New	Old	New	Old	Working	Total
Occupation						
Professional, Technical	86 %	79 %	14 %	17 %	-	26 %
Manager, Sales, Administrative	14	21	32	38	-	21
Clerical	-	-	53	5	-	27
Crafts	-	-	1	2	12 %	3
Operatives, Laborer	-	-	*	2	30	8
Service	-	-	-	36	58	16
N =	(174)	(9)	(456)	(42)	(222)	(908)
Family Income						
$ 75,000 or Over	2 %	8 %	3 %	3 %	-	2 %
$ 50,000 - $ 74,999	12	17	8	10	3 %	8
$ 35,000 - $ 49,999	28	17	14	23	10	16
$ 22,500 - $ 34,999	43	17	31	13	20	30
Less Than $ 22,499	15	42	44	50	67	44
N =	(136)	(12)	(349)	(30)	(164)	(691)
Relative Financial Status						
Above Average	23 %	29 %	16 %	15 %	7 %	15 %
Average	56	36	50	51	50	51
Below Average	22	36	34	34	43	34
N =	(173)	(14)	(453)	(41)	(218)	(899)
Education						
17 Years or More	39 %	50 %	10 %	10 %	1 %	14 %
16 Years	29	14	18	24	7	18
12 - 15 Years	29	29	66	52	70	59
0 - 11 Years	3	7	7	14	21	10
N =	(174)	(14)	(456)	(42)	(222)	(908)

*Less than 0.5 percent.

Fair-sized differences also appear with respect to party identification. Among the marrieds, as seen in Table A.4, the gender gap
amounted to five points. Among the nonmarrieds, overall, the gap is
twice that figure.

Several lessons may be drawn from this brief review: First, on the
whole, the nonmarried segments, both the men and the women, have
less-satisfying circumstances than the comparable marrieds. Second,
husbands and wives appear to share economic circumstances, class

Table A.7
Class Identification and Party Identification: Not Currently Married Men
and Women by Class, Full-Time-Employed, Single, Separated, Widowed,
and Divorced Combined (NORC–GSS: 1990–1994)

| | Respondent's Class | | | | | |
| | Upper Middle | | Lower Middle | | | |
	New	Old	New	Old	Working	Total
Class Identification	Percentage Middle and Upper Class					
Men	72 %	100 %	49 %	50 %	20 %	41 %
N =	(104)	(9)	(227)	(74)	(292)	(706)
Women	54	50	35	51	23	37
N =	(172)	(14)	(453)	(41)	(222)	(902)
Party Identification	Percentage Republican[a]					
Men	49 %	75 %	44 %	45 %	41 %	44 %
N =	(101)	(8)	(220)	(74)	(286)	(689)
Women	38	15	36	37	27	34
N =	(168)	(13)	(451)	(41)	(216)	(889)

[a]Other categories are "Democratic" and "Independent."

identifications, and party identifications. Put differently, the gender
gap appears to be very limited within this context. Third, some important differences in condition and outlook appear between men and
women of the same class among the nonmarrieds. Although, by definition, *sharing* class position, the gender-linked differences indicate
that some other things are not equal.

One should, accordingly, keep the following things in mind when reading Chapter 3. The class categories used there combine marrieds and
nonmarrieds. Those two categories differ somewhat in socioeconomic
status, and the combination hides that division. The combination also
obscures two other facts linked to marital status: Within a given class,
married men and women tend to share outlooks, and, among the
nonmarrieds, one finds some fair-sized and diverse differences. Put
differently, this means the much-discussed gender gap is not a general
phenomenon. It exists largely among the nonmarrieds. In addition to
class, one must clearly pay attention to the range of determinants, the
advantages and disadvantages, linked to marital status.[2]

For our class categories, for our combination, we have taken the
following:

1. Married men with full-time employment.
2. Married women whose husbands are employed full time. They have been classified by their husbands' occupations.
3. Single, separated, divorced, and widowed persons who are employed full time. They have been classified by their own occupations.

This means we have excluded the following:

1. Retired persons. Their incomes are derived from another system.
2. Single, separated, divorced, and widowed who are not employed full time. They are difficult to classify in class terms. Some are receiving income or support through family connections. Some are receiving transfer income through some welfare arrangement. Some are in transitional roles, having not yet taken on full-time adult positions.

NOTES

1. On those "deviant cases," the highly educated workers, see Richard F. Hamilton and James D. Wright, "The College Educated Blue-Collar Workers," *Research on the Sociology of Work* 1 (1981): 285–334.

2. For additional discussion of these points, see Richard F. Hamilton and James D. Wright, *The State of the Masses* (New York: Aldine, 1986), chs. 4–6.

Bibliography

Abrams, Mark, and Richard Rose. *Must Labour Lose?* Harmonsworth, U.K.: Penguin, 1960.

Adams, Walter, and James W. Brock. "The Automobile Industry." In *The Structure of American Industry*, edited by Walter Adams. 8th ed. New York: Macmillan, 1990.

Adams, Walter, and Hans Mueller. "The Steel Industry." In *The Structure of American Industry*, edited by Walter Adams. 8th ed. New York: Macmillan, 1990.

Adler, Dorothy R. *British Investment in American Railways, 1834–1898.* Charlottesville: University Press of Virginia, 1970.

Ahlbrandt, Robert S., Richard J. Fruehan, and Frank Giarratani. *The Renaissance of American Steel: Lessons for Managers in Competitive Industries.* New York: Oxford University Press, 1996.

Ajzenstat, Janet, and Peter J. Smith, eds. *Canada's Origins: Liberal, Tory, or Republican?* Ottawa: Carleton University Press, 1995.

Allen, Frederick Lewis. *The Big Change: America Transforms Itself, 1900–1950.* New York: Harper, 1952.

Allen, William Sheridan. *The Nazi Seizure of Power.* Rev. ed. New York: Franklin Watts, 1984.

Anderson, Margaret Lavinia. "The Kulturkampf and the Course of German History." *Central European History* 19 (1986): 82–115.

Arblaster, Anthony. *The Rise and Decline of Western Liberalism.* Oxford: Basil Blackwell, 1984.

Arnold, Guy. *Held Fast for England: G. A. Henty, Imperialist Boys' Writer.* London: Hamish Hamilton, 1980.

Arpan, Jeffrey S., José de la Torre, and Brian Toyne. *The U.S. Apparel Industry: International Challenge, Domestic Response.* Research Monograph no. 88. Atlanta: College of Business Administration, Georgia State University, 1982.

Artz, Frederick B. *Reaction and Revolution, 1814–1832.* New York: Harper, 1934.

Bain, Trevor. *Banking the Furnace: Restructuring of the Steel Industry in Eight Countries.* Kalamazoo, Mich.: Upjohn Institute, 1992.

Bairoch, Paul. *Cities and Economic Development: From the Dawn of History to the Present.* Translated by Christopher Braider. Chicago: University of Chicago Press, 1988.

———. *Economics and World History: Myths and Paradoxes.* Chicago: University of Chicago Press, 1993.

Baran, Paul A. *The Political Economy of Growth.* New York: Monthly Review Press, 1957.

Baran, Paul A., and Paul M. Sweezy. *Monopoly Capital: An Essay on the American Economic and Social Order.* New York: Monthly Review Press, 1966.

Barnett, Donald F., and Robert W. Crandall. *Up from the Ashes: The Rise of the Steel Minimill in the United States.* Washington, D.C.: Brookings, 1986.

Beaumarchais. *The Barber of Seville and the Marriage of Figaro.* Translated and with an introduction by John Wood. London: Penguin, 1964.

Bechhofer, F., and B. Elliott. "The Petite Bourgeoisie in Late Capitalism." *Annual Review of Sociology* 11 (1985): 181–207.

Becker, Eugene H. "Self-Employed Workers: An Update to 1983." *Monthly Labor Review* 107, 7 (1984): 14–18.

Beer, Thomas. *Hanna.* New York: Knopf, 1929.

Beisner, Robert L. *From the Old Diplomacy to the New: 1865–1900.* 2d ed. Arlington Heights, Ill.: Harlan Davidson, 1986.

———. *Twelve against Empire: The Anti-Imperialists, 1898–1900.* 1968. Reprint Chicago: Imprint Publications, 1992.

Bellamy, Richard. *Liberalism and Modern Society: An Historical Argument.* University Park: Pennsylvania State University Press, 1992.

Bender, Frederic L., ed. *The Communist Manifesto.* New York: Norton, 1988.

Bennoune, Mahfoud. *The Making of Contemporary Algeria, 1830–1987: Colonial Upheavals and Post-Independence Development.* Cambridge: Cambridge University Press, 1988.

Berelson, Bernard F., Paul F. Lazarsfeld, and William N. McPhee. *Voting: Study of Opinion Formation in a Presidential Campaign.* Chicago: University of Chicago Press, 1954.

Bernstein, Eduard. *Die Voraussetzungen des Sozialismus und die Aufgaben der Sozialdemokratie.* Stuttgart: Dietz, 1899.

———. *Evolutionary Socialism: A Criticism and Affirmation.* Translated by Edith C. Harvey. New York: B. W. Huebsch, 1909.

———. *The Preconditions of Socialism.* Edited and translated by Henry Tudor. Cambridge: Cambridge University Press, 1993.

Betts, Raymond F. *France and Decolonisation, 1900–1960.* New York: St. Martin's, 1991.

Bhagwati, Jagdish. *A Stream of Windows: Unsettling Reflections on Trade, Immigration, and Democracy.* Cambridge: MIT Press, 1998.

"Big Public Funds Reap Gains." *Pensions & Investments,* 9 March 1998, 2, 68.

Blackbourn, David, and Geoff Eley. *The Peculiarities of German History: Bourgeois Society and Politics in Nineteenth-Century Germany.* New York: Oxford University Press, 1984.

Cranny, C. J., Patricia Cain Smith, and Eugene F. Stone. *Job Satisfaction: How People Feel About Their Jobs and How It Affects Their Performance*. New York: Lexington Books, 1992.

Cuneo, Carl J. "Has the Traditional Petite Bourgeoisie Persisted?" *Canadian Journal of Sociology* 9 (1984): 269–301.

Daalder, Hans, ed. *Party Systems in Denmark, Austria, Switzerland, The Netherlands, and Belgium*. London: Frances Pinter, 1987.

Dacquel, Laarni T., and Donald C. Dahmann. *Residents of Farms and Rural Areas: 1991*. U.S. Bureau of the Census, Current Population Reports, P20-472. Washington, D.C.: U.S. Government Printing Office, 1993.

Davenport, Russell W., and Editors of *Fortune*. *U.S.A.: The Permanent Revolution*. New York: Prentice Hall, 1951.

Davis, James Allan, and Tom W. Smith. *General Social Surveys, 1972–1993: Cumulative Codebook*. Chicago: National Opinion Research Center, 1993.

Davis, Nancy J., and Robert V. Robinson. "Do Wives Matter? Class Identities of Wives and Husbands in the United States, 1974–1994." *Social Forces* 76 (1998): 1063–1086.

Dawson, Carl A., and Warner E. Gettys. *An Introduction to Sociology*. New York: Ronald Press, 1929.

Deane, Phyllis. *The First Industrial Revolution*. 2d ed. Cambridge: Cambridge University Press, 1979.

Desai, Ashok V. *Real Wages in Germany, 1871–1913*. Oxford: Clarendon Press, 1968.

Diamond, Larry, and Seymour Martin Lipset. "Colonialism." *Encyclopedia of Democracy*. Vol. 1. Washington, D.C.: Congressional Quarterly, 1995.

Dickerson, Kitty G. *Textiles and Apparel in the International Economy*. New York: Macmillan, 1991.

Doyle, Michael W. *Ways of War and Peace: Realism, Liberalism, and Socialism*. New York: Norton, 1997.

Doyle, William. *The Oxford History of the French Revolution*. Oxford: Clarendon Press, 1989.

Draper, Hal. *Karl Marx's Theory of Revolution*. Vol. 2, *The Politics of Social Classes*. New York: Monthly Review Press, 1978.

Draper, Theodore. *American Communism and Soviet Russia*. New York: Viking, 1960.

Duiker, William J. *Sacred War: Nationalism and Revolution in a Divided Vietnam*. New York: McGraw-Hill, 1995.

Dunae, Patrick A. "Boys' Literature and the Idea of Empire, 1870–1914." *Victorian Studies* 24 (1980): 105–121.

———. *Dictionary of Literary Biography*. Vol. 18, *Victorian Novelists after 1885*. Edited by Ira B. Nadel and William E. Freedman. Detroit: Gale Research, 1983.

Duncan, Otis Dudley. "Ability and Achievement." *Eugenics Quarterly* 15 (1968): 1–11.

Dye, Thomas R. "Who Owns America: Strategic Ownership Positions in Industrial Corporations." *Social Science Quarterly* 64 (1983): 863–870.

Easterlin, Richard A., Christine M. Schaeffer, and Diane J. Macunovich. "Will the Baby Boomers Be Less Well Off Than Their Parents? Income, Wealth, and Family Circumstances Over the Life Cycle in the United States." *Population and Development Review* 19 (1993): 497–522.

Blake, Robert. *Disraeli*. 1967. Reprint New York: Carrol and Graf, 1987.

Blank, R. "Die soziale Zusammensetzung der sozialdemokratischen Wählerschaft Deutschlands." *Archiv für Sozialwissenschaft und Sozialpolitik* 20 (1905): 507–550.

Blaug, Mark. "Economic Imperialism Revisited." *Yale Review* 50 (1960): 335–347.

Blumenberg, Werner, ed. *August Bebels Briefwechsel mit Friedrich Engels*. The Hague: Mouton, 1965.

Bluntschli, J. C., and K. Brater. *Deutsches Staats-Wörterbuch*. Vol. 2. Stuttgart and Leipzig: Expedition des Staats-Wörterbuchs, 1857.

Böhme, Helmut. "Thesen zur Beurteilung der gesellschaftlichen, wirtschaftlichen und politischen Ursachen des deutschen Imperialismus." In *Der moderne Imperialismus*, edited by Wolfgang J. Mommsen. Stuttgart: Kohlhammer, 1971.

Bosher, J. F. *The French Revolution*. New York: Norton, 1988.

Bottomore, Tom, ed. *A Dictionary of Marxist Thought*. 2d ed. London: Basil Blackwell, 1991.

Bottomore, Tom, and Robert J. Brym, eds. *The Capitalist Class: An International Study*. New York: Harvester Wheatsheaf, 1989.

Bourdieu, Pierre. *The Logic of Practice*. Translated by Richard Nice. Stanford: Stanford University Press, 1990.

Bradford, Sarah. *Disraeli*. New York: Stein and Day, 1982.

Bradley, Ian. *Breaking the Mould? The Birth and Prospects of the Social Democratic Party*. Oxford: Martin Robertson, 1981.

Brahms, Johannes. *Briefwechsel mit dem Mannheimer Bankprokuristen Wilhelm Lindeck 1872–1882*. Sonderveröffentlichung des Stadtarchivs Mannheim, no. 6. Heidelberg: Heidelberger Verlagsanstalt und Druckerei, 1983.

Braunbehrens, Volkmar. *Mozart in Vienna: 1781–1791*. Translated by Timothy Bell. New York: Grove Weidenfeld, 1990.

Braverman, Harry. *Labor and Monopoly Capital: The Degradation of Work in the Twentieth Century*. New York: Monthly Review Press, 1974.

Bregger, John E. "Self-Employment in the United States, 1948–62." *Monthly Labor Review* 86, 1 (1963): 37–43.

———. "Measuring Self-Employment in the United States." *Monthly Labor Review* 119, 1 (1996): 3–9.

Brewer, Anthony. *Marxist Theories of Imperialism: A Critical Survey*. 2d ed. London: Routledge, 1990.

Brewer, John. *The Sinews of Power: War, Money and the English State, 1688–1783*. Cambridge: Harvard University Press, 1990.

Brinton, Crane. *English Political Thought in the Nineteenth Century*. London: Benn, 1933.

Brittan, Samuel. *Capitalism with a Human Face*. Aldershot, U.K.: Edward Elgar, 1995.

Brooks, Clem, and Jeff Manza. "Class Politics and Political Change in the United States, 1952–1992." *Social Forces* 76 (1997): 379–408.

Brown, Michael Barratt. *After Imperialism*. Rev. ed. New York: Humanities Press, 1970.

Bruneau, Thomas C. *Politics and Nationhood: Post-Revolutionary Portugal*. New York: Praeger, 1984.

Bry, Gerhard. *Wages in Germany, 1871–1945*. Princeton: Princeton University Press, 1960.

Burch, Philip H., Jr. *Managerial Revolution*. Lexington, Mass.: D. C. Heath, 1972.

Burns, E. Bradford. *A History of Brazil*. New York: Columbia University Press, 1970.

Burns, James MacGregor, J. W. Peltason, Thomas E. Cronin, and David B. Magleby. *Government by the People*. 17th ed. Upper Saddle River, N.J.: Prentice Hall, 1998.

Butler, Marilyn. *Romantics, Rebels, and Reactionaries: English Literature and Its Background, 1760–1830*. New York: Oxford University Press, 1981.

Buttinger, Joseph. *Vietnam: The Unforgettable Tragedy*. New York: Horizon Press, 1977.

Cain, P. J. "J. A. Hobson, Cobdenism, and the Radical Theory of Economic Imperialism, 1898–1914." *Economic History Review*, 2d ser., 31 (1978): 565–584.

————. *Economic Foundations of British Overseas Expansion, 1815–1914*. London: Macmillan, 1980.

Cain, P. J., and A. G. Hopkins. "The Political Economy of British Expansion Overseas, 1750–1914." *Economic History Review*, 2d ser., 33 (1980): 463–490.

————. "Gentlemanly Capitalism and British Expansion Overseas. I: The Old Colonial System, 1688–1850." *Economic History Review*, 2d ser., 39 (1986): 501–525.

————. "Gentlemanly Capitalism and British Expansion Overseas. II: New Imperialism, 1850–1945." *Economic History Review*, 2d ser., 40 (1987): 1–26.

————. *British Imperialism: Crisis and Deconstruction, 1914–1990*. London: Longman, 1993.

————. *British Imperialism: Innovation and Expansion, 1688–1914*. London: Longman, 1993.

Cairncross, A. K. *Home and Foreign Investment, 1870–1913: Studies in Capital Accumulation*. Cambridge: Cambridge University Press, 1953.

————. *The British Economy since 1945: Economic Policy and Performance, 1945–1990*. Oxford: Basil Blackwell, 1992.

Cameron, Rondo. *A Concise Economic History of the World*. 3d ed. New York: Oxford University Press, 1997.

Carosso, Vincent P. *The Morgans: Private International Bankers, 1854–1913*. Cambridge: Harvard University Press, 1987.

Carroll, Paul. *Big Blues: The Unmaking of IBM*. New York: Crown, 1993.

Carsten, Francis Ludwig. *Eduard Bernstein, 1850–1932: Eine politische Biographie*. Munich: C. H. Beck, 1993.

Cassidy, John. "The Next Thinker: The Return of Karl Marx." *The New Yorker*, 12 January 1998, 248–259.

Caton, Hiram. *The Politics of Progress: The Origins and Development of the Commercial Republic, 1600–1835*. Gainesville: University of Florida Press, 1988.

Cecil, Lamar. *Albert Ballin: Business and Politics in Imperial Germany, 1888–1918*. Princeton: Princeton University Press, 1967.

Centers, Richard. *The Psychology of Social Classes*. Princeton: Princeton University Press, 1949.

Chamberlin, T. C. "The Method of Multiple Working Hypotheses." *Science* 148 (1965): 754–759.

Chapman, Stanley. *Merchant Enterprise in Britain: From the Industrial Revol to World War I*. Cambridge: Cambridge University Press, 1992.

Chase-Dunn, Christopher. *Global Formation: Structures of the World-Eco* Oxford: Basil Blackwell, 1989.

Chernow, Ron. *The House of Morgan: An American Banking Dynasty and t of Modern Finance*. New York: Atlantic Monthly Press, 1990.

————. *Titan: The Life of John D. Rockefeller, Sr.* New York: Random 1998.

Chirot, Daniel, ed. *The Crisis of Leninism and the Decline of the Left: Th tions of 1989*. Seattle: University of Washington Press, 1991.

Chirot, Daniel, and Thomas D. Hall. "World-System Theory." *Annu of Sociology* 8 (1982): 81–106.

Christman, Henry M., ed. *The American Journalism of Marx and Enge tion from the New York Daily Tribune*. New York: New America 1966.

Clark, Grover. *The Balance Sheets of Imperialism: Facts and Figures (* New York: Columbia University Press, 1936.

Clark, Samuel. "Nobility, Bourgeoisie and the Industrial Revolu gium." *Past and Present* 105 (1984): 140–175.

Clawson, Dan. *Bureaucracy and the Labor Process: The Transformation try, 1860–1920*. New York: Monthly Review Press, 1980.

Cobban, Alfred. "The Influence of the Clergy and the 'Institutev in the Election of the French Constituent Assembly April *Historical Review* 58 (1942): 334–344.

————. *A History of Modern France*. 2d ed. Vol. 2. Harmondswo guin, 1965.

————. *France Since the Revolution and Other Aspects of Moder don*: Jonathan Cape, 1970.

Cobden, Richard. *England, Ireland, and America*. Edited by Rich 1835. Reprint Philadelphia: Institute for the Study of 1980.

Cochran, Bert. *Labor and Communism: The Conflict That Shaped* Princeton: Princeton University Press, 1977.

Collier, Peter, and David Horowitz. *The Rockefellers: An Ameri* York: Holt, Rinehart, and Winston, 1976.

Connor, Walker. *The National Question in Marxist–Leninist T* Princeton: Princeton University Press, 1984.

Conot, Robert. *A Streak of Luck: The Life & Legend of Thoma* York: Seaview, 1979.

Conversations-Lexikon. 10th ed. Vol. 9. Leipzig: F. A. Brock

Cottrell, P. L. *British Overseas Investment in the Nineteen* Macmillan, 1975.

Council of Economic Advisers. *Economic Report of the P* D.C.: U.S. Government Printing Office, 1993.

Crafts, N.F.R. *British Economic Growth during the Industri* Clarendon Press, 1985.

Craig, Gordon A. *Germany, 1866–1945*. New York: Ox 1978.

Eckland, Bruce. "Genetics and Sociology: A Reconsideration." *American Sociological Review* 32 (1967): 173–194.

Edelstein, Michael. *Overseas Investment in the Age of High Imperialism: The United Kingdom, 1850–1914*. New York: Columbia University Press, 1982.

———. "Imperialism: Cost and Benefit." In *The Economic History of Britain since 1700*, edited by Roderick Floud and Donald McCloskey. 2d ed. Vol. 2. Cambridge: Cambridge University Press, 1994.

Edwards, Alba M. "Social–Economic Groups of the United States." *American Statistical Association Quarterly* 15 (1917): 643–661.

Edwards, Richard. *Contested Terrain: The Transformation of the Workplace in the Twentieth Century*. New York: Basic Books, 1979.

Eldridge, J.E.T., ed. *Max Weber: The Interpretation of Social Reality*. New York: Scribner's, 1971.

Elliott, Charles F. "Quis custodiet sacra? Problems of Marxist Revisionism." *Journal of the History of Ideas* 28 (1993): 71–86.

Engels, Friedrich. "Germany: Revolution and Counter-Revolution." In *The German Revolutions*, edited by Leonard Krieger. Chicago: University of Chicago Press, 1967.

———. *Role of Force in History*. New York: International Publishers, 1968.

Erikson, Robert, and John H. Goldthorpe. *The Constant Flux: A Study of Class Mobility in Industrial Societies*. Oxford: Clarendon Press, 1992.

Esherick, Joseph. *The Origins of the Boxer Uprising*. Berkeley and Los Angeles: University of California Press, 1987.

Etherington, Norman. *Theories of Imperialism: War, Conquest and Capital*. London: Croom Helm, 1984.

Eyck, Erich. *A History of the Weimar Republic*. Translated by Harlan P. Hanson and Robert G. L. Waite. Vol. 1. New York: Atheneum, 1970.

Fain, T. Scott. "Self-Employed Americans: Their Number Has Increased." *Monthly Labor Review* 103, 11 (1980): 3–8.

Fairbank, John King. *The Great Chinese Revolution: 1800–1985*. New York: Harper & Row, 1986.

———. *China: A New History*. Cambridge: Belknap-Harvard, 1992.

Fairbank, John King, Edwin O. Reischauer, and Albert M. Craig. *East Asia: The Modern Transformation*. Boston: Houghton Mifflin, 1965.

Fall, Bernard B. *The Two Viet-Nams: A Political and Military Analysis*. 2d rev. ed. New York: Praeger, 1967.

Falter, Jürgen W. *Hitlers Wähler*. Munich: C. H. Beck, 1991.

Farwell, Byron. *The Great Anglo–Boer War*. Toronto: Fitzhenry and Whiteside, 1976.

Fedyshyn, Oleh S. *Germany's Drive to the East and the Ukrainian Revolution, 1917–1918*. New Brunswick: Rutgers University Press, 1971.

Feinstein, C. H. *National Income, Expenditure and Output of the United Kingdom, 1855–1965*. Cambridge: Cambridge University Press, 1972.

Feis, Herbert. *Europe the World's Banker, 1870–1914*. 1930. Reprint New York: Norton, 1965.

Feldman, Gerald D. "The Social and Economic Policies of German Big Business, 1918–1929." *American Historical Review* 75 (1969): 47–55.

———, ed. *German Imperialism, 1914–1918: The Development of a Historical Debate*. New York: Wiley, 1972.

Ferns, H. S. "Britain's Informal Empire in Argentina, 1806–1914." *Past and Present* 4 (1953): 60–75.

Feuersenger, Marianne, ed. *Gibt es noch ein Proletariat?* Frankfurt/Main: Europäische Verlagsanstalt, 1962.

Feyerabend, Paul. *Against Method: Outline of an Anarchistic Theory of Knowledge*. London: Verso, 1978.

Field, James A., Jr. "American Imperialism: The Worst Chapter in Almost Any Book." *American Historical Review* 83 (1978): 644–668.

Fieldhouse, D. K. "'Imperialism': An Historiographical Revision." *Economic History Review*, 2d ser., 14 (1961): 187–209.

———. *Economics and Empire, 1830–1914*. London: Weidenfeld and Nicolson, 1973.

Firebaugh, Glenn. "Growth Effects of Foreign and Domestic Investment." *American Journal of Sociology* 98 (1992): 105–130.

Firebaugh, Glenn, and Frank D. Beck. "Does Economic Growth Benefit the Masses?" *American Sociological Review* 59 (1994): 631–653.

Firebaugh, Glenn, and Brian Harley. "Trends in Job Satisfaction in the United States by Race, Gender, and Type of Occupation." In *Research in the Sociology of Work*. Greenwich, Conn.: JAI Press, 1993, 5 (1995): 87–104.

Firey, Walter. *Land Use in Central Boston*. Cambridge: Harvard University Press, 1947.

Fischer, Louis. *The Life of Lenin*. New York: Harper & Row, 1964.

Flechtheim, Ossip K. *Die KPD in der Weimarer Republik*. Frankfurt: Europäische Verlagsanstalt, 1969.

Fletcher, Roger. *Revisionism and Empire: Socialist Imperialism in Germany, 1897–1914*. London: George Allen and Unwin, 1984.

———. "The Life and Work of Eduard Bernstein." In *Bernstein to Brandt: A Short History of German Social Democracy*, edited by Roger Fletcher. London: Edward Arnold, 1987.

Floud, Roderick, Kenneth Wachter, and Annabel Gregory. *Height, Health and History: Nutritional Status in the United Kingdom, 1750–1980*. New York: Cambridge University Press, 1990.

Form, William. "The Sociology of a White-Collar Suburb: Greenbelt, Maryland." Ph.D. diss., University of Maryland, 1944.

———. "Self-Employed Manual Workers: Petty Bourgeois or Working Class?" *Social Forces* 60 (1982): 1050–1069.

———. "On the Degradation of Skills." *Annual Review of Sociology* 13 (1987): 29–47.

———. "Mills at Maryland." *American Sociologist* 26 (1995): 40–67.

Frank, Andre Gunder. *Capitalism and Underdevelopment in Latin America*. New York: Monthly Review Press, 1969.

Franklin, Mark N., Thomas T. Mackie, and Henry Valen. *Electoral Change: Responses to Evolving Social and Attitudinal Structures in Western Countries*. Cambridge: Cambridge University Press, 1992.

Friedman, Milton. *Capitalism and Freedom*. Chicago: University of Chicago Press, 1982.

Galbraith, John Kenneth. *The Affluent Society*. Boston: Houghton Mifflin, 1958.

———. *The New Industrial State*. Boston: Houghton Mifflin, 1967.

Galbraith, John S. "The 'Turbulent Frontier' as a Factor in British Expansion." *Comparative Studies in Society and History* 2 (1960): 150–168.

Gallagher, John, and Ronald Robinson. "The Imperialism of Free Trade." *Economic History Review*, 2d ser., 6 (1953): 1–15.

Gallup Poll Monthly 307 (April 1991): 39.

Gann, L. H., and Peter Duignan. *Burden of Empire: An Appraisal of Western Colonialism in Africa South of the Sahara*. Stanford: Hoover Institution Press, 1967.

Gans, Herbert. *The Urban Villagers: Group and Class in the Life of Italian-Americans*. New York: Free Press, 1962.

Garaudy, Roger. *Peut-on être communiste aujourd'hui?* Paris: Bernard Grasset, 1968.

Garraty, John A. *Right-Hand Man: The Life of George W. Perkins*. New York: Harper, 1960.

Gay, Peter. *The Dilemma of Democratic Socialism: Eduard Bernstein's Challenge to Marx*. New York: Columbia University Press, 1952.

Geiger, Theodor. "Panik im Mittelstand." *Die Arbeit* 7 (1930): 637–654.

German, James C., Jr. "Taft, Roosevelt, and United States Steel." *The Historian* 34 (1972): 598–613.

Gerschenkron, Alexander. *Bread and Democracy in Germany*. Berkeley and Los Angeles: University of California Press, 1943.

Gifford, Prosser, and William Roger Louis, eds. *Britain and Germany in Africa: Imperial Rivalry and Colonial Rule*. New Haven: Yale University Press, 1967.

Gilcher-Holtey, Ingrid. *Das Mandat des Intellektuellen: Karl Kautsky und die Sozialdemokratie*. Berlin: Siedler, 1986.

Girard, Alain, and Henri Bastide. "Niveau de vie et répartition professionelle." *Population* 12 (1957): 37–70.

Girifalco, Louis A. *Dynamics of Technological Change*. New York: Van Nostrand, 1991.

"Give and Take." *Chronicle of Higher Education*, 12 June 1998, A37.

Goff, Richard, Walter Moss, Janice Terry, and Jiu-Hwa Upshur. *The Twentieth Century: A Brief Global History*. 4th ed. New York: McGraw-Hill, 1994.

Goldthorpe, John H. "Women and Class Analysis: In Defence of the Conventional View." *Sociology* 17 (1983): 465–488.

———. "Women and Class Analysis: Replies to the Replies." *Sociology* 11 (1984): 491–499.

Goldthorpe, John H., David Lockwood, Frank Bechhofer, and Jennifer Platt. *The Affluent Worker: Political Attitudes and Behaviour*. Cambridge: Cambridge University Press, 1968.

———. *The Affluent Worker: Industrial Attitudes and Behaviour*. Cambridge: Cambridge University Press, 1968.

———. *The Affluent Worker in the Class Structure*. Cambridge: Cambridge University Press, 1969.

Goody, Jack. *The East in the West*. Cambridge: Cambridge University Press, 1996.

Gould, Lewis L. *Reform and Regulation: American Politics from Roosevelt to Wilson*. New York: Knopf, 1986.

————. *The Presidency of Theodore Roosevelt*. Lawrence: University Press of Kansas, 1991.

Gourevitch, Peter A. "Breaking with Orthodoxy: The Politics of Economic Policy Responses to the Depression of the 1930s." *International Organization* 38 (1984): 95–129.

————. *Politics in Hard Times: Comparative Responses to International Economic Crises*. Ithaca: Cornell University Press, 1986.

Granovetter, Mark. "Small Is Bountiful: Labor Markets and Establishment Size." *American Sociological Review* 49 (1984): 323–334.

Grimal, Henri. *Decolonization: The British, French, Dutch and Belgian Empires, 1919–1963*. Translated by Stephan De Vos. 1965. Reprint Boulder, Colo.: Westview, 1978.

Guttsman, W. L. *The German Social Democratic Party, 1875–1933: From Ghetto to Government*. London: George Allen and Unwin, 1981.

Haber, Sheldon E., Enrique J. Lamas, and Jules H. Lichtenstein. "On Their Own: The Self-Employed and Others in Private Business." *Monthly Labor Review* 110, 5 (1987): 17–23.

————. "Industrial Districts: The Road to Success for Small Businesses." *Monthly Labor Review* 115, 2 (1992): 46–47.

Hahn, Hans-Werner. *Geschichte des Deutschen Zollvereins*. Göttingen: Vandenhoeck and Ruprecht, 1984.

Halberstam, David. *The Reckoning*. New York: William Morrow, 1986.

Hamilton, Richard F. "Affluence and the Worker: The West German Case." *American Journal of Sociology* 71 (1965): 144–152.

————. *Affluence and the French Worker in the Fourth Republic*. Princeton: Princeton University Press, 1967.

————. "Einkommen und Klassenstruktur: Der Fall der Bundesrepublik." *Kölner Zeitschrift für Soziologie und Sozialpsychologie* 20 (1967): 250–287.

————. *Class and Politics in the United States*. New York: Wiley, 1972.

————. *Restraining Myths: Critical Studies of U.S. Social Structure and Politics*. New York: Sage–Halsted–Wiley, 1975.

————. *Who Voted for Hitler?* Princeton: Princeton University Press, 1982.

————. *The Bourgeois Epoch: Marx and Engels on Britain, France, and Germany*. Chapel Hill: University of North Carolina Press, 1991.

————. Review of *Hitlers Wähler*, by Jürgen W. Falter. *Contemporary Sociology* 22 (1993): 543–546.

————. *The Social Misconstruction of Reality: Validity and Verification in the Scholarly Community*. New Haven: Yale University Press, 1996.

Hamilton, Richard F., and Lowell L. Hargens. "The Politics of the Professors: Self-Identifications, 1969–1984." *Social Forces* 71 (1993): 603–627.

Hamilton, Richard F., and James D. Wright. "The College Educated Blue-Collar Workers." *Research on the Sociology of Work* 1 (1981): 285–334.

————. *The State of the Masses*. New York: Aldine, 1986.

Harding, Neil. *Lenin's Political Thought*. Vol. 2, *Theory and Practice in the Socialist Revolution*. London: Macmillan, 1981.

Hareven, Tamara K. *Family Time and Industrial Time: The Relationship between the Family and Work in a New England Industrial Community*. Cambridge: Cambridge University Press, 1982.

Hareven, Tamara K., and Randolph Langenbach. *Amoskeag: Life and Work in an American Factory-City.* New York: Pantheon, 1978.

Harr, John Ensor, and Peter J. Johnson. *The Rockefeller Century.* New York: Scribner, 1988.

Harrington, Michael. *The Other America: Poverty in the United States.* New York: Macmillan, 1962.

Hartmann, Heidi. "The Unhappy Marriage of Marxism and Feminism." In *Women and Revolution,* edited by L. Sargent. Boston: South End Press, 1981.

Hartwell, R. M., ed. *The Industrial Revolution.* New York: Barnes and Noble, 1970.

Hartwell, R. M., G. E. Mingay, Rhodes Boyson, Norman McCord, C. G. Hanson, A. W. Coats, W. H. Chaloner, W. O. Henderson, and J. M. Jefferson. *The Long Debate on Poverty: Eight Essays on Industrialisation and "The Condition of England."* London: Institute of Economic Affairs, 1972.

Hayek, Friedrich A., ed. *Capitalism and the Historians.* Chicago: University of Chicago Press, 1954.

Hayes, Carleton J. H. *A Generation of Materialism.* 1941. Reprint New York: Harper Torchbooks, 1963.

Heberle, Rudolf. *From Democracy to Nazism: A Regional Case Study on Political Parties in Germany.* Baton Rouge: Louisiana State University Press, 1945.

——. *Landbevölkerung und Nationalsozialismus: Eine soziologische Untersuchung der politischen Willensbildung in Schleswig-Holstein 1918 bis 1932.* Stuttgart: Deutsche Verlags-Anstalt, 1963.

Henderson, W. O. *The Zollverein.* Cambridge: Cambridge University Press, 1939.

——. "British Economic Activity in the German Colonies, 1884–1914." *Economic History Review* 15 (1945): 56–66.

——. "The Labour Force in the Textile Industries." *Archiv für Sozialgeschichte* 16 (1976): 283–324.

——. *The Life of Friedrich Engels.* London: Frank Cass, 1976.

——. *The German Colonial Empire, 1884–1919.* London: Cass, 1993.

Hennessy, Peter. *Never Again: Britain, 1945–1951.* New York: Pantheon, 1993.

Hennessy, Peter, and Anthony Seldon. *Ruling Performance: British Governments from Attlee to Thatcher.* Oxford: Basil Blackwell, 1987.

Heritage Foundation. "How 'Poor' Are America's Poor?" *Backgrounder,* no. 791, 21 September 1990.

——. "The Myth of Widespread American Poverty." *Backgrounder,* no. 1221, 18 September 1998.

Herring, George C. *America's Longest War: The United States and Vietnam, 1950–1975.* 3d ed. New York: McGraw-Hill, 1996.

Hessen, Robert. *Steel Titan: The Life of Charles M. Schwab.* New York: Oxford University Press, 1975.

Hidy, Ralph W., and Muriel E. Hidy. *Pioneering in Big Business, 1882–1911.* New York: Harper, 1955.

Hinde, Wendy. *Richard Cobden: A Victorian Outsider.* New Haven: Yale University Press, 1987.

Hinkle, Roscoe C. *Founding Theory of American Sociology, 1881–1915.* London: Routledge and Kegan Paul, 1980.

——. *Developments in American Sociological Theory, 1915–1950.* Albany: State University of New York Press, 1994.

Hobsbawm, Eric. *The Age of Empire, 1875–1914*. New York: Pantheon, 1987.

Hobson, C. K. *The Export of Capital*. London: Constable, 1914.

Hobson, John A. *Imperialism: A Study*. Edinburgh: Ballantyne, Hanson, 1902; 2d ed., London: Archibald Constable, 1905; 3d ed., London: George Allen and Unwin, 1938; 4th ed., Ann Arbor: University of Michigan Press, 1965.

Hodge, Robert W., Paul M. Siegel, and Peter H. Rossi. "Occupational Prestige in the United States, 1925–1963." In *Class, Status, and Power*, edited by Reinhard Bendix and Seymour Martin Lipset. 2d ed. New York: Free Press, 1966.

Hodson, Randy. "Workplace Behaviors: Good Soldiers, Smooth Operators, and Saboteurs." *Work and Occupations* 18 (1991): 271–290.

———. "Organizational Ethnographies: An Underutilized Resource in the Sociology of Work." *Social Forces* 76 (1998): 1–34.

Hoerr, John P. *And the Wolf Finally Came: The Decline of the American Steel Industry*. Pittsburgh: University of Pittsburgh Press, 1988.

Hofstadter, Richard. *The Age of Reform: From Bryan to F.D.R.* New York: Vintage Books, 1955.

Holmes, Stephen. *Passions and Constraint: On the Theory of Liberal Democracy*. Chicago: University of Chicago Press, 1995.

Holub, Robert C. "Young Germany." In *A Concise History of German Literature to 1900*, edited by Kim Vivian. Columbia, S.C.: Camden House, 1992.

Horowitz, Irving Louis. *C. Wright Mills: An American Utopian*. New York: Free Press, 1983.

Houser, Robert M., and John Robert Warren. "Socioeconomic Indexes for Occupations: A Review, Update, and Critique." *Sociological Methodology* 27 (1997): 177–298.

Hovde, Brynjolf J. "Socialistic Theories of Imperialism Prior to the Great War." *Journal of Political Economy* 38 (1928): 569–591.

Howard, Michael. *War and the Liberal Conscience*. New Brunswick: Rutgers University Press, 1978.

Hugo, Victor. Preface to *Hernani*, edited by David Owen Evans. London: Thomas Nelson, 1936.

Hunley, J. D. *The Life and Thought of Friedrich Engels*. New Haven: Yale University Press, 1991.

Huttenback, Robert A. *The British Imperial Experience*. New York: Harper & Row, 1966.

"Industrial Districts: The Road to Success for Small Businesses." *Monthly Labor Review* 115, 2 (1992): 46–47.

Inglehart, Ronald. *The Silent Revolution: Changing Values and Political Styles among Western Publics*. Princeton: Princeton University Press, 1977.

———. *Culture Shift in Advanced Industrial Society*. Princeton: Princeton University Press, 1990.

International Labour Organization. *Working Conditions in the Textiles Industry in the Light of Technological Changes*. Report 2. Geneva: International Labour Office, 1991.

Investment Company Institute. *1999 Mutual Fund Fact Book*. 39th ed. Washington, D.C.: Investment Company Institute, 1999.

Irwin, Douglas A. *Against the Tide: An Intellectual History of Free Trade*. Princeton: Princeton University Press, 1966.

Isaacs, McAllister, III. "World Class Manufacturers Cut Labor Needs in Half." *Textile World* 139, 10 (1989): 71–76.

———. "Manufacturing: Pace of Change Is Breathtaking." *Textile World* 140, 10 (1990): 21–30.

Jack, Ian. *English Literature: 1815–1832*. Oxford: Clarendon Press, 1963.

Jackson, Kenneth T. *Crabgrass Frontier: The Suburbanization of the United States*. New York: Oxford University Press, 1985.

Jarausch, Konrad H., and Larry Jones, eds. *In Search of a Liberal Germany: Studies in the History of German Liberalism from 1789 to the Present*. New York: Berg, 1990.

Jay, Richard. *Joseph Chamberlain: A Political Study*. Oxford: Clarendon Press, 1981.

Jefferson, J. M. "Industrialisation and Poverty: In Fact and Fiction." In *The Long Debate on Poverty: Eight Essays on Industrialisation and the Condition of England*, by R. M. Hartwell, G. E. Mingay, Rhodes Boyson, Norman McCord, C. G. Hanson, A. W. Coats, W. H. Chaloner, W. O. Henderson, and J. M. Jefferson. London: Institute of Economic Affairs, 1972.

Jenks, Leland H. "Britain and American Railway Development." *Journal of Economic History* 4 (1951): 375–388.

Jones, Howard Mumford. *Revolution and Romanticism*. Cambridge: Harvard University Press, 1974.

Josephson, Matthew. *Edison: A Biography*. New York: McGraw-Hill, 1959.

———. *The President Makers: The Culture of Politics and Leadership in an Age of Enlightenment, 1896–1919*. 1940. Reprint New York: Frederick Unger, 1969.

Judd, Denis. *Radical Joe: A Life of Joseph Chamberlain*. London: Hamish Hamilton, 1977.

Kagan, Donald, Steven Ozment, and Frank M. Turner. *The Western Heritage*. 4th ed. New York: Macmillan, 1991.

Kahin, George McTurnan. *Nationalism and Revolution in Indonesia*. Ithaca: Cornell University Press, 1952.

Kahler, Miles. *Decolonization in Britain and France: The Domestic Consequences of International Relations*. Princeton: Princeton University Press, 1984.

Kann, Robert A. *Habsburg Empire: A Study of Integration and Disintegration*. New York: Praeger, 1957.

Karnow, Stanley. *In Our Image: America's Empire in the Philippines*. New York: Random House, 1989.

———. *Vietnam: A History*. Rev. and updated. New York: Viking Penguin, 1991.

Kautsky, Karl. *Das Erfurter Programm*. 3d ed. Stuttgart: Dietz, 1892.

———. *Bernstein und das sozialdemokratische Programm: Ein Antikritik*. Stuttgart: Dietz, 1899.

———. *The Road to Power*. Translated by A. M. Simons. Chicago: S. A. Bloch, 1909.

———. *The Class Struggle* (Erfurt Program). Translated by William E. Bohn. Chicago: C. H. Kerr, 1910.

———. *The Social Revolution*. Translated by A. M. Simons and May Wood Simons. Chicago: Charles H. Kerr, 1912.

———. *The Dictatorship of the Proletariat*. Translated by H. J. Stenning. 1964. Reprint Westport, Conn.: Greenwood Press, 1981.

Kelf-Cohen, Reuben. *British Nationalisation, 1945–1973*. London: Macmillan, 1973.

Keller, Maryann. *Rude Awakening: The Rise, Fall and Struggle for Recovery of General Motors*. New York: William Morrow, 1989.

———. *Collision: GM, Toyota, Volkswagen and the Race to Own the 21st Century*. New York: Currency-Doubleday, 1993.

Kelly, George Armstrong. "The Machine of the Duc D'Orléans and the New Politics." *Journal of Modern History* 51 (1979): 667–684.

Keltie, J. S., ed. *Statesman's Yearbook 1911*. London: Macmillan, 1911.

Keltie, J. S., and M. Epstein, eds. *Statesman's Yearbook 1922*. London: Macmillan, 1922.

———. *Statesman's Yearbook 1926*. London: Macmillan, 1926.

Kennedy, A. L. *Salisbury, 1830–1903: Portrait of a Statesman*. London: John Murray, 1953.

Kennedy, W. P. "Foreign Investment, Trade and Growth in the United Kingdom, 1873–1913." *Explorations in Economic History* 11 (1974): 415–444.

Kent, Marion, ed. *The Great Powers and the End of the Ottoman Empire*. Boston: Allen and Unwin, 1984.

Kerbo, Harold R. *Social Stratification and Inequality: Class Conflict in Historical and Comparative Perspective*. 3d ed. New York: McGraw-Hill, 1996.

Kiernan, V. G. *Marxism and Imperialism*. London: Edward Arnold, 1974.

Kindleberger, Charles P. *The World in Depression, 1929–1939*. Rev. ed. Berkeley and Los Angeles: University of California Press, 1986.

Kitschelt, Herbert. *The Transformation of European Social Democracy*. Cambridge: Cambridge University Press, 1994.

Klotzbach, Kurt. *Der Weg zur Staatspartei: Programmatik, praktische Politik und Organisation der deutschen Sozialdemokratie 1945 bis 1965*. Berlin/Bonn: Dietz, 1982.

Koch, H. W., ed. *The Origins of the First World War*. 2d ed. London: Macmillan, 1974.

Kocka, Jürgen. *White Collar Workers in America, 1890–1940: A Social–Political History in International Perspective*. Translated by Maura Kealey. Beverly Hills, Calif.: Sage, 1980.

Koebner, Richard, and Helmut Dan Schmidt. *Imperialism: The Story and Significance of a Political Word, 1840–1960*. Cambridge: Cambridge University Press, 1964.

Kolakowski, Leszek. *Main Currents of Marxism*. Translated by P. S. Falla. Oxford: Clarendon Press, 1978.

Komlos, John, ed. *Stature, Living Standards, and Economic Development: Essays in Anthropometric History*. Chicago: University of Chicago Press, 1994.

Kossmann, E. H. *The Low Countries, 1780–1940*. Oxford: Clarendon Press, 1978.

Krüger, Horst, ed. *Was ist Heute Links?* Munich: Paul List Verlag, 1963.

Krugman, Herbert E. "The Role of Hostility in the Appeal of Communism in the United States." *Psychiatry* 16 (1953): 253–261.

Laderman, Jeffrey M. *1991 Business Week's Annual Guide to Mutual Funds*. New York: McGraw-Hill, 1991.

Landes, David S. "Some Thoughts on the Nature of Economic Imperialism." *Journal of Economic History* 21 (1961): 496–512.

———. *The Unbound Prometheus: Technological Change and Industrial Development in Western Europe from 1750 to the Present*. Cambridge: Cambridge University Press, 1969.

———. *The Wealth and Poverty of Nations: Why Some Are So Rich and Some So Poor*. New York: Norton, 1998.

Langer, William L. "A Critique of Imperialism." *Foreign Affairs* 14 (1935): 102–119.

———. *Political and Social Upheaval, 1832–1852*. New York: Harper & Row, 1969.

———. *The Diplomacy of Imperialism, 1890–1902*. 2d ed. 1951. Reprint New York: Knopf, 1972.

Langewiesche, Dieter. *Liberalismus in Deutschland*. Frankfurt am Main: Suhrkamp, 1988.

———, ed. *Liberalismus im 19. Jahrhundert: Deutschland im europäischen Vergleich*. Göttingen: Vandenhoeck and Ruprecht, 1988.

Laqueur, Walter. *Europe in Our Time: A History, 1945–1992*. New York: Penguin, 1992.

Lebovics, Herman. *The Alliance of Iron and Wheat in the Third French Republic*. Baton Rouge: Louisiana State University Press, 1988.

Leech, Margaret. *In the Days of McKinley*. New York: Harper, 1959.

Leege, David C., and Lyman A. Kellstedt. *Rediscovering the Religious Factor in American Politics*. Armonk, N.Y.: M. E. Sharpe, 1993.

Leites, Nathan. *On the Game of Politics in France*. Stanford: Stanford University Press, 1959.

Lemaitre, George. *Beaumarchais*. New York: Knopf, 1949.

Lemke, Christiane, and Gary Marks, eds. *The Crisis of Socialism in Europe*. Durham, N.C.: Duke University Press, 1992.

Lenin, V. I. *Imperialism: The Highest Stage of Capitalism: A Popular Outline*. New York: International Publishers, 1939.

———. *Collected Works*, edited by George Hanna. Vols. 22, 35. Moscow: Progress Publishers, 1964.

Lenski, Gerhard. *The Religious Factor*. Garden City, N.Y.: Doubleday, 1961.

———. "Marxist Experiments in Destratification: An Appraisal." *Social Forces* 57 (1978): 364–383.

———. "New Light on Old Issues: The Relevance of 'Really Existing Socialist Societies' for Stratification Theory." In *Social Stratification: Class, Race, and Gender in Sociological Perspective*, edited by David B. Grusky. Boulder, Colo.: Westview, 1994.

Levy, Marion J., Jr. *Our Mother-Tempers*. Berkeley and Los Angeles: University of California Press, 1989.

Licht, Walter. "How the Workplace Has Changed in 75 Years." *Monthly Labor Review* 111, 2 (1988): 19–25.

Lichtenberger, James P. *The Development of Social Theory*. New York: Century, 1925.

Lichtheim, George. *Marxism: An Historical and Critical Study*. New York: Praeger, 1961.

———. *Imperialism*. New York: Praeger, 1971.

Liebknecht, Wilhelm. *Socialism: What It Is and What It Seeks to Accomplish*. Chicago: Charles H. Kerr, n.d.

Linder, Marc, and John Houghton. "Self-Employment and the Petty Bourgeoisie: Comment on Steinmetz and Wright." *American Journal of Sociology* 96 (1990): 727–735.

Lindert, Peter H., and Jeffrey G. Williamson. "English Workers' Living Standards During the Industrial Revolution: A New Look." *Economic History Review*, 2d ser., 36 (1983): 1–25.

Link, Arthur S. *Woodrow Wilson and the Progressive Era, 1910–1917*. New York: Harper, 1954.

Linz, Julian. "The Social Bases of West German Politics." Ph.D. diss., Columbia University, 1959.

Lipset, Seymour Martin. *Agrarian Socialism: The Cooperative Commonwealth Federation in Saskatchewan*. Berkeley and Los Angeles: University of California Press, 1950.

———. *Political Man: The Social Bases of Politics*. Garden City, N.Y.: Doubleday, 1960.

———. *Revolution and Counterrevolution: Change and Persistence in Social Structures*. New York: Basic Books, 1968.

———. "Why No Socialism in the United States?" In *Sources of Contemporary Radicalism*, edited by Seweryn Bialer and Sophia Sluzar. Boulder, Colo.: Westview, 1977.

———. *Continental Divide: The Values and Institutions of the United States and Canada*. New York: Routledge, 1990.

———. "No Third Way: A Comparative Perspective on the Left." In *The Crisis of Leninism and the Decline of the Left: The Revolutions of 1989*, edited by Daniel Chirot. Seattle: University of Washington Press, 1991.

Lipset, Seymour Martin, and Reinhard Bendix. *Social Mobility in Industrial Society*. Berkeley and Los Angeles: University of California Press, 1959.

Lipset, Seymour Martin, Martin A. Trow, and James S. Coleman. *Union Democracy*. Glencoe, Ill.: Free Press, 1956.

Long, Roger D., ed. *The Man on the Spot: Essays in British Imperial History*. Westport, Conn.: Greenwood Press, 1995.

Longford, Elizabeth. *The Life of Byron*. Boston: Little, Brown, 1976.

Louis, William Roger. *Great Britain and Germany's Lost Colonies, 1914–1919*. Oxford: Clarendon Press, 1967.

———, ed. *Imperialism: The Robinson and Gallagher Controversy*. New York: New Viewpoints, 1976.

Lowe, C. J. *The Reluctant Imperialists: British Foreign Policy, 1878–1902*. New York: Macmillan, 1969.

Luethy, Herbert. *France Against Herself*. Translated by Eric Mosbacher. New York: Praeger, 1955.

Lustick, Ian S. *Unsettled States, Disputed Lands: Britain and Ireland, France and Algeria, Israel and the West Bank–Gaza*. Ithaca: Cornell University Press, 1993.

Lynch, John. *The Spanish American Revolutions: 1808–1826*. 2d ed. New York: Norton, 1986

Mace, Myles L. *Directors: Myth and Reality*. 1971. Reprint Boston: Harvard Business School Press, 1986.

Machin, Howard, ed. *National Communism in Western Europe: A Third Way to Socialism?* London: Methuen, 1983.

Macionis, John J. *Sociology*. 7th ed. Upper Saddle River, N.J.: Prentice Hall, 1999.

Mack Smith, Denis. *Italy: A Modern History*. Rev. ed. Ann Arbor: University of Michigan Press, 1969.

———. *Modern Italy: A Political History*. Ann Arbor: University of Michigan Press, 1997.

Maehl, William Harvey. *August Bebel: Shadow Emperor of the German Workers*. Philadelphia: American Philosophical Society, 1980.

Magdoff, Harry. *The Age of Imperialism: The Economics of U.S. Foreign Policy*. New York: Monthly Review Press, 1969.

Mankiw, N. Gregory. *Principles of Microeconomics*. Fort Worth: Dryden, 1998.

Mann, Michael. *Sources of Social Power*. 2 vols. New York: Cambridge University Press, 1993.

Manners, William. *TR and Will: A Friendship That Split the Republican Party*. New York: Harcourt Brace Jovanovich, 1969.

Manza, Jeff, and Clem Brooks. "Does Class Analysis Still Have Anything to Contribute to the Study of Politics?" *Theory and Society* 25 (1996): 717–724.

———. "The Religious Factor in U.S. Presidential Elections, 1960–1992." *American Journal of Sociology* 103 (1997): 38–81.

Manza, Jeff, Michael Hout, and Clem Brooks. "Class Voting in Capitalist Democracies: Dealignment, Realignment, or Trendless Fluctuation." *Annual Review of Sociology* 21 (1995): 137–163.

Marcus, Steven. "Marx's Masterpiece at 150." *New York Times Book Review*, 26 April 1998, 39.

Marks, Harry. "The Sources of Reformism in the Social Democratic Party of Germany, 1890–1914." *Journal of Modern History* 11 (1939): 334–356.

Marlowe, John. *Milner: Apostle of Empire*. London: Hamish Hamilton, 1976.

Marshall, Gordon, Howard Newby, David Rose, and Carolyn Vogler. *Social Class in Modern Britain*. London: Hutchinson, 1988.

Martin, Stephen. "The Petroleum Industry." In *The Structure of American Industry*, edited by Walter Adams. 8th ed. New York: Macmillan, 1990.

Marx, Karl. *Capital: A Critique of Political Economy*. New York: International Publishers, 1975, *MECW*, 35.

Marx, Karl, and Friedrich Engels. *Letters to Americans: 1848–1895*, edited by Alexander Trachtenberg. New York: International Publishers, 1953.

———. *Werke*. Berlin: Dietz Verlag, 1964.

———. *Collected Works*. New York: International Publishers, 1976.

Mathew, W. M. "The Imperialism of Free Trade: Peru, 1820–70." *Economic History Review*, 2d ser., 21 (1968): 562–579.

Mathias, Peter. *The First Industrial Nation: An Economic History of Britain, 1700–1914*. 2d ed. London: Methuen, 1983.

Matthew, H.C.G. *The Liberal Imperialists: The Ideas and Politics of a Post-Gladstonian Elite*. London: Oxford University Press, 1973.

———. *Gladstone 1809–1874*. Oxford: Clarendon Press, 1986.

———. *Gladstone 1875–1898*. Oxford: Clarendon Press, 1995.

May, Ernest R. *American Imperialism: A Speculative Essay*. New York: Atheneum, 1968.

McCloskey, D. N. "Did Victorian Britain Fail?" *Economic History Review*, 2d ser., 23 (1970): 446–459.

McConnell, Grant. *Steel and the Presidency, 1962.* New York: Norton, 1963.

McKenzie, Richard B. *What Went Right in the 1980s.* San Francisco: Pacific Research Institute for Public Policy, 1994.

McKibbon, Ross. "Why Was There No Marxism in Great Britain?" *English Historical Review* 99 (1984): 298–331.

McLellan, David. *Karl Marx: His Life and Thought.* London: Macmillan, 1973.

——— *Marxism after Marx: An Introduction.* New York: Harper & Row, 1979.

Mehring, Franz. *Deutsche Geschichte vom Ausgange des Mittelalters.* 1910. Reprint Berlin: Dietz Verlag, 1947.

Mény, Yves. *Government and Politics in Western Europe: Britain, France, Italy, and Germany.* Translated by Janet Lloyd. 2d ed. Oxford: Oxford University Press, 1993.

Merton, Robert K. *Social Theory and Social Structure.* Rev. ed. Glencoe, Ill.: Free Press, 1957.

Messinger, Gary S. *Manchester in the Victorian Age.* Manchester: Manchester University Press, 1985.

Meyer, Michael C., and William L. Sherman. *The Course of Mexican History.* 5th ed. New York: Oxford University Press, 1995.

Michels, Robert. "Die deutsche Sozialdemokratie. I. Parteimitgliedschaft und soziale Zusammensetzung." *Archiv für Sozialwissenschaft und Sozialpolitik* 23 (1906): 471–556.

———. "Die deutsche Sozialdemokratie im internationalen Verbande: Eine kritische Untersuchung." *Archiv für Sozialwissenschaft und Sozialpolitik* 25 (1907): 148–231.

———. *Political Parties: A Sociological Study of the Oligarchical Tendencies of Modern Democracy.* Translated by Eden Paul and Cedar Paul. Glencoe, Ill.: Free Press, 1958.

Mickelson, Sig. *The Northern Pacific Railroad and the Selling of the West: A Nineteenth Century Public Relations Venture.* Sioux Falls, S.D.: Center for Western Studies/Pine Hill Press, 1993.

Miliband, Ralph. "Socialism and the Myth of the Golden Past." In *The Socialist Register: 1964*, edited by Ralph Miliband and John Saville. New York: Monthly Review Press, 1964.

Miller, Ann R., Donald J. Treiman, Pamela S. Cain, and Patricia A. Roos, eds. *Work, Jobs, and Occupations: A Critical Review of the Dictionary of Occupational Titles.* Washington, D.C.: National Academy Press, 1980.

Miller, S. M., and Roy Bennett. "A New-Imperialism Critique: Do the Rich Nations Need the Poor?" New York University, *Center for International Studies Policy Papers* 4, 1 (1971).

Mills, C. Wright. *White Collar: The American Middle Classes.* New York: Oxford University Press, 1951.

Miner, Horace. *St. Denis: A French-Canadian Parish.* 1939. Reprint Chicago: University of Chicago Press, 1967.

Mitchell, B. R. *Abstract of British Historical Statistics.* Cambridge: Cambridge University Press, 1962.

———. *European Historical Statistics 1750–1970.* Cambridge: Cambridge University Press, 1975.

Mommsen, Wolfgang J. *Der europäische Imperialismus*. Göttingen: Vandenhoeck and Ruprecht, 1979.

———. *Theories of Imperialism*. Translated by P. S. Falla. New York: Random House, 1980.

Morgan, David W. "The Father of Revisionism Revisited: Eduard Bernstein." *Journal of Modern History* 51 (1979): 525–532.

Morgan, Kenneth O. *Labour in Power, 1945–1951*. Oxford: Clarendon Press, 1984.

Morgan, Wayne. *William McKinley and His America*. Syracuse: Syracuse University Press, 1963.

Mowery, David C., and Nathan Rosenberg. *Technology and the Pursuit of Economic Growth*. Cambridge: Cambridge University Press, 1989.

Namier, Lewis. *1848: The Revolution of the Intellectuals*. London: Oxford University Press, 1946.

Nelson, Ralph L. *Concentration in the Manufacturing Industries of the United States*. New Haven: Yale University Press, 1963.

Neumann, Sigmund. "Germany." In *European Political Systems*, edited by Taylor Cole. 2d ed. New York: Knopf, 1959.

———, ed. *Modern Political Parties: Approaches to Comparative Politics*. Chicago: University of Chicago Press, 1956.

Nevins, Allen. *John D. Rockefeller: The Heroic Age of American Enterprise*. 2 vols. New York: Scribner, 1940.

———. *John D. Rockefeller: A Study in Power*. 2 vols. New York: Scribner, 1953.

New York Stock Exchange. *Shareownership 1990*. New York: New York Stock Exchange, 1991.

———. *Fact Book for the Year 1995*. New York: New York Stock Exchange, 1996.

———. *Fact Book for the Year 1998*. New York: New York Stock Exchange, 1999.

Noyes, P. H. *Organization and Revolution: Working-Class Associations in the German Revolutions of 1848–1849*. Princeton: Princeton University Press, 1966.

Nutt-Powell, Thomas E. "The House That Machines Built." *Technology Review* 88, 8 (1988): 30–37.

O'Brien, Patrick. "European Economic Development: The Contribution of the Periphery." *Economic History Review*, 2d ser., 35 (1982): 1–18.

O'Brien, Terence H. *Milner: Viscount Milner of St. James's and Cape Town, 1854–1925*. London: Constable, 1979.

Oneal, John R., and Bruce M. Russett. "The Classical Liberals Were Right: Democracy, Interdependence, and Conflict, 1950–1985." *International Studies Quarterly* 41 (1997): 267–294.

O'Neill, William L. *The Last Romantic: A Life of Max Eastman*. New York: Oxford University Press, 1978.

Padgett, Stephen, and William E. Paterson. *A History of Social Democracy in Postwar Europe*. London: Longman, 1991.

Paish, George. "Great Britain's Investments in Other Lands." *Journal of the Royal Statistical Society* 72 (1909): 456–480.

———. "Great Britain's Capital Investments in Individual Colonial and Foreign Countries." *Journal of the Royal Statistical Society* 74 (1911): 167–200.

Pakenham, Thomas. *The Boer War*. London: Weidenfeld and Nicolson, 1979.

———. *The Scramble for Africa, 1876–1912*. New York: Random House, 1991.

Park, Robert E., and Ernest W. Burgess. *Introduction to the Science of Sociology*. 2d ed. Chicago: University of Chicago Press, 1924.

Parsons, Talcott. *The Structure of Social Action: A Study in Social Theory with Special Reference to a Group of Recent European Writers*. Glencoe, Ill.: Free Press, 1949.

Peemans, Jean-Philippe. "Imperial Hangovers: Belgium—The Economics of Decolonization." *Journal of Contemporary History* 15 (1980): 257–286.

Pelling, Henry. *The Labour Governments, 1945–51*. London: Macmillan, 1984.

"Pension Assets Grow." *Pensions & Investments*, 20 January 1997, 3, 96.

Pirker, Theo. *Die SPD nach Hitler: Die Geschichte der Sozialdemokratischen Partei Deutschlands 1945–1964*. Munich: Rütten and Loening, 1965.

Platt, D.C.M. "The Imperialism of Free Trade: Some Reservations." *Economic History Review*, 2d ser., 21 (1968): 296–306.

———. "Further Objections to an 'Imperialism of Free Trade,' 1830–60." *Economic History Review*, 2d ser., 26 (1973): 77–91.

———. *Britain's Investment Overseas on the Eve of the First World War: The Use and Abuse of Numbers*. London: Macmillan, 1986.

———. *Mickey Mouse Numbers in World History: A Short View*. London: Macmillan, 1989.

Popenoe, David. "American Family Decline, 1960–1990: A Review and Appraisal." *Journal of Marriage and the Family* 55 (1993): 527–555.

Pratt, Julius W. *The Expansionists of 1898: The Acquisition of Hawaii and the Spanish Islands*. 1936. Reprint. Chicago: Quadrangle, 1964.

Price, Richard. *An Imperial War and the British Working Class: Working-Class Attitudes and Reactions to the Boer War 1899–1902*. London: Routledge and Kegan Paul, 1972.

Przeworski, Adam. *Capitalism and Social Democracy*. Cambridge: Cambridge University Press, 1985.

Purcell, Victor. *The Boxer Uprising: A Background Study*. Cambridge: Cambridge University Press, 1963.

Quinn, Robert P. , Thomas W. Mangione, and Stanley E. Seashare, "1972–73 Quality of Employment Survey." Ann Arbor: Survey Research Center, 1975.

Ralph, Philip Lee, Robert E. Lerner, Standish Meacham, Alan T. Wood, Richard W. Hull, and Edward McNall Burns. *World Civilizations: Their History and Their Culture*. 9th ed. Vol. 2. New York: Norton, 1997.

Ray, Robert N. "A Report on Self-Employed Americans in 1973." *Monthly Labor Review* 98, 1 (1975): 49–54.

Reid, Anthony. *The Indonesian National Revolution, 1945–1950*. Hawthorn, Victoria, Australia: Longman, 1974.

Reuss, Martin. "The Disgrace and Fall of Carl Peters: Morality, Politics and Staatsräson in the Time of Wilhelm II." *Central European History* 14 (1981): 110–141.

Rigby, S. H. *Engels and the Formation of Marxism: History, Dialectics and Revolution*. Manchester: Manchester University Press, 1992.

Rippy, Merrill. "The Economic Repercussions of Expropriation: A Case Study: Mexican Oil." *Inter-American Economic Affairs* 5 (1951): 52–72.

———. *Oil and the Mexican Revolution*. Leiden, The Netherlands: Brill, 1972.

Ritter, Gerhard A. *Die Arbeiterbewegung im Wilhelminischen Reich: Die sozialdemokratische Partei und die freien Gewerkschaften 1890–1900.* Berlin: Colloquium Verlag, 1963.

Roberts, Clayton, and David Roberts. *A History of England.* 3d ed. Englewood Cliffs, N.J.: Prentice Hall, 1991.

Robertson, Priscilla. *Revolutions of 1848: A Social History.* Princeton: Princeton University Press, 1952.

Robins, Robert S., ed. *Psychopathology and Political Leadership.* New Orleans: Tulane Studies in Political Science, 1977.

Robins, Robert S., and Jerrold M. Post. *Political Paranoia: The Psychopolitics of Hatred.* New Haven: Yale University Press, 1997.

Robinson, Ronald, John Gallagher, and Alice Denny. *Africa and the Victorians: The Climax of Imperialism.* New York: St. Martin's, 1961.

Rogow, Arnold A. *The Labour Government and British Industry, 1945–1951.* Ithaca: Cornell University Press, 1955.

Rose, Richard, ed. *Electoral Behavior: A Comparative Handbook.* New York: Free Press, 1974.

Rosenberg, Arthur. *The Birth of the German Republic, 1871–1918.* Translated by Ian Morrow. London: Oxford University Press, 1931.

Rosenberg, Nathan. *Inside the Black Box: Technology and Economics.* Cambridge: Cambridge University Press, 1982.

Ross, George, Stanley Hoffmann, and Sylvia Malzacher, eds. *The Mitterrand Experiment: Continuity and Change in Modern France.* Cambridge: Polity Press, 1987.

Rotberg, Robert I. *The Founder: Cecil Rhodes and the Pursuit of Power.* New York: Oxford University Press, 1988.

Roth, Guenther. "Weber the Would-Be Englishman: Anglophilia and Family History." In *Weber's Protestant Ethic, Origins, Evidence, Contexts,* edited by Hartmut Lehmann and Guenther Roth. Cambridge: Cambridge University Press, 1993.

———. "Heidelberg–London–Manchester: Zu Max Webers deutsch–englischer Familiengeschichte." In *Heidelberg im Schnittpunkt intellektueller Kreise,* edited by Hubert Treiber and Karol Sauerland. Opladen: Westdeutscher Verlag, 1995.

Routh, Guy. *Occupation and Pay in Great Britain, 1906–1960.* Cambridge: Cambridge University Press, 1965.

Rühle, Jürgen. *Literature & Revolution.* New York: Praeger, 1969.

Russell, James W. *Introduction to Macrosociology.* 2d ed. Upper Saddle River, N.J.: Prentice Hall, 1996.

Sagarra, Eda. *Tradition and Revolution: German Literature and Society, 1830–1890.* New York: Basic Books, 1971.

Salvadori, Massimo. *Karl Kautsky and the Socialist Revolution, 1880–1938.* Translated by Jon Rothschild. London: NLB, 1979.

Sassoon, Donald. *One Hundred Years of Socialism: The West European Left in the Twentieth Century.* New York: New Press, 1996.

Scarr, Sandra, and Richard A. Weinberg. "The Influence of 'Family Background' on Intellectual Attainment." *American Sociological Review* 43 (1978): 674–692.

Schalk, David L. *War and the Ivory Tower: Algeria and Vietnam*. New York: Oxford University Press, 1991.

Schama, Simon. *Citizens: A Chronicle of the French Revolution*. New York: Knopf, 1989.

Schellenger, Harold Kent, Jr. *The SPD in the Bonn Republic: A Socialist Party Modernizes*. The Hague: Martinus Nijhoff, 1968.

Scherer, Frederick M. "Industrial Structure, Scale Economics, and Worker Alienation." In *Essays on Industrial Organization*, edited by Robert T. Masson and P. David Qualls. Cambridge, Mass.: Ballinger, 1976.

———. *Industrial Market Structure and Economic Performance*. 2d ed. Chicago: Rand McNally, 1980.

Scheuerman, William. *The Steel Crisis: The Economics and Politics of a Declining Industry*. New York: Praeger, 1986.

Schrank, Robert. *Ten Thousand Working Days*. Cambridge: MIT Press, 1978.

Schumpeter, Joseph. "Imperialism." In *Imperialism and Social Classes*, edited by Paul M. Sweezy. New York: A. M. Kelley, 1951.

Scoville, James. "The Development and Relevance of U.S. Occupational Data." *Industrial and Labor Relations Review* 19 (1965): 70–79.

Sennett, Richard, and Jonathan Cobb. *The Hidden Injuries of Class*. New York: Knopf, 1973.

Service, Robert. *Lenin: A Political Life*. Vol. 2, *Worlds in Collision*. Bloomington: Indiana University Press, 1991.

Sheehan, James J. *German Liberalism in the Nineteenth Century*. Chicago: University of Chicago Press, 1978.

Smelser, Neil. *Sociology*. 5th ed. Englewood Cliffs, N.J.: Prentice Hall, 1995.

Smith, Adam. *An Inquiry into the Nature and Causes of the Wealth of Nations*. Edited by C. J. Bullock. 1776. Reprint New York: Collier, 1937.

Smith, David G. "Liberalism." In *International Encyclopedia of the Social Sciences*. Vol. 9. New York: Macmillan, 1968.

Smith, Helmut Walser. *German Nationalism and Religious Conflict*. Princeton: Princeton University Press, 1995.

Smith, Michael R. *Power, Norms, and Inflation: A Skeptical Treatment*. New York: Aldine de Gruyter, 1992.

Sørensen, Annemette. "Women, Family and Class." *Annual Review of Sociology* 20 (1994): 27–47.

Sorokin, Pitirim. *Social Mobility*. New York: Harper, 1927.

Spector, Paul E. *Job Satisfaction: Application, Assessment, Cause, and Consequences*. Thousand Oaks, Calif.: Sage, 1997.

Spence, Jonathan D. *The Search for Modern China*. New York: Norton, 1990.

Sperber, Jonathan. "The Shaping of Political Catholicism in the Ruhr Basin, 1848–1881." *Central European History* 16 (1983): 347–367.

———. *Popular Catholicism in Nineteenth-Century Germany*. Princeton: Princeton University Press, 1984.

———. *The European Revolutions, 1848–1851*. New York: Cambridge University Press, 1994.

———. *The Kaiser's Voters: Electors and Elections in Imperial Germany*. Cambridge: Cambridge University Press, 1997.

Spitz, David. *The Real World of Liberalism*. Chicago: University of Chicago Press, 1982.

Stanworth, Michelle. "Women and Class Analysis: A Reply to John Goldthorpe." *Sociology* 18 (1984): 159–170.

Statistisches Bundesamt. *Bevölkerung und Wirtschaft: 1872–1972*. Stuttgart: Kohlhammer, 1972.

Steckel, Richard H., and Roderick Floud. *Health and Welfare during Industrialization*. Chicago: University of Chicago Press, 1997.

Steenson, Gary P. *Karl Kautsky, 1854–1938: Marxism in the Classical Years*. Pittsburgh: University of Pittsburgh Press, 1978.

———. *After Marx, before Lenin: Marxism and Socialist Working-Class Parties in Europe, 1884–1914*. Pittsburgh: University of Pittsburgh Press, 1991.

Steger, Manfred B. *The Quest for Evolutionary Socialism: Eduard Bernstein and Social Democracy*. New York: Cambridge University Press, 1997.

Steinbeck, John. *The Grapes of Wrath*. New York: Viking, 1939.

Steinmetz, George, and Erik Olin Wright. "The Fall and Rise of the Petty Bourgeoisie: Changing Patterns of Self-Employment in the Postwar United States." *American Journal of Sociology* 94 (1989): 973–1018.

———. Reply to Linder and Houghton. *American Journal of Sociology* 96 (1990): 736–740.

Stern, Fritz. *Gold and Iron: Bismarck, Bleichröder, and the Building of the German Empire*. New York: Knopf, 1977.

Stern, Philip M. *The Great Treasury Raid*. New York: Signet, 1965.

Stewart, Robert, ed. *Dictionary of Political Quotations*. London: Europa Publications, 1984.

Strohmeyer, John. *Crisis in Bethlehem: Big Steel's Struggle to Survive*. New York: Penguin, 1987.

Strouse, Jean. *Morgan: American Financier*. New York: Random House, 1999.

Sturgis, James L. *John Bright and the Empire*. London: Athlone, 1969.

Sturmthal, Adolf. *Left of Center: European Labor Since World War II*. Urbana: University of Illinois Press, 1983.

Suits, Daniel B. "Agriculture." In *The Structure of American Industry*, edited by Walter Adams. 8th ed. New York: Macmillan, 1990.

Swafford, Jan. *Johannes Brahms: A Biography*. New York: Knopf, 1997.

Talbott, John. *The War without a Name: France in Algeria, 1954–1962*. New York: Knopf, 1980.

Tan, Chester T. *The Boxer Catastrophe*. New York: Columbia University Press, 1955.

Taylor, A.J.P. *The Struggle for Mastery in Europe: 1848–1918*. London: Oxford University Press, 1954.

Taylor, Arthur J., ed. *The Standard of Living in Britain in the Industrial Revolution*. London: Methuen, 1975.

Temin, Peter. *Lessons from the Great Depression*. Cambridge: MIT Press, 1989.

Thompson, John M. *Russia, Bolshevism, and the Versailles Peace*. Princeton: Princeton University Press, 1966.

Thornton, A. P. *The Imperial Idea and Its Enemies: A Study in British Power*. London: Macmillan, 1959.

Toller, Ernst. *Hinkemann: Eine Tragödie*. Potsdam: Kiepenheuer, 1924.

Toutain, J.-C. *La Population de la France de 1700 à 1959*. Supplement no. 133. Paris: Cahiers de l'institut de science économique appliquée, 1963.

Traugott, Mark. *Armies of the Poor: Determinants of Working-Class Participation in the Parisian Insurrection of June 1848*. Princeton: Princeton University Press, 1985.

Tudor, Henry, and J. M. Tudor, eds. and trans. *Marxism and Social Democracy: The Revisionist Debate, 1896–1898*. Cambridge: Cambridge University Press, 1988.

Turner, Bryan S. "Asiatic Society." In *A Dictionary of Marxist Thought*, edited by Tom Bottomore. 2d ed. London: Basil Blackwell, 1991.

Turner, Henry A., Jr. *German Big Business and the Rise of Hitler*. New York: Oxford University Press, 1985.

———. "Hitler's Impact on History." In *From the Berlin Museum to the Berlin Wall: Essays on the Cultural and Political History of Modern Germany*, edited by David Wetzel. Westport Conn.: Praeger, 1996.

Turner, Jonathan H. *Herbert Spencer: A Renewed Appreciation*. Beverly Hills, Calif.: Sage, 1985.

Turner, Jonathan H., Leonard Beeghley, and Charles H. Powers. *The Emergence of Sociological Theory*. 3d ed. Belmont, Calif.: Wadsworth, 1995.

Underwood, Kenneth. *Protestant and Catholic: Religious and Social Interaction in an Industrial Community*. Boston: Beacon, 1957.

United Nations. *Statistical Yearbook*. 42d ed. New York: United Nations, 1997.

U.S. Bureau of the Census. *Historical Statistics of the United States: Colonial Times to 1957*. Washington, D.C.: U.S. Government Printing Office, 1960.

———. *Historical Statistics of the United States: Colonial Times to 1970*. Part 1. Washington, D.C.: U.S. Government Printing Office, 1975.

———. *Statistical Abstract of the United States, 1981*. Washington, D.C.: U.S. Government Printing Office, 1981.

———. *The Relationship between the 1970 and 1980 Industry and Occupation Classification Systems*. Technical Paper 59. Washington, D.C.: U.S. Government Printing Office, 1989.

———. *Statistical Abstract of the United States, 1992*. Washington, D.C.: U.S. Government Printing Office, 1992.

———. *Residents of Farms and Rural Areas: 1991*, Current Population Reports. Washington, D.C.: U.S. Government Printing Office, 1993.

———. *Statistical Abstract of the United States, 1996*. Washington, D.C.: U.S. Government Printing Office, 1996.

———. *Statistical Abstract of the United States, 1998*. Washington, D.C.: U.S. Government Printing Office, 1998.

U.S. Department of Commerce. "Concentration Ratios in Manufacturing." Subject Series MC87-S-6. In *1987 Census of Manufactures*. Washington, D.C.: U.S. Government Printing Office, 1992.

U.S. Department of Labor. *Dictionary of Occupational Titles*. 4th rev. ed. Washington, D.C.: U.S. Government Printing Office, 1991.

van den Berg, Axel. "Creeping Embourgeoisement? Some Comments on the Marxist Discovery of the New Middle Class." *Research in Social Stratification and Mobility* 12 (1993): 295–328.

Vincent, John. *The Formation of the Liberal Party, 1857–1868*. London: Constable, 1966.

Volkogonov, Dmitri. *Lenin: A New Biography*. Translated by Harold Shukman. New York: Free Press, 1994.

von Strandmann and Hartmut Pogge. "Domestic Origins of Germany's Colonial Expansion under Bismarck." *Past and Present* 42 (1969): 140–159.

Wade, Mason. *The French Canadians: 1760–1967*. Rev. ed. Vol. 1. Toronto: Macmillan, 1968.

Wald, Kenneth D. *Religion and Politics in the United States*. 3d ed. Washington, D.C.: CQ Press, 1992.

Wall, Joseph Frazier. *Andrew Carnegie*. 1970. Reprint Pittsburgh: University of Pittsburgh Press, 1989.

Wallerstein, Immanuel. *The Modern World System*. 3 vols. New York: Academic Press, 1974, 1980, 1988.

———. "The Collapse of Liberalism." In *Socialist Register 1992*, edited by Ralph Miliband and Leo Panitch. London: Merlin, 1992.

Warner, W. Lloyd, and Paul S. Lunt. *The Social Life of a Modern Community*. New Haven: Yale University Press, 1941.

Warren, Bill. *Imperialism: Pioneer of Capitalism*. Edited by John Sender. London: NLB, 1980.

Wattenberg, Ben J. *The Good News Is the Bad News Is Wrong*. Rev. ed. New York: Simon & Schuster, Touchstone, 1985.

Weber, Adna. *The Growth of Cities in the Nineteenth Century*. Ithaca: Cornell University Press, 1899.

Weber, Max. *From Max Weber, Essays in Sociology*. Edited and translated by H. H. Gerth and C. Wright Mills. London: Routledge and Kegan Paul, 1948.

Wehler, Hans-Ulrich. *Bismarck und der Imperialismus*. Cologne: Kiepenheuer and Witsch, 1969.

Weinberg, Arthur S. "Six American Workers Assess Job Redesign at Saab-Scandia." *Monthly Labor Review* 98 (1975): 52–54.

Weingarten, Renée. *Writers and Revolution: The Fatal Lure of Action*. New York: Franklin Watts, 1974.

Weinstein, James. *The Corporate Ideal in the Liberal State: 1900–1918*. Boston: Beacon, 1968.

Weintraub, Stanley. *Disraeli: A Biography*. New York: Truman Talley/Dutton, 1993.

Wesseling, H. L. "Post-Imperial Holland." *Journal of Contemporary History* 15 (1980): 125–142.

———. *Imperialism and Colonialism: Essays on the History of European Expansion*. Westport, Conn.: Greenwood Press, 1997.

Wesson, Robert G. *Why Marxism? The Continuing Success of a Failed Theory*. New York: Basic Books, 1976.

Whiteley, Paul. *The Labour Party in Crisis*. London: Methuen, 1983.

Whyte, William Foote. *Street Corner Society*. Enl. ed. 1943. Reprint Chicago: University of Chicago Press, 1955.

Wiebe, Robert H. "The House of Morgan and the Executive, 1905–1913." *American Historical Review* 65 (1959): 49–60.

Williamson, Harold F., and Ralph L. Andreano. "Competitive Structure of the Petroleum Industry, 1880–1911: A Reappraisal." In *Oil's First Century*. Cambridge: Harvard Graduate School of Business Administration, 1960.

Wolfbein, Seymour L. "The Pace of Technological Change and the Factors Affecting It." In *Manpower Implications of Automation*. Washington, D.C.: U.S. Department of Labor, 1965.

Wolfe, Bertram D. *Marxism: One Hundred Years in the Life of a Doctrine*. New York: Dial, 1965.

Wright, Erik Olin. *Class, Crisis and the State*. New York: Schocken, 1978.

———. *Classes*. London: Verso, 1985.

———. *Class Counts: Comparative Studies in Class Analysis*. Cambridge: Cambridge University Press, 1997.

Wright, Erik Olin, and Bill Martin. "The Transformation of the American Class Structure, 1960–1980." *American Journal of Sociology* 93 (1987): 1–29.

Yergin, Daniel. *The Prize: The Epic Quest for Oil, Money, and Power*. New York: Simon & Schuster, 1992.

Young, Michael, and Peter Willmott. *Family and Kinship in East London*. Harmondsworth, U.K.: Penguin, 1957.

Zeitlin, Maurice. "Corporate Ownership and Control: The Large Corporation and the Capitalist Class." *American Journal of Sociology* 79 (1974): 1073–1119.

———. *The Large Corporation and Contemporary Classes*. Cambridge: Polity Press, 1989.

Zimmermann, Ekkart, and Thomas Sallfeld. "Economic and Political Reactions to the World Economic Crisis of the 1930s in Six European Countries." *International Studies Quarterly* 32 (1988): 305–334.

Zvesper, John. "Liberalism." In *Blackwell Encyclopaedia of Political Thought*, edited by David Miller. Oxford: Blackwell Reference, 1987.

Index

ABOUT THE AUTHOR

Richard F. Hamilton is Professor Emeritus of Sociology and Political Science at The Ohio State University. He specializes in comparative and historical studies of political institutions and mass political behavior, and he has published many books and articles over the course of the last forty years. His most recent books are *The Bourgeois Epoch: Marx and Engels on Britain, France, and Germany* (1991) and *The Social Misconstruction of Reality: Validity and Verification in the Scholarly Community* (1996).